THE
COUNTRY
HOUSE
GUIDE

THE COUNTRY HOUSE GUIDE

Historic Houses in Private Ownership
in England, Wales and Scotland

**Robin Fedden
and John Kenworthy-Browne**

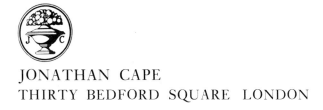

JONATHAN CAPE
THIRTY BEDFORD SQUARE LONDON

First published in Great Britain 1979
Copyright © 1979 by John Kenworthy-Browne,
Mrs Katharine M'Seffar and Mrs Frances Fedden Eckl
Designed by Adrienne Gear

Jonathan Cape Ltd, 30 Bedford Square, London WC1

British Library Cataloguing in Publication Data

Fedden, Robin
  The country house guide.
  1. Country homes – Great Britain – Guide-books
  I. Title   II. Kenworthy-Browne, John Anthony
  914.1'04'857   DA660

ISBN 0-224-01359-9

Printed in Great Britain by Jolly & Barber Ltd, Rugby

Contents

The Contributors

ALEC CLIFTON-TAYLOR's book *The Pattern of English Building*, a comprehensive study of English traditional buildings from the aspect of their materials, is the acknowledged classic on this subject. Other books include *The Cathedrals of England*, and *Parish Churches as Works of Art* - described by Sir John Betjeman as 'the best book on its subject I have ever read'. Apart from numerous articles and reviews, Mr Clifton-Taylor is widely known for his radio and television programmes, particularly his contribution to the B.B.C.'s symposium *Spirit of the Age* and his series *Six English Towns*. As a lecturer he has travelled all over the world, though not yet in Antarctica.

JOHN HARVEY trained as an architect under Sir Herbert Baker and has specialised in conservation; he has been Consultant Architect to Winchester College since 1947. More widely known as a scholar, his research into Gothic architects and master masons is pioneer work of fundamental importance. Among his numerous books have been *English Mediaeval Architects* (a dictionary), *Gothic England*, *The Gothic World*, *The Cathedrals of Spain*, *Mediaeval Craftsmen*, *Conservation of Buildings*, *Early Nurserymen*, and the latest, *The Perpendicular Style*. He contributed chapters to *The National Trust* (1945) and *The National Trust Guide* (1973). In 1976 he received the honorary degree of Doctor of the University of York.

JOHN CORNFORTH has been writing about country houses in *Country Life* since 1961, as well as being Architectural Editor from 1967 to 1977. This led to his membership of the Properties Committee of the National Trust, and of the Historic Buildings Council since 1970. A desire to combine historical research with work on practical problems led to his collaboration with John Fowler on *English Decoration in the 18th Century* (1974) and to produce in the same year *The Country Houses of Britain – Can they Survive?*. He continues to work on the complex problems of historic houses, and is currently producing a follow-up to his country house report, on the conservation of historic towns.

COLIN MCWILLIAM is in charge of history and conservation at the Heriot-Watt University Department of Architecture in the Edinburgh College of Art. Born in London in 1928, he graduated in Architecture at Cambridge and was successively director of the Scottish National Buildings Record (now SNMR) and assistant secretary (concerned with historic buildings and their contents) to the National Trust for Scotland. A founder member and subsequently for five years chairman of the Scottish Georgian Society, he is now editor and part-author of the Penguin *Buildings of Scotland* series.

Preface

When Robin Fedden died in 1977, he had written rather more than a quarter of this book. It is something for which he was particularly well suited. During an association of thirty years with the National Trust he had worked to preserve, arrange and open a great number of historic houses; and, besides, he was a frequent and valued guest in many of the private houses that are described in this book. Robin Fedden's outlook was supremely urbane. He had a love of tradition, a detestation of boredom, and impeccable taste. In addition, a finely tuned ear for language made him one of our most remarkable contemporary writers of prose. The success of *The National Trust Guide* (first published in 1973) shows only a small part of his achievements. The present book, on the other hand, is not a National Trust publication. It is concerned with privately owned houses, and he was working on it independently.

The houses included here are all open to the public. In describing properties that are still privately owned – the definition extends to those belonging to family trusts – a certain emphasis has been placed on the history of a building and the family or families that occupied and contributed to it. At the present time, social and financial pressures are combining to give the private country house a most uncertain future. Many have disappeared altogether during the last fifty years, while others have been stripped of their contents and family association. Nearly all that survive do so under considerable strain. The pessimistic view is that our generation will be the last to enjoy them.

Yet magnificent houses, great and small, survive today. There will be found in the English section of the book several Norman and Gothic castles, and fine manors that still keep their mediaeval character; three of the largest 'Jacobethan' prodigy houses, two houses associated with Inigo Jones, the three best known houses by Vanbrugh, four with interiors by Robert Adam, and two by Soane; as well as Chatsworth, Houghton and Holkham, three splendid works of the Gothic revival and five great Victorian creations. No less gratifying are the numerous smaller houses, palimpsests of all periods, which for centuries have been the focal points of country life. As to Scotland, the houses range from the 13th-century fortress of Dunvegan on Skye to the Edwardian opulence of Manderston – the Georgian period being particularly well represented.

We decided to limit the book to properties advertised as regularly open for a minimum of twenty days in the year. Thus, those open only by appointment have not been included, nor those which open only their gardens. A few houses have been added which fall below the twenty-day rule. Either they seemed too good to leave out, or they were houses for which Robin Fedden had a particular affection. They make a bonus.

The definition of a 'country house' is very imprecise. Syon House, though now quite urban, is undoubtedly a country house; but of two properties described (Malmesbury House and Churche's Mansion), one is in a cathedral close, the other in a country town. Uninhabitable ruins have been left out, but some houses that are restored but empty (Hedingham Castle, Stokesay, Markenfield, Seaton Delaval) have considerable historic interest and are therefore included. An inflexible ruling would have been pedantic and unhelpful.

More houses are opened to the public every year, and sometimes houses are removed from the list. Contents and their arrangement may change; so too, in the longer run, will gardens and parks. Although the book will never be quite up to date, it is hoped it may be found interesting and useful. A great deal of information has had to be sifted, digested and diluted; errors will undoubtedly have crept in, and the author will be grateful if these can be brought to his notice. For opening times and precise locations, visitors should always refer to *Historic Houses, Castles & Gardens*, an indispensable spring catalogue by ABC Publications Ltd that grows in size from year to year, or to the booklet published by the Automobile Association.

The author has incurred numerous debts of gratitude. This is due in the first place to those owners of houses who have given their time and knowledge, who have checked facts and supplied photographs. Scholarly contributions to the house descriptions have been supplied by John Martin Robinson, Michael Trinick, John Cornforth and Clive Aslet; John Robinson, Mark Girouard, Gervase Jackson-Stops and Colin McWilliam have kindly corrected some of the texts. Mary Clare Wilson of the Historic Houses Association has considerably eased a voluminous correspondence, and Sarah Hahn of Country Life has patiently supplied photographs. Jeremy Whitaker, and Bernard Wood of English Life Publications (Derby) are among others who have been consistently helpful with photographs. The labour of travelling has been reduced by the help and encouragement of Antonia Yates and John Robinson; Mrs Stirling of Keir gave valuable hospitality in Scotland. Lastly (or firstly), the book would not have been completed without the kindness of Mrs Fedden, who also offered Robin Fedden's library for the use of his successor.

JOHN KENWORTHY-BROWNE

November 1978

Private Houses and their Visitors

by John Kenworthy-Browne

In 1785, John Byng (who eventually succeeded as 5th Viscount Torrington) called at Wroxton Abbey near Banbury, and was very much put out that Lord Guilford refused him admission. 'Very rude this, and unlike an old courtly Lord,' he commented. The excuse had been feeble. It was unusual to be kept out after taking the trouble to visit a fine house, and no other had yet been denied him.

Tourists' accounts from the 18th century are not so plentiful as one would like, but in the Torrington Diaries there survives a kaleidoscopic and delightfully personal view of the country at that time. In his middle age, Torrington would spend a month or two each year seeing some part of England 'from the outside of a horse', and he recorded everything for the amusement of his old age and of his descendants. His contemporary, Mrs Lybbe Powys, also wrote about houses, at greater length but with less originality. She would base her excursions from houses of friends or relations; whereas Torrington valued his independence and preferred to stay at inns. On reaching a fine house he would send in his name, the housekeeper would appear, and generally he could see all he wished. A complete account of just such a visit is given in *Pride and Prejudice*, where Elizabeth Bennett calls at 'Pemberley' (often thought to have been based on Chatsworth) and is most kindly received by the housekeeper and gardener. We are told everything except the tips that were given to these obliging people. In a much visited house these could be considerable. The housekeeper at Warwick Castle, who died in 1834, had during seventy years collected more than £30,000, and had even lent money to the Earl of Warwick when there was a danger of pictures having to be sold.

Some houses were open regularly on stated days. Thus Woburn Abbey could be seen only on Mondays. This was a convenient arrangement, Torrington thought, though it must have involved careful planning in the days of horse transport. However, there seems never to have been any difficulty in entering a park; and in those days, when every park in the country either had been or was about to be improved, it was the landscape that claimed the ordinary visitor's chief interest. So many people came to Henry Hoare's pleasure grounds at Stourhead that he built the inn to accommodate them, and this was often full. Mrs Lybbe Powys noted that, in 1775, 2,324 visitors had been to Wilton House. Country houses, in short, were immensely popular and by the end of the century there were guide books to some of the finest collections and parks.

All this had resulted from the improvement of the roads. Before that, dedicated sightseers were rather few. The antiquary John Leland made his *Itineraries* in 1534–43; they were expensive, and had been sponsored by King Henry VIII. Two centuries later, Horace Walpole's visits were, similarly, serious rather than curious. By contrast with these scholars, the indefatigable Celia Fiennes had begun her journeys through England in 1685 for the sake of her health. She caught the travel-bug, wrote breathless, fascinating descriptions of many houses that came in her way, and recommended that all her countrywomen should do the same as 'a souveraign remedy to cure or preserve from these epidemick diseases of vapours, should I add Laziness'. Besides, Miss Fiennes insisted, everybody should be properly informed about their own country, and few people actually were.

By the later 19th century, it seems, houses were not so easily available. Already in 1835 the German scholar G. F. Waagen had been given only a grudging view of Woburn. The housekeeper had hurried him from room to room and could hardly be persuaded to open the shutters. Eventually, to judge from the scarcity of Victorian accounts, the general interest in houses seems to have died away. Perhaps the railway age had defeated the casual traveller of curiosity and leisure. For their own part, owners of houses had become more exclusive, and considered their surroundings as personal territory to be guarded jealously from casual intruders.

During the last thirty years the wheel has turned again, and we are in the middle of an astonishing revival of interest in country houses. Every year more become available, and in the most popular of them the sheer quantity of visitors is extraordinary. Who has not experienced jostling crowds at Chatsworth, Longleat, Woburn or Holkham? Apart from the nagging worry that such numbers may not be in the best interests of these houses themselves, the serious sightseer must plan his visit for a quieter day (and remember that most private houses are shut during half, or more, of the year). On an August weekend there will nearly always be some smaller house close by, less attractive for coach parties, perhaps, but unexpectedly rewarding in its own way. Monastic rooms at Ixworth and Little Malvern, Renaissance work at Nether Winchendon, Cromwellian stables at Peover, Carolean plasterwork at Eye and Georgian Gothic at Milton, and the painted rooms at Avington Park: these are examples of the unexpected pleasures that can be found in so many of our smaller country houses.

For centuries in the past, country houses were the spine and pivot of English life. They were not merely the luxurious and personal property of their owners. Such an attitude came about partly because of 19th-century attitudes towards privacy, and partly through the advance of democracy which by degrees has released the lord of the manor from certain responsibilities. In the past, the style and grandeur of a house reflected the status, whether local or national, of the squire. The types of houses most familiar today originate from periods of influence, affluence or optimism: feudal castles, for instance; the wool merchants' houses of the 15th and 16th centuries; 'prodigy' houses built by Queen Elizabeth's statesmen; magnificently solemn palaces of Stuart courtiers; and the august mansions of Georgian oligarchs. Rather less familiar, but no less intriguing, is the opulence of the Victorian age; but the survival of this group is more of a problem because in the long run they have proved to be the most difficult to maintain.

The vast majority of country houses described in this book existed in some form by the 16th century, and of these a great number were manors recorded in Domesday Book. But nearly every manor mentioned in Domesday (though not every castle) had already been in existence, in some cases for hundreds of years. The historical value of our country houses is therefore very considerable. Unfortunately the links cannot be traced further back. As yet there is no certain case of a Saxon manor having developed from a Roman villa – though in several cases (Chalcot, Dewlish and Littlecote) there was Roman occupation very close by.

The mediaeval system of manorial ownership depended on feudal dues to an overlord, and ultimately to the king. Well before the 16th century the pattern of private ownership had begun to take on its modern form, and whatever remained of feudal dues was finally relinquished by Charles II. Many houses had formerly been held on lease, and a few continued to be so; Thomas Coke, for instance, acquired the full title to Melbourne as late as 1704. But the country house in its familiar sense implies freehold ownership. Few occupiers would be prepared to lay out a fortune in building and improving unless they had full security of the property, not only for themselves but for their heirs.

The greatest change in ownership that England has witnessed since 1066 came with the Dissolution of the Monasteries. We say, with hindsight, that something of the kind had become inevitable. When it happened, the operation was speedy, ruthless, and performed with astonishing efficiency. In 1536–40, over one quarter of the country's cultivated land was put on the market at an easy valuation and greedily absorbed. Monasteries and priories, manors and granges changed hands overnight. The landed class was greatly increased and vast fortunes were made; the lawyers did particularly well. Yet many old families remained aloof, especially in the North of England where the need to toe the official line seemed less urgent. Such families generally remained Catholic and were frequently allied by inter-marriage. Raby and Alnwick Castles were Catholic until their disastrous rebellion in 1569; Yorkshire and Lancashire are closely studded with houses that have never lost their allegiance to Rome, in spite of recusancy fines and confiscations of property. Richard Gillow, the Lancaster cabinet-maker, was also of Catholic descent, and his family settled at Leighton Hall in 1822.

The upheaval of the 17th century, the Civil War, left its scars over England in the series of ancient castles that were ruined or 'slighted' by Cromwell and Fairfax. Most landed families, though by no means all, had given their support to the King, and their strongholds could not be allowed to remain as centres of a potential reaction. At Berkeley the Norman keep was breached; at Rockingham and in the castles of the Royalist West – Tiverton, and Bickleigh – the keep was removed altogether. But this was to prove the last period of wholesale destruction until the 20th century. The political dispute resolved itself into diplomatic rivalry between the Tory and

Whig parties; the great country palaces of the late 17th and early 18th centuries were built either by the Stuart court or by Whig aristocrats. Their character and existence depended on conditions of peace.

In the 18th century a house was not thought to be complete unless it stood in dignified surroundings. Thus Castle Howard was left unfinished because the money was diverted towards the park buildings. Many owners came to value the park and pleasure grounds as much as, or more than the house, and well before 1750 the grounds of Mount Edgcumbe and Hagley equalled in reputation those of Stowe and Stourhead. Then came Lancelot Brown with his revolutionary conception of a park, refashioning its contours, plantations, brooks and ponds. A 'Capability' Brown park relies chiefly on the arrangement of these 'natural' features and not, like Mount Edgcumbe, on its ornaments – temples, ruins and other diversions. Yet even Brown could not resist the grandeur of a bridge marching across a river or lake, and he built one at Burghley. Brown's parks at Burghley, Longleat, Alnwick, Dodington and above all at Blenheim have been maintained in all their splendour. By the early 19th century there was scarcely a gentleman's seat in England whose park had not followed suit. So what did they look like before? The rough pastoral surroundings at Haddon give some idea. When Torrington visited Raby in 1792, the park was still unimproved. He found 'very few single trees; and all the plantations are mean, of ill make, and without bold sweeps; the river, likewise, running thro' the park, which should form a Thames, is turn'd to no account.'

For the way houses were actually used, and for the development of their

Haddon Hall from the River Wye

plans, the reader can do no better than to take the recent book by Mark Girouard.* Here he will understand the mysteries of the mediaeval house, with its hierarchical succession of hall, dining rooms, chambers and lodgings; the grandeur of the Great Apartment of the Baroque age; and the movement towards informality that began in the 18th century. This book will answer many teasing questions: the exact purpose of a mediaeval Hall; why Torrington referred to the Parlour at Haddon as 'the steward's room'; the disposition of the King's and Queen's several lodgings at Hatfield; what is English and what French about Ragley; the nature of state rooms; the advantages of close stools over garderobes and water closets; and why Torrington dreaded being made to converse 'in a circle' for an hour before dinner.

In the romantic age of the 19th century, mediaeval and Tudor houses were regarded with nostalgia and reverence, and their rooms were given evocative titles. The name 'Banqueting Hall' seems to occur first in Sir Walter Scott's *Waverley* (1814), and in many cases it has stuck. It is certainly a misnomer because in the 16th and even 17th centuries a banquet was not the abundant affair suggested by the novels of Scott and Lytton, where the entire household was entertained by music and ballads from the 'Minstrels' Gallery', but a private table of sweetmeats taken at leisure in a tower-room-with-a-view or summer house. In 1806, the antiquarian John Britton described the two recently built Halls at Arundel and Corsham (neither of which remains today) as 'Barons' Halls', a term that surely was never used in the Middle Ages. However, it seems permissible for such romantic creations as those, or for the enlarged 'Barons' Hall' of the 1840s at Raby Castle. The Great Chamber at Lord Lytton's Knebworth became the 'Presence Chamber'. Even 'solar', a word used rather vaguely for the withdrawing rooms of mediaeval houses, has not been found in use earlier than the 19th century. At the same time, many houses appear to have raised their status. A yeoman's house might now be known as 'The Manor', granges and priories called abbeys, and fortified manors and Pele towers were elevated to castle rank.

In the period after 1680, the finest feature of the house was not the Hall but the Great Apartment. There are magnificent examples of these grand suites of rooms *en enfilade* at Boughton, Burghley and Chatsworth, but by Walpole's day they had become mere curiosities. At both Castle Howard and Blenheim, Vanbrugh built twin Apartments placed either side of the central Saloon, and this is the ultimate development of grand Baroque planning in England. Yet in both these houses the original character of the rooms, and also their purpose, was lost when the Apartments were turned into a ridiculously large number of reception rooms. It is understandable that these magnificent houses attract large numbers of visitors; and the need for directing a visitors' route can destroy the effect intended by the architects. At Chatsworth, for instance, one should ideally make the ascent from the Hall up the Great Staircase, and arrive at the Great Chamber at the

*Mark Girouard, *Life in the English Country House*, Yale University Press, 1978.

top, whence the Apartment begins. As it is, one enters with the servants through the closet and dressing room. The Apartments at Burghley, Holkham and Woburn are likewise seen in the wrong order. Another effect that is generally lost to visitors is that of passing from the grandeur of the Hall into the contrasting splendour of the Saloon that lies behind it. Unless this is done at Kedleston, for instance, the full impact of Adam's domed saloon cannot be appreciated.

By the end of the 18th century the English were already moving away from formality. Rigid ceremony was no longer expected; its place was taken by an exaggerated sense of decorum, from which Victorian snobbery developed. Informality and ease of manner became the rule, and the great 19th-century houses are often entirely in accordance with present-day behaviour – except in their size. The layout of Dodington, designed by Wyatt in 1797, is no different in its essentials from Victorian Thoresby, or 20th-century Port Lympne. The reception rooms move in an easy progression from hall to library, drawing room, breakfast room and dining room. The smaller, more intimate rooms are uncomfortably tucked out of sight. Such houses are not difficult to understand. Yet they have proved to be a most difficult group to preserve. They were built for constant entertaining of house parties. The entire house was intended for everyday living, and few state rooms and no apartments can be conveniently shut off. They depended on regiments of servants, and the labyrinthine service wings are of no use today.

A house that is privately owned has a unique flavour that cannot survive under a public body, not even the National Trust. Apart from the warmth of family occupation, the house will contain treasures, keepsakes and eccentri-

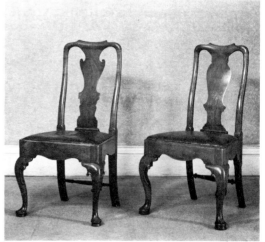

Furniture by Gillows of Lancaster. Left: *A games table, and* right: *early Georgian chairs (Leighton Hall)*

Grand Tour portraits. Left: *Thomas Coke, Earl of Leicester, by Trevisani, 1717 (Holkham Hall); and* right: *Thomas Giffard by Batoni, 1784 (Chillington Hall)*

cities that have accumulated down to the present generation, and these will be found even in the State Rooms of the grandest and most Augustan houses. The State Rooms of Holkham and Kedleston stand apart from the family wing; they were built to show works of art, and have little use except to be walked through. Yet they should not be regarded as museums. The paintings at Corsham hang in 18th-century style right up to the cornice of the gallery, in a manner that no modern museum would imitate. Later accretions are not necessarily to be cleared away. At Chatsworth, a discordant note is struck in the sombre Great Apartment by gaudy malachite and gilt furniture that was given by the Tsar of Russia in 1844; yet one would not wish this to be removed. And besides works of art there will be found objects of association and affection that show individual tastes. These too have their place in the history of the house.

In medium-size and even small houses, the number and range of family portraits can be astonishing. At Arbury, Doddington, Knebworth, Norton Conyers, Sherborne Castle and Stanford Hall (to name only a few) they are profuse, ranging from Elizabethans, through Kneller, Hudson, Reynolds and Gainsborough to the Victorians. The paintings at any of these houses could stock a museum; but if they were removed, much of their interest and all their association would be lost. The portraits that cover the walls of the stairs, halls and drawing rooms provide a vivid link between past and present. In their own houses, among ancestors, relations and living descendants, they greet their visitors with charm and courtesy. They would go to a museum cold and lifeless, like corpses to a mortuary.

Whether a certain picture was actually painted by Holbein, Cornelius Johnson, Van Dyck or Kneller, or whether it is a fine copy is a question for

Court portraits by Lely. Left: *The Duchess of Richmond as Minerva (Goodwood);* and right: *the Earl of Arlington (Euston Hall)*

experts, and this book does not attempt to give the latest attribution or re-attribution. Here, the relevance of a portrait lies generally in its family connection. Sometimes even this can be in doubt. Horace Walpole remarked of a collection of portraits that 'most of them seem christened by chance, like children at a foundling hospital'. The Duke of Wellington, ever practical, said that the identity of a picture should always be written on the back for the benefit of posterity, and it is a pity that this was not always done. A house and its heritage can be enhanced by legends and traditions. Sometimes these have grown tall over the years; sometimes they are revived and embellished to provide a spurious interest. One may be told that Queen Elizabeth slept in a certain Charles II bed, in a room that never existed in her day. From the amount of embroidery worked by Mary Queen of Scots it seems that this gay lady never left off her stitching. Charles I took a quite extraordinary number of valuables on to the scaffold that cold January morning; the Old and Young Cavaliers were surprisingly liberal with their snuffboxes, watches and waistcoats. It should be realised that fine furniture is no finer because it is labelled 'Chippendale' or 'Vile'; its authorship becomes interesting only when it can actually be proved. Likewise there is no purpose in pushing the date of a building back a few decades or even centuries. The truth is bound to emerge sooner or later.

When he invites the public to see his house, the private owner is taking certain risks. Naturally he must guard against the very real possibility of art thefts – an occurrence, incidentally, that was virtually unknown in the 18th century. But also he is vulnerable to the comparisons and criticisms that visitors will inevitably make. Those who stand in the rooms are often perplexed by the curious information offered, ex gratia, by the gyrating public. Usually, however, the attendants are able to return in kind, and they can give better than they get. Some owners prefer to have the polymorphous body of visitors drilled in formations. Guided tours, though generally liked by organised groups, are anathema to the well-informed individual who asks nothing more than to be left in peace with a reliable guide book; though, in addition, an attendant who is genuinely knowledgeable yet sparing of anecdote is always welcome. As for the necessary paraphernalia of house opening: ropes, druggets and notices – these, if carefully chosen, need not be hideous. They are preferable to finding an 18th-century Savonnerie carpet lying unguarded in the public route, which the writer has recently seen. Let us remember too that many fine old floors have been permanently scarred by stiletto heels, a brutal and thoughtless fashion that threatens to come back. The exhibitions and side shows which are increasingly offered to attract a mass of visitors – costumes, dolls and toys, 'banquets', game parks and nature trails – may or may not interfere with the character of the house. For the most part they are beyond the scope of this book. In all cases, visitors may realise that opening a house can be expensive, and always involves the owner in a great deal of hard work.

Neo-classical sculpture. Left: *The Duchess of Rutland, 1826, by M. C. Wyatt (Belvoir Castle); and* right: *The Greek Slave, 1844, by Hiram Powers (Raby Castle)*

The value of Britain's country houses was stated in unequivocal words in the Gowers Report of 1950:

> They represent an association of beauty, of art and of nature – the achievement often of centuries of effort – which is irreplaceable, and has seldom, if ever, been equalled in the history of civilisation. Certainly, nowhere else are such richness and variety to be found within so narrow a compass.

After 1950, the destruction of houses became greater than ever before, and this was demonstrated in a memorable exhibition in London in 1975;* further depredations and sales of contents have resulted from relentless and punitive taxation. To whatever uses country houses may be put, they were all created by private individuals, and they keep their true spirit only as long as they are privately owned. The following pages tell something of many abandoned or decaying houses that have been rescued by new, far-sighted owners. The system of repairing grants from the Historic Buildings Council has been of the greatest benefit, not only in finance but also in making more houses available to the general public. Yet apart from such grants, owners have had every possible discouragement. It is up to the nation whether our showpieces will continue to exist. They could easily and quickly be lost for ever.

---

* 'The Destruction of the Country House 1875–1975' at the Victoria and Albert Museum.

The Building Materials

by Alec Clifton-Taylor

Some years ago an ill-advised scheme for road widening in one of our provincial towns included the demolition of a pleasant terrace of Georgian houses. 'Oh yes', said the advocates, 'it's a pity, we admit, but there are so many other Georgian terraces, all exactly alike, that this one will hardly be missed.' Apart from the fact that if a Georgian terrace is destroyed it will *always* be missed, wherever it is, the assertion that Georgian terraces are 'all exactly alike' is ludicrous. If built of brick, as many of them are, they will have, admittedly, a family likeness, but the more one studies them the more one is aware of their manifold differences. There were, in a word, almost infinite possibilities of variation within a well-accepted convention.

For the country houses, this is still more strikingly the truth. Happily, some six thousand still survive, and every year an increasing number open their doors to the public. Nothing is more evident than the infinity of their differences. Houses built at about the same date will often have stylistic affinities, but no two will ever be found to look alike. Apart from the changes of setting, which play such an important part in the impact of any house, there are variations of scale, contrasts of local fashion, and above all an immense choice of building materials, yielding a marvellously subtle range of colours and textures, constantly changing as we move from one part of Britain to another. It is this which makes the pattern of our native buildings a subject of unending and inexhaustible fascination.

The contrasts of material are paramount for a very sound economic reason. Let us suppose that, in thinking of erecting a house, the costs are separated under three headings: labour, materials and the cost of transporting those materials. Today, the last item will always be the least expensive of the three. Before the Industrial Revolution, it was quite otherwise. Labour was cheap; materials were also reasonably cheap provided that one built with what was on or near the site. But bricks and, still more, stone were heavy; start to shift them about, and up rocketed the costs. Only if the new house were close to a river or to the sea-coast might it be possible to move these heavy materials some distance without vast expenditure, for the only way to transport them at a reasonable cost was by barge. The outcome of this was that, wherever possible, all but the very rich built with whatever they had on or very near to the site. And there was always something. Until the seventeenth century most parts of the country still had good supplies of oak, so timber-framing was all but universal for people of modest means, and was sometimes employed for larger houses too: places such as the Old Hall at Gawsworth, Churche's Mansion at Nantwich,* and Great Dixter at Nor-

* Churche's Mansion has recently been de-blacked: a very welcome undertaking. The vogue

Great Dixter; a 15th-century timber-frame house

thiam in Sussex, all described and illustrated in this book. Over broad areas stone, not always of the finest quality but at best very good indeed, was also readily available, and for grand houses like Chatsworth or Castle Howard the usual practice was to open up a quarry on the estate. Where there was no stone, not even flint from the chalk, there was generally clay suitable for brick-making; many a house in East Anglia is today surrounded by a moat which would never have been dug out had not the clay been required for the house's bricks, fired in a small kiln built expressly for the purpose. In short, the provision of the materials was, for all but the most spectacular houses, an intensely local activity, with the result that the country house usually settles most harmoniously into its environment, being part and parcel of a country-side in which, as often as not, it is the focal point.

There are, it must be admitted, houses which 'belong' in colour and texture but which, nevertheless, are stylistically exotic. This is surely true of all the Palladian houses of the Georgian period. As 'incidents' in the landscape these houses are often a delight, but they are nevertheless a curious aberration in the English scene. Our climate certainly does not suggest the need for porticoes; yet it is undeniable that houses which possess them have a 'presence', a self-assurance, beyond the reach of their more economically designed fellows. Nor should it be forgotten that the land-owners of the eighteenth century – and all who do not have to live in their houses today must surely honour them for it – were prepared to make

---

for 'black and white', mainly to be found in the Welsh Border counties and Lancashire, was a purely Victorian phenomenon. Such houses make specially bad neighbours, visually, in towns.

considerable sacrifices of comfort and convenience in the cause of Art, with a capital A.

In the planting and laying out of their estates some of them, as is now well known, were inspired by poetry and by paintings, in which the house itself might be little more than a major feature. A little later a great pile such as Eastnor Castle in Herefordshire might aspire to recreate the age of feudal grandeur. Eastnor was built by Sir Robert Smirke for the 2nd Baron Somers between 1811 and about 1820, on a surpassingly beautiful site at the southern end of the Malvern hills. It was intended to impress, and from across the lake it certainly does so. It will also be observed that, although the skyline is Romantic, the composition has, like the Houses of Parliament a generation later, a strictly Classical symmetry. The architectural style of the nineteenth-century castles might be regarded as more 'English' than that of the Palladian houses, but the sacrifices of amenity were still greater. Sometimes a genuine mediaeval castle would be 'modernised', as was Raby in County Durham for the Duke of Cleveland, mainly by William Burn in the 1840s. Set in its large and splendid park, embellished by a Georgian landscape gardener with two lakes, the huge pile looks highly picturesque; its silhouette is splendid. Within, the finest room is the mediaeval kitchen, a remarkable rib-vaulted structure with a tall stone louvre. It is perhaps enough to add that in the Victorian age the food had to travel over a hundred yards along an underground railway, swathed in blankets, to reach the dining room.

Another kind of aberration, by which I mean the sacrifice of common sense and convenience on the altar of social ambitions, is represented by those houses in non-stone districts for which even the best brick was not considered good enough. During the hundred years between 1750 and 1850, stone was regarded by many landowners as the only socially acceptable material for a country house, a view reinforced on aesthetic grounds by a number of architectural writers: Isaac Ware's objections to the 'fiery' colour of red brick, which 'in summer has an appearance of heat that is very disagreeable', are familiar. (They occur in his *Complete Body of Architecture*, published in 1756.) One solution was to use 'white' bricks (so-called: in reality they are usually a pale yellowish brown), but this was only practicable where the local clays had a high lime content and little or no iron, for the redness of most bricks derives from the presence of particles of iron in the large majority of the brick clays. Such a situation occurred at Holkham in Norfolk, where the subsoil is chalky. The uppermost beds, it is true, did contain iron and yielded bright red bricks which were used to face the internal courtyard that nobody was supposed to see. Externally Holkham makes an exceedingly sober impression, which was thoroughly in accord with Palladian ideas, and the fact that at the base storey every fourth course of bricks is boldly chamfered to give an impression of rusticated stone blocks leaves no room for doubt that stone would have been employed if it had been available. At nearby Houghton it was used: the Aislaby sandstone, a fine material, was brought by sea all the way from Whitby in Yorkshire to King's Lynn, and then dragged overland for some thirteen miles. But

Houghton was, after all, the country residence of the Prime Minister.

More usual, when brick was considered undesirable, was the resort to stucco. No English county, unless it be Kent, has more beautiful brickwork than Sussex, yet at Sheffield Park, in 1779, James Wyatt (whose client, John Baker Holroyd, was significantly – for such people always like to be 'in the swim' – a rising politician who, at that time President of the Board of Agriculture, was soon to be created Baron and later Earl of Sheffield) faced the base storey with stone and all the rest with stucco. Elsewhere, as at Althorp about 1790, red brick was concealed under 'white' mathematical tiles; shortly afterwards, Horace Walpole wrily observed that 'the pretty outside is demolished: Mr Holland has so much of the spirit of a lucrative profession in him as to prefer destroying to not being employed.' The late Lord Spencer told me that he would have dearly liked to remove this 'white' overcoat; but the original brickwork was found to have been so much damaged at the time when the tiles were added that restoration proved to be impossible.

Wherever smooth stucco was applied in England, the usual practice was to add a network of smooth ruled lines, done with the edge of the trowel or some pointed instrument while the plaster was still wet, to simulate blocks of stone. It is therefore evident that originally stucco was always regarded as a substitute material for stone. Nowadays such an attitude is quite out of date; in repainting, the old lines are ignored and gradually become fainter, as stucco is recognised for what it is: a delightful material in its own right, provided that it is repainted at fairly frequent intervals.

Roughcast, a less urbane form of rendering, has a different aesthetic base. Here the intention was not to imitate stone but to mask it, and for two reasons: to provide additional protection from the weather and to endow the building with greater artistic unity. In England roughcast is not often applied to country houses, but in Scotland, where it is known as harling, it is, in an admittedly more rigorous climate, quite common. An excellent example included in this book is Muchalls Castle north of Stonehaven, which was reharled about 1955. Brick made a very tardy appearance in Scotland: even as late as 1800 it was comparatively rare. The harling covers not brick but stone. For, although in Scotland, as in Wales, almost every large house is built of stone, most parts of both countries were devoid of freestone: of stone, that is, which can be cut freely with a saw, i.e., ashlared. Often, therefore, the stonework is markedly rubbly, as can be seen in Wales at Gwydir Castle. And even where the stone itself is, like granite, extremely durable, the surface may be decidedly rough. Harling is therefore appreciated in Scotland as a material which can endow a house with a greater artistic coherence; when our attention is not diverted by the separate stones of which the building is composed, we are better able, so the argument runs, to appreciate the formal qualities of the whole. In England so many kinds of stone can be ashlared that the need to apply a unifying surface material did not normally arise.

England has, however, one material which in Scotland would unhesitatingly be harled, and that is flint. And who is to say that roughcast over flint would not be an improvement? The answer, in my view, depends upon quality – the quality both of the roughcast and of the flint. Flint is not a very common material for large country houses, but two major examples are represented in this book: Littlecote and Goodwood House. When the third Duke of Richmond commissioned James Wyatt to rebuild Goodwood, he expressly stipulated that flint should be used, because on the South Downs it was the local material. Hurrah for the *genius loci*? For once, alas, no. Flint, perfectly appropriate for a cottage, is, especially when unknapped, as here, much too humble a material for a big house. At Goodwood Chambers's stables, of excellent knapped flint with stone dressings, steal the show. For large houses flint is best used in combination with limestone, in bands or chequers, or in that sometimes highly accomplished product of East Anglia, flushwork.

These aberrations, as I have termed them, are interesting, and not always aesthetically unsuccessful. Nevertheless, we may be glad that the large majority of British houses exhibit none of them, but conform to the general pattern of displaying, often to excellent advantage, the material which was most readily at hand. Many of the most seductive are of Jurassic limestone. In Dorset a notable example from the Tudor period is Athelhampton Hall, built of a fine light grey oolite quarried neither at Portland nor at Purbeck (the two best known Dorset limestones) but at Portesham, near Abbotsbury. The early Elizabethan wing has dressings in the rich golden brown Ham Hill stone, which figures so prominently along the Dorset-Somerset border. At Brympton d'Evercy the combination of mansion, chantry house and modest little church displays this stone to perfection. Wiltshire's limestone houses include several of major importance: Wilton House, Longleat and

Littlecote; the Elizabethan wing, built mainly of flint

Corsham Court in particular. But mention must also be made of a sandstone of very individual character, sarsens, which can be seen at Avebury Manor.

In the Cotswolds the limestones are deservedly famous. At Upper Slaughter Manor, which is mostly Elizabethan (and has, incidentally, one of the lovely stone-slated roofs for which this part of the country is justly renowned), the ashlar of the two-storeyed porch and the characteristic refinement of the dressings – window-frames, drip-moulds, gable copings and finials – stand out very effectively against the roughly coursed rubblestone of the main walling. Chastleton, a Jacobean house, exhibits a similar contrast. Dodington, on the other hand, as befits its date (1796–1817), is of impeccable ashlar throughout. So also, moving north-east from the Cotswolds, are several of the great Northamptonshire houses: Boughton, Deene Park and Burghley. At Deene much of the pale brown Weldon stone is dusted with lichen, so that the house tends to look more grey than brown. Burghley, built with prodigious extravagance by William Cecil, Lord Treasurer and Secretary of State to Elizabeth I, of Barnack oolite quarried on the estate, ceased to be in Northamptonshire in 1965 and, improbable as it may seem, is now officially in Cambridgeshire. Belton House is a superb Lincolnshire example of ashlared limestone, for this is built of Ketton stone, structurally the purest of all our oolites.

The Jurassic limestones sweep across England from Dorset to Yorkshire in a great ogee curve. To the south-east of it are the younger stones, of which Wealden sandstone is the best: this is well seen at Penshurst Place. Most of the important sandstones, however, are more ancient than the Jurassic

Deene Park; the courtyard, of Weldon limestone

Harewood House; the garden front, of sandstone

limestones and are to be found in the Midlands, West and North; Arbury Hall, Weston Park, Chatsworth, Harewood House and Seaton Delaval are among the leading English examples, while across the Border, in a pink sandstone, are Kellie Castle, Arbroath (where the stone was quarried on the estate) and a more spectacular house than any of these: Drumlanrig Castle in Dumfriesshire. Heavy sandstone slates endow many roofs in these regions with splendid authority, including even houses like Adlington Hall near Macclesfield, which are wholly or partly timber-framed.

Mountain (Carboniferous) limestone is chiefly to be found in the Peak District and in the far North. Usually it is rubbly and very tough, as at Haddon Hall, where this light grey stone has stood up to centuries of weathering even better than the buff-coloured gritstone, also quarried locally, which was employed here for the dressings. An unusually refined and delightful example of this limestone is Dalemain in Cumbria, where the presence of ferric oxide in the strata that once covered it has tinged its Georgian front with pink. Still older, but less reliable, are the grey Silurian limestones, confined in England to Wenlock Edge and the Ludlow district, but widely distributed in Wales and the Lowlands of Scotland. These too could only be employed as rubblestone, as at Shipton Hall and Stokesay and Gwydir Castles.

For granite, on the other hand, we must go to the South-West. An interesting Cornish example dating from the seventeenth century is Godolphin House near Helston. Somewhat akin to granite and also employed for building in Cornwall, is a local quartz-porphyry known as elvan, which mostly came from the Pentewan quarry north of Mevagissey. Trewithen, a delightful early Georgian house built of this light grey stone, is nevertheless on the garden side almost wholly pink. This surprising effect is due to a very smooth lichen, growing here in profusion.

The finest brick houses are mostly in the South and East, where good stone is not so readily available and where the clays are the best for brick-making. But there is at least one highly enjoyable example of Tudor brickwork on the west side of the Jurassic limestone belt: Compton Wyn-yates, where, admittedly, the dressings and the roofs are of stone. Contemporary with this in Essex is that extraordinary Tudor skyscraper, Layer Marney Tower, where it is no surprise to find no stone at all, for no county is so devoid of it as Essex. At Layer Marney the principal windows are of terracotta, but Ingatestone Hall, not far away, is brick in its entirety, even to the copings of its gables and the mullions and transoms of every window.

Under Elizabeth I and James I the bricks still remained comparatively narrow ($9 \times 4\frac{1}{2} \times 2\frac{1}{4}$ inches was somewhere near the average) and fairly rough, but for these very reasons rich in textural quality. Among a good many fine examples from this period Hatfield House and Burton Agnes Hall are outstanding, but Doddington Hall near Lincoln and two big houses which in the nineteenth century were badly damaged by fire, Kentwell Hall in Suffolk and Breamore House in Hampshire, yet preserve handsome red brick fronts. In the early Georgian period the brick craftsmanship reached the apogee of subtlety and refinement, and in the entire country there is scarcely one example finer than Chicheley Hall in Buckinghamshire, where two fronts are entirely faced with orange-red rubbed bricks. Including the garden walls, nearly a million of them were required for this house, and it is practically certain that they were specially made on the site, for the clay here is ideal for brickmaking.

On this absorbing subject a great deal more could of course be added, but enough has, I hope, been said to indicate what is indeed the truth: that, with eyes wide open, it is almost impossible to exhaust the architectural delights of our island. I find grounds for optimism in the increasing interest in visual education: for when more people are aware of what they are looking at and of what there is to be seen, the prospects of preservation, and where necessary of scholarly restoration, are improved. In this respect, and even though demolitions have occurred which are greatly to be deplored, the country houses have, on the whole, during the past thirty years, an honourable record. Some, like Chatsworth, have restored Georgian glazing bars to windows so misguidedly deprived of them during the nineteenth century; others have greatly improved their appearance by the removal of in-appropriate Victorian accretions. The opening of more and more houses to the public has also had, I do not hesitate to say, a beneficial effect, for it has meant that owners have been put on their mettle. 'How good of you,' my mother once said to the owner of a spectacular collection of Japanese cherry trees, 'to open your garden to the public.' 'Not at all,' he replied; 'that's the one way in which I can be sure of getting my gardeners up to scratch.' *Mutatis mutandis*, the same may be true of some at least of the rich cross-section of houses which this book so enthusiastically describes.

The Middle Ages: From House in the Country to Country House

by John Harvey

The unique institution of the English Country House is rooted in the Middle Ages. What are now considered 'country houses' do not conform to a single type but have several different origins. Firstly there are defensive strongholds such as Alnwick, Arundel, Raby or Warwick Castles; numerous in England, this type is all but universal in Scotland (Cawdor, Glamis, Traquair). Then there are houses on the sites of monasteries dissolved under Henry VIII: in this category are Beaulieu, Forde, Longleat, Syon, Wilton and Woburn among others. Finally there are the strictly domestic mansions whose main purpose has always been residential. This class, in England by far the most numerous, includes many relatively small homes though a few, such as Haddon Hall and Compton Wynyates, are large and complex buildings.

The term country house has wide social connotations apart from its literal meaning, and these overtones derive in considerable measure from mediaeval systems of land ownership. Scotland had different forms of tenure, and so had independent Wales, but we are here concerned primarily with England and with its history after the Norman Conquest of 1066. The vague Anglo-Saxon theory of royal ownership of the country was replaced by the hard reality of the feudal system, imported from the continent. The free communities of England, though dominated by men of wealth and lineage, had been essentially independent and based upon the association of tribes, families or ships' companies which had combined to conquer Britain before the 11th century. Superimposed upon this English system, largely homogeneous in origins and language, was an alien French-speaking stratum of Normans, Bretons, Flemings and others, owing their position to force of arms. In a few cases (e.g. Sudeley) estates remained in the hands of Saxon families.

The new lords were bound to one another and to the king by the incidents of feudal tenure whereby each knight (mounted warrior) owed loyalty and service to a superior. On the continent this system was largely self-defeating, in that subordinates of a great lord might be led by him against the sovereign: loyalty to an immediate overlord was not controlled by any higher patriotism. William the Conqueror, so far as England was concerned, changed the system radically. Towards the end of his life, in 1086, he caused the whole country to be surveyed, recording both ownership and valuation in Domesday Book; and he called together all the tenant lords and required

Haddon Hall, showing the 14th-century Hall

them to take an oath (the 'Oath at Salisbury') to obey him as king rather than any intermediate lord. From this point England diverged from continental usage in the direction of insularity and of personal loyalty to the Crown.

Thus Norman rule in England was the regime of a powerful monarch based upon a military oligarchy of great lords who, in turn, derived power from the services and payments of subordinate tenants. The fundamental service was that of fighting in the king's wars, and of bringing a body of knights as a private contingent, supported by socially inferior men-at-arms and archers, the infantry of the period. Under the Norman kings the great landowners were mainly men who had fought with the Conqueror at Hastings and who were rewarded by grants of large areas of land. In most cases the cautious king scattered his gift over a wide area to afford less scope for the formation of rebellious interests in particular regions. To the Crown were reserved many, but not all, of the places which had belonged to the defeated Anglo-Saxon House of Wessex, the 'ancient demesne of the Crown'.

Many of the agglomerations of estates in the hands of magnates were termed 'Honors', which might comprise many manors spread over several counties. In such cases the lord would move from one possession to another, imitating the constant travels of the king himself. Provisions were best eaten fresh and the cost of transport precluded bringing large amounts of food to a single centre. It was cheaper for king or nobleman to ride to one estate after another, devouring its stock, than to live in a single home off transported produce. This way of life had two results that deeply affected the development of the English country house. At strategic points in each major collection of scattered manors large dwellings had to be built, capable of containing the lord, his family, and a substantial number of servants and followers. In second place, this gave rise to the leasehold system, whereby some of these large houses (e.g. Deene, Sheldon) could be let to tenants, usually on condition of entertaining the lord and his retinue for a limited time at stated intervals. Eventually these leased houses were bought outright by their tenants.

As a general rule the English country house is the home of the lord of a manor. It is what is commonly known as a manor-house, the *caput manerii* of the old lawyers; but it grew far beyond this into a treasury of personal possessions of a family, surrounded by a pleasance of gardens. The process of development has been one of imitation, as taste and fashion emanated from the Court and steadily penetrated the country. A process which began at royal palaces and passed to the castles of the great earls, went on to enrich the homes of the lesser nobility and the gentry. The system of feudal tenure, combined with the constant travels of the royal Court and of the greater landowners, ensured the rapid dissemination of ideas.

The lords of manors, whether of the higher nobility or not, had heavy responsibilities and played an important part in mediaeval government. Long before the creation of our Justices of the Peace, local administration was largely in the hands of the manor court presided over by the lord's steward. The ancient system of mutual responsibility termed *Frankpledge*, inherited from Saxon England, was incorporated into the post-conquest jurisdiction of the lord. Every householder had to belong to his *tithing* or group of ten and, in theory, ten such tithings formed the *hundred*, one of the subdivisions of each county. The more powerful lords of manors obtained from the Crown a grant of the View of Frankpledge or Court Leet, in which the lord and his tenants jointly appointed a Constable and assistant Tithing-men. Law and order throughout the country were maintained by the Courts

Ightham Mote; a mediaeval courtyard house

Leet and the Hundred Courts, while the quality and fair measure of the staple foods, bread and ale, were tested by the Ale-conner, also appointed for the year at the Michaelmas Court.

By the thirteenth century the uneasy tension between the English and their French-speaking lords was becoming a more settled partnership. Many intermarriages had taken place between the invaders and the descendants of the Saxon landowners, so that there was no longer any sharp hostility between two nations in one land. Generally the lay manors were held by *military tenure* or else were in *socage*, essentially the same as a normal freehold. There might also be special duties as well as the obligation to pay a *heriot*, the best beast or its cash value, on the death of the holder, the forerunner of death duties. These heavy dues at death affected high and low in all walks of life.

Subordinate manors, besides owing service to their chief lord, might owe him money rents, periodic duties of *Castle Guard* at the chief castle of his estates (as at Northborough), and a heriot, as well as a *fine* in cash payable by the heir for his right to succeed. A few special cases were of manors held in *serjeanty*, that is by some particular service, such as finding tents for the king when on campaign or keeping the king's hawks or hounds (at Purse Caundle). *Leasehold*, as applying to supernumerary manors forming part of a great estate, has already been mentioned. Many special conditions might be included in leases, sometimes the right to hold courts as if the lessee were himself lord of the manor; sometimes provisions regarding the maintenance of the house and its park and gardens. Occasionally this might go

Purse Caundle Manor; 15th century, with Tudor additions

so far as to stipulate numbers of forest or fruit trees to be planted each year.

Between the Norman Conquest and 1290 it was possible for the lord of a large manor to sell off parts of it, conveying manorial rights over each part to the purchaser. After 1290 this was not allowed and the number of separate manors in England remained the same. Originally there may have been as many manors as there were parishes, some 11,000 or so in all. But by the end of the thirteenth century the total must have been far greater, since many large parishes consisted of several manors. On the other hand there were a few enormous manors like Wakefield in Yorkshire, which spread into over a dozen parishes, comprised 36 sub-manors, and over 50 townships.

All this was supported by the labour, fines and rents of the men who worked the land and who supplied the needed craftsmanship in various trades. Most of these men held houses with larger or smaller amounts of land under the copyhold system of customary tenure. Each manor had its own customs but every transaction passed through the lord's hand in the manorial court (or Court Baron) held by a steward on his behalf, and was entered in the court roll; a copy of the entry was handed to the tenant as his title. The lord could not turn all the land of his manor into copyholds: if he did not keep at least two freehold tenants the manor became a mere lordship and the manorial rights reverted to his overlord or to the Crown if he held of the king in chief. The principle of forfeiture in case of disloyalty or disobedience to the custom of a particular place was fundamental to the whole system. While a great lord might forfeit his gigantic estate to the Crown if he became a traitor, so the humble copyholder would lose his few acres if he felled a timber tree for repairs without his lord's licence.

Whereas copyholds had normally, from Saxon times, descended to the youngest son ('Borough English'), the Norman lords brought with them the custom of primogeniture in which the eldest son inherited. When estates, great or small, descended to daughters for lack of male heirs, the wardship and marriage of daughters became a valuable commodity, sold in the open market. The king would grant the right to the marrying of his wards, in effect to the highest bidder, and the fortunate suitor would have to pay handsomely for his chance to acquire by marriage an estate otherwise unobtainable. One unexpected effect of this acquisition by marriage was biological: the tendency to have girl children rather than sons was sometimes genetic and inheritable, so that an estate would repeatedly pass to the female line and the surname of the holding family change again (e.g. Athelhampton, Burton Agnes, Warwick Castle).

Many estates were not inherited by blood relatives: those in the hands of churchmen. Some of the larger country homes of the Middle Ages belonged to archbishops and bishops (Saltwood, Sherborne) or archdeacons (Lympne), others to abbots or priors of monasteries (Boughton, Burghley, Deene, Gaulden, Gorhambury, Ingatestone); smaller manors might comprise the glebe land of the rectors of wealthy parishes (Buckland). Such lands were held in *mortmain* by the tenure called *Frankalmoign* or Free Alms. If a man wished to ensure his welfare in the next world he might give a whole manor to the Church, on the undertaking that masses would be said

Buckland Rectory; once owned by the Abbey of Gloucester

perpetually for his soul and the souls of his parents, wife, children or other relatives and friends. To effect such a transaction the king's licence had to be obtained; a large fee was paid to the Crown in compensation for the loss of the expectation of forfeiture, not only for misbehaviour but owing to the eventual dying out of a family. The '*mort main*' or dead hand of the Church would hold for ever, come what might; and in the case of educational foundations like the Oxford or Cambridge Colleges, Eton, Winchester, and a few hospitals such as St Cross, this tenure in mortmain has survived. It was the steady increase in the proportion of land that thus passed to ecclesiastical landlords that was the chief factor provoking Henry VIII's ultimate decision to abolish monasticism altogether.

The king obtained fees for various subsidiary privileges of lords of manors. Among these the principal were the rights to hold Markets and Fairs; the Court Leet already mentioned; permission to *crenellate*, that is to embattle the walls of a dwelling to form a castle (Belvoir, Broughton, Hever, Markenfield, Penshurst, Raby, Sherborne, Stokesay); to enclose a Park for fallow deer (red deer were reserved to the king), as at Boughton Monchelsea, Berkeley, Knebworth, Powderham; or to have *Free Warren*, the privilege of preserving game such as roe deer, hare and rabbit. The lords of manors enjoyed two other rights: the keeping of pigeons and doves and erection of a Dovecote (Athelhampton, Aston Munslow, Avebury, Hellen's, Shipton Hall; and, converted to a cottage, at Powderham); and the appointment of Gamekeepers. Until modern times all gamekeepers were licensed, and few but the lords of manors could obtain this licence.

Certain major aspects of the country estate were common to all, whether military or civil, lay or ecclesiastical. Many, indeed almost all, of the major houses were surrounded by parks, for preserving deer, but also rather for aesthetic love of the combination of trees, grassland and pools or lakes of water. The pools might serve as fishponds, but they were also things of beauty. All country homes had gardens and these too served a double or triple purpose. Vegetable garden and orchard provided the lord's table; in the south there might also be a vineyard producing grapes for wine. A herb garden was added for the medicinal value of its plants from the earliest times, and from the beauty and rich perfume of some species: rose, lily, wallflower, flag iris, there arose the high appreciation of flower gardens which has become so characteristically English.

Paradoxically, it is from far off that this typical outlook came to us by surprising routes. From Arabo-Norman Sicily came the oriental paradise-garden: a walled park with animals and an inner sanctuary of pools, arbours and flower-beds. A foretaste of English horticulture already existed about 1092 at Romsey, where William Rufus and his courtiers sought to enter the nuns' garden 'to see its roses and other flowering herbs'. In the case of the later nuns' garden at Syon there was actual continuity with the botanical garden started there by William Turner for the Protector Somerset in 1548 and flourishing ever since. Henry I introduced the Persian zoological

Berkeley Castle; the 14th-century Chapel, now the Morning Room (chimneypiece and doorways are recent importations from France)

Markenfield; view from the east, showing the 14th-century Chapel window

paradise when he had a stone wall built about Woodstock (now Blenheim) Park in 1110, and appointed a royal gardener at Havering in Essex, named from its characteristic pleasure garden or arbour 'atte Bower' to this day. In 1165 Henry II was creating the original Rosamund's Bower for his mistress beside the spring of Everswell in Woodstock Park, and by 1190 Randolph, earl of Chester, was appointing a head gardener for the castle garden and securing the future of the stock apple-tree from which grafts would be taken. Early in the reign of Henry III the newly rich Paulin Peyvre was lampooned by Matthew Paris for apeing the luxury of earls at his manor-house of Toddington in Bedfordshire, which he 'beset with orchards and pools'. Evidently the country house had already arrived and long before the end of the Middle Ages was assuming that special guise which, in spite of many changes of style and fashion, it still wears today.

Private Ownership and the Future

by John Cornforth

There is a deceptive lull on the historic house scene. Every year more and more houses in Britain are open, and gifts and bequests of houses to the National Trust and the National Trust for Scotland still go through, so to most visitors all seems well, particularly as the standards of presentation and of the facilities for visitors generally go up. But visitors should not be assured that all is well, and that the existing package of highly technical arrangements for exemption from Capital Transfer Tax, treatment of opening operations for purposes of income tax, repair grants, and so on, is either a possible or an acceptable one to owners. It is not. But owners are holding on to see what the Government will do; and the Government is waiting to see if the little they have done is sufficient to prevent total collapse. However, it is no longer a straight game of cat and mouse: public opinion is a force that the Government has to reckon with as well. Public participation is one of the theoretical corner stones of the new planning machine, and the awakening of opinion since the autumn of 1974 when a Wealth Tax was proposed, and its development into a wide-ranging vocal lobby, could be and should be crucial in the achievement of a fair deal for historic houses in private ownership.

The achievement of that fair deal looks simple enough on paper, but it is only right to point out some of the difficulties. As far as the public is concerned, it is not always clear how significant 'a crisis' may be. The announcement of the impending sale of a large house and its possibly valuable contents immediately creates a shudder, but the shudder may be down the wrong spine. If the contents are particularly good, they may include individual objects that national and regional museums would like to buy but cannot afford, and such institutions fear a future tussle over export licences. On the other hand even now quite a high proportion of the objects are likely to find new owners in this country and take their place in growing collections. On occasions such as these the problem may not be a historic house problem at all.

What is much more serious is the sale from clearly recognised historic collections in historic houses of significant things such as the Canaletto views of Warwick Castle. Rightly there is considerable dismay that the pictures should leave the Castle; but the fact that is hard to accept is that the family had foresight in realising that one day it might want to sell them, and so paid the death duty liability rather than seek exemption; and that now the family has the foresight to sell them before it is prevented from so doing by some future legislation of unknown severity. People do not want to see that the argument has that particularly nasty tail. There is much more to be said about the whole problem of Warwick Castle, its importance, its repair, and its contents, and all this concerns the responsibilities involved in the preservation of what has come to be called the National Heritage. The nation still pays incredibly little towards the total upkeep of houses, gardens and collections, and all the running costs fall on the owner: so while the nation talks about National Heritage it conveniently forgets who pays for it. Most owners feel that they are only trustees of their houses and collections, but they feel that way not only because of their sense of tradition and indebtedness to the past but also out of a sense of responsibility to the future – which means their family as well as the nation. They are caught in a web of legislation and social pressures, and they must see some kind of a future for both their houses and their families if they are to be expected to soldier on. If they don't, they won't.

That is what the Warwick sales have been about: cash and confidence. For about 20–25 years, from the late 1940s to the early 1970s, there was a remarkable recovery of confidence among country house owners, and it is to be seen not only in the number of houses that visitors can now enjoy but the truly remarkable number of massive restoration programmes carried out in the face of great difficulty. Indeed it will prove to be one of the most fascinating periods in the history of the English country house. The announcement in the summer of 1974 of the proposed Capital Transfer Tax and Wealth Tax seriously undermined if not actually destroyed that confidence; but, coming as it did at a time of unprecedented inflation, the effect was disastrous and there is little doubt that owners' confidence was in fact destroyed. As a result of a great deal of public pressure, certain significant concessions were made to the CTT proposals as regards historic houses, but their significance has to be interpreted in two ways.

Warwick Castle about 1750; view in the Courtyard by Canaletto

Warwick Castle about 1750; the Driveway, by Canaletto

As far as the Government has been concerned, it has felt that the concessions were sufficient to ensure the preservation of historic houses in private hands, or anyway were as far-reaching as it could afford or dared to go. As far as private owners are concerned, the concessions do not go far enough to provide a realistic economic basis for the future, but at least they form a basis for negotiation and a position from which to exert pressure.

That is the reason for the uneasy pause following the public fever from the autumn of 1974 to the autumn of 1976. Things seem quiet, but the stock pot is kept close to boiling point: every time a major house appears to be in difficulties the Press seizes on it, and the obituary columns of *The Times* have a new significance. To my mind the surprising thing is that there have not been more pictures like the Warwick Canalettos put up for sale, and that, apart from Mentmore, no other great house or historic collection has yet become a public crisis. But one, or six, could at any moment.

As far as owners are concerned, the future does not just depend on a workable arrangement for their houses, collections and the assets to support them: it depends on their heirs, how they think their heirs will react and whether the heirs will actually want to carry on. Many of the houses that have been demolished in this century or have been adapted for some new purpose have belonged to people who did not want to carry on or felt that their children would not want to, or the children themselves decided to leave. I do not think that before 1974 this was recognised as a significant part of the future problem. Now, however, I am sure it is, and when there is talk of a sense of trusteeship and confidence and a working relationship with the Government, the willingness of heirs to continue is much more important. Indeed it could be as significant as day to day cost problems. Owners will not necessarily wish to be shackled to a house open to the public, and if their farm or estate is not large enough – and many will not be after CTT – they will want and have to pursue a full time career elsewhere that cannot be combined with proper running of a house or its opening.

As far as the Government and its advisers are concerned, the problem is an appalling one. It is now stated policy to encourage private owners, and it is acknowledged that private ownership is in the best interests of the houses as well as being the most economical both in terms of income and capital. The costs involved in the acquisition of a major house, its contents and its park, are now enormous, as are the repair, maintenance and running costs, and naturally the Government wishes to have to take on as few as possible. Furthermore historic houses without their historic contents are much less significant as well as being of much less appeal to visitors; but there is no way of tying contents to houses, or land to houses. For the smaller houses a new owner could be a good solution, but there is no way of encouraging their owners to maintain the thread of continuity and further extend it. All that we have is negative legislation to protect the fabric of such houses. Each crisis has to be fought out agonisingly blow by blow.

That, however, is no solution to the general problem, and what is needed is a policy that will reduce the number of crises and make the best use of resources. The possibility of light at the end of the tunnel must be turned into a tunnel properly lit. Otherwise the Warwick Canalettos will be followed by a rapid acceleration of sales, and if two or three owners of major houses decided to sell and depart the fever would spread. It would then be too late for any Government to act. In less than a generation houses would be stripped and abandoned, and much of the point of country house visiting in Britain would have gone. That is why the present lull is so deceptive and so disturbing. The grey clouds could quickly turn to thunder.

Since this was written in 1978, Warwick Castle with its surviving contents has been sold and is no longer in private ownership.

Houses in
England and Wales

Adlington Hall, Cheshire
(Mr Charles Legh)

Five miles north of Macclesfield (A523)

Leghs have been at Adlington for over six-and-a-half centuries. They fought with the Black Prince, campaigned in Scotland, served with distinction under Essex at the siege of Cadiz. Royalists in the Civil War, they saw Adlington twice besieged, and their property sequestered. On nine occasions they filled the office of High Sheriff of the County of Cheshire.

The architecture of the house reflects this long tenure. The wide brick entrance front, centred on a huge pedimented portico, was finished in 1757. It was built by Charles Legh, dilettante and friend of Handel, who was perhaps his own architect (for the portico is too tall for the facade and its Ionic columns stand uneasily on their octagonal pedestals). Behind this front lies a flagged courtyard, and here a far older house is revealed. The transition from the formality of the 18th century to the black and white timbering of Tudor times offers a surprising contrast. One is confronted across the courtyard with a hall completed in 1505. Originally timbered it was refaced in brick some eighty years later, when the large windows with stone mullions were inserted. At the same date the gabled jettied porch was added, and the black and white timbered house was built that forms the rest of this front and the whole of the east wing. This characteristic Cheshire work is highly picturesque.

The Hall, composed of diverse elements, is the most remarkable feature of Adlington. The hammerbeam roof is 1500, though the shield-bearing angels which look down benevolently from the hammers are said to be later. The two great octagonal spere trusses, a Cheshire and Lancashire speciality, are elaborately carved (unlike those at Chorley Old Hall). They mark the site of the screen which was no doubt movable and stood between them, as the movable screen still does at Rufford Old Hall. The oak trees which form the speres are said never to have been felled but shaped *in situ*. At the end of the hall where the dais was once situated, there is an extraordinary coved and panelled canopy. This also is a feature original to the hall of 1500, though much of the armorial decoration is later. The mullioned and transomed windows, as we have seen, were inserted in about 1580. Further important changes occurred in the late 17th century, when the Baroque organ, built by the most notable of 17th-century organ builders, Father Smith, was installed. This noble instrument terminates in a splendid flourish with the family arms, surmounted by their white unicorn crest, set between trumpeting angels. The balusters of the organ gallery, which breaks forward in the

Adlington Hall; left: *the portico, dated 1757, and* right: *the Hall, showing the spere truss and later organ gallery*

centre to allow room for the organist's seat, are carved with great refinement, as are those of the galleries added at the same time on either side of the Hall. Handel himself played on the organ when staying at Adlington in 1741–2. The final additions to the Hall, if one excepts the early-18th-century fireplace, were the large murals depicting scenes from the *Iliad*. They can hardly be before about 1700 for at least one lady, dressed in the fashion of that time, has joined the heroes in classical costume. Plastered over at an unknown date, the murals were rediscovered in 1859; though crudely painted, they make their contribution to the warmth and colour that characterise this unusual hall.

One or two smaller rooms have Carolean panelling, and must have been done up at about the time that the organ was introduced into the Hall. By contrast, the Main Staircase (with a good portrait of John Legh, 1668–1739, by Pieter Van Reyschoot) and the formal apartments in the west range date from the mid-18th century and are contemporary with the porticoed Entrance Front. The Drawing Room has a plaster ceiling and wainscot of that date, the latter punctuated by fluted Corinthian columns and hung with Legh portraits. The overmantel surprisingly combines the realistically carved fruit and foliage typical of late Carolean times with rococo elements. In the Dining Room, panelled more simply but at the same date, there are a convincing full-length portrait by Cornelius Johnson of Thomas Legh, who made the black and white timbered additions to the house, and three portraits by Thomas Hudson which include a likeness of Charles Legh who both created this room and built the Entrance Front.

A la Ronde, Devon
(Mrs Ursula R. Tudor Perkins)

Two miles north of Exmouth (A377)

One of the less-known curiosities among English houses, A la Ronde was built by two maiden ladies. Jane Parminter, the daughter of a successful Devon merchant, took her young cousin Mary on an exhaustive European tour lasting ten years. Returning in 1794, they designed this sixteen-sided house. The tradition that its singular plan was inspired by the Byzantine church of San Vitale in Ravenna is supported chiefly by Jane's intelligence and invention, evident in every part of the building. Later they also built the nearby chapel 'Point in View', with its almshouses and Minister's Manse.

Much more than a mere *cottage orné*, the house is bigger than it appears and within the solid stone walls there are twenty rooms. The roof was originally thatched; the dormers are modern, and the square basement windows 19th century. On the main floor, eight rooms radiate from a high octagonal Hall, their diamond-barred windows all built on angles; the lozenge windows belong to wedge-shaped closets between the rooms. All kinds of ingenuities like folding seats and sliding doors help to save space. The Hall, when seen from the gallery above, gives a curious illusion of being nearly twice its actual height, which is thirty-six feet.

The decorations were carried out by the cousins themselves, and are a fine survival of ladies' accomplishments that had been made fashionable in London by Mrs Delany and others. The entire Gallery floor is covered with shell-work, the shells having mostly come from Guernsey, and feather pictures of birds set against backgrounds of coloured sand. Shell- and feather-work also feature in some of the rooms, besides sand-and-seaweed

A la Ronde

pictures and some skilful pictures of cut paper. The Parminters' furniture and pictures remain here, including chairs that were specially designed for the Hall, while the cousins' tour of Italy is recalled in sixteen framed etchings of Rome and Paestum by Piranesi. All this has passed by family descent to the present owner.

Alnwick Castle, Northumberland
(The Duke of Northumberland, K.G.)

In the town of Alnwick

No name in Northumberland is more illustrious than Percy. The family came to England in 1066, and have lived at Alnwick since 1309 when they succeeded the de Vescys as hereditary Wardens of the Scottish Marches. Their history became one of Border wars, invasions and counter-invasions, hostilities and bloodshed, and the Northumbrian people depended on the Percys for their very survival. In the more settled 16th century the family were mostly Catholic, and they suffered much for taking part in the Northern Rebellions. The free-thinking 10th Earl of Northumberland supported Cromwell on constitutional grounds, but was strongly opposed to the execution of Charles I and later helped to restore Charles II to the throne. He will be seen here, as Lord High Admiral of England, in a magnificent portrait by Van Dyck.

In 1750, the male line died out and the vast Percy estates were divided. Lady Elizabeth Seymour inherited the Northumberland property as well as Syon and the house in London. She had married Sir Hugh Smithson, a Yorkshire Baronet reputed to be the most handsome man in England. He assumed the name of Percy and became the 1st Duke of Northumberland. Full-length portraits by Reynolds of the Duke and his Duchess are given the place of honour in the Dining Room.

The Castle occupies a natural defensive position on a rocky precipice above the Alne. From the main roads there are superb views of the park, whose rocky crags were reduced to green slopes by Capability Brown. The Norman castle of the de Vescys was mostly rebuilt by the Percys in the early 14th century. The Keep was remodelled with semi-circular bastions and given a strong and imposing entrance with twin octagonal towers. The Percys also rebuilt the curtain wall to the enceinte, and the long, threatening defile of the Barbican, or main entrance. The figures of soldiers on the battlements seem to be 18th-century replacements of mediaeval originals.

Inside the gate the outer and inner baileys lie either side of the Keep. Much of the fabric is mediaeval, but since the 18th century it has been extended twice. Robert Adam remodelled all the rooms, and, to please the Duchess, they were made delightfully Gothic. But most of his work was swept away by the 4th Duke, who in the 1850s spent a quarter of a million pounds in modernising the whole building. The architect was Anthony Salvin, who added to the exterior the Chapel, and the Prudhoe Tower that

Alnwick Castle from the River Alne; (see also colour plate 1)

rises above the height of the old castle. He removed part of the wall and
built the north Terrace with its fine view of Adam's bridge over the river.
Inside the Keep there remains a Norman arch and the draw-well of 1310,
but Salvin's massive arcade supporting a towering structure is much more
impressive. He showed a genius in constructing palatial state rooms within a
decidedly cramped shell. The Library takes up the whole length of the
Prudhoe Tower, and the Dining Room is in the position of the original
Great Hall.

The 'building' 4th Duke was a sailor, a dedicated traveller, and a per-
fectionist. Though the outside remained a feudal stronghold, he wanted the
interior to be both modern and enduring. Italian palaces, he noticed, had the
right combination of ruggedness outside and polish within, so the style
decided upon was Renaissance and Italians were employed for the interior
features. The Drawing Room is hung with gold and scarlet damask from
Italy. As for the noble coffered ceilings, they were designed in Italy but
mostly carried out by the 'Alnwick School' that was established under a
talented local carver, John Brown. The unpainted Dining Room ceiling was
carved from cedar and pine imported from New Brunswick. The result of all
this is probably the finest Victorian interior in England.

In 1754 Canaletto was employed to paint the 1st Duke's inheritance of
three houses: Northumberland House (London), Syon and Alnwick, and
these paintings will be seen in the Music Room. Northumberland House
was demolished in 1874, and its contents, including Kent and Adam
furniture, were divided between Alnwick and Syon. But the most famous
pieces here are a pair of French cabinets, made by Cucci at the Gobelins

factory in 1683 and incorporating Florentine *pietre dure*. They had belonged to Louis XIV, but at the Revolution were looted from the Tuileries, and later were bought in Paris by the 3rd Duke. The most impressive porcelain is a Meissen dinner service of 1740, boldly painted with animals and birds, and another of 1780 with gentle scenes from Aesop. Many Italian paintings were bought in Italy by the 4th Duke, including works by Titian, Sebastiano del Piombo, Tintoretto, Andrea del Sarto and Palma Vecchio. The long series of family portraits extends from Van Dyck and Dobson into the 19th century.

Althorp, Northamptonshire
(The Earl Spencer)

Seven miles north-west of Northampton (A428)

The Spencers lived at Wormleighton in Warwickshire, and became rich from extensive sheep farming. They bought Althorp, a moated courtyard house, in 1506, and Sir John Spencer added the forecourt wings in 1575. By the mid-17th century the internal courtyard had been covered over and became the Grand Staircase, which is the earliest visible part of the building. Henry Lord Spencer lent £10,000 to Charles I at the outset of the Civil War, in return for which he was created Earl of Sunderland, only to be killed four months later, aged twenty-three, at the Battle of Newbury. His brilliant son Robert, a man of few scruples, became indispensable to Charles II, James II and William III in turn, and during his extraordinary career was Ambassador to Paris, Cologne and Madrid. A great collector of paintings, he Italianised the house, held secret political meetings in the Great Room, and gave splendid entertainments for Cosimo III de' Medici and William III. The rooms and furnishings, John Evelyn wrote, were 'such as may become a great prince'.

The great survival from that period is the long Picture Gallery. The oak-panelled walls are entirely hung with portraits, the most notable being by Van Dyck whose double portrait on the end wall of the young Earls of Bristol and Bedford is popularly known as 'War and Peace'. It seems to prophesy the time when the Parliamentarian Bedford came to sack Sherborne Castle. The series of Hampton Court Beauties by Lely are in carved frames of a type invented by Lord Sunderland and which still bear his name.

Through his aunt a later Earl of Sunderland succeeded as Duke of Marlborough in 1733; the Althorp property passed to the younger brother John. At that time the Entrance Hall was being remodelled: its lofty coving is crisply stuccoed in the best Palladian manner, and the Ducal coronet was included in the carving above the inner door. The walls were designed for horse paintings by John Wootton, which fill the spaces exactly. Sarah, Duchess of Marlborough, doted on her Spencer grandson and left him houses, pictures, and the famous Marlborough plate which had travelled with the General on his campaigns in the Low Countries. His heir, the 1st Lord Spencer, also collected works of art, and built and furnished Spencer

Althorp

House (now used as offices) overlooking Green Park in London. During a ball at Althorp in 1755 he had secretly married Georgiana Poyntz in the Oak Room upstairs. The marriage proved happy, and their daughters were those famous leaders of Whig Society, the Duchess of Devonshire and the Countess of Bessborough.

When the 2nd Earl, an active Whig, succeeded in 1783, Althorp was in need of extensive repairs. For a Whig the natural choice of architect was Henry Holland, who had not only built Brooks's Club but was working on Carlton House and Brighton Pavilion for the Prince of Wales. Holland's designs for Althorp were fine and more work was done than Lord Spencer had intended. The red brick and stone disappeared behind pale mathematical tiles baked at Ipswich, which Holland made fashionable. The width of the forecourt was reduced by communicating corridors. The Oak Gallery was papered green and fitted with bookshelves, and the state rooms, formerly on the first floor, were moved downstairs. Holland's succession of Dining Room, Yellow Drawing Room and Long Library filled the west side of the house. He also designed furniture that is decidedly French in character, and it stands well with the superb French lacquer commodes by Saunier and Weisweiller that were bought at the same time.

The present appearance of these rooms is deceptive because later alterations fit in extremely well. Some ceilings and wide door openings were put in around 1870; 18th-century doors and marble chimneypieces designed by John Vardy and 'Athenian' Stuart were moved here from Spencer House after the last war, together with wonderful 18th-century furniture and portraits. The gilded chairs in the Marlborough Room were made for the great ballroom at Spencer House, and the two famous pedestals, pioneer works of English neo-classicism, were designed for its painted room about 1760 by 'Athenian' Stuart.

Althorp; William Poyntz (Gainsborough); and Lady Spencer with her daughter Georgiana (Reynolds)

To enter the Marlborough Room, where all the portraits are by Reynolds and Gainsborough, is like taking a journey back to 18th-century London. Here is Reynolds's tender portrait of Lady Spencer with her daughter, the future Duchess of Devonshire, painted at the same time as Gainsborough's portrait of her brother, William Poyntz. Reynolds painted three generations of this family. The 2nd Earl appears, full length, as a youth of seventeen in Van Dyck dress and with copious auburn hair. His sister, Lady Bessborough, hangs next to the four-year-old Viscount Althorp who grew up to become the ardent promoter of the Reform Bill and Leader of the House of Commons under Lord Grey. A later portrait of him by Hayter hangs by the staircase. The Spencers had a gift of choosing talented painters, and were also painted by Maratti and Batoni, Copley, Orpen, Sargent, Nicholson and Augustus John.

The Grand Staircase is entirely hung with more portraits. Other rooms show the vast collection of old master paintings that have been acquired over two centuries, among them the large canvases by Salvator Rosa and Guercino in the Dining Room and the striking Pourbus in the South Drawing Room of the Duc de Chevreuse. In the Yellow Drawing Room there are portraits by Rubens of Charles V, Philip IV and Elizabeth of Spain, and the Archduke Albert.

After the last war, the late Lord Spencer found the house almost in danger of collapse. Eighteen tons of bedroom walls, injudiciously built by Holland into the first floor, were removed and the fine 17th-century woodwork was once more revealed. When the treasures from Spencer House were brought to Althorp, cases were built for the superb porcelain in which nearly all the 18th-century factories are represented, notably Chelsea, Meissen and Sèvres. The house has been completely re-arranged by the present Lord and Lady Spencer in the last few years, and it is all lived in as a family home.

Arbury Hall, Warwickshire
(Mr Humphrey FitzRoy Newdegate)

Three miles south-west of Nuneaton (B4102)

In the built-up area between Coventry and Nuneaton, once part of the Forest of Arden, a baronial gateway of dark red sandstone leads into an oasis of park. George Eliot was brought up on this estate, and Arbury appears in her early work, *Scenes of Clerical Life*, as 'Cheveril Manor'. She describes its benevolent and cultivated squire transforming it 'from plain brick into the model of a Gothic manor-house'. This was Sir Roger Newdigate, who owned the property for seventy-two years. A painting by Arthur Devis shows him as a young man seated in his newly Gothicised library. Romney's later full-length presents him as a man of letters, and his Oxford University gown is a reminder of the Newdigate Prize that is still awarded annually for verse.

None of our 18th-century Gothic houses remains so complete or so spectacular. Sir Roger began Gothicising by 1750, so the earlier rooms are contemporary with Horace Walpole's Strawberry Hill and the very start of the Gothic Revival. This movement began as a kind of nostalgic archaeology, but it took root because the pointed style was both novel and pretty. Both Walpole and Newdigate seized upon the decorative late-Perpendicular style, and, as at Strawberry Hill, the details at Arbury were copied from known mediaeval buildings, notably from Henry VII's chapel at Westminster Abbey. The result was gaiety, exuberance, and a light heart. The structural basis of true Gothic decoration was unnoticed, or at least unheeded. At Arbury the vaults are not of stone but plaster, not vaults so much as fragile canopies hovering in space.

Over half a century room after room was Gothicised. Sir Roger's architects were, first (probably) Sanderson Miller; then Henry Keene, Surveyor to Westminster Abbey and an acknowledged expert in the Gothic; and finally, after Keene's death, Henry Couchman of Warwick, who finished the

Arbury Hall; left: *the fan-vaulted Dining Room, and* right: *the bow window in the Saloon*

exterior. The patron and his architects became progressively more resourceful. Keene's Drawing Room of 1762 has a pretty vault, and a fireplace based on a tomb at Westminster. The large and lofty Dining Room was constructed ten years later out of the former Hall, and has a bold fan-vault, while an aisle was thrown out towards the garden like a loggia. Here is another monumental chimneypiece, and canopied niches that hold casts of incongruous classical sculpture. The Saloon ceiling is the most elaborate of all, its tracery and pendant drops extending like petrified lace into the bow window.

The house had originally been built on the site of a former Augustinian Priory by Edmund Anderson, one of Queen Elizabeth's more ruthless and ambitious judges. Finding that he must live nearer to London, Anderson exchanged properties in 1586 with John Newdegate, the ancestor of the present owner. Newdegate's son married Anne Fitton, a Maid of Honour to the Queen and sister to Mary Fitton who is still the most popular candidate for the 'Dark Lady' of Shakespeare's sonnets. (On being created Baronets by Charles II, the family changed the spelling of their name until the 19th century.)

The old house, with the stable block behind, can be seen in a drawing of 1708. It was a routine Elizabethan structure, built round the courtyard, with the main door and hall to the south, on the site of the present Dining Room. The original Long Gallery remains over the north entrance. The other room which remains ungothicised is the Chapel. Its foliage ceiling was made by Edward Martin, who also worked at a Wren City church and at Burghley. The door is fitted with a pierced brass lock signed by Wilkes of Birmingham. The chapel was enlarged in the 18th century, and furnished with chairs in the Gothic style.

The paintings are numerous, and begin with Tudor portraits of the first John Newdegate and his wife by Hans Eworth, and a striking picture of Queen Elizabeth. The series then includes Anne Fitton, and later Newdegates by Lely and Dahl, while some of the 17th-century portraits were enlarged and fitted into the decoration of the Gothic Drawing Room. A double portrait by Mercier called *The Card Players* belongs to the 18th century, as do those of the building 5th Baronet. His cousin and heir, the Rev. Francis Parker Newdigate, was painted by the mercurial American artist, Gilbert Stuart, and the portraits continue into the 19th century. Dozens of needlework chair covers were worked by the ladies of the family. A cedar cabinet is carved in the 17th-century mannerist style, and has the coat of arms of Archbishop Laud.

Arreton Manor, Isle of Wight
(Count Slade de Pomeroy)

Three miles south-east of Newport (A3056)

Tucked below the chalk downs, Arreton lies on the edge of a belt of greensand that must have always been exceptionally rich farmland. Alfred

Arreton Manor

the Great owned the manor, as did Edward the Confessor, and at the Dissolution of the Monasteries it became Crown property for nearly a century. Sir Thomas Bennet, who bought it in 1629, was probably responsible for the H plan of the little manor house which stands today.

The south front, with its mullioned windows and its porch dated 1639, is an attractive and unchanged example of the work of the first half of the 17th century. The most interesting rooms are the Dining Parlour and Entrance Hall, both with panelling *c.* 1630. The Dining Parlour has pilasters with a crisply carved vine pattern and a swagger overmantel with the carved arms of Sir Thomas Bennet set between lively panels depicting Mars and the Goddess of Plenty. The oak furniture in these rooms, collected by the present owner, is predominantly Jacobean.

In the Attic storey, and in the East Wing (which possibly antedates the Jacobean house), there are collections of dolls and byegones, and in the nearby Dairy is an unusual museum celebrating the early history of wireless and television.

Arundel Castle, West Sussex
(The Duke of Norfolk)

Between Chichester and Worthing

The best view of Arundel is from the train as it crosses the water meadows after bursting through the Axun gap. Towers and battlements overlook the trees, the Norfolk standard flying from the keep, the red-roofed town below

Arundel Castle; a photograph taken before 1870; (see also colour plate 2)

and an Amiens-vision of the cathedral on the sky-line. Of the mediaeval castle, only the keep on its conical hump, the barbican and some bits of walling survive. Arundel's chief interest lies in its being one of the grandest achievements of the 18th- and 19th-century Romantic imagination. In solidity and scale it is exceeded only by Windsor and Alnwick.

Founded by Roger de Montgomery after the Norman Conquest, Arundel came into the possession of the Fitzalans in 1243 and passed to the Howards as a result of the marriage of Lady Mary Fitzalan, daughter of the 12th Earl of Arundel, to Thomas, 4th Duke of Norfolk in 1556. Much of the original castle was destroyed by besieging Parliamentarians in the winter of 1643. It was not until 1777 that the idea of restoring the ruins as the principal Ducal seat was seriously considered. The 10th Duke got no further than raising money for building work, and it was left to his son Charles, the 11th Duke, to start the grandiose reconstruction that was to continue for one-and-a-half centuries.

In 1787 he made the park and built Hiorne's Tower to the design of Francis Hiorne. Between 1791 and 1815 he rebuilt the quadrangle to his own design, assisted by craftsmen from his Cumberland estate specially trained in London for this task. Various 19th-century architects were employed, such as William Burn, who in 1850 designed the curtain wall and Upper Lodge, and M. E. Hadfield, a leading Catholic church architect. But Henry, the 15th Duke, was largely responsible for the Castle as eventually completed. He began in 1870 and finished in 1910. Besides restoring the keep and barbican, he largely reconstructed the quadrangle to the design of C. A. Buckler.

The result of all this is vast, feudal, and somewhat chilling. Nevertheless, much of it fulfils the expectations raised by the distant views. Overall, it is in the 'Early English' style. The 15th Duke's Private Chapel, with Hardman's stained glass, is one of the finest of those 'celestial fanes' which Victorian Catholic aristocrats 'more than dreamed of raising to the revealed Author of Life and Death'.* The other interiors are monumental but less excitingly Gothic, except for the Library, built in 1802. Constructed by Jonathan Ritson, it is entirely of mahogany and vaulted, looking like the inside of a huge model for a church. Most work of this date was later replaced, but the Library was too good to throw away.

These huge rooms form a setting for family portraits, of which the Mytenses and Van Dycks are outstanding. The soldier-poet Earl of Surrey, beheaded by Henry VIII for alleged treason, was painted by Stretes and is at the head of the staircase. In the Drawing Room, the collector Earl of Arundel is shown in his famous gallery of ancient marbles. Quantities of 18th-century furniture came to Arundel in 1938 when Norfolk House in London was sold to raise death duties, while the Gainsborough portraits came from Worksop. The Boulle, exuberant Italian furniture and ivory cabinets were considered the essence of luxury during the late 19th century. Among the historic relics is the rosary of Mary Queen of Scots, given to the 4th Duke of Norfolk who was later beheaded for attempting to marry her.

A visit concludes with the Fitzalan Chapel, part of the parish church but separated since the Reformation and still Catholic. It contains remarkable Fitzalan and Howard monuments. In these elegiac surroundings one can feel the tenacity of the illustrious Howards, who, despite executions, martyrdom, treason, attainder and a steadfast refusal to conform to the Established Church, have retained their pre-eminence at the head of the English Peerage for 500 years.

Athelhampton, Dorset
(Mr Robert Cooke)

Six miles east of Dorchester (A35)

The house lies low among water meadows, and the River Piddle forms a boundary to the garden. The forecourt is one of the most picturesque sights of Dorset. With ornaments of golden Ham Hill stone set like jewels against light grey, it exemplifies the skill and artistry of the Wessex masons.

The Martyns came here about 1350 through a marriage with the de Pydele heiress. The chained ape that first appears on the gate piers was their punning crest, 'Martin' being the familiar name for a monkey as 'Reynard' was for a fox. The ape will also be seen on two very lovely alabaster tombs in Puddletown church. The house has a centrepiece of purest Gothic, built about 1485 by Sir William Martyn, Lord Mayor of London in 1493. His battlemented front survives intact, and the oriel bay has slender three-tier windows. Within lies the Hall, where all the windows contain heraldic glass,

---

* Disraeli, *Lothair*.

Athelhampton; the forecourt

much of it a restoration, of the Martyns and their allied families. The unique feature of the Hall is its roof, where the principals were fashioned in the form of bounding trefoil arches.

The long wing that flanks the forecourt is early Tudor, and its Renaissance detail is paralleled at Sandford Orcas and elsewhere in Dorset. Formerly a massive gatehouse stood in the court. It was removed in 1862, perhaps because it darkened the house and hid the view, but the fine carving, closely resembling that at Montacute and Bingham's Melcombe, has been preserved for future use.

By 1848 when the house was sold, the internal courtyard had been partly destroyed and the house was derelict. The new owner, George Wood, restored the Hall, and much more restoration and rebuilding was done by Alfred Cart de Lafontaine after 1891. The rooms are well panelled and ceiled, and it is hard to tell what is original and what has been brought in. The linenfold panelling in the Hall has some unusually long pleatings. The King's Room also has linenfold panelling, while in the State Bedroom the wainscot fits neatly round a 15th-century stone overmantel with the Martyn crest and shields that once were painted. In the wing, a newel staircase (stone at the bottom and oak at the top) leads to the Great Chamber whose ceiling reproduces the 'Reindeer Inn' design, so called from the Jacobean example in an inn at Banbury.

The late Mr Robert Cooke, FRCS, rescued Athelhampton from a new period of decay in 1957, and he and his son continued the restoration. There is much fine furniture, with oak, walnut and Georgian mahogany, and one of Kirckman's splendid inlaid harpsichords (1761) on its original carved stand. The Gothic Revival chairs and Puginesque metalwork go well with rich Pugin wallpapers that were designed for the House of Lords. De Lafontaine employed Inigo Thomas to lay out the garden with terraces and pavilions, ponds and parterres. Though famous in their day, they were sadly neglected after 1939. Under its present restoration, the garden expands year by year.

Avebury Manor, Wiltshire
(The Marquess of Ailesbury)

Just west of Avebury Church

Over four thousand years ago Avebury was a centre of civilisation, and its megalithic Circle is one of the most impressive prehistoric monuments in Europe. In mediaeval times the Circle was regarded with suspicion, and the older parts of the village, including the church and manor, were built outside it. At the time of the Conquest Avebury was royal property, and for some three hundred years it contained a small Benedictine cell.

During the reign of Henry VIII the manor came into the grasping hands of Sir William Sharrington, owner of Lacock Abbey; but the house was actually rebuilt by William Dunch, an auditor of the London Mint, who bought it in 1551. Of his building there remains the long low range facing the church, with its steeply pitched gables and the low beamed Parlour within. In 1595 there was a dispute over the manorial rights, and in particular over the right to own the dovecote (standing near the gate). The rival house, lying further west, is known as Truslowe Manor. Sir James Mervyn, who had married Walter Dunch's widow, as High Sheriff of Wiltshire was able to settle the matter in his own favour, and shortly after, he rebuilt the entire south side of the house. His initials and the date 1601 are above the porch. As for materials, the old rendering has been partly removed revealing limestone walls; but in the older parts, and in garden walls and paving, sarsens were used – the local sandstone that was used for the prehistoric megaliths.

After 1700 the house belonged to Sir William Holford, a Master in Chancery, who is said to have remodelled the Hall and the Chamber above

Avebury Manor; the south front of about 1600

it in preparation for a visit from Queen Anne. That may be, but what decorations these rooms now have are chiefly in the style of William Kent, i.e. *circa* 1745. Otherwise the interior is Elizabethan or earlier, and the walls are panelled. In the south wing are Mervyn's airy Great Parlour and a bedroom above, both having fine chimneypieces of white Compton Bassett stone and ribbed plaster ceilings. The staircase is late 17th century and has dog gates.

From 1798 the manor was let as a farmhouse and repairs were minimal until Colonel Jenner bought and restored it early in this century. The imposing 'Queen Anne' bed has sumptuous needlework hangings made by Mrs Jenner in a single year (1910). In the 1930s the manor belonged to Mr Alexander Keiller, who did so much in restoring the megalithic Circle and converted the stables by the gate into a museum. Lord Ailesbury bought the house in 1976. In this house are such family portraits as are suitable, having been removed from a much larger place, Tottenham House in Savernake Forest (now let as a school). The most striking are two full-lengths of the 1st Earl and Countess of Elgin by Paul van Somer, hung in the Dining Room. The 1st Marquess of Ailesbury, in Van Dyck dress, and his Marchioness, are by Angelica Kauffmann. There is much oak furniture, including Cromwellian chairs with their original leather seats, and some beautiful Queen Anne walnut. The garden is large and divided by walls, hedges and avenues. The unusual curved wall is early 18th century and shelters box and yew topiary of the same date. The Monks' Garden has recently been redesigned in the traditional formal style.

Avington Park, Hampshire
(Mr J. B. Hickson)

At Itchen Abbas, four miles north-east of Winchester (B3047)

William Cobbett, who had seen more of England on horseback than most people, thought Avington one of the prettiest places in the country. Though only five miles from Winchester, the surroundings have changed little in a century and a half. The park, entered through early-18th-century gates, is flanked by the quiet-moving Itchen; the Lebanon cedars, tulip trees, and part of the great lime avenue, were planted by the 3rd Duke of Chandos over two hundred years ago; and the house still looks across water meadows to generously wooded hills.

On the west, the brick entrance front, dating probably from the early 18th century, has been attributed to John James who built St George's, Hanover Square. The central recess is entirely occupied by a vast Doric portico, with four giant columns and pediment in painted wood. The three voluptuous goddesses that surmount the pediment were added by the Duke of Chandos fifty years later. This imposing centrepiece recalls the portico of Wren's Chelsea Hospital which must have been built some two decades earlier. It is flanked by projecting wings in finely gauged brick, with windows set between pilasters. The north and south facades, designed in the late 18th

Avington Park; the entrance front

century as elements in a scheme that was never completed, are not distinguished. Two conservatory-pavilions on the south front, small and early echoes of the Crystal Palace, make amends.

Today, former owners – such as Robert Brydges, friend of Charles II, husband of the notorious Countess of Shrewsbury, and who drowned in the lake trying to save his pet dog in 1713; the 3rd Duke of Chandos, the Croesus who succeeded in 1751; the poet Shelley's brother, who bought Avington in 1848 – seem ghostlike figures. A generation ago the estate was broken up and the contents of the house dispersed. The architectural bones remain, most notably the 3rd Duke's Staircase with its inlaid handrail and lead balusters incorporating a Grecian honeysuckle motif. But the great feature of Avington is its painted rooms. The Entrance Hall was beautifully decorated before 1800 with murals by French craftsmen. Above it, the Saloon is a remarkable room with gilded decoration of the late 18th century, fine doors with infants and foliage, and a ceiling that preserves some earlier painted panels in the late-17th-century manner of Verrio. The Red Drawing Room, with a deep frieze boldly decorated with sunflowers and cornsheaves, has on its painted walls historic figures in the romantic taste of *circa* 1840. Happily, the gilded pelmets have remained, and four vast plate looking-glasses that stand over carved consoles and Victorian chimneypieces.

Close by, the red brick Georgian church, completed in 1771, has miraculously preserved its original furnishings, with gallery, reredos, three-decker pulpit and box pews made of mahogany. This was planned and paid for by the Marchioness of Carnarvon, whose monument, with a long and charming inscription, stands on the left of the altar.

Badminton, Avon
(The Duke of Beaufort, KG)

Five miles east of Chipping Sodbury

Great encircling tree belts, model villages with apricot-washed cottages, and William Kent's magnificent domed Worcester Lodge, proclaim the existence of a feudal demesne. The park, though flat and decimated by elm disease, still retains sections of the 1st Duke's immense network of avenues, in addition to Capability Brown's 18th-century plantations. The house at the heart of all this comprises a substantial late-17th-century building by an unidentified architect, altered in about 1740 by William Kent who added the pediments, cupolas and rusticated pavilions that give this complicated building a special scenic quality.

The manor had been bought in 1608 by Edward Somerset, 3rd Earl of Worcester, one of the largest landowners in Wales and a direct descendant in the male line of John of Gaunt, but it was only after the Restoration that Badminton became the chief family seat and building and planting started on a princely scale. This was because Raglan Castle had been so badly damaged in the Civil War that it had had to be abandoned.

The 3rd Marquess of Worcester was created 1st Duke of Beaufort in 1682. He lived at Badminton in semi-royal state surrounded by a household of over two hundred souls. This pomp extended even into death, and the most striking thing in the church, attached to the south-east corner of the house, is his monument by Grinling Gibbons, a gigantic marble structure over twenty-five feet high, crowned with a ducal coronet on a tasselled cushion.

The tour of the house begins in William Kent's Entrance Hall where the game of Badminton was evolved. This is covered in magnificent Baroque plasterwork, and the walls are lined with huge hunting scenes painted by John Wootton. The Library was remodelled by Wyatville in 1811, and the

Badminton; the Hall, designed by William Kent

chimneypiece is surmounted by a carved panel of instructive botanical specimens. In the Oak Room, carved panelling from Raglan Castle was brought here in 1896.

The Dining Room is the most complete 17th-century survival, with luscious carvings of lobster, fruit and game by Grinling Gibbons, and a charming view of the Garden Court through the windows. Smaller Drawing Rooms, hung with mellow Regency flock papers, are crammed with family portraits, Dutch and Italian Grand Tour paintings, and historical relics and objects including a wax model of Bébé, the 18th-century French dwarf who was only twenty-four inches high when he died at the age of twenty-three.

The last room seen by visitors is the much gilded Great Drawing Room by Wyatville, hung with green brocade by the last Duchess and embellished with a rare Italian chimneypiece of porphyry and ormolu, and lit by 18th-century Bristol glass chandeliers. The enormous Florentine cabinet of *pietre dure* was bought by the 3rd Duke on his Grand Tour for £500. Among the paintings are full-length portraits by Reynolds and Lawrence and the two famous Canaletto views of Badminton commissioned by the 4th Duke about 1750.

The stables and hunt kennels are open to visitors and their scale is an impressive testimony to Badminton's long-established association with horses and the chase; an association which is continued today in the annual Three-Day Event Horse Trials, initiated by the present Duke. They have become world-famous and through television have made the north front of Badminton one of the best-known English country house views.

Bamburgh Castle, Northumberland
(The Lord Armstrong)

On the coast, east of Belford (B1340)

Gripping a long narrow outcrop of rock, the castle looks in the distance, seen against the sky and the chilly Northumbrian seas, like a vast crouched animal. A natural fortress of unusual strength, the site was occupied from very early times. But the great period was the 7th century, when Bamburgh was the seat and capital of the powerful Northumbrian kings, who ruled from the Firth of Forth to below the Humber. King Oswald founded the monastery on Holy Island, within sight and under the protection of the fortress, and to this we owe the beautiful Lindisfarne Gospels. St Oswald's right arm was preserved in a silver shrine in his chapel on the castle rock. But Northumbrian power faded, and the Castle was sacked and the chapel desecrated by Vikings.

Bamburgh yielded to William the Conqueror without a siege, and through-out feudal times remained almost always in the hands of the Crown. Though the Castle had resisted attack for some 400 years, it fell eventually to Edward IV after a sustained bombardment by the King's new artillery. This was one of the first occasions when the walls of a great English castle were successfully breached by gunfire. The age of such fortified castles was

Bamburgh Castle; the Norman keep, from the outer bailey; (see also colour plate 3)

drawing to an end. In Tudor times Bamburgh was reported ruinous and decayed.

Early in the 18th century, when little remained standing but the Keep, Bamburgh was bought from the Crown by Nathaniel Liewe, Bishop of Durham, one of the richest and most powerful churchmen of his day. On his death he left Bamburgh as part of a charitable trust. One of his trustees, Dr John Sharp, Archdeacon of Northumberland, conceived a particular affection for the place and carried out extensive restoration. This remarkable man also created within the walls something like a miniature welfare state, providing a free library, dispensary and hospital, a free school, and distributing food to the poor. Perhaps even more important, he turned the castle into a pioneer coastguard station.

By the late 19th century the charitable endowment proved inadequate, and in 1894 the Trustees sold the castle to Lord Armstrong, whose descendants own it today. A costly programme of restoration and rebuilding followed, and Bamburgh became a country seat until 1914. All the main rooms now contain Lord Armstrong's furniture, pictures and armour, and the remainder is divided into apartments.

The castle follows the natural shape of the rock, and a long defile leads to two outer wards or baileys. The Inner Ward stands on the highest ground, and in its eastern extremity are the ruins of St Oswald's Chapel. Parts of the walls, gates and towers are mediaeval, and the massive Norman Keep survives almost intact, still the proud nucleus of the fortress. It was built over a Saxon well, dug in the basalt to a depth of 70 feet, that gave water 'sweet to the taste and most pure to the sight'.

The Keep is built of local rosy sandstone. The other buildings round the Inner Ward are partly of the same (and basically 18th century), and partly of grey sandstone brought from Lord Armstrong's estate near Rothbury. In this restored state, the castle gives some idea of what it may have looked like in the 14th century; the excesses of romanticism have been avoided, both outside and within. The King's Hall is new and lofty, with a hammerbeam roof. It has an interesting series of portraits, including those of Dr John Sharp and Lord Armstrong, and several Royal Dukes, the sons of George III, that formerly belonged to the Duke of Cambridge.

Barford Park, Somerset
(Mr and Mrs Michael Stancomb)

Five miles west of Bridgwater, between Enmore and Four Marks

Barford lies in the gentle valleys along the edge of the Quantock Hills. The subtle change from farmland to park is hardly noticed before this dream house appears as though by magic, with rosy brick walls set like gems in the surrounding green. Part of its fascination is due to its scale: it is a miniature of a country seat, with facade and forecourt complete to every detail. Not a manor originally but a modest farm, it took on its present form early in the 18th century. The stone dressings to the centre were improvements to the earlier house, whose sloping roof can be traced on one side. But the real character comes from the addition of curved wings and pavilions, with classical details of moulded brick. The designer may have been Benjamin Holloway, who in 1723 was building Castle Street in Bridgwater; or, perhaps, Nathaniel Ireson of Wincanton, who was later to build Crowcombe Court in this county.

The lanterns over the pavilions do not quite match, and the dates on the weather vanes, 1666 and 1775, are certainly not those of the facade. The left-hand wing was the kitchen; that on the right had coach house and stables,

Barford Park

with doors opening at the back. This side of the house is more roughly built, using red Quantock sandstone. A large bow window has been inserted to add light and space to the Drawing Room within. Inside, the decoration of the rooms is on the whole simple, and the stable wing has been converted into a Library.

The first recorded owner is James Jeanes, who died here in 1759, so perhaps it was he or his father who had improved the house some thirty-five years earlier. His family lived here until 1958, but during the last war the building fell into bad repair. The new owner has made extensive restorations, but the brickwork on the wings remains a problem on account of the prohibitive cost of remaking the different mouldings. The back overlooks an enclosed garden, whose walls are contemporary with the house front. A Victorian pleasure ground has been cleared of undergrowth, revealing an archery lawn under the pine trees and a water garden.

Beaulieu Abbey
See Palace House

Belle Isle, Cumbria
(Mr Edward Curwen)

On Lake Windermere, at Windermere

Both island and house are a delight. The porticoed rotunda was designed in 1774 by John Plaw. Though he later left his mark on London, notably with Paddington Church, his masterpiece stands here embowered by trees on the waters of Windermere. His patron was a certain Mr English, who (so Wordsworth maintained) was the first person to visit the Lake District solely for its scenery. In 1781 Belle Isle was sold to Isabella Curwen, young, enchanting, and rich. She and her husband, John Christian Curwen, later planted the island in the romantic taste to the design of Thomas White, and their fortunate descendants live there today.

Belle Isle, a confident but highly unusual exercise in neo-classicism, is circular in plan and crowned with a dome and lantern. Admiral Byng compared it to a tea-canister. It directly influenced, and antedated by some twenty years, the Earl-Bishop of Derry's inflated oval mansion at Ickworth, the only extant building of the time that remotely resembles it.

Carried on Ionic columns, a white pedimented portico looks out across the lake. Behind this frontispiece, two niches with statues of 'Summer' and 'Autumn' by R. Rinaldi, flank the entrance. Between the round-headed windows on the ground floor, a Venetian window neatly punctuates each quadrant. There is nothing one would wish to change.

One can say the same of the architectural features of the interior. The curving staircase that rises to the lantern is possibly a little cramped, but the ground floor rooms express, on an intimate scale, the measured elegance of their time. The Drawing Room has a neo-classical ceiling, simple plaster

Belle Isle

panels on the walls, and chimneypiece with *giallo antico* marble. The white and yellow Dining Room strikes the same cool note. Here the frieze of the entablature carries foxes' masks, instead of the traditional rams' skulls. Both rooms have documented Gillow furniture – notably a set of Gothic chairs in the Dining Room – made originally for the Curwens' principal house at Workington (now gutted). In the Entrance Hall a landscape by Loutherburg shows the house soon after it was built. Apart from unobtrusive alterations at the back and the growth of trees, almost nothing has changed.

Belton House, Lincolnshire
(The Lord Brownlow)

Two miles north-east of Grantham (A607)

Asked to name their favourite late Stuart house, many people would choose Belton. Dignified yet friendly, confident but without a trace of Baroque swagger, it is an example of all that most commends itself to us in the architecture of the time. Stonework that has mellowed almost to amber, clean lines, hipped gables, pediments giving precisely the right weight to the two main facades, and not least a lucid plan – all these combine to create an effect of calm assurance.

The house was built between 1685 and 1688 by Sir John Brownlow whose

Belton House

great-grandfather had bought the property in 1620 and whose descendants still live at Belton. The architect is unknown, though the name of William Winde has been suggested. The house at one time lost its roof-balustrade and cupola, features essential to the design and characteristic of their period, but mercifully they were replaced in the late 19th century. Otherwise, apart from a simple neo-classical doorway by James Wyatt on the entrance front, and a 19th-century porch on the courtyard, the elevations have seen no change in three hundred years.

The sombre yet glowing colours of the interior, the panelled rooms, the profusion of carved wood and stuccowork, portraits in full-bottomed wigs, all evoke the late Stuart period. There are few more convincing expressions of the richness and warmth that we associate with the 1680s. The note is struck as soon as one enters the Marble Hall: 17th-century overmantels with a riot of naturalistic carving, resembling in its virtuosity the work of Grinling Gibbons, and bold bolection-moulded panelling. The room is hung with portraits which include versions of a Charles II by Lely and of the well-known self-portrait by Reynolds. Among the family portraits is another Reynolds of Sir John Cust, Speaker of the House of Commons; and two of his sons are here, painted by Romney and Hoppner. The Speaker acquired as a perquisite of office a vast service of plate engraved with the royal arms. Part of this service, including a massive wine-cooler is displayed on early-18th-century giltwood sidetables supported on greyhounds, the Brownlow crest. The device reappears on the beautiful brass door-furniture in many of the state rooms.

The Saloon has more 17th-century fireplaces with the same rich 'Gibbons' carving above; among the portraits are full-lengths by Riley of Sir John, the builder, and his wife. The warmth of the room owes much to Boulle writing desks, with inlay of brass and silver on tortoiseshell, to a flowered Aubusson carpet with dark red ground, and late Stuart chairs upholstered in faded red velvet.

The particular quality of Belton is most marked in the Chapel and Chapel

Gallery. Both have superb 17th-century plaster ceilings by Edward Goudge and on their cedar wainscot cascades of flowers and fruit brilliantly carved in limewood. The massive reredos, painted to simulate marble, frames an Italian 15th-century Virgin and Child and on the wall hangs a Deposition by Tintoretto. With a view down a mile of chestnut avenue to an 18th-century folly on the skyline, the Chapel Drawing Room effortlessly evokes its period. The panelling is grained in green and gold to imitate a rich marble, and this rare survival, though it may be of early 18th-century date, accords perfectly with the taste of the 1680s. It frames Soho tapestries by Vanderbank who was in charge of the factory from 1689, and the oriental motifs of the tapestries are precisely such as one finds engraved on the silver of the time.

The Staircase Hall has another fine plaster ceiling by Goudge, but the staircase itself introduces the later work at Belton. James Wyatt was employed in about 1776 and his nephew, Sir Jeffry Wyatville, in the early 19th century. The latter was responsible for the staircase, very tactfully done, and for the Red Drawing Room with its painted *trompe l'oeil* frieze and crimson damask panels set in white and gold wainscot. The paintings here provide a contrast to the family portraits in the other rooms, and include works attributed to Rembrandt, Titian, Ruysdael, Van Dyck (a study of the noble white horse which figures in many of his equestrian portraits), and a version of the 'Mona Lisa' which once belonged to Sir Joshua Reynolds.

The boldly painted floor of the Tyrconnel Room, probably of about 1800, depicts the Brownlow arms flanked by honeysuckle motifs and other formal decoration. Few examples of such painted floors have survived. The Library, with barrel-vaulted ceiling and delicate plasterwork, is by James Wyatt and contains a collection of objects associated with Edward VIII to whom Lord Brownlow was Lord-in-Waiting. The Blue Bedroom contains notable furniture, such as a tall 17th-century state bed probably made for the wife of Sir John, the builder of Belton, a late Stuart daybed and matching chairs recorded in an inventory of 1690, and an early-18th-century walnut bureau of the finest workmanship.

The Orangery across the garden is by Wyatville, and the church is full of Brownlow monuments including a powerful work by Canova.

Belvoir Castle, Leicestershire
(The Duke of Rutland)

Seven miles west of Grantham

Crowning a limestone outcrop, the castle majestically surveys the green, yet ominously threatened, Vale of Belvoir. Though essentially of the Regency period, its towers and bastions rising above the tree-clad slopes look from below as though they had stood from time immemorial. The view appealed to Turner's sense of the romantic, and his painting of Belvoir wakes the same image of cloud-capped towers and airy terraces as delights the visitor today.

Turner's vision, the sense of an heroic past, was not misplaced. Belvoir

Belvoir Castle

was granted to the standard bearer who scrambled ashore at Hastings. On account of its noble setting the Normans christened it *Belvedere*. It was a setting that cried for fortification. By the 13th century an older motte and bailey had become an embattled stone stronghold. This passed by marriage to the Manners family, already long prominent in Northumberland. Some two hundred years later they saw their new castle-house demolished by the Parliamentarians in the Civil War. Unperturbed they built again and yet another Belvoir, finished in 1688, survived until the early 19th century.

John, 9th Earl of Rutland, had acquired a dukedom in 1703, and it was the 17th-century house that was known by his famous great-grandson, the Marquess of Granby, whose signal achievements in the Seven Years' War so endeared him to popular esteem that more pubs bear his name than that of any other English worthy. The immense rebuilding that created the Belvoir we know was the conception of the 5th Duke and his talented Duchess. Begun in 1801 soon after the Duke's coming of age, it is among the outstanding monuments of the Regency period. James Wyatt, then at the height of his success and still employed on building Fonthill for William Beckford, was the architect. His assignment at Belvoir was vast and progress correspondingly slow, but when he died in 1813 at least two fronts were finished, the gaily crested and turreted chapel contrasting with an enormous neo-Norman tower. Only three years after his death an appalling fire swept the castle, destroying not only much of Wyatt's interior but a great part of the collection of old master paintings acquired by the 4th Duke, the close friend of Reynolds and a discriminating collector.

When work was resumed it was under the direction of the Rev. Sir John Thoroton, the Duke's domestic chaplain, with the co-operation of Wyatt's sons, Benjamin, Philip and Matthew Cotes. The clergyman was perhaps

1 Alnwick Castle;
the 19th-century
Dining Room

2 Arundel Castle;
the Library

3 Bamburgh Castle

4 Brympton d'Evercy; the Forecourt

more distinguished for his Gothic scholarship than his architectural sensibility, but the immense castle, when finished some ten years later, justified the comment of the diarist Charles Greville: 'so grand as to sink criticism in admiration'. Noble builders of great castles saw no reason why a crenellated 'mediaeval' exterior should not conceal the elegance and comfort of an interior in classical taste. Belvoir became a mixture of the feudal and the classical.

In the Entrance or Guard Room, the visitor meets Thoroton's work, a complex arrangement of arches and steps and self-indulgently Gothic. Much of the display of arms, armour and military equipment is associated with the Leicestershire Militia. On the Grand Staircase above hang portraits of the 5th Duke and Elizabeth, his Duchess, who played so important a role in the creation of the Regency Castle. Beyond, in the vaulted Ballroom, are portraits of four of the first Dukes by Closterman, Jervas, and Hoppner.

The true delights of the interior lie ahead. The Elizabeth Saloon, and more particularly the Regent's Gallery, are among the most alluring examples of the taste of their time. The Duchess Elizabeth employed Matthew Cotes Wyatt, best known as a sculptor, to decorate the Saloon and to paint the ceiling with mythological scenes showing the unedifying love-life of Jupiter and Juno. The white and gold panelling, much of it genuine Louis XV, has the Manners peacock in the coved frieze, and Louis XV seat furniture upholstered in rose-red damask silk, placed on an Aubusson carpet, creates an effect gloriously rich and very much of its period. The Duchess, sculptured at full-length by Wyatt, seems about to step down into the room she created.

If the Duchess's Saloon be thought over-elaborate, the Regent's Gallery admits of no such criticism. Designed by James Wyatt, it was saved from destruction by the fire and architecturally, decoratively, and in its furnish-

Belvoir Castle; left: *the Guard Room;* right: *the Regent's Gallery; (see also p. 17)*

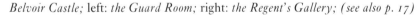

ings it is one of the great conceptions of its time. The length of this vast gallery, named after the Prince Regent who visited Belvoir soon after its completion, is broken by an enormous bay, the projection of the neo-Norman keep. The proportions are perfect. The ceiling, apart from a richly gilded frieze, is unadorned; the doors are inlaid maplewood; the windows have their original red silk-damask pelmets and curtains, and the red carpet woven with arum lilies is also of the period. The walls are hung with Gobelins tapestries depicting *The Adventures of Don Quixote* (after designs by Coypel) on a rose *damas* ground. Below are a series of white marble busts, mostly by Nollekens, which suitably include his likenesses of the Prince Regent and the martial Marquess of Granby. Blue and white oriental porcelain, rococo pier glasses and Regency furniture complete this wholly satisfying room.

Despite a heavy coffered ceiling, the Dining Room seems all reflection, for the walls are set with huge arched mirrors. There is more fine Regency furniture here, mahogany sideboards and colza lamps. Two full-length portraits by Reynolds flank the chimneypiece. A silver wine cooler of 1662 stands on an astonishing plinth by M. C. Wyatt, covered by a film of white marble that convincingly simulates a draped table cloth.

The Picture Gallery would be of importance for its Poussins alone, bought by the 4th Duke on the advice of Reynolds in 1786. They represent three of the Seven Sacraments (two more hang in the Chapel). There are also portraits of the Earl of Southampton, to whom Shakespeare dedicated *Venus and Adonis*, and his wife by Johnson, a contemporary version of Holbein's portrait of Henry VIII, an excellent van de Velde, a Jan Steen, an outstanding Teniers, and other paintings of importance which include three landscapes by Gainsborough and early miniatures by Hilliard and Oliver. Not least, three early-19th-century portraits by Shannon testify to a remarkable talent. They hang without embarrassment among the earlier masterpieces. The Great Bed, recently restored, is hung with Venetian velvet and is one of the few pieces of furniture to survive from the 17th-century castle.

The Bedrooms bring us back to the Regency. Though hung with a series of Chinese hand-painted silks and wallpapers that could be slightly earlier, they are chiefly remarkable for their early-19th-century furniture and unusual lacquered wardrobes.

Berkeley Castle, Gloucestershire
(Mr R. J. Berkeley)

Between Bristol and Gloucester, west of M5 and A38

With the passing of centuries this venerable building has become mellow and benign; its turbulent early years, even the murder of an English king within its walls, seem remote and graceless legends. The Berkeleys, we read, were a peaceful family. They seldom led a dispute, but had the knack of following the winning side. Their ancestry can be traced to Saxon times;

their castle is mediaeval; but their treasures belong to a later and easier age.

'Rose red and grey, the colour of old brocade', the buttressed walls and towers huddle round a cliff-top whose uncouth face has been terraced and alleyed, and lined with flowers. The meadows below could be flooded from the River Severn in case of assault. Berkeley, still contained by its old defensive walls, grew around the motte built by the powerful Norman, William FitzOsbern. Owing to Roger FitzOsbern's support of King Stephen, in 1153 the Castle was granted by Henry II to Robert Fitz-Harding, from whom the Berkeley family are descended. The Keep is said to have been rebuilt the same year, a circular shell-keep with a solid wall sixty feet high. From the outer courtyard you see the breach in the wall imposed by the Parliamentarians during the Civil War, which may only be repaired through an Act of Parliament. Within the gate, a Norman doorway survives.

Most of the work jostling round the Inner Courtyard is of the 14th century. The Great Hall stands opposite the Keep, private rooms to the right of it, offices to the left. There have been, of course, alterations, the last during the 1920s when the 8th Earl of Berkeley brought stone doorways, windows, and chimneypieces from France. Two doorways in the Court belonged to some ancient *château* and, though undeniably picturesque, are alien to an English castle.

The gruesome murder of King Edward II (1327) was carried out by his gaolers, the diplomatic Lord of Berkeley having, as we may well believe, absented himself. The rooms in the Keep, where the murder took place, have been altered beyond recognition, but the bottle-dungeon is a grim reminder of how prisoners were treated. From here there follows a warren of rooms large and small, which take in the original Kitchen, polygonal in plan with a high beamed roof, and buttery. A large low room is now a Picture Gallery, and another is set out as a Dining Room. There are many excellent

Berkeley Castle from the terraces, showing the 'slighted' keep; (see also p. 33)

pictures, notably a portrait of the 4th Earl by Batoni, a fine painting by Stubbs, and *The Old Berkeley Hunt* by Benjamin Marshall. In the 18th century the Berkeleys could hunt on their own land all the way to London. Their hunting coats are traditionally of canary yellow, and so they appear in Sir William Orpen's portrait of the 8th and last Earl, and a later picture of the present owner.

The 14th-century Great Hall has a timber roof, not very high, and windows and doors in the form of the 'Berkeley' arch, with distinctive polygonal heads that are also found at Bristol. The screen is 16th century, but was brought here from Pembrokeshire, Berkeley coats of arms having been added to the original paint. The fireplace was originally at Wanswell Court. A 17th-century stair leads to the private rooms, and the landing is hung with embroidered wall hangings of scarlet cloth that once graced a Tudor bed-chamber.

The three 'state' rooms are of great beauty. Loveliest of all is the Morning Room, which was designed as the Chapel of St Mary. Its graceful timber roof with cusped arches on carved stone corbels is painted with texts from Revelations in the translation by John Trevisa, who was buried in Berkeley church. All this is 14th-century work, but the fireplace is a French importation. Two Drawing Rooms follow, with stone walls and beamed ceilings. The first now contains the King's Pew, removed from the Chapel, a commanding late Gothic work of oak. Separating the rooms is a stone doorway brought from France.

The works of art in this wing are notably fine. An opulent tone is set by the early Georgian furniture of carved and gilded gesso: side tables and exquisite pier glasses, and chairs, sofas and stools all covered with contemporary needlework. Among the Flemish tapestries, most attractive are the lush garden scenes with mythologies from Ovid, woven by Jan Cobus. The Spanish carpets are fine and very rare. In the Morning Room there is a French walnut cabinet in the Loire style. Family portraits here are by Kneller, Cotes, Reynolds and Hoppner.

With the death of the 8th Earl of Berkeley in 1942, the title passed to a distant relation, and the heir to the estate, the late Captain R. G. Berkeley of Spetchely, Worcestershire, was a 13th cousin. The connection goes as far back as the 15th century, but he too was a direct descendant of Robert FitzHarding. His son now lives in the Castle.

Bickleigh Castle, Devon
(Mr and Mrs O. N. Boxall)

Four miles south of Tiverton (A396)

As the beautiful valley of the River Exe narrows, Bickleigh Castle appears below the village of its name, against a background of hanging woods: a cluster of cottages, with a mighty Gatehouse of pink stone. The thatched building on the river bank is the Norman Chapel, and may be the oldest complete building in Devon. Its walls, door and east windows are *circa* 1100,

Bickleigh Castle; the gatehouse

other windows and the chancel roof 15th century.

About 1410 the Castle became the property of the great Courtenays of Powderham and Tiverton, who rebuilt it and used it for their younger sons. Early in the next century young Elizabeth Courtenay eloped with her cousin, Thomas Carew. Being 'young and lusty, of an active body, and a courageous mind' he greatly distinguished himself at the Battle of Flodden (1513), so the abduction was forgiven and the Castle became his property. But during the Civil War it was 'slighted' by Fairfax, and all that now remains is the Gatehouse and Chapel. Sir Henry Carew repaired these, and built the adjoining farmhouse, not grandly but in the local style of cob and thatch. The clock on the main barn is also mid-17th century. Like so many old buildings, Bickleigh deteriorated and when its rescue began in 1925 the ivy was eight feet thick. The taste of the inter-war period has left its imprint on the interior, particularly on the chapel furnishings.

The Gatehouse has a fine vault, a Guard Room, Armoury (stripped of its plaster) and a long room upstairs. The one interesting feature that remains from the time of the Carews is now in the farmhouse, namely a stone overmantel intricately carved with buildings and groups of people, between heraldic lions. The subject of this extraordinary work has not been convincingly identified. Oak and walnut furniture has come with the owners, who bought the property in 1970, and their garden makes use of the old moat. Among all this vernacular work, a pair of very lovely wrought-iron gates come as a surprise. They are Italian, rococo, and of great delicacy.

Blenheim Palace, Oxfordshire
(The Duke of Marlborough)

At Woodstock, eight miles north of Oxford

The gift of a sovereign to a triumphant general, Blenheim is a symbol of national achievement and royal satisfaction. The greatest of English palaces (George III understandably remarked that he had 'nothing to equal this'), its Baroque grandeur and state recall palaces abroad, such as the Belvedere in Vienna built a few years later by Prince Eugene, Marlborough's companion in arms, rather than anything in this country.

For the quit-rent of a silken Bourbon standard embroidered with three *fleurs de lys* (still tendered to the reigning sovereign on August 13th each year), Queen Anne presented the royal manor of Woodstock to the Duke of Marlborough in 1705 with the intention that the Crown should meet the expense of building a mansion worthy to celebrate both the notable victory of Blenheim in the previous year and, by implication, the glory of the Queen's reign. At the time of the gift the Duke was fifty-five and hardly less high in the royal esteem than his Duchess, who had obtained an extraordinary ascendancy over the Queen. Great victories still lay ahead – Ramillies, Oudenarde, Malplaquet; so too political eclipse, self-imposed exile in 1712, and after return to England the long crippling illness which led to the Duke's death in 1722. His widow was to live on at Blenheim for nearly a generation more.

Blenheim might well have been merely an extravagant pile; that it proved an architectural masterpiece was due to the imagination of John Vanbrugh, the heroic genius of English Baroque, who had recently at Castle Howard designed his first house. Throughout the long building operations he was able to rely on the talent and experience of Nicholas Hawksmoor, and to enlist the services of the outstanding specialists of the time: Thornhill and Laguerre for decorative painting, Grinling Gibbons for stone carving, and Henry Wise, the Queen's gardener at Hampton Court, for the creation of a great formal garden. The one thing he was unable to secure was the co-operation of the Duke's masterful wife. Architect and Duchess were temperamentally unsuited, but accord with a lady who embarked on over four hundred lawsuits cannot have been easy. When his running conflict with the Duchess led in 1717 to his furious resignation, the palace fortunately was nearly finished.

On the road from Oxford to Woodstock the east gates, with their monumental piers set diagonally, are a first intimation of the Baroque, but the present approach to Blenheim is through the village, past Chambers's seemly town hall, to a triumphal arch. At this point a breathtaking view is sprung on the visitor. Greensward falls away steeply to a great lake on which a wooded island seems to float 'like a becalmed frigate', in the middle distance. Seen against a background of hanging woods, an enormous bridge spans the waters, while the fretted skyline of Blenheim rises some way off to the left. The bridge, recalling some triumph of Roman engineering, was built by Vanbrugh across the valley through which flowed the Glyme. The

Blenheim Palace; the Great Court and main entrance

lake and hanging woods came half a century later when Capability Brown dammed the stream to create the lake and landscaped the setting. In so doing he half-submerged the towering piers of Vanbrugh's bridge.

As soon as work got under way, Blenheim attracted visitors, and in 1712 when going abroad Marlborough left instructions 'that all persons may see ye whole Building to their Satisfaction'. Today the visitor enters through the massive east gate from which the house-flag flies when the Duke is in residence. The urns over the gate and probably the statues were the work of Grinling Gibbons, who provided most of the carved stonework at Blenheim to the designs of Vanbrugh or Hawksmoor. The east or service courtyard, in Vanbrugh's words 'regular, decent and clean', provides a telling contrast to the heroic facade of the main building which is abruptly revealed as the visitor steps under the clocktower into the Great Court beyond. The full impact of the design can only be appreciated if one stands well back at the outer end of the Great Court. From there the scale and drama, the grouping of component masses, the sense of movement conveyed by calculated recessions and projections, and the climax of the central portico with an unusual clearstory rising above and behind it, inspire something like awe. This they were surely meant to do. The narrowing perspective is achieved with calculated precision: the flanking service and stable courts linked by colonnades to the wings of the house, and these in turn by quadrant arcades sweeping inward to the centrepiece with its giant Corinthian order, and Marlborough's coat of arms proudly displayed on the pediment. The Baroque movement terminates in the flourish of the roofscape, busy with statuary and punctuated with unlikely pavilions, topped with thirty-foot finials, that Vanbrugh's genius alone renders acceptable.

The Great Hall, resembling a wide nave with two ranges of superimposed arcades below a clearstory, has the same imposing scale. The ceiling, painted by Thornhill, depicts Marlborough pointing to a map of the Battle of Blenheim and receiving a laurel wreath from Britannia. Vanbrugian features, reminiscent of Castle Howard, are the ironwork gallery supported on huge carved brackets and the stone corridors leading off the hall. A collection of classical busts and statuary looks particularly well in this architectural setting. (Sir Winston Churchill was born at Blenheim in November 1874 and off the west corridor there is an exhibition devoted to his memory and to his association with Blenheim. It includes some irresistible early photographs.)

The Saloon is decorated with murals of the Four Continents set in a feigned architectural framework and a ceiling depicting the apotheosis of Marlborough. The paintings are by Louis Laguerre, and the murals, derived from the theme of the Escalier des Ambassadeurs at Versailles, are his masterwork. Bold marble doorcases by Hawksmoor incorporating two-headed eagles, an emblem to which Marlborough was entitled as Prince of the Holy Roman Empire, complete a Saloon that in conception and execution 'can vie (as James Lees-Milne says) with the most splendid palace rooms in Europe'.

The arrangement of rooms is the ultimate in Baroque planning. As at Castle Howard, a great apartment extends either side of the Saloon; when such apartments became redundant, all the rooms were turned into Drawing Rooms. Their chief feature perhaps is the series of Brussels tapestries which hang on the walls. Woven by de Vos, with an extraordinary concern for detail, they depict scenes from Marlborough's campaigns. The rooms to the east of the Saloon have ceilings designed by Hawksmoor, though the armorial cartouches in the coves are 19th-century additions; there are also chimneypieces supplied by Sir William Chambers who in 1764 also redecorated the private apartments in the east wing where the family live. In the Green Drawing Room hang a Romney of the 4th Duke who not only employed Chambers but called in Capability Brown to landscape the park and waters, a Reynolds of his pretty wife Caroline, and a Kneller of the formidable Sarah, 1st Duchess, in a mantilla and looking as though butter would not melt in her mouth. In the Red Drawing Room, the 4th Duke and his Duchess appear again, with their six children, a great set-piece by Reynolds which faces, for deliberate contrast, a family group of no less panache commissioned by the 9th Duke and his wife, born Consuelo Vanderbilt, from John Sargent. In the Green Writing Room beyond hangs Kneller's best portrait of Marlborough, which prompted the Duke in old age to murmur, 'This once was a man'.

The rooms west of the Saloon, where most of the famous Marlborough tapestries hang, were elaborately decorated by the 9th Duke in the Louis XIV style soon after he succeeded in 1892. While it is no doubt sad that such famous rooms were altered, the pastiche is accomplished and the craftsmanship meticulous. The rooms provide a setting, as do the State Rooms to the east, for some remarkable objects: a Savonnerie carpet contemporary with the house, Boulle furniture, signed commodes by Migeon and Rousseau, pier glasses and giltwood side tables by Ince and Mayhew, and by James

Moore (who enjoyed the Duchess's confidence after Vanbrugh departed), ormolu-mounted neo-classical blue-john candelabra by Matthew Boulton, an inkstand of alarmingly rococo design by Paul de Lamerie, and a quantity of bronzes, including works attributed to Giovanni Bologna and a delicious kneeling Venus by Coysevox.

Since Vanbrugh built from east to west, the vast Gallery in the west wing with a great bow window was not finished until the 1720s. The huge marble doorways and the plaster ceiling were designed by Hawksmoor. A decade later Duchess Sarah commissioned from Rysbrack the full-length marble statue of Queen Anne and the bust of the Duke. Though intended as a picture gallery, the room has always been used as a library: the present bookcases are copies of the originals, put here by the 9th Duke who did so much to restore the palace after a period of 19th-century neglect.

Reached by an open colonnade on the west side of the Great Court, the Chapel, though much altered since, was the last element in the majestic design to see completion. In 1732 the Duchess wrote that it was finished, and twelve years later she was buried there with her husband in the magniloquent marble tomb which William Kent had designed for her, and Rysbrack executed to a standard worthy of Rome.

Vanbrugh's great parterre south of the house was sacrificed to the fashionable informality of the later 18th century, but the 9th Duke, between two World Wars, made noble amends with the creation of the water-terraces on the west front. Laid out by Achille Duchêne, clearly a designer of talent, they introduce a formal note that is wonderfully effective when seen from the Long Gallery.

Blenheim Palace; left: *the Saloon, painted by Laguerre, and* below: *Rysbrack's monument to the Duke of Marlborough*

73

Blithfield Hall, Staffordshire
(Nancy, Lady Bagot)

Four miles north of Rugeley (B5013)

Famous for an ancient herd of black-necked Schwarzhal goats and for enormous oak trees, Blithfield has been the home of the Bagots since 1360 (with only one short break, in this century). Before 1360 they lived three miles away at Bagots' Park and their ancestry can be traced without affectation to 1067. The family arms are accompanied by the apposite motto 'Possessing Antiquity'. The recent history of Blithfield adds a romantic postscript to their story of ancient tenure. At the end of his life the 5th Lord Bagot sold the house to the South Staffordshire Water Works so that the reservoir, which now enhances the immediate environs, could be built in the park. Many of the contents too were sold in 1945. It seemed likely that the house would be demolished, like so many others in the post-war years, but in 1946 the 6th Lord Bagot and his wife bought it back and slowly restored it with care and affection.

Venerably low, straggling and quadrangular with clusters of tall Elizabethan chimneys, the old ranges were given unity and a pretty Gothic dress by the 2nd Lord Bagot in 1822 probably to the design of John Buckler, the topographical artist. The Gothic casing is of Roman Cement worked by Francis Bernasconi and provided by its inventor Charles Wyatt, cousin and brother-in-law to the well-known architects James and Samuel Wyatt who owed the origins of their success to the patronage of the Bagots. Samuel Wyatt himself worked at Blithfield in 1768, building the neo-classical orangery to the design of 'Athenian' Stuart and designing various additions

Blithfield; the Hall

to the house, including the New Drawing Room in the South West corner, when the moat was drained. Most of the house, however, dates from the 16th century and beneath later accretions much of the original structure survives, including timber framing in the walls and the Hall roof (now out of sight) with 'carved crooks and rafters'.

The present appearance of the Great Hall is a *chef d'oeuvre* of Bernasconi's art with tabernacled niches for statues, an heraldic chimneypiece and elaborate vaulted ceiling. The plaster vaulted cloisters round the inner quadrangle are further specimens of excellent Regency Gothic, inspired by the 2nd Lord Bagot's antiquarian enthusiasms. Good pre-Regency interiors include the Great Chamber with 16th-century panelling and chimneypiece flanked by bookcases made by Samuel Wyatt; the 17th-century staircase made of carved oak grown on the estate; and the study added in 1738, with handsome architectural wainscot divided by fluted Doric pilasters. The prettily decorated rooms in bright colours and cheerful chintzes contain appropriate furniture. Family portraits by Richardson, Reynolds, Owen and other artists were painstakingly traced and bought back after the 1945 sale.

In manorial proximity to the house, the interesting 13th-century church contains a large array of Bagot memorials in stone, marble, brass and stained glass spanning six centuries and terminating with the 6th Lord Bagot in 1961.

No mention of Blithfield would be complete without a reference to the Abbots Bromley horn dance, a pre-Christian custom, performed on the lawn every September by six men wearing reindeer horns, a hobby horse, 'Maid Marion', a jester, a musician, and two boys, one with a triangle and one with a crossbow.

Bodrhyddan Hall, Clwyd
(Colonel the Lord Langford)

Three miles south-east of Rhyl (A5151)

The family's name is Rowley-Conwy, and they have two crests that are much in evidence. The Saracen's head was awarded to the Conwys for valour during the Crusades; the second is a pelican in her piety. The Conwys were appointed Hereditary Constables of Rhuddlan Castle in 1399, this being Sir Henry's condition for his quiet surrender of the Castle's keys to the usurping forces of Bolingbroke; the family still keep the office today. Bodrhyddan, a farmhouse two miles distant, seems to have been their retreat from the responsibilities of castle life. It stands near an ancient freshwater spring, a traditional holy well on which the most ancient trees in the park are aligned. The 17th-century well-house is very dubiously inscribed with the name of Inigo Jones. Bodrhyddan has always passed by descent, though several times this was through the female line. In the 18th century it came by marriage to William Shipley, Dean of St Asaph for fifty-two years, whose more famous father, Dr Jonathan Shipley, was the Bishop. The Irish barony

Bodrhyddan Hall; Nesfield's entrance front, early 1870s

of Langford was not associated with this house until the present owner inherited the title from a cousin in 1953.

The Entrance Front, a trim pavilion of brick and stone, was designed by William Eden Nesfield (son of the landscape gardener) in 1873–4. Its vigorous centrepiece rises past a balcony to a high gable that carries the pelican crest. This very accomplished work, predominantly Dutch in style, came at the start of the 'Queen Anne' revival and was *avant-garde* in its day. Yet Augustus Hare had regrets that 'the quaint old peculiar character' of the house had gone. Before Nesfield's enlargements the entrance was on the south side that now looks across a formal garden towards the old gate piers. There is 17th-century brickwork here, and the old front door, dated 1696, has been removed to one side. Yet even the 17th-century work recased a late Elizabethan house from which yet another doorway survives. Of stone and sturdily columned, it has been degraded to the cellar on the other side of the house.

The Front Hall is filled with armour, among which are two Nuremberg suits of about 1485, flintlock rifles, swords and other arms. The document in a glass case is the original Charter of Rhuddlan, granted by Edward I and dated 1284. In an adjoining room there are two Egyptian mummy cases of the 18th dynasty, one containing the embalmed body of a young priest. They were acquired in Egypt by Mrs Rowley (*née* Conwy) about 1830.

Nesfield dressed the old Hall in light oak panelling and gave it a cosy inglenook lined with gilt leather. The best paintings are the two portraits by de Troy dated 1696, of the young Duc d'Anjou (later King Philip V of Spain) and his brother the Duc de Berry. The Chinese enamel altar set in *famille rose* colours came from Spain and was captured with the French baggage train in the Peninsular War. Upstairs, the White Drawing Room was until recently the Library and stained chocolate brown. Two fireplaces are surrounded by Flemish carvings, and one overmantel is in fact an Italian picture frame. Such cobbling of old woodwork was very much to the taste of the 1840s.

It was probably Dean Shipley who added the Big Dining Room in the late 18th century. This is notable chiefly for family portraits by Dahl, Vanderbank, Hudson, Ramsay and others. The Dean was painted by Beechey, his father, the Bishop, by Reynolds. The portrait of Mrs Rowley, the traveller, is by Sir Francis Grant.

Boughton House, Northamptonshire
(The Duke of Buccleuch and Queensberry)

3 miles north of Kettering (A43)

This legendary Ducal seat is vast but unostentatious and has a magic all its own. Grey walls and mysterious courts push out in all directions as though this were the palace of Minos. Under a low and unadventurous roof-line, most of the fabric is in the simple vernacular style seen in the colleges of Oxford and Cambridge. Yet this merges into structures that are urbane and courtly: a rusticated gateway, now set off-centre; a domed stable block; and, most important, the principal facade that forms an open court, with an arcaded loggia but no obvious door. This front is the focus of Boughton's mystery. It is a Louis XIV château, transplanted to English soil.

Boughton remains today almost as it was left in 1709 by the Duke of Montagu, a nobleman with a declared taste for all things French. When his title died out the house passed into what has been aptly described as a deep sleep. The estates were responsibly maintained, but their owners lived in Scotland or London. After more than a hundred years the house came back to life, a dignified survival from an earlier age which the 19th century had passed by.

Sir Edward Montagu, one of the most successful of Tudor lawyers, bought the manor from St Edmondsbury's Abbey in 1528. The plan of his house is no longer apparent, but the Hall he built still looks over the Fish Court, and two Renaissance chimneypieces are to be seen in downstairs rooms. Four generations later the 3rd Lord Montagu a man of singularly 'good address', was appointed Ambassador to France in 1669. The Gallic character of Boughton is due to his love of French architecture, decoration and manners. Yet strangely Montagu remained a resolute protestant and Whig, and was on very equivocal terms with the Stuart kings. William III and Queen Anne advanced his titles by degrees until, in 1705, he reached his ambition of becoming a Duke. Meanwhile he maintained his fortune, though not without legal disputes, by marrying a succession of rich widows.

Additions to the old house were begun by 1688. If the main front was not actually by a French architect, it was certainly based on a French design, and the fenestration of the wings is distinctly un-English. The left wing was never finished: it is beamed inside, but not floored or ceiled. For decoration Montagu brought a team of painters from abroad. He had introduced Verrio

Boughton House; the main front, begun in 1688

to this country in 1672, and for Montagu House in London he employed Frenchmen. Gaudy mythological ceilings and the staircase walls at Boughton were all painted by Louis Chéron. When Montagu House became the British Museum, flower paintings by Baptiste and much else besides came to Boughton. Yet the rooms, for all their fine oak panelling, are sober and show nothing of French ostentation. On the ground floor they run all round Fish Court to the Hall, where Chéron's *Marriage of Hercules* hides the old timbered roof. The Great Apartment, directly above the arcaded front, consists of five rooms *en enfilade* with wantonly pagan ceilings, and on the floors is the earliest use in England of 'Versailles' parquet. This impressive apartment, by comparison with its near contemporary at Chatsworth, is simple and the frieze above the panelling is painted, not carved.

As examples of late Stuart taste, the furnishings are probably without equal. Walnut, marquetry and gilded gesso, velvet upholstery, Boulle and lacquer fill these rooms, together with fine Italian paintings and an astonishing collection of early Persian carpets. We may note two carpets, Persian in style but woven in England in 1584; an early Boulle writing table, a gift from Louis XIV; two massive *verre eglomisé* pier glasses; and a pair of white japan cabinets in the style of Stalker and Parker. In that age the tapestries would probably have been the most highly valued of all. Montagu bought the management of the Mortlake factory in 1674, and the series of *Elements* (after Le Brun) and the beautiful table cover woven with Montagu's arms and Earl's coronet date from that period. (Another set of Mortlake tapestries, woven after the Mantegna cartoons, have been removed to Bowhill.) Two sets of Bacchanal Infants and the *Acts of the Apostles*, though also Mortlake, are earlier. Many of the Italian paintings were acquired in the 18th century. In the Drawing Room there are a pair of Carlin's writing tables or *bonheurs du jour*, encased with Sèvres porcelain.

The grounds, laid out on a grand scale with a lake, water gardens and broad avenues, were begun by the 1st Duke and extended by his son, who is said to have planted seventy miles of elm and lime. The 2nd Duke's contribution to the house was chiefly in chimneypieces overloaded with the heraldry of his descent. His only surviving child, Mary, married Lord Cardigan of nearby Deene Park, who was created Duke of Montagu in 1766. Their heir, the cultivated Marquess of Mouthermer, travelled in Italy where he collected paintings, and was himself portrayed by Mengs and Batoni before his early death in 1770. Boughton then devolved on his sister, Lady Elizabeth Montagu (whose portrait is by Gainsborough). She had married the 3rd Duke of Buccleuch, so the name and estates of Montagu joined those of the Douglas-Scott family. Their Scottish properties include Drumlanrig and Bowhill.

Boughton Monchelsea Place, Kent
(Mr Michael Winch)

Five miles south of Maidstone (from A229)

The drive winding through chestnut coppice and beech grove gives no hint of what awaits, until one emerges near the house to sense the great expanse of air that lies beyond. Poised on the lip of the Kentish greensand ridge, with a vast view over the Weald, Boughton Monchelsea is wonderfully placed. Below the house, the slopes of the deer park, scattered with large oaks and walnuts, fall abruptly to a distant lake, and a rural landscape stretches unbroken to Tenterden thirteen miles away.

Robert Rudston, a Lord Mayor of London, bought Boughton Monchelsea from the son of the poet, Sir Thomas Wyatt, in 1551. The house reflects the changes that he and his descendants made over the next three centuries, until it was sold in 1888. Robert Rudston built the ragstone entrance front in about 1570. It retains much of the character of the period, with his porch, attractive gabled dormers, and a curious undecorated frieze below the gables. The Gothic fenestration, the drip-moulds above the ground-floor windows, and the battlements, were added about 1790. Some thirty years later, the adjoining facade that overlooks the Weald was wholly rebuilt in

Boughton Monchelsea Place

the same spirit (and with wooden mullions and transoms to the windows).

The interior derives its architectural character predominantly from changes made late in the 17th and 18th centuries. About 1690 the handsome staircase with twisted balusters was introduced. The staircase ceiling is of the same date, as is the Gun Room with bolection-moulded panelling at the foot of the stairs. The tall windows which light the staircase contain a quantity of fragmented German glass of about 1600 originally in the nearby church.

Rather over a century after the alterations of 1690, and possibly under the influence of James Wyatt's famous Lee Priory, built a few years earlier, the Entrance Hall and Dining Room were given a Gothic dress. The change, which introduced shallow vaulting and cluster columns, was carried out with sensitivity. The attractive Dining Room, which has a screen of these columns, is hung in dark red, and furnished with mid-18th-century giltwood mirrors, late Mortlake tapestry, and Regency dining chairs with ebony inlay. Elsewhere in the house there is a good deal of Regency furniture, and a few early oak pieces. In the Drawing Room, an elegant giltwood rococo mirror hangs over the mid-18th-century chimneypiece.

Bramham Park, West Yorkshire
(George Lane Fox)

Five miles south of Wetherby (A1)

About 1698, Robert Benson, later created Lord Bingley, acquired six hundred acres of Bramham Moor. Within little more than a decade he had built his house and laid out the grounds. During his Italian travels Lord Bingley had learnt much about architecture and he was probably his own architect, even though Thomas Archer is known to have supplied some designs. The house is grandly austere, distinctly Italian in character, and gives interesting effects of space, light and shadow. Specially pleasing are the open colonnades that lead to the wings. The gate piers in the forecourt, with their clusters of 'clipped' columns, are more overtly Baroque and may have been designed by Archer. On the left is a vigorous and dramatic stable block with a Tuscan portico, and wings added by James Paine.

Bramham is still owned by the descendants of Lord Bingley. A delightful series of water-colours, painted by Ziegler about 1825, gives an idea of the house and its occupants as they were then. But three years later a fire gutted the building, and owing to the heavy debts run up by George Fox it was not restored until 1906. The outside is now as originally built, except for the garden side where a central door and staircase, designed by Detmar Blow, have replaced an early-19th-century bow window. Inside, the stone cube of the Hall, with Corinthian pilasters and a rich cornice, survives from the original, and some fine carved woodwork of the York school is in the Sitting Room. But most rooms had to be replaced by Blow, and an imposing Gallery has taken the place of three that formerly looked over the garden.

Lord Bingley was Chancellor of the Exchequer in the Tory Government

Bramham Park; the garden front

of Queen Anne, and next to his father's portrait hangs one of the Queen herself, presented on the occasion of a Royal visit. The quality of the many family portraits may be judged by their artists, among whom have been Kneller, Highmore, Hoppner, Beechey, Benjamin West, Hayter, Sir Francis Grant and Henry Lamb. As a bonus there is a full-length portrait of the Duke of Cumberland, the notorious hero of Culloden, by Reynolds. The sporting pictures on the staircase and a bedroom hung with engravings of notable families, chiefly Whig, show the interests and connections of this house.

The garden at Bramham is very special. Capability Brown was not asked to make improvements, and as a result it remains almost unique as an English imitation of the style of Le Nôtre. The walks were laid out by about 1710. As in its smaller contemporary at Melbourne, French formality was modified by English refinements. Broad grassy rides with high clipped hedges join and divide, but the deliberate lack of symmetry and, originally, of terminal features gives the impression of a vast wilderness. A vista, temple, or view of the house always comes as a surprise. Those who remember the garden in the beauty of its Indian summer are fortunate, because in 1962 four hundred beech trees were brutally felled by a gale. Replanting, which would in any case have become necessary before long, has already been done, and the present appearance somewhat resembles that seen by the original designer.

The old parterre in front of the house is now a sunken rose garden. The Baroque Four Faces Urn stands farther off, at the meeting of five walks. By 1725, Lord Bingley added the T-canal, directed obliquely towards the house, which is fed from a spring in the woodlands away to the south-east. The original plan for a long cascade gave way to a complex system of hanging ponds, water terraces and carved fountains, very much in the tradition of Le Nôtre's early work at Vaux and Chantilly. Temples in various shapes were introduced by 1750. One is a columned rotunda, another an open Doric arbour, a third is octagonal and Gothic, and the best of all, designed by James Paine, stands close to the house and is now the domestic Chapel. From here a long vista extends southwards towards the distant obelisk, erected in memory of the 2nd Lord Bingley's only son who died in 1768.

Breamore House, Hampshire
(Sir Westrow Hulse, Bart.)

Seven miles south of Salisbury (A338)

The intoxicating draught of the Renaissance did not always make for sobriety; there is something wild and unmannerly about many late Tudor houses. But in contrast to the ostentatious and the wilful, a graver tradition of building expressed a new sense of scale and symmetry without excess. The south elevation of Breamore is a notable example of this tradition.

The long brick front beneath its five gables, and on the familiar E-shaped plan, is carefully proportioned. Big mullioned and transomed windows of six or eight lights, judiciously balanced, break up the wall spaces, and stone quoins, emphasising the three projecting bays, provide just the right decorative touch. Here is nothing lacking, nothing superfluous: a clean job completed in 1583. Even the central doorway, added in the second half of the 17th century, is suitably restrained.

The house was built by a rich merchant, William Dodington, who, to the great scandal of Elizabethan society, climbed the tower of St Sepulchre's church in Holborn on April 11th 1600, 'threw himself over the battlements and brake his neck'. His successor, another William Dodington, was knighted by James I: but ill-fate dogged the family and he lived to see his son hanged at Winchester for matricide. After passing by marriage to the Grevilles, who held it for nearly a century, Breamore was bought in 1748 by Sir Edward Hulse, 1st Baronet. Son of Dr Edward Hulse, physician to William of Orange, he was himself physician to no less than three sovereigns: Queen Anne, George I and George II. The property has remained in the Hulse family ever since.

A great fire that swept the house in 1856 destroyed William Dodington's interior, but stone Renaissance fireplaces and overmantels survive in the Dining Room and Hall. Following the fire the house was extended northwards and a new entrance on this side replaced the old Tudor entrance on the south front.

Happily most of the contents were saved from the fire and the furnishings of Breamore represent today the acquisitions of ten generations. Some fascinating Mexican objects are said to derive from a Spanish galleon captured by a Westrow buccaneer who presented them to his niece, Dorothy, wife of the physician Edward Hulse. They comprise a 17th-century hexagonal table-top of painted alabaster mounted with silver plaques; the 'Races of Mexico', a set of fourteen paintings, perhaps by Juan Tinoco, which to judge by the costumes of the Europeans must date from about 1700 or soon after, and illustrate the results of intermarriage between whites,

Breamore House; the Hall

blacks, and native Indians; and finally a 17th-century Indian featherwork fan. As rare as it is beautiful, this fan portrays Pyramus and Thisbe and the legend of Perseus and Andromeda. Its colours have lost nothing in three hundred years.

The outstanding English rarity is a pile table-carpet woven in 1614 with a pattern of scrolling stems bearing fruit and flowers on an apple-green ground. Good furniture made in this country includes a large set of Charles II high-back chairs and early examples of the use of mahogany, while a marriage towards the middle of the 18th century brought in Dutch marquetry, over-elaborate as such pieces usually are, but of the first quality. There is a sumptuous K'ang Hsi armorial service painted in gold, blue and rose, and a rare Derby 'hunting' service of about 1800.

Family portraits begin with Dr Edward, founder of the Hulse fortunes, by Riley, and a brilliant pastel of his son, Sir Edward, by Francis Cotes. There are also a number of historical portraits such as a full-length by Gheeraerts of Sir Thomas Coningsby and his dwarf painted in 1601, another full-length by Cornelius Johnson of Sir Norton Knatchbull (1636) and two kitkats by the same of the Lord Keeper Coventry and his wife, a fine likeness of George IV as a young man, painted by Thomas Beech in 1797 when the Prince still retained something of his figure and his early charm, a sensitive head by Lucas of the Duke of Wellington (said to have been the Duke's favourite portrait), and a work that is an understandable favourite, 'The Boy with the Bat' (W. H. Fawkes of Farnley Hall). Executed by Thomas Hudson soon after the middle of the 18th century, when the game was still in its infancy, it is one of the earliest representations of a cricketer. There are landscape and genre paintings by David Teniers, J. M. Molenaer, and Jan

Miel, while P. A. Rysbrack, brother of the famous sculptor, contributes four large still lifes.

The stables and outbuildings house a Carriage and Countryside Museum. The latter is designed to illustrate both the historical development of agricultural tools and machinery, and the yearly farming cycle.

Broughton Castle, Oxfordshire
(The Lord Saye and Sele)

Three miles south-west of Banbury (B4035)

An island-house islanded in past time. Still approachable only across a bridge, and in mediaeval fashion through an embattled gatehouse, the weathered buildings have not materially changed in appearance since 1600. Even the defensive waters, too wide really for a moat yet hardly broad enough for a lake, are of venerable antiquity and probably saw the building of Sir John de Broughton's large fortified manor early in the 14th century. Much of his mediaeval house survives; even the Elizabethan Entrance Front preserves at the east end a two-light window in the private chapel, for which Sir John obtained a licence in 1331. The next development, in the early 15th century, was the enclosure of the manor in a defensive curtain wall, as happened at Penshurst. From the gatehouse it followed the line of the moat, but was largely demolished long since.

In 1451 the Fiennes family, who still own Broughton, made their appearance in the person of Sir William Fiennes, 2nd Lord Saye and Sele, to whom the property came by marriage. The curious title of the barony, created in 1447, is both personal and territorial, deriving from Saye, a family name, and Sele a property in Kent. It was over a hundred years later, between 1554 and the end of the century, that the family transformed their mediaeval manor into a handsome Elizabethan mansion. Externally the transformation is most evident on the Entrance Front. Here appear the typical gabled roof-line and the large mullioned and transomed windows of the time. To achieve a Renaissance balance, a large bay was added at one end as counterpoise to the old chapel at the other, and two-storey bays were set between these features. A central accent was obtained by a shield of arms and an oriel window incorporating Ionic and Corinthian columns; in the further interests of visual symmetry the front door, which could not be centrally situated, was discreetly tucked into the flank of one of the two-storey bays.

With the 17th century building activity ceased, but though besieged and briefly occupied by Royalist forces in the Civil War the house suffered little damage. Though William, the Lord Saye and Sele of the day, was an active Parliamentarian, he so strongly opposed the execution of the King that he found it wise for a time to retire to the Isle of Lundy. The 18th century also left little mark on the outside of the house, though one or two sash windows with Gothic glazing on the Entrance Front are of this period. In the 19th century when Broughton might have suffered disastrous 'improvement' it

Broughton Castle

was probably spared, paradoxically enough, by the accession of the 15th Baron. This extravagant rake is most often recalled for the succinct instructions he once gave his valet: 'Place two bottles of sherry by my bedside and call me day after tomorrow.' He so wasted the family fortune that there was nothing left for building, and in 1837 even the contents of the castle were auctioned, the final lot being the swans on the moat. Minor changes carried out both later in the century and in recent years have been unobtrusive.

The Great Hall was once obviously the mediaeval hall, but to appreciate what has happened one must realise that the Elizabethan transformation turned the plan of the house arsy-versy. Their entrance (the visitor's entrance today) is at the dais end of the hall, but instead of creating their state apartments here in the mediaeval domestic wing, they built them on the site of the kitchens and buttery at the other or service end of the hall. This happily meant that important 14th-century features survived in the solar wing. Most notable are the Chapel with Decorated windows, a number of mediaeval floor-tiles, and its original stone altar; a vaulted Undercroft, now used as a dining room and wainscoted with 16th-century linenfold; and two curious vaulted passages. When putting new windows in the Great Hall and a chimney to replace the central hearth, the Elizabethans lowered the height of the ceiling, but the decorative plasterwork is mid-18th century. Like other Gothic work at Broughton it may be by Sanderson Miller, who was a neighbour at Edgehill less than ten miles away. Two mediaeval doorways still lead from the dais end of the hall to the solar wing, and at the screens end are the doorways that once communicated with kitchens and buttery. The adjoining Tudor arch leads to two large, light, airy rooms, the most imposing apartments to emerge from the 16th-century transformation.

85

Broughton Castle; left: *interior porch in the Oak Room, and* right: *the Renaissance overmantel in the Star Chamber*

The Oak Room has wainscot with large geometric panels set between Ionic pilasters, and is entered through an interior porch, reminiscent of that which survives in a bedroom at Sizergh Castle in Cumbria. Surmounted by obelisks and strapwork, the oak porch carries a Latin inscription added at the Restoration by William Fiennes, the Parliamentarian. It may be translated, 'There is no pleasure in memory of the past.' Tact was rewarded, for he was pardoned and became Lord Privy Seal. Perhaps he also bought, in a spirit of conciliation, the painting by Johannes Peeters of Charles II setting sail from Scheveningen on his return from exile in 1660. It is set in the overmantel above a fine stone chimneypiece that incorporates vases of flowers carved in relief, but must surely be later than the room. A painting of Mrs Nathaniel Fiennes is of interest for its associations. She was the mother of Celia Fiennes, the inveterate traveller whose observations of English country houses are of such interest.

In the White Room on the first floor, once the Elizabethan Great Chamber, the ceiling dated 1599 with pendants and elaborately moulded strapwork shows that the plaster decoration of the period could be exuberantly rich yet strictly controlled. The bold early Victorian wallpaper must be among the finest surviving examples. One would like to have seen the room before its vivid colours faded, and when George Gilbert Scott's white dado and doors of the 1860s were parcel-gilt.

The Long Gallery on the same floor is an Elizabethan addition in the fashion of the time, but was given slender trefoil columns and a Gothic dress in the mid-18th century. There are marble plaques of Inigo Jones and Ben Jonson at either end, and the walls are hung with family portraits which include William, the Parliamentarian. Some are in dashing rococo frames.

James I slept in the Star Chamber off the Gallery, now hung with Chinese

18th-century hand-painted paper. It contains a stucco overmantel of great importance. Closely related to work executed for Francis I at Fontainebleau, it has now no close parallel in England. A central medallion of dancing figures in a landscape is supported by naked boys, and on either side between Ionic columns stand symbolic figures. No one knows how or when it reached Broughton. The fireplace below is a plainer version of that in the Oak Room. The ceiling looks Elizabethan though it may be, like that in the Great Hall, a sensitive 18th-century pastiche.

Brympton d'Evercy, Somerset
(Charles E. B. Clive-Ponsonby-Fane)

Two miles west of Yeovil (A3088)

The name Brympton d'Evercy suggests mystery and romance, and its cluster of Ham-stone buildings is certainly one of the most memorable sights in Somerset. The d'Evercys were a Norman family who came here in 1220, and have left their record in the diminutive church where, among many fine monuments, there are a cross-legged knight and a wimpled and kerchiefed lady. Just next to the church, the detached house (now in use as a museum) is a rare example of a 15th-century residence, with a newel stairway rising to the Hall and Solar. It seems to have been in use about 1480 as a Dower House for Joan Sydenham (*née* Stourton), whose father had bought the estate on her marriage some fifty years earlier. The Sydenhams remained at Brympton for nearly three hundred years. They were Somerset landowners of considerable fortune, but eventually their wealth disappeared through an unaccountable prodigality. By 1640 their estates were mortgaged for £50,000, and, impoverished, they finally departed in 1722. Yet

Brympton d'Evercy; the garden front of the 1670s; (see also colour plate 4)

between these two dates, the means and ambition were found to rebuild the long garden front. Large as it is, it is only a part of what had been intended.

The mediaeval house has gone, but was probably a long courtyard, with a gateway on the site of the present entrance. The highly decorated Tudor building on the left, with a bay window, stair turret and the Royal arms, can be dated about 1520, and was kept for his own use by John Sydenham when he made the house over to his son ten years later. The plainer but more prominent Hall block was an Elizabethan in-filling of the old gateway. In 1722–3, for no very obvious reason, the Elizabethan porch was rebuilt as a detached loggia under a clock house. The airy substitute porch is clearly made up from an old oriel window.

The famous garden front was built by Sir John Posthumous Sydenham in the 1670s. It has the compelling, almost fatal attraction of so much provincial work of this period, for, though ostensibly in the Palladian style of Inigo Jones, its architect was not quite conversant with the rules and conventions of classical architecture.

Delusions of grandeur become more obvious inside. A great parade of State Rooms ends with a large Bed Chamber and Closets. This planning is in the Versailles manner that had only recently become high fashion but wide double doors, set down the centre of the enfilade, take up much of the wall space. The cross-mullioned windows are unusually broad and light. Oak wainscot turns into walnut in the Bedroom, but some bolection panelling and chimneypieces were put in later. The lordly oak Staircase extends for more than half the length of the wing. The Kitchen is vast and makes up the east side of an intended courtyard.

A prosperous barrister, Francis Fane, bought the estate in 1731. It descended through the Earls of Westmorland to Lady Georgiana Fane, who early in life had rejected the hand of a 'lowly soldier'. As he rose to be Duke of Wellington she would have done better to accept him. Georgiana remained unmarried and they kept up a life-long correspondence. Her treatment of the property, however, showed better judgment. She did not interfere with the house, but improved the garden by a terrace and lake, and planted many trees. In 1966 Brympton was leased to Clare School, but recently the present owner decided to return to his family seat, which by then was in need of much restoration.

Bryn Bras Castle, Gwynedd
(Mr R. D. Gray-Williams and Mrs M. Gray-Parry)

At Llanrug, between Caernarfon and Llanberis (A4086)

Before the house was built there was a farmstead here and a tavern, frequented by quarrymen but owned by the Williams family of Cae Poeth. The old name was Coed Goleu ('pale trees'), but before 1800 it was changed to Bryn Bras ('fertile hill'). The Llanberis valley, leading into the heart of Snowdonia, was much visited for its outstanding beauty by the 18th-century picturesque artists, including the young Turner. After 1800 the slate quar-

Bryn Bras Castle

ries of Llanberis greatly increased, and Bryn Bras might well be supposed the house of some newly prosperous quarry owner. It was no such thing. Thomas Williams, the owner, was an attorney of Bangor, and in 1828 he married Lauretta Panton, the youngest and favourite daughter of Jones Panton, High Sheriff of Anglesey. Both were descended from eminent Welsh antiquaries: he from Lewis Morris, the poet and recorder of Welsh history and mythology, while Lauretta's grandfather was Paul Panton, the collector of ancient manuscripts. What could be more fitting than a house, or rather castle, evoking the 13th century, the time of bards and Princes and Edwardian conquest?

The 'castle' is built of stone and brick, but faced with roughcast of dour grey. It was designed in two stages. The three-bay centre, originally with a ground floor only and square turrets standing up like matchsticks, would have resembled a toy fort. Building had begun by 1830, but this fantasy pavilion was very soon enlarged by an additional floor and flanking towers, to become a sizeable house.

The castle was completed about 1835. Inside the style is Norman, with sturdy arches and wall arcading, mouldings of bird's head, billet and cable, and beams faced with chevron ornament. Undoubtedly there is a relationship with Penrhyn Castle near Bangor, which was built at exactly the same time to designs by Thomas Hopper. Bryn Bras is modest by comparison, but it has an arched front door and two massive chimneypieces of slate (now painted over) almost identical to those at Penrhyn. The floors were originally paved with slate. Flashy Penrhyn Castle was built for a rich quarry owner, and Thomas Williams must have borrowed his craftsmen and designs.

Williams lived until 1874, and then or shortly after the woodland garden took the place of former farmland. Bryn Bras was sold in 1897 to Captain Frank Barnard, and again in 1918 to an oil millionaire from New Zealand,

Duncan Elliot Alves. Both left their mark on the house. The former fitted up the library, which he found ruined and overgrown, with panelling and liturgical stained glass, and the drawing room with an *art nouveau* frieze and a fine Louis XVI chimneypiece. Alves put in more stained glass, and imported a motley collection of old panelling for the Dining Room. After the wartime interregnum, and the consequent dilapidation, the property was bought by the present owners in 1964. Repairs to the structure are still in hand. Among the furniture are two lavishly carved Eisteddfod chairs (1902 and 1904), and a historical seascape by Bernard Gribble.

The two statues in front of the house are good copies of Canova's little known Pugilists. They will repay study because the originals in the Vatican Gallery, completed in 1802, cannot be properly seen.

Buckland Rectory, Gloucestershire
(The Rev. Michael Bland, M.A.)

Two miles south-west of Broadway (A46)

This comfortable Cotswold building, all faced with freestone, is the oldest parsonage house in the county that is still in use as such. The nucleus, to the left of the front door, is an upright square building of perhaps the early 15th century. It was originally timbered, and surprisingly enough a complete face, with overhang or jetty, survives inside. From the garden side, the old doorway leads up by stone steps (visible under modern wooden treads) to a hall or chamber that was later divided into four rooms. The roof timbers were of hornbeam.

Buckland belonged to the Abbey of Gloucester, for the dignity of whose Abbot, it seems, a fine new Hall was built against the old house. This can be dated by the stained glass in two windows, with the *rose en soleil* badge of King Edward IV (1461–83), the arms of Gloucester Abbey, and the rebus of

Buckland Rectory (also illustrated on p. 32)

the Rector, William Grafton (1466–1510). These are set against a rare pattern of those mysterious birds, the blackcocks. The lofty Hall is of two bays, and as in a church the hammerbeams have carved angels bearing shields.

Later the Rectory was improved and modernised. The cross wing on the north is 17th century, while the old part to the south was altered and extended, with discreet Gothic decoration, in 1849. Restorations have been carried out by the present Rector.

Burghley, Cambridgeshire
(The Marquess of Exeter)

South-east of Stamford (Lincs) (B1443)

The mighty building stands on high ground, with Capability Brown's beautiful deer park sloping gently towards the lake. Two ancient manors of Burghley were bought by Richard Cecil, an officer at the court of Henry VIII, and one of them formed the basis of the house built by Richard's son William, who was born nearby in 1520.

William Cecil did more to shape English history than any man of his time. As a successful young lawyer he became secretary to the Protector Duke of Somerset. Queen Elizabeth made him Secretary of State in 1558, Baron of Burghley in 1571, and Lord High Treasurer the next year. A master of intrigue both at home and abroad, Cecil settled every detail of policy, accomplished the execution of Mary Queen of Scots, and, by means of informers, ruthlessly hunted down the Catholics. By contrast, his eldest son Thomas, later Earl of Exeter, had 'very ordinary abilities'. Much of the wealth Cecil gained through his office was spent in building four houses (of which Burghley was by no means the largest) and in entertaining the Queen, which he did twelve times. He wrote that he 'meant to exceed his purse' to please Queen Elizabeth, who used her subjects' houses and money for the lodging and entertainment of the whole court on annual Royal progresses. But in addition to his inheritance of great estates that once had been monastic lands, Cecil made vast profits from his various offices and could well afford his buildings.

Cecil was building at Burghley from 1556, and during the next ten years he raised the east side of the house. As Lord Burghley he completed the vast rectangular courtyard block about 1577–87, and it seems that the Hall and Kitchen were rebuilt during this period. With its confused and prickly skyline of turrets and column chimneys, Burghley is decidedly more picturesque and Gothic than the slightly earlier Longleat, but both keep to the English tradition of vast windows. Specially fine are the principal gatehouse facing west (fitted later with magnificent gilded iron gates wrought by Tijou) and the 'corona' entrance in the north forecourt, both these features being derived from late Gothic sources. The design of the house seems to have been largely Burghley's own.

Only two original rooms will be seen, and a staircase. The Hall is decidedly Gothic, with a steep double-hammerbeam roof and very tall windows, but the soaring chimneypiece is classical. (Its panelling is much later.) A lofty stone vault in the Kitchen rises to a central louvre. The Roman Staircase, which is probably of 1577, is vaulted in stone and has geometrical decoration of a French character. Outside the Chapel on the upper floor there is a glimpse of the courtyard. This will not appear again because the internal windows were blocked during the 17th-century conversion.

In 1680 the 5th Earl of Exeter began to transform all the private and state rooms into fashionable Baroque. He was related to the Dukes of Montagu and Devonshire, who were at the same time modernising Boughton and Chatsworth; he was a great traveller, an indefatigable collector and a notable patron of Vanderbank's tapestries. On two sides of the courtyard the rooms have very fine plaster ceilings, probably made by Edward Martin, and superb carved panelling. Grinling Gibbons is known to have worked at Burghley, but this luxuriant work in oak and lime is thought to be by Thomas Young. The room evocatively known as 'Queen Elizabeth's Bedroom' was actually part of the Long Gallery in the 16th century. It has a splendid James II bed, and carved chairs with covers to match.

The Great Apartment was known as the 'George Rooms' at least a hundred years before it was prepared for the Prince Regent. As his visit failed to take place, it is sad that the state bed, a very elaborate affair eighteen

Burghley; left: *wrought-iron gate by Jean Tijou, and* right: *the Heaven Room, painted by Verrio; (see also colour plate 5)*

feet high, was discarded in favour of a Regency piece, later adapted for Queen Victoria and Prince Albert. The long-established visitors' route takes the five George Rooms in their reverse order, passing from the smallest to the greatest instead of the other way round. The Neapolitan Antonio Verrio, having already decorated Windsor Castle, came to paint the ceilings, and lived like a prince at Lord Exeter's expense for ten years until, to his patron's evident relief, he left to work at Hampton Court.

The ceiling subjects were chosen more or less to suit the use of the rooms. The first George Room, a dressing room, has *Day chasing away Night*. In the Bedroom, where the walls are hung with Vanderbank's tapestries of *The Elements*, there is *Romulus received on Olympus*, but the Great Drawing Room, with *Cupid and Psyche* actually contained the state bed. The Dining Room has *The Marriage Feast of Jupiter*. The fifth George Room is Verrio's undoubted masterpiece. Known as the Heaven Room, both walls and ceiling show *The Rage of Vulcan* (as related in the *Odyssey*). All the gods have come to see Venus and Mars caught together, naked, in Vulcan's net, while Neptune, prominent in the centre wall, offers to take her as his own wife. In 1697 Celia Fiennes was shocked by the nudity of the figures. Under the rainbow, close to the Cyclops' forge, Verrio himself sits in classical undress. On the Grand Staircase, he finished only the ceiling, showing *Tartarus* or Hell. For over a century the staircase remained incomplete, and the apartment was said to be unfloored until Capability Brown designed the new stairs. Eventually the walls were painted, and not unsuccessfully, by Stothard in 1801, with *War*, *Intemperance* (Antony and Cleopatra), and *Orpheus descending to the Underworld*.

When visiting Italy, Lord Exeter spent much time with Cosimo III, Grand Duke of Tuscany, who gave him the superb Florentine cabinet (on the grand Staircase) made of *pietre dure*, the most expensive product of the Medici workshops. Exeter's portrait bust, carved in classical style by Monnot in Rome, is in the George Rooms, and his vast monument by the same sculptor is in St Martin's Church, Stamford. As for the astonishing number of paintings, they were collected by the 5th and 9th Earls, and as an introduction to these the printed list is essential. No other seat in England shows so completely, and on so grand a scale, the taste of the English collectors. The names of Carracci, Guido Reni, Gentileschi, Carlo Dolci and Luca Giordano are only a handful of what are here. The *Rent Day*, probably by Jan Breughel, and Rembrandt's portrait of his Mother are in the west wing. As for portraits, William Cecil himself hangs in the Pagoda Room, close to Queen Elizabeth and Cranach's *Luther*. The Billiard Room was used by the 5th Earl's 'Little Bedlam Club', whose members, including Newton, Hobbes, Verrio and Kneller, were painted by Kneller. There are later portraits by Hudson, Dance and Gainsborough, and the large family group of the 1st Marquess of Exeter was painted by Lawrence.

The 9th Earl lived here for forty years and employed Capability Brown as both architect and landscapist. From this period come most of the Georgian chairs, pier glasses and marquetry commodes. The Chapel, though redesigned in the 1770s, retains its 'Gibbons' carvings, and is furnished with

Gothic Revival chairs; the altarpiece by Veronese was among the 9th Earl's purchases. The chimneypiece in the second George Room was made in Rome to a design of Piranesi, and above it there are two paintings by Benjamin West. The portrait of the present (6th) Marquess of Exeter by Sir Oswald Birley is in the Great Hall, next to his athletic trophies and the Olympic Gold Medal that he won for hurdles at Amsterdam in 1928.

Burton Agnes Hall, Humberside
(Mr M. W. Wickham-Boynton)

Between Great Driffield and Bridlington (A166)

Burton is Old English for 'fortified manor', and this hill on the edge of the Wolds, overlooking the North Sea, was well chosen for defence. 'Agnes' appears to have been the daughter of Roger de Stuteville who probably built the Old Hall in the 12th century. This building actually survives, though it was later encased in dingy brick when used as a laundry. The undercroft has a ribbed vault on sturdy Norman pillars, and the newel stairway leads to the hall, mostly reconstructed three hundred years later. The stone is chalk.

The property passed by descent to the Griffiths, a Welsh family long established in the Midlands, and then in 1654, again by marriage, to Sir Matthew Boynton, the Squire of Barmston six miles away on the coast. The present owner's family have thus been at Burton Agnes for over eight hundred years. A tragic story concerns Anne Griffiths who, walking in the grounds shortly after the house was built, was mortally attacked by vagrants. As she was dying she willed that her head should remain in the house that she loved so dearly. First she was buried entire in the churchyard; and then, years later, a servant threw out her skull. On each occasion the 'manifestations' in the house were so alarming that the head was retrieved and kept ever since as she wished. The triple portrait of Anne and her sisters is attributed to Gheeraerts.

The dates carved on the front doorway and panelling tell us when it was built: between 1601 and 1610. The Gatehouse survives complete as a substantial two-storey lodge with domed turrets and a centrepiece carved with the arms of James I between Justice and Prudence. The lawns and topiary in the forecourt lead 'up a pretty ascent' (as Celia Fiennes described it) to the house, a splendid and glittering composition of exceptionally fine brick and stone. It is one of the later houses designed by Robert Smithson, the architect of Longleat and Hardwick, but much of its cheerful character comes from the brightness of the whitened window frames. Sashes were fitted during the 18th century, filled with sepulchral plate glass in the 19th, and returned to whitened window bars more recently.

The house is of a compact plan built round a courtyard, and has much in common with its contemporary, Chastleton House in Oxfordshire. The dominating feature is the tall pair of 'compass' window bays – an advance on the more usual polygonal form – and the front door is placed, as at Chastleton, at one side of a projection.

Burton Agnes Hall (see also colour plate 6)

The interior was extensively modernised during the 18th century, but many of the rooms still have their original carved panelling in excellent condition. The open staircase has the unusual feature of arched and carved posts. As for the chimneypieces, they are carved with so many figures of Virtues and Vices and other sententious motifs – a macabre *Dance of Death* is, of all places, in the Drawing Room – that the house is like a perpetual sermon. The screen in the Great Hall is particularly elaborate in religious allegory, but the alabaster chimneypiece with the Wise and Foolish Virgins is perhaps more interesting because it is in fact earlier, and was brought here from Barmston.

The Queen's Bedroom has a delightfully modelled ceiling with scrolling honeysuckle, and all along the tunnel of the Long Gallery is a similar but larger design of roses. Most of the Gallery's plaster collapsed in 1810, and it was later divided up as bedrooms. Fortunately enough survived to be copied, and since 1951 a complete restoration of the ceiling has been carried out by a Leeds firm. The 18th-century Venetian windows add grandeur, and look well with the Georgian panelling which has come recently from a demolished Yorkshire house.

As with the outside, the character of the old rooms is considerably brightened by later work, and the tone is set in the Great Hall by a Palladian ceiling and two full-length portraits of Sir Griffith and Lady Boynton painted by Francis Cotes. It was perhaps Sir Griffith who lined the Chinese Room with fine coromandel lacquer screens, and panelled the Upper Drawing Room. The furniture, including French and 'French Hepplewhite' chairs, is of good quality; the beds, hung with blue silk, are of *circa* 1700, and there is a fine collection of 18th-century porcelain. Mr Wickham-

Boynton is a collector of paintings, mostly of the modern French school, and large numbers of them are on view. They range from Courbet and Boudin, through familiar Impressionist painters, and then past Derain and Sickert to contemporary works. The Long Gallery makes an excellent room in which to hang the larger canvases.

Burton Constable, Humberside
(Mr John Chichester-Constable)

Ten miles east of Beverley (*via* A165)

The Constables, from nearby Halsham, acquired the manor of Burton by marriage early in the 12th century. Thus for more than eight centuries they have lived here, and when the male line failed, as it has done four times since 1719, nephews or cousins have always assumed the name of Constable. Like so many other northern families they remained Catholic after the Reformation; yet they kept their property despite the fines and penalties imposed on recusants.

At first sight the grand brick building looks typical of many a country seat built by ambitious and newly rich Elizabethans. It proves to be nothing of the kind. It is larger than first appears because the centre block is built round an internal courtyard. Two embattled towers will be seen above the roof-line, whose unequal size implies the presence of an earlier house. Stephen's Tower on the right is said at bottom to be 12th century.

Alterations made early in the 18th century to the entrance front are hardly detectable except by comparison with an early painting. The main door was moved to the centre, an attic floor added and also two bay windows rising to onion domes. The garden front is more of a problem, but some Elizabethan brickwork remains. Brick was thought unworthy in the 18th century and the whole building was faced with stucco painted yellow until 1896.

Nearly all the rooms are 18th century. Cuthbert Constable made the Long Gallery about 1740 out of a series of bedrooms. He was a scholar and built the bookcases for his library, while the plaster frieze that looks Jacobean was in fact copied from one in the Bodleian Library. Cuthbert's son William was an able scientist, and his portrait by Liotard shows him in a fur-trimmed cap and gown, the clothes habitually worn by his friend J. J. Rousseau. Prevented by his religion from taking any part in politics, William Constable devoted himself to his studies and to modernising the house. The present Museum rooms were built for his scientific collection.

William Constable employed an astonishingly large number of architects and craftsmen. Designs were commissioned, but not used, from Carr of York and Robert Adam; the architects actually employed were Thomas Lightoler, James Wyatt, Capability Brown and Thomas Atkinson of York. The gradual transformation proceeded room by room over more than twenty years, during which time Constable made visits to Italy and bought paintings. As for plasterers and furniture makers, some worked in London but wherever possible local talents were encouraged. Lightoler's recon-

5 Burghley; the North Front

6 Burton Agnes Hall; the Jacobean Gatehouse

7 Finchcocks

8 Glynde Place from the park

Burton Constable; left: *the Long Gallery, and* right: *the Hall*

struction of the Great Hall (1763) is open and lofty. Capability Brown's ceiling design was rejected* in favour of one in Elizabethan style by James Henderson of York. The coat of arms in the overmantel contains thirty-seven quarterings. Plaster statues of Hercules and Demosthenes, representing the active and contemplative life, were supplied by John Cheere.

The best of the state rooms is the Ballroom (formerly the Great Drawing Room), designed in 1775–6 by the brilliant young James Wyatt in a rather austere version of Adam's style. The gilded furniture was designed and made by Thomas Chippendale, whose bill amounted to £1,000. The Chapel, originally a Billiard Room, is by Thomas Atkinson, and also the delightful Blue Drawing Room with its airy bow window. Lightoler's Dining Room is seen last, its chaste walls containing an abandoned relief of *Pan and the Graces* by William Collins and a gilded ceiling by Cortese of York. The table and chairs here were made by John Lowry of Burton Constable, the sideboard and gilded 'cisterns' by Jeremiah Hargrave of Hull.

To this bewildering number of craftsmen more names were added during the 1840s, when Lady Constable redecorated many of the rooms. Much furniture ordered from Hull seems in these classical settings excessively rococo and gilt, and the Blue Drawing Room now carries a distinctly 19th-century air. Plenty more furniture of this date is in the Long Gallery; a set of William and Mary walnut chairs was gilded, and the result is overpowering.

Numerous family portraits of the 16th and later centuries hang all along the Gallery, where the outstanding work is that of Lady Constable by Gheeraerts, dated 1599. Nineteenth-century portraits hang in the Ballroom, while the Blue Drawing Room is filled with William Constable's collection of Dutch and Flemish paintings. The Staircase Hall was built by Lightoler in one end of the courtyard as a picture gallery. Most prominent

* But was later used at Corsham Court.

here are three very large canvases of obscure historical subjects by Andrea Casali, an Italian who spent many years in England in the 18th century. These were originally at Fonthill Splendens.

The Stable Block was designed by Lightoler. Capability Brown made additions to the south side, and also advised on the park though the designs actually adopted came from his pupil Thomas White in 1768. Two lakes were shaped in picturesque style, and across one of them marches a noble bridge of five arches.

Burton Court, Hereford and Worcester
(Lieut.-Commander R. M. Simpson)

Six miles west of Leominster (between A44 and A4112)

The hill-top manor stands close to an ancient British settlement, and was a look-out point in 1402 when the future King Henry V was campaigning against Owen Glendower. However, the fabric is mainly of the early 19th century, when it belonged to the Brewster family. A Brewster heiress married the Rev. Canon W. E. Evans, naturalist and author of *The Song of Birds* (1845), but the house was sold in 1865 to John Clowes. Nearly a hundred years later it was bought by the present owner.

Victorian modifications were carried out in 1865 by Kempson, but his entrance front was redesigned in 1912 by the late Sir Clough Williams-Ellis of Portmeirion, whose neo-Tudor porch bears the Clowes initials. Behind

Burton Court

this lies the surprise of the house, the survival of a five-bay Hall dating from the early 14th century. The lofty timbered roof has cusped braces. The oak overmantel, dated 1654, is elaborately carved in the traditional style and has three puritanical portrait figures. The angels that support it are Flemish Baroque work.

A cantilevered staircase floats up a cylindrical well, lit from overhead. In the Library the Gothic bookcase was built for Canon Evans by the Chester firm of Samuel Gardner, and is matched by the oak window pelmets. The high-Victorian Dining Room furniture – table, chairs and sideboards – has delicate bronze mounts and was made about 1882 for a house in Sutton Coldfield.

Cadhay, Devon
(Mr Oliver William-Powlett)

Half a mile west of Ottery St Mary (B3176)

The most interesting Tudor house in the county, Cadhay passed by marriage from the original family, the de Cadehayes, to the Haydons in 1527. John Haydon, a successful lawyer of Lincoln's Inn, traded well in the suppressed Priories around Exeter. Mediaeval stone fragments found in the walls of this house appear to have come from the College of Ottery St Mary, dissolved in 1547, so this may be taken as the date of the building. Three sides of the courtyard, including of course the Hall, were built by John

Cadhay from the north east

Haydon; the fourth, narrower side containing the Long Gallery was almost certainly added by his son Robert, who succeeded him in 1587.

Salcombe sandstone was used, but the corners and dressings are of limestone from Beer (also used at Exeter Cathedral). On the east side, where mullioned windows remain, there is a central newel stair turret. What is curious is that the work added by Robert after 1587 was still in the Gothic style of some forty years earlier. The very interesting Hall fireplace, for instance, is perfectly Gothic, yet it may be dated by the arms of Robert Haydon's wife, Joan Poulett.

The delightful Courtyard was faced (by Robert) in chequer-work of sandstone and flint – a style associated with East Anglia rather than Devon. Even more curious are the four ornamented niches, one of them dated 1617, containing statues of four Tudor monarchs. Henry, Edward, Mary and Elizabeth stand rather stiffly, crowned and cloaked, and give the enclosure the name of the 'Court of the Sovereigns'.

An 18th-century floor has divided the Hall into two rooms, but the old chestnut roof remains as the best internal feature of the house. Its former hammerbeams and arched braces have been removed, but sweeping arches are still there to support the principal rafters.

By the Restoration period the Haydons seem to have become extravagant; they lost their fortune and sold Cadhay in 1736. In the next year the new owner, Pere Williams, divided the Hall as has been described, and re-modelled the entrance front, facing it with Beerstone ashlar and giving it stepped gables and a 'Gibbs' front door. The result is well balanced and imposing. The change from mullions to sash windows seems to have come later. During the 19th century the house was divided up as a farm and small residence, and remained so until 1910 when Dampier Whetham, a Fellow of Trinity College, Cambridge, bought it. By now its condition was bad, but he restored it, revealing once more the old fireplaces and roof. Cadhay was let in 1924 to Major William-Powlett who bought the house outright nine years later, and now it belongs to his grandson.

Callaly Castle, Northumberland
(Major A. S. C. Browne)

Five miles north of Rothbury, near Whittingham

Callaly lies beyond the crags and forests of Rothbury, among valleys of remote and melancholy beauty. Its owners, the powerful Norman family of de Burgh, adopted the name of Clavering in the 13th century and lived here for more than six hundred years. Traces of their original circular castle survive close to the house, but the present castle, more correctly described as a Pele tower, replaced it by 1415. The Claverings were allied to many distinguished families. They remained Catholic, raised troops for Charles I, and as Jacobites were heavily involved in the 1715 Rebellion. Fines and penalties may explain their piecemeal and spasmodic improvements to the house. Yet by the mid-18th century they were prosperous enough to

Callaly Castle; the left-hand projection was the Pele tower

consolidate the building, remove the village, and enclose the park by a stone wall. When the male line died out in 1877, the estate was sold to Major A. H. Browne, whose family have been considerable landowners in the county since the 17th century.

An apparently regular stone exterior covers a patchwork of buildings constructed over nearly five hundred years. The house was recased in ashlar about 1750, when roofs and gables were lowered to the level of a parapet. The ancient Pele tower survives in the almost detached south wing, but has lost its top floor. Left of it, in an open courtyard, is a heavily keyed doorway dated 1727.

Passing on to the right, the recessed range facing south bears the date 1676 on the sundial, and is doubtless the work of the Newcastle architect, Robert Trollope. The facade is a delightful work of 'artisan baroque'. It has four bays, with a door squeezed into the centre. Ralph Clavering's richly mantled coat of arms is flanked by windows and broken pediments bearing trophies of arms, flowers and dolphins. The former Catholic Chapel, whose foundation stone is dated 1750, protrudes further to the north and is now the Ballroom. There yet remains a huge range built in 1890 as servants' quarters and a museum.

The interior is as confusing as the outside. The Smoking Room, with walls seven feet thick, is the original ground floor of the Pele tower. This will formerly have had a stone vault. The lofty Drawing Room is one of the most remarkable interiors in the county. The coat of arms over the fireplace celebrates the marriage of Ralph Clavering in 1757, but otherwise the lavish plasterwork resembles that at Wallington, and might, therefore, have been made by the Francini brothers at an earlier date. The overmantel is of a spirited Baroque, and the curious protruding looking glasses between the windows are even richer in ornament. The medallion portraits, perhaps a little crude, are of poets and philosophers, with Pope, Prior, Newton and

Virgil just recognisable. High above the fireplace is Shakespeare, with Kings Henry IV and V below. Galleries with *chinoiserie* railings at either end imply that it was once the Hall. Recently a priest's hiding hole was discovered near the fireplace.

The strangest room of all is the Music Room of 1890. It looks more like a courtyard, as indeed it once was, and this position may have been chosen as being soundproof. The organ has gone, but the iron stairs and gallery remain complete.

The paintings, furniture and tapestries all come from the Browne family. In the Drawing Room, the scagliola table tops were made in Florence. On one of them the signature of Laurentius Bon Ucelli will be found in a design of playing cards, music and trinkets. The chandeliers are of about 1760. Sporting pictures include works by James Seymour, Sartorius and George Morland. Four large canvases in the Smoking Room were part of the original 18th-century decorations to the supper boxes at Vauxhall Gardens. Three of them, of pretty rococo subjects, are by Hayman. The fourth, of *Fairies Dancing by Moonlight*, now cut into two parts, may be by Hogarth.

Capesthorne, Cheshire
(Lieut.-Col. Sir Walter Bromley-Davenport)

Between Wilmslow and Congleton, south of Manchester (A34)

Capesthorne could be a house in a Disraeli novel, particularly when seen across the park. With the turrets, gables and chimneystacks of the main house rising above wide spreading wings and service courts, it is almost aggressive about the romantic impact it wants to make on the Cheshire plain, and it is not difficult to imagine Disraeli describing it as the home of an early Victorian tycoon. In fact all is not what it seems, nor was its creator cast in that mould. The house itself is a dressing up of an early-18th-century building, and its builder Edward Davenport was the head of an ancient

Capesthorne

Cheshire family with roots going back to the Conquest. His great-grandfather had married Penelope Ward, the heiress to Capesthorne, which had belonged to her family since 1386, and thus acquired the house built for her father by William Smith of Warwick between 1719 and 1731.

The Smith house, a rectangular box with two large flanking courts, must have seemed decidedly dull to the young Edward Davenport when he succeeded in 1837, and immediately he called in Edward Blore to remodel all except the Chapel, which still survives, in a style that is perhaps best described as free Old English or Elizabethan Revival: contemporaries were not quite sure. His rearrangement of the plan was carried out in similar spirit, with the entrance ending up under a corner tower, so that a friend of the family commented on the crab-like approach. The entrance and Hall survived the fire of 1861 that gutted most of the house, and they influenced the reconstruction carried out by Anthony Salvin for Edward Davenport's nephew, William Bromley-Davenport, who succeeded him in 1867. Salvin was a more distinguished architect than Blore, but he did not have a free enough hand, and the results have not impressed pundits of Victorian architecture. That, however, is not the point of Capesthorne.

The intercommunicating rooms that Salvin planned for entertaining provide a handsome setting for a country house collection of considerable diversity. Edward Davenport had reacted against the upbringing of a Tory squire and became a Radical MP, but, more relevant to Capesthorne, he went in for Etruscan antiquities, Greek vases, Roman marbles and fine books. His younger brother, the Rev. Walter Davenport Bromley, was a well known collector of early Italian pictures. Sadly, that collection was dispersed by his son, Salvin's patron, and later many of Edward Davenport's acquisitions were sold; but what survives gives an unusual insight into the independence of mind of an early Victorian, and it is fascinating to see what the house looked like in Edward's day through a series of watercolours of the interior done soon after it was completed. However, there is a strong recent period at Capesthorne: the scholarly tastes of the brothers, the bold array of family portraits and varied relics of its history have been woven together with unusual skill and enthusiasm by Lady Bromley-Davenport. She has approached with an American freshness of eye, and arranged it so that what sounds esoteric becomes part of an enjoyable family chronicle.

Carlton Towers, North Yorkshire
(The Duke of Norfolk)

Six miles south of Selby (A1041)

Carlton Towers has passed down entirely by inheritance since the Norman Conquest, through the Bruces, Bellews and Stapletons, to the present Duke of Norfolk through his mother, the last of the Stapletons and 11th Baroness Beaumont in her own right. It is perhaps the largest, most spectacular and most complete of inhabited Victorian Gothic country houses.

The overwhelming Victorian appearance is, however, only skin-deep and

Carlton Towers

beneath the stunning array of battlements, turrets, towers, coats of arms and gargoyles remains the fabric of the original 1614 house and the stables and chapel added by Thomas Stapleton in 1777. The house was first Gothicised in the 1840s by the 8th Lord Beaumont, to celebrate the successful re-surrection of the dormant barony of Beaumont in his favour. He was heir through the marriage of his ancestor Sir Bryan Stapleton to Joan Lovel, niece of the 7th Baron Beaumont who had died without direct issue in 1507. The Beaumonts were descended from the princely house of Brienne and claimed kinship with the last Christian King of Jerusalem, as well as the Royal House of France.

This illustrious but complicated genealogy furnished material for the heraldic decoration which was worked out by General John de Havilland, York Herald of Arms, and is remarkably extensive even by Victorian antiquarian standards.

The exterior was again remodelled by E. W. Pugin for Henry, 9th Lord Beaumont, in 1873 to 1876. Both patron and architect were slightly un-balanced and both of them died bankrupt in their forties. They quarrelled while work was in progress and Lord Beaumont chose a different, younger architect to decorate the interior, namely John Francis Bentley, the most accomplished Catholic architect of his time and designer of Westminster Cathedral. His work at Carlton is his only major country house commission and remains largely as he left it. Bentley also designed much of the furnish-ing down to such details as pokers, curtains and towel rails.

The great Victorian state rooms, Armoury, Venetian Drawing Room, Card Room and Picture Gallery, open up to form an enfilade of nearly 200 feet, which would have been twice as long if Lord Beaumont's money had not run out. These rooms with their original dark rich colour-schemes contain interesting furniture as well as a collection of paintings by obscure Italian Masters typical of English Catholic houses.

Carlton also retains a number of smaller 18th-century rooms, such as the Bow Drawing Room and the Dining Room, and it is these with their chintzes, Turkey carpets, silver-framed photographs and Edwardian family portraits which give the house much of its charm and its happy lived-in atmosphere – an agreeable contrast to the Gothic megalomania of the exterior.

Castle Ashby, Northamptonshire
(The Marquess of Northampton)

Six miles east of Northampton (A428)

No trace survives of the mediaeval castle from which Castle Ashby derives half its name, and the front of the house speaks with the comfortable assurance of the great mansions of the Elizabethan and Jacobean age. The landscape too is comfortable, undulating Northamptonshire at its mild and verdant best. Two immense rides, dating from the time of William III, radiate from the house. On the noble south ride, at any summer weekend, the village cricket team – white figures on green sward – is engaged in the stately hieratic ballet that is cricket. The formal terraced garden on the east and north, of Italian inspiration, dates from the 1860s and is none the worse for that. Among the most elaborate designs of its sort in the country, it replaces a landscape devised by Capability Brown over a century earlier.

The Comptons, who had been settled at Compton Wynyates since the early 13th century, bought Castle Ashby in 1512, but the house in which they still live was not begun until 1574 by Henry, 1st Lord Compton. His Elizabethan building with its two polygonal staircase towers and its mullioned and transomed windows, occurred after 1620 when the Comptons, by that time Earls of Northampton and living in high state with eighty-three household servants, four chaplains and three musicians, were in touch with the advanced architectural taste of the Court. The first of the lettered

Castle Ashby

balustrading on the roof appeared about 1624, and at the same time the central section of the east front was given a classical dress though still with strong Jacobean overtones. The open loggia on the upper storeys was sealed in 1691 and turned into rooms.

In 1635 came the elegant classical screen on the entrance front, closing the open side of the old Elizabethan courtyard. With two storeys of the Doric and Ionic orders, and with a Venetian window (one of the first in England), this screen is attributed to Inigo Jones. It was to have been merely the central feature in a larger scheme for the whole of the south front which unhappily was never executed. As it stands, the famous facade is architecturally restless.

The inside of the house chiefly evokes the late 17th and late 19th centuries. Of the Elizabethan interior an undercroft alone survives, and of the interesting work that preceded the Civil War the most important survival is the plaster ceiling in the Great Chamber. The middle decades of that century have left even less, for the 2nd Earl died heroically in the first engagement of the Civil War, the Compton estates were sequestrated, and the east side gutted by the Roundheads.

It was about 1675 that renovation was undertaken. In 1688 when William of Orange had landed at Torbay, Princess Anne, aged twenty-three and already a determined Protestant, was willingly whisked away one night from St James's Palace. The coach that carried her belonged to a Compton, the martial Bishop of London, an ecclesiastic as happy with the sword as the crozier. When the future queen reached Castle Ashby she must have climbed the new Grand Staircase with its panels of luxuriant carved foliage to find the State Apartments much as they are today. Their walls are hung with Flemish and Mortlake tapestries or lined with panelling. Two rooms are decorated with swags of carving in the contemporary manner of Grinling Gibbons. Much of the furniture – elaborately carved high-back chairs, Charles II cabinets on stands, coromandel lacquer, seaweed marquetry and two scriptors – is also of the period.

The most imposing of these rooms is the Great Chamber (King William's Dining Room). It contains interesting furnishings of later date such as the thirteen large panels of mid-18th-century needlework depicting scenes of rural life and worked by the ladies of the house, 18th-century Italian silver wall sconces, carved and gilded rococo mirrors and superb torchères of about 1760, the latter designed by Chippendale. The great oak chimney-piece of 1601 was inserted in the late 19th century, and came from Canonbury, a London property of the Comptons.

Substantial changes occurred in the second half of the 19th century. The Great Hall was then shorn of its 18th-century decoration and reinstated in sumptuous Jacobethan, the Chapel largely repanelled, and the Long Gallery (the upper storey of Inigo Jones's south front) was given a genteel and watery classical dress. The gallery now houses an outstanding collection of ancient Greek vases.

One of the delights of Castle Ashby are the paintings. For the visitor, they begin with a Flemish triptych of the early 16th century in the Chapel, and continue with a series of portraits in the east wing that include Antonis Mor's likeness of Mary Tudor, a sensitive Cornelius Johnson of the 2nd Earl, good Hoppners, and two outstanding works by Ramsay and Reynolds (Lady Mary Compton and Mrs Drummond-Smith). On the Grand Staircase hangs an arrogant full-length of the 3rd Earl by Dobson (again an outstanding example of this artist's work), and the head and shoulders of the 1st Duke of Buckingham, paler than ivory, painted by Van Dyck after the Duke's assassination. There are elsewhere Dutch cabinet paintings by such masters as Gerard Dou, Isaac Ostaade, and Jan Steen, and an important Dosso Dossi. Finally, the Great Hall contains two masterpieces: a Giovanni Bellini of the Virgin and Child, and a curious but most moving Adoration by Mantegna.

Castle Howard, North Yorkshire
(Mr George Howard)

Thirteen miles north-east of York; five miles west of Malton

Castle Howard is never disappointing. The approach along a five-mile avenue, with limes and beeches and bizarre arched lodges, reaches a turning where a huge obelisk was erected to commemorate the rebuilding and replanting. This is the site of old Henderskelfe Castle, an ancient property of the Dacres but secured by marriage, in 1571, to Lord William Howard, a younger son of the Duke of Norfolk. His descendants, the Earls of Carlisle, became front-line Whigs in the 18th century.

When Henderskelfe was gutted by fire in 1693, the 3rd Earl of Carlisle decided on a complete rebuilding. William Talman submitted designs, but was dismissed after a dispute over his charges. Carlisle's next action had great consequences for English architecture: the commission was given to a witty and convivial playwright of rather bawdy comedy, John Vanbrugh. Before plunging into architecture, Vanbrugh had undoubtedly secured the help of Nicholas Hawksmoor, the most able and erudite man in Wren's office. As a result, country house architecture exploded into wild Baroque of a kind quite new to England. While the grand ideas must surely have been Vanbrugh's, the scholarly Hawksmoor worked out the details. Perhaps he did more. Yet Vanbrugh was always given the credit, and often the discredit, for the magnificent, ponderous buildings that resulted from their combination. There is a freshness and innocence in Castle Howard that is not found in their later houses. Vanbrugh was never to be so young again.

The new site was dramatic, on high ground overlooking the north valley. Designs for the house were made in 1699 and work started the next year. Fine local stone was used, pale yellow in colour with the faintest blush. The central block in the forecourt depends upon four groups of pilasters. It is ornamented by niches, round-headed windows and chanelled masonry, enlivened by sculpture, and triumphantly crowned by a drum and dome. To the left, beyond the private wing, is the laundry court where walls, gates, domes and turrets are seen in fantastic variety. The misfortune is that, in

Castle Howard; Vanbrugh's garden front

spite of the architect's entreaties, Carlisle never began the chapel wing and stable block on the right. He had become more interested in the park buildings, and money was running short. The west wing was finally built in the 1750s by Sir Thomas Robinson. Though worthy enough in the Palladian way, it lacks the excitement of Vanbrugh's first masterpiece.

The long garden front looks oddly European, but no convincing prototype can be found. The pedimented centrepiece was copied many years later by Frederick the Great at Potsdam. There is a constant repetition of round-headed windows with chunky keystones, and the frieze is closely packed with carving. As for planning, the centre contained the saloon, and an apartment extended at either side, making a total length of 300 feet. Blenheim Palace was given the same format.

The Hall is a *tour de force*, with giant arches like the crossing of a church and light pouring down from the lantern of the dome. Twin staircases just visible through side openings make a genuinely Baroque effect of extended space, and four stone-clad corridors vanish towards mysterious quarters. The carving was done by Samuel Carpenter, from Yorkshire, and Nadauld, a Huguenot refugee; the iron balustrade is by Tijou. The gay rococo chimneypiece was made by the Italian stuccoist Bagutti in 1710 – a singularly early date for this style – and the niche opposite is by his assistant, Plura. The antique sculpture was collected in Rome. All available wall spaces are filled by frescoes by Pellegrini, one of the most talented of the Venetian painters, who had been brought to England by Lord Manchester. The dome is a recent and happy reconstruction, for the original fell in after the tragic fire in 1940, when the house was in use as a girls' school. Two-thirds of the garden front was gutted and Pellegrini's frescoes in the High Saloon were lost for ever. Let us not dwell on this appalling tragedy.

Of Vanbrugh's state apartments, only two rooms survived the fire. Two more had already been reduced to matter-of-fact Palladianism during the 1750s. The west wing was unfinished until after 1800, when the Gallery was at last completed by Tatham. It was intended for sculpture as well as paintings, and is so well proportioned that one forgets Vanbrugh's unfulfilled intentions. The three sections give interesting effects of light and shade, and the wide floorboards add to the perspective.

Frederick, 5th Earl of Carlisle, reigned here for sixty-seven years. As a young man he was painted as Knight of the Thistle by Reynolds; fifty years later Jackson showed him, a distinguished statesman who had long since sown many wild oats, standing in his gallery. Carlisle was an indefatigable collector, and bought many of the paintings. Some came from the Orléans collection, which was sold in London during the French Revolution. Most striking, perhaps, is the *Salome* by Rubens, which once belonged to Reynolds. Of the portraits, front place must be given to Holbein's *Henry VIII* and his *3rd Duke of Norfolk*, but there are also courtly paintings by Van Dyck, Lely and Kneller. From the 18th century there is Gainsborough's *Countess of Carlisle*, and his *Girl with Pigs* which, to the delight of the artist, was bought by Reynolds. Here too is Reynolds's painting of *Omai* (the 'Gentle Savage'), a youth brought to England from Tahiti who became the rage of London society. As for the 19th century, Lord Carlisle's alliance with other great Whig families will be recognised in the busts by Nollekens, portraits by Lawrence, and the mass of pictures arranged in Lady Georgiana's rooms (seen first in the tour). She was the eldest daughter of the Duke of Devonshire, and married the 6th Earl of Carlisle.

The Chapel was much altered in 1870. Crowded with columns, it has paintings by pupils of Kempe and stained glass made to Burne-Jones's designs by William Morris. The 9th Earl, a notable painter himself, counted these among his friends.

Castle Howard; the Hall

The formal garden, re-created in 1850, makes a fine complement to Vanbrugh's long facade, and the fountain was carved to Nesfield's design by William Thomas. Statues on Vanbrugian pedestals are original with the house, and they march in line up to the Temple of the Winds, also designed by Vanbrugh and one of his last works. It is a useless, utterly delectable building that would not look out of place at Bomarzo in Italy. Inside, the plaster and the Cosmatesque floor of scagliola are the work of Vassalli. The view from this *belvedere* shows what Lord Carlisle was doing instead of completing the house. Vanbrugh's lake is crossed by a cyclopean bridge, and further off stands Hawksmoor's magnificent and costly Mausoleum. But Vanbrugh's work does not end here. There are yet his nightmare gates to the walled garden, the pyramids, the castellated park wall punctuated with turrets, and the gated lodges across the avenue.

Chalcot House, Wiltshire
(Mrs Anthony Rudd)

Two miles south-west of Westbury (A3098)

The park rises steeply up to the house, and the drive passes close by a dry river valley. This was once the site of a Roman-British settlement, and during the recent renovations two thousand coins of the 3rd century A.D. were found. Chalcot has probably been in continuous occupation since then but the mediaeval manor is no longer recognisable. The distinctive feature of this brick and stone house is its classical front, which is very curious and perhaps unique. Of five bays, the pedimented windows are framed by pilasters, all linked in vertical lines. The capitals have a Renaissance flavour,

Chalcot House; a Georgian facade with Elizabethan stonework

and suggest Allen Maynard and the craftsmen who were working nearby at Longleat during the 1560s and 1670s.

On the other hand the doorcase, the attic panels carved with drapery and cockleshells, and the brickwork are mid-18th century. The probable explanation is that when the Phipps family came here in the Georgian period they rebuilt the facade but retained most of the existing stonework. The fine Kentian urn above the doorway is carved with the Phipps crest.

A hundred years ago the house was enlarged by a wing at the back, and many rooms were increased in height. The part of the stables that remains has a pleasing dormer window and a rain-head bearing the date 1872. The usual fate of such Victorian additions has occurred here: they were not only unsuitable to modern conditions, but proved to be badly decayed. The present owners bought the property in 1971, and in removing much of the 19th-century work have created a new entrance on the north. The Victorian rooms, with marble chimneypieces and plaster ceilings, have been restored with great care, and the hall and staircase are now lit by circular skylights. This preservation gained for the owner and architect a European Architectural Heritage Year Award in 1975.

Chambercombe, Devon
(Mr R. Hayward)

Just south of Ilfracombe (B3230)

The setting was a delightful one, in a steep valley running down to Hele Beach with high cliffs either side. But proximity to the sea has been its undoing. Caravans now fill the floor of the valley, and this small ancient

Chambercombe

house has to cope with the crowds who flock to Ilfracombe during its short holiday season. The needs of the visitor are adequately catered for here amid newly laid out gardens, which have yet to settle into the landscape.

Built round a cobbled court, this reluctant showpiece was originally a sequestered farmhouse. Champernons owned the manor from the 12th to the 15th centuries and may have lived in this house, the older part of which appears to be late 15th century. Alterations were made a hundred years later. The beamed Hall and seven rooms contain good furniture, mainly 17th century but including some later pieces. A well-attested story of a corpse discovered in a walled-up chamber is told by the guide in grisly detail. The Chapel, licensed in 1404 and only ten feet long, still retains the spirit of that time in spite of later alterations.

Chastleton House, Oxfordshire
(Mrs Clutton-Brock)

Four miles west of Chipping Norton (A44)

The fascination of Chastleton is that it has survived unaltered since the death of its builder, Walter Jones, in 1632. The ancient manor had come by marriage in the 15th century to the Catesbys. As recusants they were heavily taxed, and after Robert Catesby's involvement in the Essex Plot he was forced, in 1602, to sell Chastleton for £4,000 in order to realise his fine. Three years later he was executed as leader of the Gunpowder Plot. Jones, the new owner, seems also to have come under suspicion, for he obtained a signed document from James I that recognised his total innocence.

Walter Jones was a successful wool merchant from Witney. His family had come from Wales, and he produced a pedigree satisfactorily proving his descent from Brutus, the ancient King of Britain, and from Priam of Troy. The house may have been designed largely by himself, for the Cotswold builders, like a well-trained orchestra, could work from the simplest of instructions.

The front, though scarcely ornamented, is of a sophisticated design. Projections and recessions give it a vertical emphasis, and the windows are set at different levels. The coping runs continuously round the top of the walls, taking the gables in its way like so many hurdles. The front door, slightly enriched, is set round a corner – a curious mannerism that is often found in houses of this date and size. The tall battlemented projections either side contain staircases. It is symptomatic of Chastleton that inside the house one easily loses all sense of direction.

The Hall is of the single-storey type with a generous bay window, but its courtyard windows are now blocked. Fireplace and panelling are simple, but the screen, carved with columns, satyrs and acanthus scrolls, is refined and courtly. The refectory table, like most of the furniture of the house, has always been here, and was clearly made before the screen was set up. Another table is in the Great Parlour, now a dining room. There are a great number of parlours and chambers, the finest being the Great Chamber on

Chastleton House; the Great Chamber (lithograph by Joseph Nash, 1840)

the first floor. Its walls are entirely panelled, lavishly carved with strapwork and arches taken from Flemish pattern books, and painted with prophets and sybils. The chimneypiece is even more elaborate, and bears the arms of Walter Jones and his wife, Eleanor Pope. The plaster ceiling, with numerous ribs and drops, is overpowering, and the room has been described rather unkindly as the taste of a *nouveau riche*. However it was thought very fine during the romantic period, and Nash's famous engraving of 1840 is to be seen here.

The west stairs, more rustic in style than the east, are also the more interesting, with square balusters forming a cage to the stairwell. Both staircases have prominent obelisk finials, and they lead to the tunnel of a Long Gallery, with strapwork and flowers all along the curved vault. The plasterwork seems to have been made by craftsmen employed at Oxford colleges.

The family emerged as staunch royalists. There is a story that Arthur Jones returned from the exiled King's defeat at Worcester in 1651. He was concealed in the Secret Room while his wife drugged Cromwell's troops with wine, thus allowing him to escape.

There are early lacquer cabinets, 16th-century Flemish tapestries, wall hangings in Florentine stitch, and crewel-work that was made in the house. The Jones family portraits include some by Hudson.

In the 16th century there was a family connection with Ralph Sheldon, who made the rare Elizabethan tapestries at Barcheston, his house in Worcestershire. Sheldon's coat of arms occurs over a fireplace, and, though they are no longer here, a number of Sheldon tapestries were discovered in the house. Four large tapestry maps are recorded as hanging in the Long Gallery in the probate inventory of 1633. Possibly Walter Jones had supplied the wool from which they were made.

Chatsworth, Derbyshire
(Trustees of the Chatsworth Settlement)

Nine miles west of Chesterfield (B6012)

Chatsworth is not only among the largest of our country houses, but one of the most distinguished. It stands majestically in the open valley of the Derwent, and the aura of the park extends for miles around. If you were to remove the woods and leave the turf to rankle, this setting would return to desolate Peak country that alarmed travellers in the 17th century. The approach then came over the steep precipice of the hill, and the house was described in 1681 as 'a bright diamond set in a vile socket of ignoble jet'. Just as the inhospitable moorland has been tamed into park and garden, so the hard gritstone rock has been civilised and fashioned into classical forms. Where once there was a 'houling wildernesse', now the Palace of the Peak enshrines the splendour of a great Whig dynasty. Three members of the family built it in different centuries.

During the 1550s, the ambitious Bess of Hardwick and her second husband, Sir William Cavendish, built a courtyard house of two storeys. Thirty years and two husbands later she added a top floor with grand high rooms. Not surprisingly, the walls were 'bending' by 1680, and this alone must have compelled rebuilding. Not a stone of the Tudor house will now be seen, but it survives as the skeleton of the square centre block. The courtyard format remains, as well as the Great Hall, though both wear a Baroque dress. A gallery has become the Library, and, further up, the old High Chamber and Gallery were converted into the Great Apartment.

The Baroque transformation took twenty years and was carried out by the first Duke of Devonshire. As an advanced Whig and champion of Protestantism, he had to live in retirement when James II came to the throne, and his first work was to remodel the south front (facing the long lawn and

Chatsworth; Talman's south front, 1685

fountain). The architect, William Talman, designed this in 1685 as a noble and solid *palazzo*. With its heavy keystones and ponderous cornice and balustrade, it is almost a work of sculpture, but has been criticised for lacking a central door opening. Devonshire's star rose again with the Glorious Revolution and the reign of William III. By then he had caught the building bug, and one wing after another was reconstructed in turn. Talman, famous for quarrelling, was dismissed by 1697, and the designer of the elaborate park front (*c.* 1700) is not known. But it was followed in 1704 by the present entrance, designed by Thomas Archer, where a curious bulge ingeniously hides the fact that the corners are not in alignment. Within the bulge the original kitchen became an entrance hall in 1756.

Chatsworth then is a collection of limbs uneasily jointed at the corners. It is not domestic or cosy. Ceremonious rooms and staircases, plain but palatial corridors, and rich, sombre fittings are far from present-day ideas of comfort. The most interesting interiors are due to Talman and his talented group of artists and craftsmen. The Chapel is a masterpiece of the English Baroque, its walls and ceiling painted with New Testament scenes by Laguerre, and the altarpiece by Verrio. The cedar panelling came from London, but the limewood carvings are by Samuel Watson, a highly talented young Derbyshire craftsman who worked at Chatsworth for many years. The reredos of Derbyshire alabaster, again carved by Watson, was designed by Cibber who also supplied the statues of Faith and Justice.

Talman was adroit in managing the long progression and ascent from the Great Hall – also painted by Laguerre – to the Great Apartment. Here and there his design was altered in the 19th century, but the stone staircase, with paintings by Verrio, sculpture by Cibber and ironwork by Tijou, remains intact, and leads up to the enormous Great Chamber.* Three more rooms and two closets extend the whole length of the wing. The painted mythologies on the ceilings, with their simulated architecture, recall the King's Apartment at Versailles; the luxuriantly carved and parqueted oak panelling is chiefly by Watson. This noble parade of rooms became obsolete within fifty years; Walpole wrote that they were 'vast but trist'. A second staircase, dating from after Talman's period, has a ceiling with *Phaeton* painted by the Englishman James Thornhill, who was greatly superior to Laguerre. He also decorated the entire walls and ceiling of the Sabine Room, where various deities attend the Rape of the Sabines.

From this period are the massive pier glasses by Gumley, the coromandel lacquer chests made from discarded panelling, Delft tulip vases, and the Dutch silver chandelier (1694), which was probably a present from a grateful William III. Much Georgian furniture has come to Chatsworth from Devonshire House in London, and also from Chiswick House which the family inherited through a marriage with the heiress of the 'Palladian' Earl of Burlington. This will account for the massive gilded tables designed by William Kent; and Lord Burlington himself, dignified and unbending, is to be seen in a painting by Knapton. There are excellent Italian and Dutch

---

* The Great Apartment is seen by visitors in its reverse order.

Chatsworth; left: *the Chapel and alabaster reredos, and* right: *the Great Chamber*

paintings of all sizes in the corridors and state rooms, and the group of works by Rosa, Ricci, Thomas Patch and others on the second staircase should not be overlooked. The best portraits, many of them by Van Dyck, are hung in the Dining Room.

The third of the Cavendishes to indulge in building was the genial 'bachelor' 6th Duke. Much as he loved his 'adored Chatsworth', the inflexible Baroque palace was gloomy and inconvenient, and, from 1818, Sir Jeffry Wyatville made considerable improvements. Some of these, such as the replacement of the steep horseshoe stairs in the Great Hall, the addition of corridors, and the fitting of gilt leather in the state rooms, are to be regretted. The service wing he completely rebuilt, with offices below and princely rooms above. The suite begins with a succession of libraries for the Duke's famous and ever growing collection of books, and continues with the white and gold Dining Room. This was first used when Princess Victoria made her tour of England in 1832, and the Duke described it as 'like dining in a great trunk, and you expect the lid to open'. By then he had been through a love affair with marble, and rare coloured columns, some of them from ancient Rome, support door and window openings. Next comes the Sculpture Gallery, with his unique but now, alas, unfashionable collection of mythologies, including four statues by the great Canova, and the rest by his pupils and contemporaries. The group of Bonaparte portraits, all modelled from life, are most interesting: *Madame Mère*, the first statue he bought, and Napoleon's head are both by Canova, and *Pauline Borghese* is by a Scotsman, Thomas Campbell. Continuing past the Orangery, a staircase leads to the Duke's private Theatre in the tower, and a temple attic gives splendid views over the grounds.

The garden was always big, but its former extensive parterres were removed by Capability Brown. From the 1st Duke's time there remain the long canal and the enchanting Cascade House, which, with its dolphins, fountains and sonorous descent of water, was the Baroque creation of Archer. The legendary beauty, the Duchess Georgiana, has left little mark at Chatsworth except for a grotto. Brown planted the park, and buckled the river Derwent into a serpentine course. The bridge and very fine stables were built then by James Paine.

The 6th Duke's craze for gardening developed as a result of his inspired appointment of the young Joseph Paxton as head gardener. Paxton rapidly showed himself to be an engineer, architect and man of business. The Orangery became fairyland, and Paxton constructed glass wall-cases for camellias, a rockery large enough for Brobdingnag, the Great Stove or Conservatory – forerunner of the Crystal Palace but demolished in 1920 – and the Emperor Fountain that throws a water jet 290 feet high, the second highest in Europe. This was intended to greet the Duke's friend, Tsar Nicholas I, but the visit failed to take place. Meanwhile, enormous sums of money were spent in collecting rare plants from all over the world. Though the pleasure grounds cannot exactly be described as a 'flower' garden, the groves, trees and flowering shrubs thrive and are constantly replanted; recent additions include a modern greenhouse, a sunk garden and maze on the site of the Great Stove, and a serpentine walk leading to a bronze bust of the 6th Duke. The garden is so vast that even on the most crowded days solitude can be found.

Chavenage, Gloucestershire
(Mr David Lowsley-Williams)

Two miles north-west of Tetbury

The house is in the parish of Horsley, once the property of Bruton Priory. The Prior's house stood near Horsley Church, and there are various medi-aeval fragments at Chavenage that are said to have come from it. This is the case with the Chapel behind the house, a substantial towered building (probably late 17th century with later embellishments) which shows the size of the community once attached to the house. Great old barns with steeply pitched roofs indicate that Chavenage has always been the centre of a working farm, as indeed it is today. It was bought in 1553 by Edward Stephens, one of a sheep-farming family from Eastington who were acquiring considerable estates in this part of the county. In 1712 Atkyns described the house as 'a pleasant Seat with delightful Prospects on Wiltshire'.

Clearly something of a mediaeval house remains in the forecourt, and inside there is an old newel stair. Fifteenth-century windows were used again in the Elizabethan rebuilding, the best being over the central porch; the date 1575 and initials of Edward Stephens are carved left of the front door. The form of the building is a deep Elizabethan E, but additions have been made at different periods.

The splendid stone chimneypiece in the Hall has the arms of Robert Stephens, son of Edward, who was here until 1608, and is an accomplished

Chavenage

work of the pre-Inigo Jones period. Nathaniel Stephens, successor to Robert, was a staunch Parliamentarian and Oliver Cromwell, to whom he was related by marriage, and other generals used Chavenage as headquarters during the Civil War. In the winter of 1648 Cromwell's son-in-law, Henry Ireton, came down and successfully persuaded Nathaniel to support the Impeachment of the King and thus his subsequent execution. The rooms used by Cromwell and Ireton are hung with tapestry.

Dutch stained glass (17th century) is in the porch, while the miscellany of mediaeval stained glass in the two tall windows of the Hall probably came from Horsley. Here, old wood carving has been rather unsatisfactorily cobbled on the screen and doorway in the romantic fashion of the 1840s. More interesting is the patched panelling in the Drawing Room. The date 1627 will be seen, but some parts, carved with portrait heads or allegorical figures and gilded, is Renaissance and mid-16th century. On the garden front there is a delightful confusion of building of all periods, stretching from a Gothic revival window on the 1680 Billiard Room to the bow window of the Dining Room added early in this century. The latter was built for the present family, who came here in 1894.

Chenies Manor House, Buckinghamshire
(Lt.-Col. and Mrs Macleod Matthews)

Three miles east of Amersham (A404)

Overlooking an exceptionally well preserved village, the ancient manor is of beautiful mellowed brick. In Saxon days Chenies was known as Isemhamp-stead, but the Cheyne family were living here by 1180. Some 350 years later it passed by marriage to John Russell, who was steadily and dramatically rising in the royal favour. A courtier *par excellence*, he survived the early Tudors, became Lord Privy Seal and Earl of Bedford, and his descendants, staunch Protestants and Parliamentarians, were elevated to the Dukedom by William III. Chenies was their principal seat until 1627 when they concentrated on Woburn Abbey. The magnificence of old Chenies can be judged by the monuments in the church where the Dukes of Bedford are still buried, but of the house not a great deal is left. During the 18th century it was let to farm tenants, and Horace Walpole described the building as being 'in piteous fragments'. In 1954 it was sold to the present owner, and has once more become a family home.

The present front garden was once divided into two courts. The Gatehouse was built about 1460, but may have been altered by Russell. It is an odd mixture of crow-stepped gables, angle buttresses and pinnacles. Inside, the newel staircase has a moulded brick rail and a squint window, and the stone-floored parlour, once open to the roof, may have been a hall. Leland about 1540 described the interior as 'richly painted with antique workes of white and black'.

The Gatehouse was reduced in width and overshadowed by the addition of the long high wing. Russell entertained Henry VIII here and this was necessary as lodgings and rooms of state. On the first floor each chamber has the odd arrangement of a closet or garderobe behind the chimney, one of these concealing a hiding hole and another retaining its original privy. The back of the wing is most impressive, with a long row of powerful chimney-breasts. Twenty-two chimneys are among the best rubbed brickwork of their period, and the builders responsible for them were taken over by Henry VIII for Hampton Court. The top floor, known as the Armoury, became a

Chenies Manor House; the gatehouse and Henry VIII wing

barrack room for Parliamentarian troops during the Civil War. It is 144 feet long, and may be among the earliest Long Galleries to be built in an English country house. The plasterwork has long since been removed.

According to a surveyor's report of 1745 the house was too large, in bad repair, and ought to be demolished. Owing to the Russells' ancient connection they decided to renovate it, but removed the decaying wings. Repairs in the 19th century resulted in new oriel windows, and the garden side was refaced. Under the garden, brick passages take in their way the now ruined Nursery Building. This had been put up to house the children of Henry VIII, and later, on one of Queen Elizabeth's several visits, William Cecil was accommodated there 'for his quieter lodging'.

Chicheley, Buckinghamshire
(The Hon. Nicholas Beatty)

Two miles north-east of Newport Pagnell (A422)

The early 18th-century house, red brick with stone dressings, is first seen framed by a double avenue of limes. As soon becomes apparent, the facade is decidedly unusual. Giant pilasters with Corinthian capitals support a cornice that sweeps dramatically upward to accentuate the projection of the three central bays. These are further emphasised by an exuberant frieze of grotesque masks and cornucopia, by window heads of strange profile, and by the central doorcase which has a weird segmental pediment carried on eccentric tapering pilasters. The effect, here in a quiet stretch of Buckinghamshire countryside, strangely evokes the Netherlands, though it seems that the unusual architectural features of the exterior are provincial echoes of Roman Baroque architects such as Bernini and Borromini.

No wonder that Chicheley was long attributed to Thomas Archer, among the most wilful and engaging practitioners of Baroque in this country. It was in fact built between 1719 and 1723 for Sir John Chester by Francis Smith of Warwick, who elsewhere on at least one occasion had built to Archer's designs. The house remained in the Chester family until 1952 when it was bought by the 2nd Earl Beatty, father of the present owner. The long Chester occupation, and lack of money in the 19th century, preserved Chicheley almost unchanged. Many of the windows retain the thick glazing bars of the early 18th century and their original crown glass panes; a ram, Sir John's crest, peers precariously from each end of the cornice; and on the east front his moulded lead downpipes survive with their massive decorated heads. So too on this front does his formal canal which bounds a vast lawn on three sides. Once there must have been elaborate Dutch parterres here, but today the lawn, bearing only three or four immense oaks and cedars, is simple and effective.

Entering the house the visitor steps from the Baroque to the Palladian, for the panelled Hall was designed by Henry Flitcroft and the ceiling painted by William Kent, both of whom in the 1720s were embarking on their successful careers as protégés of Lord Burlington, the dedicated promoter of the

Chicheley

Palladian movement. From the Hall, beyond a screen of marble columns, rises an excellent staircase of the early 18th century. Of oak inlaid with walnut, with elegant balusters of three differing designs, and with scroll-carved terminal brackets to the treads it is a fine example of the joinery of the time.

The joinery of the Sitting Room and Drawing Room is no less remarkable. Both have elaborate fielded panelling and the treatment is strictly architectural, with carved limewood friezes over the doors and fluted pilasters flanking the chimneybreasts. The original plasterwork ceilings and chimneypieces survive. The effect of the Drawing Room is particularly rich, and here curiously enough much of the wainscot is of elm, a wood rarely used for panelling but with flowing and decorative 'flower'. Sir John Chester's portrait (Hudson at his best) surveys furniture which he once owned, notably a pair of gilt gesso side tables and four superb giltwood mirrors with his crest. There is also a collection of mother of pearl, which includes Stuart tankards and candlesticks: unusual though perhaps not to everyone's taste.

Sir John Chester's eccentric 'Library' upstairs is also fitted with fine wainscot from floor to ceiling. But the fielded panels punctuated by pilasters prove to be an ingenious deception, for even the pilasters swing open to reveal shelves. Sir John's books were carefully concealed.

Since 1952 Chicheley has acquired a new interest through its association with the 1st Earl Beatty. There are portraits of the distinguished sailor by Sargent and de Laszlo, and in the Study many objects of association, such as the naval desk which the Admiral used on board HMS *Lion* at the battle of Jutland. In the same room hang a series of seascapes by Serres and minor masters of the genre, and a fine version of L. F. Abbott's sensitive portrait of Nelson.

Chiddingstone Castle, Kent
(Executors of the late Mr Denys Eyre Bower)

Four miles east of Edenbridge

The Streatfeilds had been established at Chiddingstone for some three hundred years when they decided, early in the 19th century, to transform their red brick Carolean house into a Gothic castle. Perhaps they hoped to emulate James Wyatt's Lee Priory in the eastern half of the county, now alas demolished but one of the foremost Gothic houses of its day. But Henry Kendall, the architect who completed the transformation of Chiddingstone, was no Wyatt and left a solid castellated sandstone mansion with some hints of the 'picturesque'.

But one does not visit Chiddingstone for its architecture, or indeed primarily as a country house. Its interest lies in the highly unusual collections assembled over a lifetime by the late owner. The average visitor will probably most appreciate the unrivalled Stuart memorabilia: paintings, miniatures (works by Hilliard and Cooper), medals, boxes by Obrisset, Jacobite glass, finely tooled Stuart bindings, and such moving objects of association as Charles I's handkerchief, the pathetic letter the Duke of Monmouth wrote to James II on the eve of his execution, and the letter, full of hope, despatched by Prince Charles Edward to his father in 1745 as he set out from France to raise the Stuart flag in Scotland.

There are also six rooms devoted to a remarkable display of Egyptian antiquities and Japanese works of art. The Egyptian Rooms contain a collection that ranges from Pre-dynastic objects to a fine porphyry head, said to represent Cleopatra. There are over 200 ushabti (tomb) figures. The Japanese Rooms contain metalwork, arms and armour (including sword blades by early masters), extensive collections of lacquer, netsukes and inros (many pieces again by well-known masters), and not least terracotta tomb figures dating from the 4th/6th centuries A.D.

Chiddingstone Castle

Chillington Hall, Staffordshire
(Mr Peter Giffard)

Seven miles north-west of Wolverhampton; two miles from Brewood

Few houses in England can prove so long a family succession as Chillington, which has passed from father to son in the Giffard family for eight hundred years. Peter Giffard, of Fonthill, Wiltshire, came here about 1178, and was descended from Giffards who, having landed in England with William I, were amply rewarded by numerous manors. We know something of the Tudor house, because it was considered as a stronghold for Mary Queen of Scots but rejected as not providing enough security. Queen Elizabeth was entertained here in 1575, but, on their discovery as Catholics and recusants, the Giffards, like so many of the Staffordshire gentry, suffered fines and imprisonment. In 1651, the family aided the escape of Charles II after the Battle of Worcester by hiding him in their nearby properties, Whiteladies and Boscobel.

No structure earlier than the 18th century is visible. The private wing of the old house was rebuilt by Peter Giffard in 1724 (the date being on the rain-heads). Three floors high, it is in the late Baroque style that is so familiar in the Midlands. The architect is thought to be Francis or William Smith. The staircase is a fine oak construction with the family's crest of a panther carved into each bracket, and plasterwork, more Italian in style than is usual, attributed to Vassalli, who also worked under Smith at Sutton Scarsdale.

Peter Giffard was succeeded by his son and grandson, both called Thomas. The younger Thomas made his Grand Tour in 1784, and his portrait by Batoni, in the confident relaxed pose of an English tourist, is one of the most pleasing late works by this artist. It hangs in the Dining Room, opposite his marble bust, also made in Rome, by Christopher Hewetson, and an earlier portrait, again by Batoni, of the elder Thomas Giffard.

Chillington Hall; Soane's entrance front, 1785; (see also illustration on p. 15)

Fresh from his Italian tour, Thomas Giffard employed John Soane in 1785 to rebuild the old house. As one of Soane's earliest country houses, Chillington is of particular interest. The sixty-year-old wing was kept, but the join at the angle seems unfinished. Soane did not favour high buildings but had perforce to keep the height of the old building in the wings. The brickwork was intended to be covered by stucco but fortunately (as we think) this was not carried out. The columned Hall and three uncompromisingly rectangular rooms show the distinction of Soane's work. Vast windows, fourteen feet high, reach almost to the floor making a flood of light, and the delicate mouldings of the cornice and windows show how Soane was already moving towards his abstraction of classical style. Some of the plasterwork and the chimneypieces are thought to have been added about 1830.

The Saloon was built within the walls of the old Tudor Hall. Soane was already experimenting with overhead lighting, and developed this idea further at the Bank of England. The effect, though somewhat chilling, is fully in accordance with mature neo-classical thought. At one end there is a vaulted bay, and it is said that the corresponding bay at the other end was omitted to make room for a service staircase. The fireplace, by tradition, is the doorcase to the old Tudor hall or, more likely, a copy of it made in 1830. It bears the family's arms and their two crests of an archer and a panther's head.

Upstairs, the corridors show how Soane loved to create spatial effects by arches and curved vaults. The painted state bed commemorates the marriage of Thomas Giffard to Lady Charlotte Courtenay in 1788. The chintz hangings, curtains and chair covers are all of an 18th-century 'Indian' pattern.

The park is very extensive. A long, wide avenue, planted about 1724, approaches the house at an angle from Brewood. Capability Brown's principal achievement was to create the 'pool', an enormous lake which James Paine described as 'one of the finest pieces of water that this Kingdom produces'. The bridge is by Paine, but the large Temple near the lodge is of uncertain authorship.

Chingle Hall, Lancashire
(Mrs M. H. Howarth)

Near Goosnargh, four miles north of Preston (B5269)

This pleasant cottage-like house with white rendering was originally a small thatched and timbered mediaeval building. Sections of the moat, and ancient timbering, survive. Chingle has a special place in the affection of English Catholics for it was a stronghold of the Old Faith. John Wall who was executed at Worcester in 1679 and was thus one of the last Catholic martyrs in England, was probably born there. It is a much haunted house, where inexplicable phenomena have repeatedly been observed.

Chorley Old Hall, Cheshire
(Mr Michael Burling)

Half a mile from Alderley Edge (A535)

This moated building, dating in part from the 14th century, is reputedly the oldest hall-house in the county. It has been restored by the present owner.

Crossing the moat, one sees the original stone-built hall, and at right angles a Tudor wing of 1560 timbered in characteristic 'black and white' Cheshire fashion. The stone building tells a complicated architectural history. The doorway with splayed and moulded reveals is 14th-century Gothic, but the gables are of varying dates. The latest, above the doorway, dates from the mid-17th century, as do the mullioned windows on this front (two earlier windows survive on the rear elevation).

Entering the 14th-century doorway one finds on one's left no less than four attractive Gothic arches. The first three led in normal fashion from the screens passage to buttery, kitchen and pantry, but the fourth gave access to a newel staircase and a solar above. The unusual situation of the solar at this end of the building is accounted for by the fact that the hall was relatively modest and never had the usual domestic wing at the dais end.

Two large speres or tree-trunks, a constructional rarity that is something of a Cheshire speciality, indicate the width of the screens passage. Rising the full height of the house, they were originally free-standing, and a movable oak screen was probably placed between them. The stone chimneypiece in the hall dates from the 16th century when a chimney replaced an open louvre in the roof, and an upper storey was inserted in the hall.

Chorley Old Hall; 14th-century arches to the service rooms

There are several 16th-century stone chimneypieces in the later black and white wing. Here also is a room with 17th-century wainscot, and an overmantel with an unusual frieze displaying mermen associated with flowing floral ornament and an enigmatic recumbent figure that nonchalantly holds a severed head under its arm.

Churche's Mansion, Nantwich, Cheshire
(Mr and Mrs Richard Myott)

In Hospital Street, Nantwich

This is not really a country house, but the town house of a successful tanner. Nantwich is a well preserved country town, and the 'wich' in its name implies that it originally grew up with the salt trade. By the 16th century it was also prosperous from wool and leather. A disastrous fire in 1583 gutted the town, but fortunately did not reach Churche's Mansion which stood near the eastern gate.

Inscriptions on the house record the owner, Richard Churche, his wife Marjery, the builder Thomas Clease and the date of its completion, May 4 1577. Churche was everything expected of the reliable middle classes of those days: diligent, pious and loyal. His timbered house is in the decorative style familiar in Cheshire, and two among the carved brackets are thought to show the heads of himself and his wife. On most of the joints the carpenter's numbering will be seen: Arabic outside and Roman numerals within. The planning is conventional and typical of its date. The beamed ceilings are fine, their diagonal dragon beams at the corners are clearly visible, and

Churche's Mansion; an Elizabethan merchant's house

several rooms retain their original panelling and floors.

The condition of the house today is so fine that one forgets the ruinous and dilapidated state of fifty years ago. Though it remained with Churche's descendants until 1930, it had been let to tenants since 1696. Much rebuilding in alien styles and materials had been done, rooms had been altered and fireplaces concealed. The late Dr Myott set out to restore the original condition, and his work, continued by his son, has been remarkably successful. The back of the house, where old beams had rotted under later accretions or been removed altogether, offered great problems, and a substantial rebuilding with old materials was done in coronation year (1953), the Queen's head being carved on a corner bracket.

A splendid piece of furniture, the Elizabethan buffet, has lately returned to its original home. The frieze matches the Hall panelling, and the front, carved with the royal arms, is inlaid with its first owner's initials. Like the panelling in the house it has been cleaned to a beautiful honey colour. The building is in use as a restaurant, and visitors are free to wander upstairs.

Clearwell Castle, Gloucestershire
(Mr Bernard Yeates)

Six miles south-east of Monmouth (B4231)

The drive leads uphill, through a castellated gatehouse and a fine stable block (shorn, alas, of its clock tower) into the courtyard. From here the main front of this solidly built structure is hidden behind the trees on the right. In three sturdy blocks, it is a competent essay in castle building during a classical age; but it is something more. Datable to *circa* 1728, this may be the earliest example of Gothic revival on such a scale. The architect was Roger Morris, later to become the designer of Inverary Castle where similar clustered columns flank the main doors. Other Gothic features are the windows on the main floor, the angled buttresses, and of course the sturdy battlements, half of which are carved with the lion's head crest of the patron, Thomas Wyndham. Round windows in the basement are a pleasing touch. All this is excellently constructed of Forest of Dean stone.

By the 18th century the old manor, a former Throgmorton property, had been acquired by a younger branch of the Wyndhams (who are better known at Felbrigg in Norfolk and Orchard Wyndham, Somerset). It passed to the Countess of Dunraven and was sold on her death in 1870. Disaster struck in 1927 when a fire gutted the entire building. Yet the four-foot walls survived unhurt, and the owner, Colonel Charles Vereker, reconstructed the rooms and designed a new staircase. After the war Clearwell fell into the ungentle hands of speculators; trees, roofs, floors and fittings were removed. Mr Frank Yeates, hearing by chance of its condition, bought it in 1953 and with the help of his able family he gradually restored the building. It is his son who now lives here. Frank Yeates was actually born in the lodge, his father having been gardener at the property. This makes a satisfying and optimistic last chapter to the story.

Clearwell Castle; an early essay in Gothic revival by Roger Morris

Behind the simple but boldly conceived facade lie a hall and two large rooms. Here the few suggestions of Gothic consist of a doorway and two niches. The ceilings are modern reconstruction, but several original chimneypieces remain. They are carved in stone with flowers and trophies, all in the Baroque manner of James Gibbs. At the back, the Long Library has its original columns, chimneypieces and frieze, but the bow window is a Victorian addition.

Compton Wynyates, Warwickshire
(The Marquess of Northampton)

Eight miles west of Banbury

Glimpsed first through the trees from the escarpment to the south, with sheep grazing on the slopes below, Compton Wynyates gives the impression of a house seen in a dream. And like a dream it is clearly unplanned. Irregular, seemingly haphazard, the tall moulded chimneys, the oriels, the mullioned windows, the rose brickwork appear to have drawn together in some natural affinity. Richly varied in outline and texture, the house appeals to the imagination rather than to a sense of formal architecture.

Compton means 'the settlement in the coombe', and Wynyates is a reference to the vineyards which once flourished on the suave slopes about the house which has descended in the Compton family in unbroken succession since 1209. Built round a courtyard, and surrounded by a moat until the middle of the 17th century, the house took shape in early Tudor times. It owes much to William Compton who was fortunate enough to be appointed page to Prince Henry, later Henry VIII. Thus arose a boyhood friendship which brought William not only honours but the ruined castle of Fulbroke near Warwick. From Fulbroke came the timber ceiling and the ample bay-

Compton Wynyates

window in the Great Hall and perhaps many of the cusped and arched window surrounds.

Some of the rooms later acquired Jacobean panelling, and early-18th-century fireplaces appeared in the Great Hall and Dining Room, but few structural changes of importance occurred (except in the east wing) for over three hundred years. Then in the second half of the 19th century, Sir M. D. Wyatt, who was also employed by the family at Castle Ashby reworked the east and south facades, built the main staircase, and inserted the rich Elizabethan panelling (from Canonbury, another Compton house) in the Dining Room. He must surely have also been responsible for a number of the plaster ceilings which are unconvincing as Tudor work. But the general effect remains highly picturesque.

The sense of past time which so informs Compton Wynyates is evoked even as one approaches the entrance porch, surmounted by the arms of Henry VIII and with an oak door of his time. The stonework still carries the grooves worn by the chains that once lowered the drawbridge, and each side of the porch incorporates a stone bench with delightfully upcurved ends where retainers sat looking out across the vanished moat.

Following a financial crisis, the contents of Compton Wynyates were unfortunately sold in the 1770s, when the house was closed for over fifty years. None the less, there is today a good deal to see in the interior: Compton family portraits, appropriate oak furniture, later Stuart pieces, tapestries, blue and white Delft. In the chapel are two dated Elizabethan oak chairs inlaid with ebony and boxwood, and a chamber organ of 1665 by Father Smith, perhaps the best known of the late-17th-century organ-makers. In the Great Hall, likenesses on panel of John Talbot, 1st Earl of Shrewsbury, and his wife must be among the earliest English portraits, and there is a copy of Holbein's famous portrait of Henry VIII, painted in 1547, four years after the artist's death.

Constable Burton, North Yorkshire
(Mr Charles Wyvill)

Six miles south of Richmond (A684)

This trim Georgian villa was the result of an expensive mistake. In 1762, Sir Marmaduke Wyvill employed John Carr to make alterations to the Elizabethan house of his ancestors at a cost of £1,500. Returning home five months later, instead of seeing the work finished, he found the entire house demolished except for its lowest walls. The complete rebuilding cost him £10,000. Yet the mistake does not seem to have damaged the architect's reputation. 'Carr of York' was for more than half a century the leading architect in the north of England, and any crisp Palladian house or lodge seen in Yorkshire will, as likely as not, turn out to be his.

Constable Burton appears to have been rebuilt largely on its old foundations. Such a Palladian villa might seem old-fashioned for the 1760s, except that the ornament has been kept to a neo-classical minimum. At basement level, only the 'Gibbs' windows are rusticated, not the wall surfaces. A double stair leads over a bridge to the pedimented loggia – an Italian feature often used by Palladio himself but rarely seen in England. The back elevation with its bow window is the most austere of all. The stonework is excellent and shows hardly any sign of weathering.

Fine proportions and restrained detail characterise the interior. There are plaster ceilings in Adam's style, good marble chimneypieces, and the original mahogany shelves remain in the Library. In the centre is a stone staircase with an elegant wrought-iron balustrade, lit from lunettes overhead. All this leaves ample wall space for pictures which are mainly Netherlandish – van Meiris, Frans Francken, Hondecoeter and Weenix – with some Italian, and of course the family portraits.

The Wyvills were allied to many Yorkshire families. A marriage in 1845 between a later Sir Marmaduke and Laura, heiress of Sir Charles Ibbetson, brought with it the Ibbetson portraits, including two by Mercier and Soldi.

Constable Burton

The Ibbetson seat, Denton Park near Otley (Leeds), became the principal family home until recently when Mr Wyvill decided to return here. Otley was the birthplace of Thomas Chippendale, who was well patronised by Yorkshire squires during his famous London career. Several pieces which came from Denton are attributed to Chippendale's workshop: two mahogany specimen cabinets, tables, and some agreeably simple painted chairs and stools. On the other hand the Dining Room was furnished by Gillow of Lancaster in about 1800.

The house is raised on a hill, round which a stream has formed a deep valley. The garden is beautifully laid out with shady walks of shrubs and lilies, and a rock garden has recently been made near the drive.

Corsham Court, Wiltshire
(The Lord Methuen)

Between Chippenham and Bath (A4)

In Corsham village, traditionally famous for the skill of its masons, an Elizabethan stone manor stands near the church. Built by Thomas Smythe, a haberdasher and Collector of Customs in London, it is E-shaped with pedimented windows, pinnacled gables and a columned porch dated 1582. Despite the gloom of the plate glass windows, the forecourt with its old stable buildings is a delight; yet inside the house it will be forgotten, for Corsham is visited chiefly for its 18th-century rooms and collections. In the 1760s Paul Methuen, having bought the house twenty years earlier, doubled the width of the wings and rebuilt the park side. The state apartment remains, hardly altered, and its architect was Capability Brown.

The Methuens, or de Methvins, had been diplomats in Scotland during the Middle Ages. Paul Methuen, a clothier from Bradford on Avon, inherited a great collection of paintings from his uncle, Sir Paul, and many more came through a marriage in 1844 to the daughter of the Rev. John Stanford. The result is one of the finest assemblies of old master paintings to survive in an English house. They are set off by furniture supplied by some of the best cabinet-makers in London.

The visitor will go at once to the state rooms. First and finest is Capability Brown's Picture Gallery, which gives an experience comparable to that of the Colonna Gallery in Rome (the impact is greater when the room is entered by the far door). Brown's curious ceiling was a rejected design for the hall at Burton Constable, and was carried out by Thomas Stocking of Bristol. It is reflected in the carpet, recently made in Madrid for the 4th Lord Methuen. This room, a triple cube, is hung in 18th-century style with pictures up to the ceiling. Brown surely designed it round the three largest: Van Dyck's equestrian *Charles I* on the end wall; the same artist's early *Betrayal of Christ*; and Guido Reni's *Baptism*. Over the chimneypiece is a spirited *Wolf Hunt* by Rubens. Every picture here is worth study. Those by Luca Giordano, Guercino and Salvator Rosa are typical of 18th-century taste, while *Tobias and the Angel* (labelled Caravaggio), a Madonna by

Corsham Court; the Picture Gallery, with Capability Brown's ceiling

Andrea del Sarto, and the *Gaddi Children* have hauntingly introspective qualities.

All this is set off by the furnishings. The walls are hung with crimson silk damask; the marble chimneypiece is by Scheemakers and on it rests the same sculptor's bust of Paul Methuen. The long set of chairs, sofas and window seats in crimson silk may be by Chippendale, while the gilded pier glasses and tables below were designed by Robert Adam. Shagreen chests, coromandel lacquer and huge jars of blue and white porcelain strike a more exotic note.

The other three rooms are smaller, but filled with treasure. The Cabinet Room is named from its three Florentine cabinets of *pietre dure*, but the outstanding furniture is a marquetry commode and two flanking torchères made in the 'French' style by John Cobb in 1772. They stand below another pier glass designed by Adam. Among the paintings, Filippo Lippi's beautiful *Annunciation* is a witness of the interest in Florentine Renaissance that was aroused in the early 19th century. The State Bedroom has paintings by Bronzino, Guercino and Salvator Rosa, two fine mahogany commodes and a pair of gilded looking glasses delicately carved with twigs, squirrels, and birds. These correspond with designs by Thomas Johnson, one of the cleverest of the London carvers during the 1750s. Finally, the Octagon Room, a boudoir enlarged about 1840, contains no less than forty paintings, mostly of cabinet size. The best are Elsheimer's *Apollo and Coronis* and Claude's *St John*, while others are by Jan Breughel and Teniers; the melancholy portrait of an aged Queen Elizabeth is of particular interest.

The rest of the house was transformed into airy Gothic by John Nash from 1798. His plans were irresistible and work began happily enough, only to end in nightmare. Progess was slow, the cost immense, and the result was instant dry rot. By 1840 everything had to be rebuilt by Thomas Bellamy, who chose a ponderous French style. His staircase is monumental but gloomy, and the two front rooms rather bleak. Here will be seen family portraits including several excellent canvases by Reynolds; a Gothic sideboard and chimneypiece by Nash; a pianoforte by Clementi; and a chamber organ made for the Bath Assembly Rooms.

In the garden a diminutive Gothic Dairy by Nash remains attached to the house, and further off is Brown's Gothic Bath House. The park, designed by Capability Brown, was improved by Repton, who planned the lake. The state of the house and its informal garden owe much to the 4th Lord Methuen, artist and Royal Academician, who lived here for more than forty years, rearranged the paintings and restored the original silk hangings and upholstery. Part of the house has been in use since the Second World War by the Bath Academy of Art.

Dalemain, Cumbria
(Mr and Mrs Bryce McCosh)

Three miles south-west of Penrith (A592)

By Ullswater the volcanic mountains of the Lake District change suddenly to pastoral country. The poet Thomas Gray on his Lakeland tour in 1769 noticed the fine lawn and wooded hills of Dalemain. The front of the house, then about thirty years old, is also part of the landscape, for the dusty pink sandstone, one of the loveliest building materials in the north, was quarried a mile away.

Dalemain; the 18th-century facade, built of pink sandstone

Dalemain was established in Saxon days, and became one of the chain of fortifications against the Border raiders, its closest neighbours being Dacre and Yanwath. The sturdy Norman Pele tower and stone staircase still form the core of the old house. The earliest recorded owner is John de Morville, whose brother Hugh took refuge here after taking part in the murder of Thomas à Becket (1172). To the Layton family, owners of the house from the 13th until the 17th centuries, is due the mixture of old building round the courtyard. The mediaeval Great Hall survives, though divided in the 16th century by a beamed floor and the upper part turned into a panelled chamber. The adjoining bedroom, sited in the old Pele tower, has a good Elizabethan ceiling. The great barn outside is 16th century.

Sir Edward Hasell (1642–1707), a member of a Royalist family, was Secretary to the famous heiress Lady Anne Clifford, and out of her substantial legacy he was able to buy Dalemain in 1679. Lady Anne's portrait is here, and also the diary of her last years. Hasell proceeded to a seat in Parliament and a Knighthood, and his descendants still live here. They have always taken a prominent part in local affairs, whether in working the estate, in forestry, the militia, the Ullswater Foxhounds, or the building of the railway.

The long entrance front enclosing the courtyard was built by another Edward Hasell after 1735. It is classical in spirit, with French quoins providing some distraction to the row of windows. Most of the oak fittings came from the estate, and the fine cantilevered staircase and the Drawing Room panelling are skilful works, perhaps by local joiners. The *chinoiserie* chimneypiece, carved with dragons, is the essence of English rococo and might well have been made in St Martin's Lane, but is curious for being carved in oak rather than softwood. It is contemporary with the Chinese wallpaper.

The family portraits are of good quality, and run continuously from the 17th century to the present day. There is a fine portrait by Kneller, and two small full-lengths by Devis and Zoffany. The furniture is partly sophisticated – witness the coromandel screen – and partly country-made. A delightful pair of ashwood 'courting chairs', with conveniently wide seats, are unusual. Local interests appear in the Victorian silver trophies presented by the Lancaster and Carlisle Railway Company to their Chairman, Colonel Edward Hasell, and in the dazzling militia uniforms in the Yeomanry Museum.

Deene Park, Northamptonshire
(Mr Edmund Brudenell)

Five miles north-east of Corby (A43)

Deene has all that one expects in an old country house: great size, a picturesque accumulation of structure, lawns round a winding lake, and a church close by in a meadow. The house has belonged to this family since it was bought in 1514 by Chief Justice Sir Robert Brudenell. During the 17th

Deene Park (also illustrated on p. 24)

century the family were Catholic and Royalist, but George Brudenell, created Duke of Montagu in 1766, became Protestant as a young man and so was able to take part in public affairs. Owing to the death of his heir* the Dukedom became extinct. The Brudenells were also Earls of Cardigan from 1661, and Marquesses of Ailesbury in 1868.

The old part of the house stands round a courtyard, and includes the large block projecting eastwards, towards the bridge. The first Great Hall of the Brudenells is on the left of the court. It dates from about 1540, but a floor was later inserted and it is now the Billiard Room. A 13th-century doorway has been found in a wall. The curious oriel window is best seen from outside. In an ambitious but unscholarly Renaissance style, it bears the initials 'E A', for Edmund Brudenell and Agnes Bussy his wife, but is clearly not in its original position. Though Agnes Bussy's fortune caused family quarrels, it allowed a greater Great Hall to be built in 1571. This is entered through a sophisticated porch and has a complex hammerbeam roof made of chestnut. The old panelling is remarkably fine but survives on only one wall. Over the chimneypiece are the arms of Edmund and Agnes. The great quantity of heraldry in the house helps to date some of the additions. The stained glass in the oriel window, for instance, was evidently put in before 1630 by Sir Thomas, the future 1st Earl of Cardigan. Close by there is his portrait by Michael Wright, 1658, which shows what he must have suffered through fines and imprisonment for his loyalty to the King. The house was plundered and damaged by Parliamentary forces in 1643.

The great length of garden front belongs to three separate building periods. The central part is of 1810, Gothic outside and classical within. Among the furniture are side tables by Gerreit Jensen. The paintings are of members and relations of the family and many of them have been collected

*The Marquess of Mouthermer (d.1770): cf. Boughton House.

quite recently, Reynolds's astonishing portrait of Lady Mary Montagu being among them. She married the 4th Earl of Cardigan, later created Duke of Montagu, and during his lifetime the estates of Deene and Boughton were united. The Duke's portrait, one of three unusually fine paintings by Thomas Hudson, is in the Ante Hall.

The Dining Room has paintings by John Ferneley of Lord Cardigan's hunters. 'Lord Cardigan' here is the 7th Earl, the hero of Balaclava, and in the painting by de Prades he is leading the Charge of the Light Brigade. The horse, Ronald, was recalled fourteen years later to lead the veteran's funeral procession, and his head and tail are preserved in the White Hall. The Ballroom was built to commemorate the Charge, but in spite of Crace's alabaster fireplace and stained glass designed by Lady Cardigan, this addition is thought to have been rather unnecessary. The monument to Lord and Lady Cardigan in the church, and some sculptured portraits in the house, are by Boehm. He was witty, arrogant, a ruthless disciplinarian; she was much younger and a beauty. They had lived together quite openly while Cardigan was waiting for his divorce, and in spite of infidelities they remained a devoted couple. Lady Cardigan outlived her husband by forty-seven years, shunned by Court and society, and delighted in shocking her neighbours by eccentric dress and behaviour. On her death in 1915 Deene passed to a nephew of the Marquess of Ailesbury. The present owner inherited the property in 1962 and since then has carried out extensive restorations. Both house and garden are in superb condition.

Detillens, Surrey
(Mr D. G. Neville)

In Limpsfield village, near Westerham

The demure Georgian front of about 1725 – rosy brick with white sash windows – surprisingly conceals traces of a typical Wealden 15th-century

Detillens

open-hall house of timber, and wattle and daub, construction. The original roof support, a king-post sitting on a massive tie beam, survives intact. The open character of the hall disappeared, as so often happened, when a floor was inserted in the 16th century to create rooms above, and a chimney replaced the open central hearth. Two or three chimneypieces with contemporary firebacks, some attractive floor tiles in the Sitting Room, and much of the simple oak panelling must date from the late 16th century or soon after.

In one of the rooms shown to visitors there is a large collection of British and Foreign orders and decorations, some of considerable rarity.

Dewlish House, Dorset
(Mr J. Anthony Boyden)

South of Dewlish, between Blandford and Dorchester (A354)

The house is a recluse, isolated in a valley formed in the chalk, by the River Dewlish. In the 18th century a Roman Villa was discovered a quarter of a mile away. The place has perhaps been continuously inhabited since then, and in the Middle Ages the farm was leased as a sub-manor. However, nothing before 1702 is visible at the house, for in that year it was rebuilt by Thomas Skinner whose father, a London merchant, had bought the property forty years earlier. The long and pleasing Queen Anne front with its shapely pediment is of grey limestone, and the columned doorway supports the Skinner arms. On the other hand, the plainer east side is of golden Ham Hill stone; and the garden front, rebuilt perhaps half a century later, is of brick.

The interior was redecorated in the mid-18th century, most likely in 1756 when the ownership changed, and is generally in the urbane style of William Kent. The best rooms are the Oak Room and an alcove Bedroom; but the show-piece of the house is the Staircase, constructed of velvet-grained

Dewlish House

Virginian walnut. It is said to have been made by a local craftsman. Mr Boyden bought Dewlish in 1962, and has had a new pine Library fitted by the East Coker Saw Mills. Also he has laid out the garden, built a ha-ha, and formed a small lake out of the river.

Doddington Hall, Lincolnshire
(Mr and Mrs Anthony Jarvis)

Five miles west of Lincoln (B1190)

Doddington appears suddenly and unexpectedly in the low and uneventful country of pastoral Lincoln. In a county which has few Renaissance buildings, this splendid Elizabethan house is a rarity. It stands behind a Gatehouse with Dutch curving gables; but the house itself, except for its three punctuating cupolas, is rectangular, functional, and almost devoid of ornament, the stone mullioned windows being large and perfectly regular. The house was built by 1600, and in its simple square outline it anticipates such buildings as Hatfield House and Quenby. The architect was probably Robert Smithson, who built many of the best Elizabethan houses including Longleat, Hardwick and Burton Agnes. Kip's engraving of 1700 shows the various buildings just as they remain today.

The first known occupants were the Pigots in the 12th century, but the house had changed hands several times before 1593 when Thomas Tailor, Registrar to the Bishop of Lincoln, bought and immediately rebuilt it. Bricks were baked from clay dug in the adjoining field, and some are clearly

Doddington Hall

over-burnt. The house passed by marriage to the Husseys, and then in 1759, again by marriage, to the ill-fated Delavals of Seaton Delaval. Sir Francis Delaval entertained lavishly at both houses until his death, but Sir John, later Lord Delaval, lived until 1808, and he modernised the interior as we see it today. A protracted lawsuit with his younger brothers resulted in his felling every tree when he thought he was about to lose the estate on which he had spent so much. Eventually the house came to Sarah Hussey Delaval, Mrs Gunman, whose portrait by Lawrence shows her considerable beauty; in 1825 she left the property to her lover, Captain George Jarvis, whose descendants continue to live here.

Though Thomas Tailor was rich and successful, the house he built was austere in its decoration. Nothing is left inside from the 16th century, but the Brown Room has oak bolection panelling of Queen Anne's day. Otherwise the interior belongs to Lord Delaval's improvements of the 1760s, carried out by the Lincoln carpenter, Thomas Lumby. The White Hall shows his simplified Palladian style and this continues in the Drawing Room above and the Long Gallery, which takes up the top floor. Lumby also reconstructed the staircase, grand in its Imperial form but of a plainness unusual in the mid-18th century.

There are plenty of fine family portraits of all dates. Among the full-lengths in the Hall are two Husseys by Michael Dahl, while royal portraits show where the Hussey sympathies lay during the Civil War. More notable are the many paintings of the Delavals. There are two groups of the Delaval children, painted in rococo style by Arthur Pond, and some of them appear again in splendid canvases by Reynolds. Sir Francis is shown wearing the red coat of the Volunteers, but the best is the family group with Sarah, later Countess of Mexborough, and her husband robed for the coronation of George III. This painting has always stood in its present position, filling the end wall of the Long Gallery. A group of views of Seaton Delaval and another of 17th-century naval pictures (from the Gunman family) are also of interest. The bed in the Tiger Room came here from Seaton Delaval, where it was occupied by the martial Duke of Cumberland (weighing 23 stone) before the Battle of Culloden. The Flemish animal tapestries are very fine, particularly an unusual verdure showing a unicorn. The rococo looking-glasses and their ribboned crestings are of papier mâché, a material much favoured by John Linnell of Berkeley Square.

Dodington, Avon
(Major Simon Codrington)

Nine miles north of Bath (M4 and A46)

An intriguing *tempietto* lodge and sturdy gate piers lead into Capability Brown's park. The Cotswold escarpment has been tempered with superb effect, and from the hills Brown's venerable trees look down over the widened brook. This setting was certainly too fine for the original house, a worthy though unadventurous 16th-century manor, but it admirably com-

Dodington

plements Wyatt's classical masterpiece which later replaced it. Six water-colour views of the house and park, made *circa* 1820, illustrate the cult of the 'picturesque', one of them showing the old house in Capability Brown's setting.

The Codringtons, distinguished as soldiers and admirals during the six centuries since Harfleur and Agincourt, lived at nearby Codrington Manor and bought Dodington in the time of Elizabeth I. When the Civil War divided the family at home, Christopher, a younger son, had already left for Barbados where he laid the basis of their later fortune. His son became Governor of the Leeward Islands, and was succeeded by another Christopher, most famous of all, the founder of the Codrington Library at Oxford where his statue is still to be seen. Codrington College in Barbados also bears his name. The West Indian estates flourished until slavery was abolished in 1832, and there is every evidence that they were well and humanely managed.

In 1796, Christopher Bethell Codrington commissioned James Wyatt to rebuild the house, and with it everything necessary to a country seat: service wings, a dairy and bath house (now the Dower House), brewhouse and laundries, a barn, stables, lodges and gates; and, linked to the house, the village church. This great work, costing £120,000, was nearly finished in 1813 when Wyatt was travelling with his patron to London, and the coach overturned near Marlborough. The architect was killed; Bethell Codrington survived unhurt. The house, completed by Wyatville, was completely modern in its day, even to the installation of a gas plant.

This is Wyatt's most mature classical work and it sums up everything he had learnt. It is certainly not Palladian in style, and is best called Roman. The main rooms have come down to ground level, and the portico is a vast *porte cochère*; the arched vault and the sweep of the conservatory all contribute towards an interesting sculptural effect. Facing the rose garden, the south front has columns in the style of William Chambers. A third, plainer facade with a generous bow window at either side overlooks the lake. The ashlar is impeccable, the windows large, and their narrow glazing bars, made of brass, were formerly gilded.

Though not austere, the interior is undeniably solemn. The Hall, a coffered *atrium*, still has its original decoration of biscuit and gilt, and at either end a raised tribune is divided by columns of porphyry-coloured scagliola. Wyatt's placing of columns was always masterly. The floor is paved in Painswick stone, with black marble, granite and brass. Bethell Codrington's Library is also unaltered, with bookshelves of mahogany, ebony and gilded brass, and its wallpaper crimson with gold stars. The doors throughout the house are magnificent, and swing not on hinges but on concealed pivots. Through the great windows of the Drawing Room there are splendid views of the park. The Staircase in the centre of the house is lit from a domed lantern overhead. This form of stair, with its three flights, is known as 'Imperial', and it rises to an arcaded gallery.

Wyatt's suite of rooms is no longer complete because the servants' wing became infested with dry rot and was demolished in 1932, the former Dining Room and Music Room being adapted as kitchen and offices. The Dining Room fireplace was brought into the Drawing Room, where its philosophers' heads strike a rather sombre note, and scagliola pilasters were fitted into the Breakfast Room, where the sideboards are of Wyatt's design. Other original fittings include bronze gasoliers with Vestal Virgins feeding the flames from urns, and the distinctive cast-iron stoves, one of which is half-way up the staircase. The tour of the house ends with St Mary's Church, seen from the family's private gallery. It was designed as a Greek cross with Italian Renaissance character, but the plasterwork is waiting for restoration.

During the 19th century, under Sir Christopher and the brilliant Lady Georgiana Codrington, the hospitality of Dodington was famous over all Europe. The present owner, their great-grandson, has adapted the house for the different pleasures of the modern visitor. A Carriage Museum in Wyatt's stables will be found interesting and instructive. Round the lake, the walk passes over Capability Brown's Gothic Cascade House. Of all the earlier buildings at Dodington, Wyatt allowed only this to remain.

Dorfold Hall, Cheshire
(Mr R. C. Roundell)

Two miles west of Nantwich (A534)

Set in the open hunting country of Cheshire, Dorfold seems on first sight a perfect example of the formal Jacobean manor. Yet the drive, which is now perfectly straight, once wound deviously round a pool (a former fishpond). The alteration was made as late as the 1860s, by William Nesfield. The extraordinary forecourt is flanked by buildings, whimsically advancing and receding under curved and arcaded gables. Of these, the L-shaped cottages

Dorfold Hall; the Drawing Room or Great Chamber

at the ends are original Jacobean, and the rest, according to the inscription, were added in 1824.

The front of the house is of diapered brick, and promises a regular H-shaped building. But in the angles there are two insertions, one for the concealed door (dated 1616), and the other for the hall bay. On the garden side the 'H' disappears, flattened out by an extra row of rooms. Such a plan is odd for a period when houses were usually only one room thick. The builder was Ralph Wilbraham, whose portrait by Cornelius Johnson is in the house. He came from a prominent family of Cheshire lawyers, who were Parliamentarians during the Civil War. Dorfold was plundered by Royalist soldiers in 1643. In the next century it was bought by James Tomkinson, a lawyer of Nantwich, from whom it passed by marriage to a branch of the Tollemache family, and so to the present owner.

The rooms downstairs were modernised by the Tomkinsons, who enclosed and vaulted the screens passage. Here and in the old hall, now the Dining Room, there is good Georgian plasterwork. The ceiling in the Library is slightly later, having been designed by Samuel Wyatt to commemorate a marriage of 1772. In the centre are a pair of billing doves, and at the corners symbols of the four seasons. Finely carved chimneypieces in the Library and Dining Room are said to have been brought from an inn in the City of London, and are in Adam's style.

Upstairs one returns to the time of James I. The staircase balustrade is carved and arcaded, but so thin as to be merely decorative. The main bedroom has a fine plaster overmantel worked with the royal arms and date 1621, set up in hopes of a visit from the King which failed to take place. Above the Hall, the Drawing Room is the finest room in the house, and would better be described as the Great Chamber. Its barrel vault has a strapwork design of an Islamic complexity. Among the heraldic emblems, what was surely intended to be the French *fleur de lys* is in fact the lily of

Florence, which supports the tradition that Italian plasterers worked here. The stone fireplace has Doric half-columns, and is painted with an odd mix of armorial bearings, all of them within Garters, of the Earl of Exeter, Earl of Derby and Sir Christopher Hatton. The panelling and carved frieze are original, but the doors are Victorian.

East Lambrook Manor, Somerset
(Mr Henry Boyd-Carpenter)

Eight miles west of Yeovil, two miles north of South Petherton

This house was either the manor or a substantial yeoman's dwelling. The roof was once of thatch, and upstairs there is a window and arched roof beams of the 15th century. Remodelling occurred in the Elizabethan age, and the date 1584 is carved on a bracket. The Hall was reduced to ground floor only, the kitchen wing extended, fireplaces inserted, and the parlour, now the Dining Room, was panelled in oak. A plank and muntin wall divides the Hall from the Kitchen. Most of the finely grained elm timbers and floors have survived, which is fortunate as this wood is notoriously attractive to worm. The house has been much patched and repaired, but the recent restorations show that traditional craftsmanship survives in Somerset.

In 1937 the house, derelict and divided into three cottages, was bought and restored by Walter and Margery Fish for their retirement. Their fine country-made furniture was collected locally. It was here that Margery Fish learnt the cultivation of plants, laid out the garden that has become world

East Lambrook Manor

famous, and wrote the books which inspire many a gardening enthusiast. She appreciated wild as well as exotic flowers, and developed the tumbling 'cottage' style. On her death in 1969, Mrs Fish left the property to her nephew. House and garden are excellently maintained, and plants may be bought from the nurseries.

Eastnor Castle, Hereford and Worcester
(The Hon. Mrs Hervey-Bathurst)

Two miles east of Ledbury (A438)

When the 1st Earl Somers inherited the manor of Castleditch in 1806, his family had owned it for two hundred years. But he found his ancestral seat unworthy and commissioned Robert Smirke to build another on a commanding position up the hill. Foundations were laid in 1812. Building proceeded quickly and the castle soon became the local wonder; the expense was enormous, but the family's banking fortune could stand it, though near the end some economies appear to have been made to the interior.

The megalomania of the Castle speaks for the somewhat aggressive character of Lord Somers. Big though it is, the massive structure appears bigger from the corner towers being set out diagonally from the main block. Like so many Georgian Gothic buildings, Eastnor lies somewhere between the mediaeval and classical. Round and pointed windows (an odd mix) set deep in the walls, battlements and towers suggest the authority of a feudal stronghold; but their symmetry and the interplay of solid blocks of masonry are classical. Indeed Smirke, who was later to design the British Museum, was already a prominent neo-Greek architect. The drive under an arched gateway is dramatic, and a cavernous *porte cochère* stands like a galilee before a cathedral. The fine Forest of Dean stone is attractively dappled with lichens, and the Virginia creeper that covers half the building is apple-green in summer, vivid scarlet in autumn.

Of Smirke's interior only about half remains because many alterations were made during the 19th century. The Great Hall, an immense half-cube sixty feet high, seems intended for giants. Smirke's rather austere design was later embellished (by George Fox in the 1860s) with coloured marbles in a Venetian romanesque style and the walls were painted with a bird pattern from a Saracenic cloth. This makes a fine setting for the collection of arms formed by the 3rd Earl Somers. In the centre is an equestrian figure wearing dress armour worked with the Visconti arms. Thirty-three half suits of armour on the walls are Italian, *circa* 1520, while next door are two very fine complete suits of fluted armour from Bavaria.

Smirke's Dining Room remains with all its original furniture, but the former arches on the end wall and over the doors have been removed to allow more room for family portraits. His architectural treatment of the room seems a little thin. Much more robust is the Gothic Drawing Room with its fan vault (of plaster, by Bernasconi); but this was transformed by the 2nd Earl who, on succeeding in 1841, commissioned Pugin for its

Eastnor Castle; the Drawing Room, decorated by Pugin

decoration. The luxuriant chimneypiece, painting and gilding, all with an abundance of family heraldry, was carried out by the firm of John Crace. Pugin designed the inlaid furniture and the immense iron chandelier which was based on one seen at Nuremburg. All this pious Gothic sets off fine Gobelins tapestries of the *Seasons* and *Alexander the Great* given to Lady Somers by her mother. How Pugin regarded such pagan intrusions is not recorded, but it seems that he never actually visited Eastnor.

The character and contents of the remaining rooms show the taste of the 3rd Earl Somers and his devotion to Italy where he bought many works of art. The Flemish tapestries in the Library were bought in Mantua, and had originally been woven by order of Catherine de' Medici. They hang above inlaid walnut bookcases constructed in Italy and two chimneypieces of Istrian stone carved in Verona. This room was designed by George Fox (whom we have already encountered in the Hall), who was shortly to do similar work at Longleat. The Baroque woodwork in the Little Library came from Siena. Massive Italian furniture was bought from the Corsini Palace, Florence and elsewhere. The State Bedroom though not exactly a comfortable room, contains interesting paintings, the most notable perhaps being Bassano's *Last Supper*.

The 3rd Countess, née Virginia Pattle, was a friend of the painter G. F. Watts, and Lord Somers is said to have fallen in love with her from seeing her portrait at the Royal Academy. This full-length likeness hangs on the Staircase together with many other family portraits by the Italophile artist (more are in the Octagon Room in the centre of the main front). The five early *Allegories*, of rather uncertain quality, were painted by Watts for the

London house, but his large *Time and Oblivion* is a mature work and as such is more interesting.

The 3rd Earl was also a great botanist. Early views of the Castle show it to have been built on an exposed site, but he planted the slopes with trees and rare conifers that now crowd round the building. When he died without male heirs the Earldom lapsed; the Castle was occupied by his daughter, the formidable philanthropist Lady Henry Somerset, and the estate passed to a cousin, the 6th Baron Somers, KCMG, a distinguished soldier in the Life Guards who succeeded Lord Baden-Powell as Chief Scout of the British Empire. He died in 1944.

Ebbingford Manor, Cornwall
(Mr D. B. Dudley Stamp)

Just south of Bude (A39)

Known until recently as Efford, the house is modest in size and humble in character; but it was indeed a manor house, of the Arundells from 1433 and the Aclands from 1768, two great West Country landowners. In 1861 Sir Thomas Dyke Acland gave it as a vicarage for the nearby church he had built in 1835. A later Vicar exchanged houses in 1953 with Sir Dudley Stamp, the well known geographer and father of the present owner. Thus it has never been sold, but passed by descent or exchange.

Parts of the mediaeval building survive on either side of the present front

Ebbingford Manor

door. Probably it was originally a two-storey Hall with a parlour and bedchamber to the right, and wings for kitchen quarters and a stable. Mullioned windows and two massive chimneystacks belong to the 1570s, and sash windows were inserted, but not everywhere, in 1758.

Mr Dudley Stamp is an enthusiast for the cause of Bude. He has set up a series of small museums which record its history and development by the Aclands. Rooms are devoted to the locally famous Bude Canal, the history of the port of Bude Haven, local industries, and to the life and work of Sir Dudley Stamp. All this shows an individual touch. There is also a shop for local crafts.

Euston Hall, Suffolk
(The Duke of Grafton, KG)

Four miles south-east of Thetford (A1088)

Euston was built by the Earl of Arlington about 1670 as a large house round three sides of a courtyard. After seventy years it was in bad repair, and the Duke of Grafton consulted William Kent. Kent designed the park, but his suggestion of rebuilding the house on the hill was not adopted. Instead it was repaired by Matthew Brettingham and entirely refaced with impeccable red brick. Much of Euston was destroyed by fire in 1902 and rebuilt, but by 1952 the new part was found to be unnecessary and demolished. What survives, therefore, is Brettingham's north wing, forecourt and stables. It is

Euston Hall; from the stable block; (see also illustration on p. 16)

not for the interior, nor even for the fine furniture that Euston must be visited, but for the magnificent series of family portraits that can hardly be equalled in any country house. Most of them are 17th century, and many are royal.

During the Civil War, Lord Arlington was wounded fighting for the King at Andover. He was proud of the scar and always wore a black patch over his nose; and so he appears, in Garter robes, in Lely's full-length portrait. Arlington contrived the marriage of his only child, Isabella, to Henry FitzRoy, natural son of Charles II by Barbara Villiers, Duchess of Cleveland. The wedding was celebrated in 1672 when Henry was eight years old. Later he was created Earl of Euston and Duke of Grafton. The most handsome of all the King's children, he was mortally wounded at the Siege of Cork in 1690.

The royal portraits begin with James I and Anne of Denmark, both by Van Somer, and a splendid full-length of James's favourite, the Duke of Buckingham, by Mytens. Van Dyck is represented by portraits of Henrietta Maria and Charles I, the well-known group of their children, and Viscount Grandison, father of the Duchess of Cleveland. Charles II was painted in exile by Philippe de Champaigne and later, as King, by Lely. The Lely portraits are particularly fine; another of the young Duke of Gloucester, robed and ribboned and wearing his own long hair, was painted in 1660 just before he died of small-pox.

The Duchess of Cleveland with her son Henry (the future Duke of Grafton), a madonna and child, is again by Lely. Evidently she was not so handsome as Nell Gwyn, who is also here. The many later portraits include a fine early Reynolds of the 2nd Duke of Grafton (also painted as Lord Chamberlain by Van Loo), and another of the 3rd Duchess, who eloped with Lord Ossory. Of the other paintings the most notable is *Mares and Foals* by Stubbs.

Ample time should be left to see the fine setting of the house. The garden is now open with lawns and terraces, but originally it was walled; the park was laid out with avenues by John Evelyn, its planting changed by Kent and Capability Brown. Kent's distant Banqueting House is a perfect Palladian work in pale brick with rustications of unknapped flints (now a private house and not open). The Church was completely rebuilt in 1676. Despite 19th-century alterations to pews and pulpit it remains complete with fine carving and plasterwork, a country cousin to Wren's City churches.

Eye Manor, Hereford and Worcester
(Mr and Mrs Christopher Sandford)

Three miles north of Leominster, between Luston and Ashton

Eye means island, and the manor and church roost together on a hill that once overlooked marshlands. The house was built about 1680 – the date is over the central window – by Fernando Gorges, a Barbados trader who decided to settle in Herefordshire. It was perhaps a modest one for a

Eye Manor; the Hall

successful merchant, but seems now a country lover's ideal. The outside is of simple brick with sandstone corners; presumably the sash windows were later improvements, for two mullions survive on the back. But the interior remains complete in its original condition, with panelling, a floor of chestnut and a walnut staircase. The arms of Gorges and his wife are painted over upstairs doors.

The great fascination of Eye lies in its plasterwork. There are nine ceilings, all of them perfect in the art. It is thought that the craftsmen of Holyrood Palace, Messrs Dunsterfield and Halbert, came to Herefordshire and worked at Holme Lacy, Eye and elsewhere. Flowers, fruits and draperies were modelled on lead wires, which were fixed to canvas stretched across the surfaces and then plastered over. There are lush acanthus scrolls, fruits, naked boys, and (in the Great Parlour) Diana and Hercules. These were the stock patterns of the time; but the branches of oak, bay and roses, hazel, plum and other trees, all worked with a botanical precision, are unusual.

The Gorges lived here for about a hundred years. After 1786, Eye Manor changed hands some six times before it was bought by the present owner in 1958. Their furniture includes Irish 'Chippendale' mahogany inherited from Mr Sandford's father and his mother, Mary, Lady Carbery. For twenty-six years (until 1959) Mr Sandford directed the Golden Cockerel Press, and a collection of his books is on show. Superb examples of the printer's art illustrated by leading artists of the time, they are eagerly collected today. Mrs Sandford's decorative straw-work, and particularly her revival of the traditional craft of corn dollies, are a special feature of the house, besides needlework pictures, paper sculpture, and period costumes and dolls. Eye has become a centre for arts and crafts, and craft schools are in residence during part of every year.

Eyhorne Manor, Kent
(Mr and Mrs Derek Simmons)

Five miles east of Maidstone (A20 and B2163)

'Manor' seems a courtesy title, for this pleasant little house, with its garden of herbs and old medicinal plants, is basically a Wealden timber-framed yeoman's dwelling of the 15th century. The entrance front announces a standard Kentish design: a hipped roof covering what was originally an open central hall, with jetties supporting a second storey at either end (one of the jetties at Eyhorne is of minimal projection). Arch-braces carry the eaves at the ends of the central hall, which consequently looks, but is not, recessed.

As so often happened, an additional floor was inserted in the open hall (in the 17th century), when a chimney stack and large open fireplace replaced the central hearth. At the same time other changes were made, including the addition of a room for smoking carcases (a necessary convenience when stock were slaughtered each autumn for lack of winter feed).

The house has been devotedly restored in recent years, and is shown with affection. Much of the furniture and embroidery are the work of the owners, and they have commissioned young artists to paint many of the pictures.

Eyhorne Manor

Finchcocks, Kent
(Mr Richard Burnett)

A mile west of Goudhurst (A262)

Though only some forty miles from London, the house lies in a stretch of country strangely unspoilt. From a little rise, cropped pasture slopes almost imperceptibly towards it; here one should leave the drive and for a moment join the grazing sheep. Only from the pasture itself does one receive the full impact of the building that rises with an architectural flourish beyond the distant ha-ha. Supported by short curving wings that firmly embrace it, the house soars with fine effect to the panelled parapet below the roof-line and the balanced chimneys above. The point of Finchcocks is this confident upward sweep, full of movement yet with a reassuring sense of stability. The detail is taken in later: giant Doric pilasters, pediment enclosing a brave martial trophy, a second cornice at attic level, round-headed windows lending authority to the central bays, and not least the different coloured bricks, ranging from rose to dark violet, used for architectural emphasis rather than decoration. The house was finished in 1725 but the builder is unidentified. No wonder that Thomas Archer's name should have been mentioned in connection with so Baroque a composition.

In 1972 Finchcocks appeared to have no future. The paintings – Italian primitives, Patinir, Bassano, Rubens, Claude, Watteau – that graced the interior in Lycett Green days had long been gone, even the large inset portrait of Edward Bathhurst and his family – he was the first owner of Finchcocks – had recently been removed and sold; the rooms were empty and the house in disrepair. A panelled hall linking the two main fronts, other rooms with simple 18th-century wainscot, and an elegant staircase with twisted balusters, alone recalled a former consequence. It was at this juncture that Providence arrived in the person of the present owner and his partner. Musicians, scholars and craftsmen, they not only saved Finchcocks but put the house to imaginative use. It now contains a collection of rare musical instruments, notably harpsichords, spinets and a unique assembly of early fortepianos. The rooms echo as they must have done in the Bathhursts' time to the formal music of the 18th century, regular concerts take place, students come to study and visiting musicians to give recitals and lectures.

Finchcocks; the Hall, with a Viennese fortepiano, c. 1810 (See also colour plate 7)

At the same time, the 18th-century stables have been transformed into a humming workshop where a small team of dedicated craftsmen restore and make replicas of fine musical instruments. It is a thriving enterprise; and in the context of the second half of the 20th century an unusually happy story.

Firle Place, East Sussex
(The Viscount Gage)

Four miles south-east of Lewes (A27)

Pheasants driven from the coverts stream high over the slate roofs, so close does the house lie to the slopes which rise to Firle Beacon. Built in the mid-16th century, Firle has always owed much to this noble setting. The builder – his descendants have lived here ever since – was Sir John Gage, a man who so enjoyed the confidence of Henry VIII that he became Governor of Calais, Constable of the Tower, a Knight of the Garter, and ultimately one of the King's executors.

Sir John's successors were uncompromising Catholics and the heavy fines to which they were subject as recusants can have left little money for new building. The Tudor house remained substantially unchanged for two hundred years. The extensive alterations, which give Firle its present character, were probably due both to William Gage, 7th Baronet, and Thomas, 1st Viscount, masters of Firle from 1713 to 1754. Converted to Protestantism they were eligible to sit in parliament; both did so, Thomas for no less than thirty-seven years. Though they gave the house sash windows and an 18th-century dress, Tudor Firle lived on in the pale limestone masonry, in the overall plan, and in odd unexplained differences of height and elevation. Even a few specifically Tudor details survived, such as a gable and mullioned window on the south front, a couple of chimney-

pieces, and a doorway in the staircase hall. On the whole the mid-18th-century changes produced a mixture of the picturesque and the formal so pleasing that it has not been tampered with since – if one excepts the garden terrace, and the balustrading interposed early in the 20th century between the house and the green expanse of the park.

The approach is on the east front, the 1st Viscount's addition and the most formal of the elevations. Through a rusticated archway, set below a Venetian window and a central pediment, one enters an internal courtyard that betrays nothing of its Tudor past. Yet the front door, demurely classical, opens into what was once the great hall of the Tudor house. A coved ceiling now conceals the original hammerbeam roof, and little indicates that this Entrance Hall, like other rooms at Firle, is anything but George II. Two superb 17th-century Beauvais tapestries hang on either side of the massive chimneypiece and Van Dyck's magnificent portrait of John, Count of Nassau, and his family dominates one end of the room. The door at the other end, set under a monumental pediment supported by Ionic columns, leads into the Staircase Hall. The impact of this Hall is immediate, for here is robust Palladianism without a trace of the ponderous that often goes with it (some of the plasterwork panels indeed have more than a hint of rococo).

Next comes the Drawing Room. With luck sun will be streaming through the south-facing windows, and one may well murmur to oneself, recalling Eliot's phrase, 'splendour of Ionian white and gold'. Splendid indeed it is with screens of Ionic columns, yet it has a welcoming warmth; the silks, the martial uniforms and civic robes of the Gages, whose full-length portraits are set in white and parcel-gilt panelling, glow with shades of rose and muted crimson. The particular quality of the room resides precisely in the combination of this warmth and colour with a masculine Palladianism. Strong ribs of guilloche pattern delimit the cove of the ceiling, the doorcases

Opposite:
Firle Place

Right:
the Staircase

with pulvinated friezes are boldly architectural and the marble Kentian chimneypiece is assured as could be. Even the 1st Viscount derives added authority from the architectural frame with broken pediment that firmly sets him off. The parcel-gilt console tables, supported by unperturbed foxes (like those at Stourhead in Wiltshire) holding swags of oak leaves, strike the same architectural note, as do a pair of massive gilt side-tables with a strange bearded mask in the aprons, and the heads of formidable mastiffs serving as knees to the legs. A memorable room.

Altogether, the brilliant quality of the contents comes as a surprise in a house of comparatively modest pretensions. In the Drawing Room a Reynolds and a Gainsborough of the 2nd Viscount are among the notable full-length portraits. But most of the fine paintings are to be found in the upper rooms where they are seen in association with French 18th-century furniture and a famous collection of Sèvres. Apart from the Gage portraits native to Firle, most of them came by inheritance from the great Cowper Collection at Panshanger near Hertford or from Fawsley in Northamptonshire.

Over the chimneypiece in the Upper Drawing Room hangs *The Holy Family and the Infant St John*, one of the last paintings by Fra Bartolomeo in private hands. Two arresting three-quarter-length male portraits are attributed to Domenico Puligo (1475–1527) a little known painter who was the Friar's contemporary. Later paintings include a 16th-century portrait-head by Moroni, the head of an apostle by Rubens, and two little 18th-century views of Venice by Guardi.

A pair of unusual English display cabinets, veneered in satinwood with highly finished marquetry, are in the Adam manner and were surely executed by Chippendale. They contain Sèvres porcelain of the 1760s and 1770s. The French furniture in the room is mostly of the same period, though there is an earlier writing-desk with rococo gilt-bronze mounts, and a table inlaid with Sèvres plaques (c.1780) in the manner of Martin Carlin. Particularly attractive are two pairs of small tables with the decoration confined to parquetry of 'domino' design in various exotic woods on a satinwood ground.

The Long Gallery, really more of a ballroom than a gallery, looks across the park to an eye-catcher on the summit of the Downs. The room was the 1st Viscount's creation but, like the Upper Drawing Room, suffered the addition of some spidery plaster panels in the late 19th century. One of David Teniers's major works, *The Wine Harvest*, hangs over the fireplace. It is flanked by English portraits which include two full-length paintings by Reynolds. The British School is further represented by Kneller, Hoppner, Lawrence, and an early Turner, while Zoffany appropriately contributes a portrait of the 3rd Earl Cowper, the great collector: he stands somewhere in Italy (where he lived for thirty years) raising his hat above his head with an air of deep satisfaction.

The room is furnished with a large gilt suite of armchairs and settees, probably Italian, and more French 18th-century furniture, notably Régence commodes and a roll-top desk in the manner of the great J. H. Riesener. There are also two beautifully simple English low cupboards of about 1740, incorporating panels of oriental black and gold lacquer. The Firle Sèvres continues here with a quantity of early wares dating from the 1750s – *bleu céleste, rose Pompadour*, apple green – and a very large dinner service decorated with the later *œil de perdrix* pattern. It is a dazzling display.

Forde Abbey, Dorset
(Mr Mark Roper)

Three miles south-east of Chard

A long, rich tapestry of a building, Forde stands among open fields that once were cultivated by Cistercian monks, who settled here in 1141. Forde became a wealthy Abbey, but its community was never very large. In 1539 the property was surrendered by Abbot Chard and thirteen monks. The church has been demolished, but the monastic buildings formed the bases for a rebuilding by Edmund Prideaux, who bought the property in 1649. He was a lawyer and an active Parliamentarian, and became Attorney-General that same year. Forde survives largely as Prideaux remodelled it, but the rebuilding was not quite complete on his death in 1658. His son, another Edmund, was unreasonably imprisoned and fined because of the friendship he had once shown to the rebellious Duke of Monmouth. The house passed by descent until 1846 when it was sold and lost its contents. Shortly after, it was bought by Mrs Bertram Evans, from whom it descended to Mr Geoffrey Roper whose son lives there today.

In one of the most fascinating houses of its kind, we have here a rare combination: half monastic and half Cromwellian, spiced here and there with Gothic revival. Part of its attraction is due to the Ham Hill stone,

Forde Abbey

weathered to dusky gold and mellowed by lichens. Though at first sight the long facade seems uncomfortable and jostling, Prideaux's remodelling will be seen to rely on symmetry and balance. Either side of the centrepiece, long ranges of Gothic windows link up with the end pavilions. Admittedly the mediaeval Gate Tower falls outside this neat scheme, being off-centre and too tall, but it was obviously too fine a thing to throw away.

Stones from the vanished church were certainly used to build up the level of the lawn, and during a recent dig for a drain two lovely 15th-century statues were found. Most of the Cloister has also gone, but the projecting building on the right contains the Norman Chapter House. It became the Chapel, and has a carved and gilded screen. Near this is the long 13th-century Monks' Dormitory. A row of lancet windows survives over the back court, as well as the vaulted undercroft which is chequered by the use of two different stones. Plain and functional, it seems the essence of the austere Cistercian ideal. After this, the 16th-century additions of Abbot Chard may well be found shocking. What remains of his Cloister is handsome enough; but the Gatehouse and Great Hall of his own lodgings are no less than magnificent. Above gorgeous windows, panels of Renaissance carving (which include Chard's own heraldic achievements) stretch out like a rich brocade. But such expensive building was one way of keeping the money that otherwise would have been lost in forced 'loans' to the Tudor King Henrys.

The Great Hall has been shortened by at least one bay, and its late-Gothic wooden roof, though beautiful, is certainly not the original intention. This room was an enormous lanthorn with windows lighting both sides. The panelling is Prideaux's 17th-century work and so are the rooms that follow. Up the Great Staircase, where the ceiling is dated 1658 and the balustrade was once partly gilded, are the Saloon and apartments above the Cloister. The plaster ceilings are thought to have been made by Richard Abbot of Barnstaple. They have leafy beams and ovals in the courtly style of Inigo Jones, but the massed foliage and rather naïve biblical scenes and *Virtues* betray a provincial hand. Again, the grained and gilded panelling attempts, but just misses, Jones's sophisticated Italian manner.

All the rooms are well and very suitably furnished. The five Mortlake tapestries of the *Acts of the Apostles* would once have been the most highly valued things in the house. They were woven from the Raphael cartoons during the 1640s and fit the Saloon walls exactly. It is odd, therefore, that in fact they came much later, as a gift from Queen Anne, and that space was made for them on the walls by removing panelling. The red velvet bed is said to have been prepared for the Queen, but her visit never took place.

The rich and unusual mixture of Forde does not end with the 17th century. The Monks' Refectory (15th century) is now a Library, with a screen made up in the 19th century from old Breton beds. The Monks' Dormitory was redesigned, perhaps about 1810, with a wide vaulted corridor and rooms reminiscent of the gentlemanly cells of monasteries in 18th-century France. The remaining range of the Cloister acts, and very suitably, as a conservatory, the knotty window bars that fill its traceried openings being Gothic revival work. The gardens are large and extraordinarily beautiful at all seasons. A series of mediaeval fishponds have been turned into water gardens, and the rock garden is a recent creation. Behind the house, the kitchen garden has become a nursery where plants are sold.

Gaulden Manor, Somerset
(Mr and Mrs Le Gendre Starkie)

Eight miles north-west of Taunton, 1 mile east of Tolland (from B3186)

Of an ageless vernacular, the house seems to have grown with nature among the remote Somerset valleys. Gaulden was apparently a sub-manor of Tolland, and in the 12th century it belonged to Taunton Priory. During the 1560s it was leased to James Tuberville, former Bishop of Exeter, who had been imprisoned for some years in the Tower of London for refusing to take the Oath of Supremacy. Between 1618 and 1630 Gaulden was owned by Christopher Wolcott, whose family then migrated to America, but the Tubervilles returned in 1639 – and remained here for a hundred years. Gaulden has always been essentially a grange or farm. Since the present owners bought it in 1966, they have cleaned and restored the house, and laid out the garden which leads up to the old fish pond.

Though no date can be fixed for the main walls (local sandstone and shale), they seem mediaeval. The kitchen wing is a Tudor addition; an outhouse with a very large fireplace could have been the earlier kitchen. The plasterwork in the Hall is a surprise. The frieze is Elizabethan, modelled with obscure symbols and Latin texts recording the Bishop's sentiments, and the alcove, separated by a carved screen, was perhaps his chapel. The elaborate overmantel, with Tuberville coats of arms set between Peace and Plenty, is of the 1640s, and so is the ceiling with a jumbo pendant drop between King David and The Last Trump. In a bedroom there is another overmantel with the Tuberville arms. This one is the more refined, but a later ceiling has cut into the scrollwork.

Gaulden Manor

Gawsworth Hall, Cheshire
(Mrs Raymond Richards)

Three miles south-west of Macclesfield (A536)

Gawsworth is not only one of the prettiest 'black and white' Cheshire houses but it has acquired more than a touch of romance by association with Mary Fitton. Maid of Honour to Queen Elizabeth and mistress of the Earl of Pembroke, to whom Shakespeare dedicated the first folio edition of his works, she was at one time identified with the 'Dark Lady' of the Sonnets. Her portrait attributed to Zucchero, hangs in the house and depicts her as a child with her mother and brother. The Fittons, whose splendid tombs are in the nearby church, owned Gawsworth from 1316 to 1662. The first reference to a building on the site dates from 1365, when John Fitton obtained a licence to hold services in his private chapel.

The architectural history of Gawsworth is complex, for it was a courtyard house until the latter half of the 17th century when the west wing and part of the south wing were demolished; later it was at one time uninhabited, and has undergone much alteration. The entrance front, with Edward Fitton's shield of arms (he was Mary Fitton's father) on the chimneybreast, has early-18th-century sashes and is relatively restrained. The big impact is round the corner to the west, where gables and oriels, leaded lights, carved bargeboards and finials, and above all the decorative use of timbering, create an effect that is irresistibly picturesque. The most remarkable feature is the jettied three-storey bay, decorated with quatrefoils and wavy studding, that breaks the roof-line. This has mullions and transoms of 'Jacobean' profile

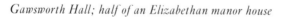

Gawsworth Hall; half of an Elizabethan manor house

and may well have been built when Mary Fitton was a girl. The leaded lights retain their original glass.

Inside the house one or two simple 16th-century plasterwork friezes survive, as do fireplaces and overmantels of the same date. The stained glass windows in the Chapel are by William Morris. There is an unusual and large collection of Victorian paintings and sculpture.

Glemham Hall, Suffolk
(Lady Blanche Cobbold)

At Little Glemham, between Woodbridge and Saxmundham (A12)

The Hall is visible from the road, a short distance from the village of Little Glemham. Glemhams were here by 1228, and the house built by Sir Henry Glemham late in the 16th century remains, though much altered. Elizabethan brickwork will be seen, chiefly on the garden front which rises to a row of gables and retains some mullioned windows. The old family left in 1708, and the house was transformed by Dudley North, a London merchant and grandson of Lord North. His wife Catherine was a daughter of Elihu Yale, whose name has world-wide renown at Yale University in the USA. The dates on the rain-heads, 1717 and 1722, presumably record the completion of the remodelled building. It is not Palladian, but rather in the Baroque tradition associated with James Gibbs. There may have been some decoration on the entrance front but now there are only two solitary pilasters, and the facade is severe and unyieldingly rectangular.

Glemham Hall, showing Elizabethan gables

Nothing Elizabethan will be seen inside except for a small panelled room and the beams in the attics. The old Hall was transformed by bolection panelling and a screen of fine Corinthian columns, once painted but stripped in 1937 to show the warm pinewood underneath. A wide arch leads to the Staircase, a splendid construction of oak inlaid with walnut, and with 'Versailles' parquetry on the landings. The walls rise almost the full height of the house to a coved ceiling, and look as though they were intended for frescoes. In the Library there are rare George I pelmets covered with damask.

Glemham Hall remained with various branches of the North family for more than two hundred years. In the 18th century they married with daughters of the Earl of Pembroke, which accounts for the plaster cast of Roubiliac's bust (the original being at Wilton House). In 1789 the house was left to Dudley Long, who took the additional name of North and was a prominent Whig politician. On his death it reverted to the Earls of Guilford.

Colonel John Murray Cobbold and Lady Blanche bought Glemham in 1923. The Cobbolds came from Ipswich, and very appropriately they have an early Gainsborough painting of a mother and daughter in a Suffolk landscape. There are some excellent lacquer cabinets, a superb Dutch marquetry cabinet of about 1700 worked with luxuriant flowers (perhaps by van Meckeren), and blue and white Chinese and Delft wares. The back staircases are hung with unusual and charming 18th-century mezzotints, mostly of dramatic subjects. Behind the house, the walled rose garden has been made by the present owner.

Glynde Place, East Sussex
(The Viscount Hampden)

Three miles east of Lewes (A27)

Not many years ago a number of papers were discovered at Glynde in a massive iron-bound chest. Among them were pages of John of Gaunt's household accounts and a list of his horses, mentioned severally by name. Were some of them, one wonders, chargers that accompanied the Duke to France and across the Pyrenees when he led a division for the Black Prince into Spain? Such speculation comes easily at Glynde which since the 12th century, except on one occasion, has passed by inheritance.* Even the exception occurred as long ago as the 15th century and was a sale within the family.

The horses that may have fought in France were dead two centuries when the present house was built in about 1568. It is an example of a courtyard-house, one of the two main formulae favoured by the Elizabethans. As such, it can be conveniently contrasted with Parham, twenty-five miles westward and nearly contemporary, which represents the other type, the E-shaped house with a central hall. The imposing entrance front at Glynde, with three

---

* Through the Waley, Morley, Trevor, and Brand families.

9 Harewood House; the Hall,
designed by Robert Adam

10 Houghton Hall; the Saloon,
decorated by William Kent

11 Kedleston Hall; the Saloon, by Robert Adam

12 Littlecote; the Calvinist Chapel

Glynde Place; the 16th-century entrance front; (see also colour plate 8)

Dutch gables, surveying beyond the ha-ha a splendid sweep of country to the east, indicates how little externally the house has changed. The leaded panes have gone from the mullioned and transomed windows, the panelled chimneys were probably a late Stuart addition, and the bow windows may have been altered in the 18th century: otherwise the facade, built like the rest of the house in Caen stone and local flint, barely recognises the passage of time. Neither does the interior courtyard, which carries the date 1569 and the arms of the builder, William Morley, over the Tudor porch. It was through this porch, from the west, that the house was originally entered.

The two most distinguished rooms speak well of the internal changes that occurred in the 17th and 18th centuries. The present Entrance Hall, which must once have been the great hall of the 16th-century house, was re-modelled in about 1758 by Richard Trevor, the handsome and amiable Bishop of Durham whom his friend George III, with an unexpected turn of wit, called the 'Beauty of Holiness'. The Bishop put in the screen of marbled columns at either end and over his two simple but excellent stone fireplaces, bronze reliefs by Francesco Bertos, a sculptor working in Italy earlier in the century. A fine Dutch conversation piece hangs in the room, depicting the Bishop's ancestor, Sir John Trevor and his family, and there are Kentian parcel-gilt pedestals and a set of early Georgian walnut chairs.

The character of the Long Gallery above, with bold fielded panelling and richly carved floral overmantel in the style of Gibbons, derives from the late 17th century. But here too the Bishop had a hand, placing his arms over the pedimented doorcase, inserting a mid-18th-century fireplace, and another bronze relief by Bertos in the overmantel. In this room he was surrounded by his Trevor ancestors: three of them painted by Cornelius Johnson (two, one on each side of the chimneypiece, in fantastically elaborated early-18th-century frames), others by Walker and Lely. Not least the Bishop himself is here in a noble Sunderland frame. Other paintings of note in the house include a Zoffany of Thomas Trevor, 2nd Viscount Hampden, and a study on panel by Rubens for the ceiling of Inigo Jones's banqueting chamber in Whitehall.

One leaves Glynde, as one entered, by a great archway, the piers surmounted by wyverns, the Trevor crest. Of mid-18th-century date, it is the benevolent Bishop bidding one farewell.

Godinton Park, Kent
(Mr A. Wyndham Green)

A mile west of Ashford (*via* A20)

Though they are so close to Ashford, both house and park, the latter landscaped in the 18th century, seem surprisingly remote from the modern world. The house, of mellowed brick, with stone dressings and mullioned windows, is first seen rising behind yew hedges, whose topiary work (designed by Sir Reginald Blomfield in 1902) echoes the prominent curvilinear gables that crown the north and east fronts.

The Toke family acquired Godinton about 1500 and lived there for some four centuries, yet the initial impression conveyed by the outside is decidedly of the first half of the 17th century. Curved gables – semi-circles set over flanking quadrants – were something of a Kentish speciality at that time. The inspiration came from Flanders, and among well known local examples are those at Knole (1605) and Broome Park (1635). The 17th-century impression is correct as far as the east front goes. Though the porch is an addition, the facade with brickwork in English bond is of the 1630s, and the rainwater heads bear the date 1628. By contrast, the north or entrance front is a professed imitation of the 17th-century work, though the bricks are laid in Flemish bond, and it dates from the early 19th century.

Behind this relatively late facade, one finds to one's surprise a mediaeval Great Hall and an atmosphere that evoke the nostalgic lithographs in volumes such as Nash's *Mansions of England in the Olden Time*. Only the little figures in 'Tudor' costume seem missing, for this hall exactly combines – and, be it said, with the same charm – the authentic and the pastiche that characterise the engravings. The 'bones' of the room are indeed 14th century, for the first Tokes acquired a timbered mediaeval hall of which the cambered tiebeam, kingpost construction and roof, survive (though the last is now hidden by a later ceiling). But the rich flavour of the hall is due to an early-19th-century Toke with antiquarian tastes. He inserted linenfold, an astonishing number of early-16th-century panels depicting Renaissance heads in profile, the 'Jacobean' arcaded screens, the finely carved overmantel, probably Flemish, with panels dated 1574, and perhaps even the marble fireplace of about the same date. The last is of the local grey fossilmarble from Bethersden which bears a resemblance to Purbeck and is found in many mediaeval Kentish churches. The overall effect is pure 'Nash', and the artist would surely have approved the late-17th-century furniture, the

Godinton Park; the romanticised Hall

splendid silver firedogs, the royal portraits (Charles I and James II, the latter by Lely), and the likenesses of bewigged members of the Toke family. Most of the paintings have been at Godinton since at least 1700.

Leading off the hall, an ornate country-made chestnut Staircase, with Jacobean balusters and heraldic beasts perched on the newels, is firmly dated 1628. But this too was bedizened by the antiquarian Toke in the early 19th century. The staircase windows contain 16th-century glass.

The Great Chamber of about 1635 on the first floor is a remarkable room. Like the east front and staircase, it was the creation of Captain Nicholas Toke, five times married and the most colourful member of the family. The woodwork is a notable example of the busy florid decoration of the time. Another Bethersden-type marble fireplace is surmounted by elaborately carved panels; the wainscot, punctuated by pilasters, alternately fluted or ornamented with strapwork, consists of bold quartered panels with a central lozenge, and is topped with a unique and entertaining frieze, possibly Flemish, depicting little military figures at musketry, pike drill, and other exercises. No doubt originally there was also a busy plaster ceiling. The room contains paintings by Cornelius Johnson, Raeburn, and a portrait of Garrick attributed to Reynolds; late-17th and 18th-century furniture; porcelain from Chelsea, Meissen, and Sèvres, and part of the extensive Godinton collection of early Worcester.

There is more panelling, a carved overmantel and marble chimneypiece of Captain Toke's time, in the Library, and yet another fine chimneypiece of Bethersden marble in the Dining Room. This room has mid-18th-century panelling, grained in the early 19th century to simulate walnut, and contains a particularly attractive set of *c.*1760 dining chairs.

Godolphin House, Cornwall
(Mr S. E. Schofield)

Between Helston and Penzance (two miles north of A394)

The home of the Godolphins is no less romantic than its name. It stands on the lower slopes of Godolphin Hill in whose woods are the remains of tin mines that made the family's fortune. A house has stood here since Norman times, and it came to the Godolphins by marriage in 1376. In the 16th century Sir William was Warden of the Stannaries which controlled the working of tin, and Leland records 'no greater Tynne workes in all Cornwall than be on Sir Wylliam Godolcan's ground'. His nephew Sir Francis brought over German mining experts who built stamps for crushing the ore and a blowing house for smelting. The grandson of Sir Francis gave shelter to Prince Charles, later Charles II, when he escaped to the Scilly Isles with Fairfax at his heels.

The great man of the family was Sidney, 1st Earl of Godolphin (d. 1712). A Tory in politics, he served Charles II (who said he was 'never in the way, never out of the way'), James II, William III, and as Lord High Treasurer to Queen Anne was one of the architects of the Union of England and Scotland. His son, the 2nd Earl, married Henrietta Churchill, Duchess of Marlborough in her own right. Then on his death in 1766 the property descended to the Dukes of Leeds. This family changed their name to Godolphin-Osborne, but they never lived in Cornwall. The house, let as a farm and largely demolished in 1805, was finally sold in 1921.

Weathered granite of grey and silver with green and gold lichen, ferns in the masonry, a roof of small slates and the lattices all contribute to a nostalgic sense of the past. The house, far gone in decay, was bought by Mr Schofield in 1937. No praise can be too high for his sensitive restoration,

Godolphin House

which is a model of the careful use of local materials. Some of the former contents have also been recovered. The house is the centre of a working farm and its future seems more secure now than at any time during the last three hundred years. Few farmers can still be using 15th-century buildings, let alone any in such good repair as these, standing west of the house.

Old oaks stand under the granite-faced banks which formed the boundary of the demesne. The dramatic first view of the house is of its granite colonnade. This feature of 1635, the last part to be added, runs along the old courtyard wall, in between two 15th-century towers; the wall itself was retained to give additional support to the rooms above. Inside the main court the arrangement of pillars is similar, and from the way the colonnade runs into the left-hand wing it is clear that this too was intended to be rebuilt. However, the Civil War brought the work to an end. The courtyard is that of the 1475 house; across it stands the old face of the Hall, Elizabethan in appearance as it was modernised about 1575. But this is only a screen, for the main range, with the second court that lay behind it, was removed in 1805.

The rooms are pleasant and filled with furniture, not grand but very suitable, and tapestries. Next to Godolphin portraits in the Dining Room hangs John Wootton's painting of the 2nd Earl's racehorse, the Godolphin Arab. All British bloodstock are descended from one of three: the Byerley Turk, the Darley Arabian, or the Godolphin Arab. Wootton shows the last, held by a despondent Turk, against a background of classical ruins; the horse is fine-boned, alert, beautifully proportioned. This is among many things recovered by Mr Schofield. Another will be seen in the King's Room in the West Wing, used by Charles II on his escape. The grand oak entablature on the far wall was made to commemorate the marriage of Sir William Godolphin and Thomasine Sidney in 1604. Sold in the 1930s, it was traced and returned to the house after the Second World War.

Goodwood, West Sussex
(The Goodwood Estate Company, Ltd)

Three miles north-east of Chichester (A285 or A286)

More famous as a race-course than for its house, the present Goodwood is a development of a Hunting Lodge bought in 1697 by the first Duke of Richmond, son of Charles II and the beautiful French spy Louise de Querouaille, Duchess of Portsmouth. In addition to the original Caroline concatenation of honours – Duke of Richmond and Lennox, Earl of March and Darnley, Baron Settrington and Torbolton – the sixth Duke of Richmond was also created Duke of Gordon by Queen Victoria in recognition of the family's vast Scottish inheritance (since dispersed). The present Duke is the 9th of Richmond and 4th of Gordon. His eldest son, the Earl of March, now lives in the house and runs the estate which is managed with great commercial efficiency.

The original Hunting Lodge was greatly enlarged and altered by the 3rd

Goodwood; the house and stable block; (see also illustration on p. 16)

Duke of Richmond in the second half of the eighteenth century. He also landscaped the park and created the race-course, and it is largely his achievement which visitors admire today. In 1757 Sir William Chambers designed the stables in the suavest classical language but executed in rustic Sussex flintwork. From the 1770s the Duke toyed with the idea of commissioning from young James Wyatt, suddenly *the* fashionable architect after the success of his London Pantheon, a lavish setting for dances, concerts and other winter entertainments. In the event, little more than the elegant Tapestry Room was built to Wyatt's early design, and the commodious kennels (now golf club) which followed in 1787. It was only about 1800 that the Duke and Wyatt turned their minds to enlarging the house in earnest. Their idea was to keep a wing of the old house as one section of a vast new structure forming a hollow octagon with eight round towers at the angles. Together with the Earl-Bishop of Bristol's rotunda at Ickworth, this is probably the most grandiose exercise in neo-classical geometry among English country houses. Unfortunately only three sections were completed and the house terminates ignominiously with an unfinished end.

The walls are of flint which, it must be admitted, lacks lustre, but the two-tiered stone colonnade is imposing enough. The rooms inside are over-austere. They were redecorated in 1970 in simple modern taste as a low-key background to the superb French furniture – lacquer and marquetry and velvet-covered chairs – clocks and Sèvres porcelain bought by the 3rd Duke when he was Ambassador-Extraordinary to the Court of Louis XV at Versailles in 1765. The Dining Room, once a rare example of the Egyptian taste of the early 19th century, was made more conventionally 'Georgian' in 1904, and now only one of the chairs still has a bronze crocodile on its back as a reminder of the lost decorative scheme.

However, Wyatt's Tapestry Room remains as he designed it, the walls hung with Gobelins tapestries of Don Quixote by Audran and Cuzotte.

Three out of the four are dated 1762–4. The winsome marble chimneypiece with its pastoral figures was made by John Bacon.

The paintings, revealed in room after room, are as fine and numerous as the furniture, and Canaletto's views of London are world famous. The family portraits begin with several Van Dycks: his group of Charles I with his family, and others of the royal children. Charles II, seated, is by Lely; and also by Lely is the full-length of Frances Theresa Stewart, Duchess of Richmond, shown as *Minerva*. She is said to have been the model for Britannia, whose image still appears on our coinage. The best portraits of the building 3rd Duke are by Reynolds and Romney.

Gorhambury, Hertfordshire
(The Earl of Verulam)

Just north of St Albans (*via* A5)

The lodge is next to the Roman theatre of Verulamium, and the house is on the crown of the hill. Built in 1777–84 by Sir Robert Taylor, it is a swollen Palladian villa, startlingly white (having recently been refaced in Portland stone) and with touches of neo-classical elegance. A massive stone stair leads to a generous portico. Once there were small flanking wings, but after 1816 one was demolished and the other increased to its present size.

A former property of St Alban's Abbey, Gorhambury was bought in 1561 by Sir Nicholas Bacon. The ruins of the house he built can be seen in the park. Ten years later Queen Elizabeth exclaimed, 'My Lord, what a little house you have gotten!' at which Bacon enlarged it against her next visit. It passed to the youngest son, the famous Sir Francis Bacon, Lord St Albans and one of the great figures of his age. Lawyer, statesman, and Lord Chancellor in 1618, he is most famous for his philosophical writings and *Essays*. The Library contains many of his books, but the precious Shakespeare Quartos are on loan to the Bodleian Library. Bacon had no direct heirs, and later the old house and its splendid contents were bought (in

Gorhambury

1652) by Sir Harbottle Grimstone. His descendants were created Viscount Grimston in 1719 and Earl of Verulam in 1815.

In the great cube of the Hall the two remarkable stained glass windows give an idea of Bacon's decorations in the old house. Datable about 1620, they show various exotic scenes and botanical plants. (Something similar survives at Lydiard Tregoze.) The walls in the Hall are hung with portraits, chiefly of great 17th-century figures contemporary with Sir Harbottle. On the right are the Royal family – including Catherine of Braganza as a Baroque St Catherine, by Huysmans – and ahead are statesmen, including middle-aged portraits of two of Shakespeare's most famous patrons, the Earls of Pembroke and Southampton. Horace Walpole noticed the portrait of George Calvert, Baron Baltimore, who planted a colony at Avalon, Newfoundland and whose son founded Baltimore. More good paintings are in the Dining Room, among them Paul Van Somer's portrait of Bacon as Lord Chancellor. In the Ball Room are a group of Dutch-style pictures by the talented amateur, Sir Nathaniel Bacon, nephew of Sir Francis. Two are large kitchen scenes with quantities of fruit and game; another is a self-portrait.

In the Yellow Drawing Room, everything is 18th century. Over the fireplace hangs the group by Reynolds of *The Grimston Children*, the youth in rose-coloured velvet being the future 3rd Lord Grimston who rebuilt the house. The chimneypiece, with antique panels of *rosso antico* marble, was designed by Piranesi and bought in Rome. These *camini* are not common, but there is another next door in the Library, and the two urns standing on it were chosen by Piranesi himself. Of the same date is the fine marble bust of Pope Clement XIV by Christopher Hewetson in the Hall. These Roman purchases were made by Grimston's father-in-law, Edward Walter.

A minute Ante-Room, painted to resemble satinwood, leads to the Library. The portraits here are not so fine; but very remarkable are three heads of painted terracotta, of Sir Nicholas Bacon, his wife, and his son, possibly Francis. They were made during the 1560s and nothing quite like them is known in England. The bookshelves are classified according to Bacon's 'divisions of knowledge'.

Great Dixter, East Sussex
(Mr Quentin Lloyd)

At Northiam, ten miles north of Hastings (A28)

The late mediaeval manor of Great Dixter was acquired in 1910 by Nathaniel Lloyd, the architectural historian. The new owner called in Edwin Lutyens, who over the next four years both restored and enlarged the house which had long been a farm and had suffered alteration. The result is a tribute to the scholarship and imagination which so often characterised Lutyens's work.

The house, approached down a flagged path between yew hedges, is a delight. The timbered half of the building, with a substantial two-storey

Great Dixter; the Hall, restored by Lutyens; (also illustrated on p. 20)

porch, is the mediaeval hall, of the Wealden type and dating from the 15th century. Parlour and solar were situated under the tall barge-boarded gable at the end. The large mullioned bay window to the right of the porch is a reconstruction, but so sensitive was the Lutyens touch that it is not always easily detected. The tile-hung section of the front is a Lutyens addition and reticently makes no attempt to compete with the timbered hall. At the rear of the house the architect re-erected a yeoman's 16th-century timbered cottage salvaged from Benenden. As was said at the time in *Country Life*, such transplantations are 'generally a meaningless proceeding, greatly to be deplored', but 'in this case . . . amply justified'.

The hall, which Lutyens restored by removing floors and partitions inserted in the late 16th century, has an open timber roof supported both by king-post trusses and by hammerbeams. The latter were normally used in conjunction with stone walls and their occurrence in a timber-framed building is unusual. A squint at the upper end of the hall indicates the position of the solar. The latter, which houses Nathaniel Lloyd's architectural library, has a 16th-century fireplace. There are agreeable furnishings in both rooms, notably a late-16th-century Flemish hunting tapestry and Jacobean tables, one having a finely carved frieze.

Lutyens also laid out the topiary garden, cleverly incorporating oast houses and farm buildings in his design. The scale is perfect. The sunk garden later added by Nathaniel Lloyd himself is no less sensitively conceived. The famous and colourful garden is now cultivated by Christopher Lloyd.

Gwydir Castle, Gwynedd
(Mr Richard Clegg)

At Llanrwst, ten miles south of Conwy (B5106)

From Llanrwst, across the romantic Conwy valley you will see a towered house standing at the foot of a high crag known as the Rock of the Falcon. A fortification existed here in about A.D. 610, when the battle was fought which may have left the name Gwead-tir or 'bloody land'. Gwydir would have controlled the valley pass, and we know that a tower was built in the 14th century, parts of which still may exist in the high building facing the river. It is a castle, however, only in name. Rather than an outpost, this is a country seat, principally of the tranquil Tudor period.

Meredith ap Jevan, who died in 1525, bought the property, and his son's name was anglicised as John Wynn. Gwydir was largely created by these two, and the date 1555 over the gate may be taken as that of its completion. Yet the diverse forms of the windows, variously Gothic, arched or rectangular, suggest modifications up to the 17th century, or maybe in the 20th. The 'tower' is the oldest part; the Tudor Hall is in the adjoining low wing. When John Wynn was enlarging the house he acquired various windows and materials from the dissolved and abandoned Cistercian Abbey of Aberconwy at Maenan, further down the valley, and the great beams in the Music Room have been traced to this source. The battlements on the chimneys are curious, and belong perhaps to improvements made in the romantic early 19th century.

Sir John Wynn, first Baronet, who died in 1626, was High Sheriff and Member of Parliament for Caernarfon. His portrait has lately returned to

Gwydir Castle; the Tower and 16th-century wing

the house, where it hangs in the Hall. In the 17th century Gwydir passed by marriage to the Duke of Ancaster, and in 1895 was sold to a cousin, the politician Earl Carrington. He planted a number of oak trees to record visits of distinguished visitors, who included King George V and Queen Mary (when Duke and Duchess of York), the Duke of Cambridge and Prince Edward of Saxe-Weimar. But disaster came in 1925 when a fire ruined the building, destroying most of the floors and roofs, and all the panelling and plasterwork. Gwydir was abandoned, then sold, and might have disappeared altogether.

The late Mr Arthur Clegg finally bought it in 1944 and at the age of sixty-three he set out to repair the entire house. The work has been continued by his son, the present owner. No trouble was spared to obtain proper materials, and the oak floors, stairs and beams are new insertions; the stone walls are unplastered. Mr Clegg's home is well furnished, for the most part with country-made pieces dating from Elizabethan to Georgian, but some of the original Wynn furniture has been recovered. The most interesting is the Wynn bed, dated 1570. It is lavishly carved, probably by Welsh craftsmen, with figures, scenes from the bible, a pious text, and a demon's mask to ward off evil spirits.

The formal garden in the forecourt and the Dutch garden have been recreated by the new owners, and are densely populated by a large and growing colony of peacocks, both white and coloured, who make a great parade during the spring showing off their tails.

Haddon Hall, Derbyshire
(The Duke of Rutland)

Two miles south-east of Bakewell (A6)

Grey walls, battlements and towers stand on a woody spur above the river, looking like an illumination of a Gothic city hung in the air. Had you come a hundred years ago, you would have found it overgrown and uninhabited; in 1819 a writer said that 'a gloomy and solemn silence pervades its neglected apartments, and the bat and the owl are alone the inmates of its remaining splendour.' That is when the story of Dorothy Vernon's elopement from Haddon with Sir John Manners was written, the 'awful and melancholy look' of the Hall supporting such romantic stories of olden time. The legend may still be believed, for it has never been disproved.

Through this famous marriage Haddon came, in 1567, to John Manners and thence to the Earls of Rutland. When they became Dukes in 1703, Haddon was abandoned in favour of Belvoir Castle. Yet the structure was not altogether neglected, and in 1912 it was possible for the future 9th Duke to restore it to its former condition. This he did as a life's work, with great expense, care and skill. So what have we now? A completely authentic survival in which nothing except the mandatory restorations is later than 17th century, and, moreover, one that shows the growth of its previous five centuries.

William I granted Haddon to his illegitimate son, Peverel, in whose ownership Domesday Book records the manor and village of Nether Haddon. The Chapel was then the village church. But Peverel's descendant lost the property through having supported King Stephen; Henry II granted it to Avenil, the steward, from whom it came to his son-in-law Richard Vernon and eventually to the Manners family. Thus Haddon has passed by descent for more than eight centuries.

Stonework of the 12th century survives in the Chapel, at the base of Peverel's Tower which stands at the opposite corner, and in much of the boundary wall. Haddon was never officially fortified, and never had to withstand a siege. The battlements, so attractive on the walls and towers, belong to the late Middle Ages. It was about 1370 that the house took on its present form, i.e. when the two courts were divided by the Great Hall. Improvements continued at regular intervals, the most obvious being those to the south or private wing carried out by Sir Henry Vernon and Sir George who between them owned Haddon for nearly a hundred years, from 1467 to 1567. The lavish hospitality given by Sir George, the last of the Vernons and father of Dorothy, earned his title 'King of the Peak'.

An uphill drive, too steep surely for horses, leads to Sir George's towered Gatehouse, the lowest as well as the tallest part of the building. Within, well-work steps rise to the Lower Court; the odd arrangement of arches and squinches in the corner shows there had been difficulty in squeezing the Gatehouse in. The Chapel in the other corner has a Norman pillar and font, and additions of various dates up to the Civil War. Its chief interest lies in the extensive wall paintings, recently revealed from puritan coats of limewash. St Christopher crosses a river well stocked with fish, against a flowery background; Saints Nicholas and Anne are on the Chancel wall.

Opposite:
Haddon Hall; view from the garden

Right:
panelling in the Long Gallery
(See also illustrations on pp. 12 and 28)

Stained glass is dated 1427; but more unusual is the complete reredos of Nottingham alabaster, its nine panels showing the Passion, which also is 15th century.

The two courts are divided by the 14th-century Hall range. Two original Hall windows survive on this side, and in the corner are two gargoyles of the same date. The first of many alterations here were the gate tower and chimneybreast (15th century). Within, to the left, the Kitchens survive, though not exactly in their original form because the beamed ceiling and fittings are Tudor. With ovens, water troughs, the salting box, chopping block and log box, these rooms remain complete and contain, besides, some rare mediaeval furniture. The Hall itself has a 15th-century oak screen and gallery, and another gallery that was inserted about 1600 to provide access between the upper floors. The roof was entirely restored by the late Duke of Rutland, who used for it forty tons of oak beams, cut on the estate as they would have been for the mediaeval original.

The Private Wing was remodelled about 1500 by Sir Henry, and both the Dining Room (the former Parlour) and the Great Chamber above have late-Gothic ceilings; in the Dining Room the original heraldic painting in black and red has been revealed. The panelling is Renaissance, that is some fifty years later, with Sir George Vernon's arms and (possibly) his portrait; while the Great Chamber has an early Elizabethan plaster frieze. From here a small Gallery, partitioned later as bedrooms for the Earls of Rutland, has timber-studded walls showing it to be a 15th-century building.

Massive semi-circular oak stairs lead to the Long Gallery, a room popularly associated with Dorothy Vernon and built originally by her father, Sir George. A festivity for her sister's marriage was, by tradition, taking place here when she left unnoticed to join John Manners who was waiting below by the bridge. Whether this be true or no, the appearance of the Gallery is the result of their son's improvements of about 1603. The panelling, with its bold and curious version of the Corinthian order, was painted to resemble walnut. In the frieze are the Vernon crest of a boar's head, the Manners peacock, and the rose of England and thistle of Scotland blooming on a single stem. The overmantel painting is by Rex Whistler, 1933, and shows the present, 10th Duke of Rutland as a boy. In the State Bedroom, the plaster overmantel of about 1603 with Orpheus charming the Beasts seems to have been made by one of the Hardwick craftsmen.

Many tapestries were, alas, destroyed in a fire, but what may have been the finest survives, namely a large French weaving of about 1460 with the arms of England against a *mille fleurs* background. It hangs above the dais in the Hall, and is thought to have been a gift from Henry VIII. There is also a set of five *Senses*, woven at Mortlake with scenes from Aesop against grotesques, which probably belonged to Charles I. Brussels verdure tapestries of the 17th century hang in the Great Chamber on Tudor iron hooks.

Perhaps the greatest pleasure comes with the garden, forming a series of three enormous terraces up the hill. At the top the balustrade is Jacobean, but the dry stone walls and massive buttresses may be much earlier. Scrub, brambles and leggy overgrown trees were removed by the 9th Duke, and the garden is now most beautifully planted, the roses being its special feature. The lattice windows in the Long Gallery will be seen to bow and make interesting reflections. This was how they had been leaded originally, and in their restoration many of the old diamond panes have been preserved.

Hagley Hall, Hereford and Worcester
(The Viscount Cobham)

Three miles south-east of Stourbridge (A456 or A491)

In 1564 the Lytteltons, a family of long standing in Worcestershire, bought Hagley at the edge of the Clent Hills. Nearly two hundred years later the dilapidated old house was rebuilt by Sir George, 1st Lord Lyttelton. His father, Sir Thomas, had married Christian Temple, sister of Lord Cobham of Stowe. Thus the Lytteltons were allied to the Opposition camp of Cobhamites, with Temples, Pitt and the Grenvilles; and when the male line of the Temples died out in 1889, the 5th Lord Lyttelton inherited their title of Viscount Cobham.

When Lord Lyttelton decided to build a new house, designs were considered from friends of Horace Walpole who belonged to the 'Strawberry Committee'. But Lady Lyttelton had strong views and would not have anything Gothic. The chosen design came from Sanderson Miller in 1753. It is plainly Palladian, the four corner towers being reminiscent of Holkham or Croome Court, and its monumental treatment makes the building appear rather larger than in fact it is. Lyttelton had written to the architect, 'we are pretty indifferent about the outside, it is enough if it is nothing offensive to the eye . . .' There is no portico but later he toyed with the idea of adding

Hagley Hall; left: *the Dining Room, and* right: *the Drawing Room*

one. Recent cleaning has shown the pristine colouring of the sandstone, a beautiful rose pink.

The plan is quite simple. Flanking the central Hall and Saloon, formal rooms lie to the right, private apartments and the Library to the left. Each side has its staircase. But nearly half the house, including the Library and private rooms, suffered from a fire in 1925, and furniture and portraits were lost. The damaged rooms were so skilfully restored that they are hardly distinguishable from the original work.

The delight of the formal rooms is their plasterwork. This dates from about 1758 and shows the English rococo at its height, just before it was to expire in the grip of neo-classicism. The Hall, with plaster medallions and statues, is restrained, but it has a wild overmantel of *Pan* signed by Vassalli, one of the best known of the immigrant Italian *stuccadores*. The former Saloon is now the Dining Room, and here Vassalli's plasterwork is both elaborate and delicate. Copious festoons on the walls are entwined with emblems of music, the arts and the chase. The chimneypiece of white and Siena marble looks like the work of Henry Cheere.

Lady Lyttelton insisted that the tapestry Drawing Room should be separated from the noise that must inevitably come from the (former) dining room. Accordingly a staircase lies between them. The Tapestry Room is among those unharmed by the fire and it remains complete. Its ceiling is French in character, even to the inclusion of pretty mythological paintings. These are by James Stuart, but the central panel was damaged by water and has been replaced. The room was designed round a remarkable set of Soho arabesque tapestries which Lyttelton had managed to buy cheaply. Pier tables, looking glasses, and picture frames round portraits of the Cob-hamites are all unashamedly rococo, and French-style chairs covered in tapestry complete this remarkable room.

The columned Gallery at the south end of the house has more good plasterwork, and some of the most interesting furniture. The mahogany chairs have applied decoration of carved boxwood. A pair of very elaborate pier glasses are generally attributed to Thomas Johnson, virtuoso of the London carvers, but the four torchères that formerly accompanied them are now unhappily dispersed among various museums. They are made of pine treated to resemble limewood and (perhaps) walnut. The picture frames are in similar style and give the appearance of a 'Grinling Gibbons revival', the more so because the Gallery pictures are 17th-century court portraits that Lyttelton had inherited from Lord Brouncker.

Among many notable portraits elsewhere there are Richard Wilson's full-length of Admiral Thomas Smith (an early work), Batoni's picture of Sir Richard Lyttelton (brother to Lord Lyttelton), and Van Dyck's Earl of Carlisle. In the Hall, the splendid pair of marble busts of Rubens and Van Dyck are by Rysbrack. Four more busts in the Library, of Spenser, Shakespeare, Milton and Dryden, all by Scheemakers, once belonged to Alexander Pope – whose portrait by Richardson hangs over the fireplace. He gave them to Frederick, Prince of Wales, who in turn bequeathed them to Lyttelton in 1751. A martial statue of 'poor Fred', the figurehead of the Tory Opposition, was placed on a column the other side of the church.

With the examples of Stowe and Mount Edgcumbe before him, Sir Thomas turned to the fashionable pursuit of improving his park, and was extolled in Thomson's *Seasons* (1743). The temples and ornaments in this once celebrated landscape multiplied, and some of the best remain today. The Rotunda dates from 1747, as does Sanderson Miller's Gothic Castle in which Horace Walpole could see 'the true rust of the Barons' Wars'. As a contrast, the Temple of Theseus, designed by James 'Athenian' Stuart eleven years later, shows the earliest use of the Greek Doric order in England; but this and the obelisk are now on the other side of the Birmingham road.

Hanch Hall, Staffordshire
(Mr and Mrs Douglas Haynes)

Four miles north of Lichfield (B5014)

The early history of the house has not yet been traced, but apparently it belonged to the Astons in the 13th century. Apart from some stout mediaeval timbers and 17th-century panelling upstairs, the building is ostensibly of Queen Anne's time and later. The garden front, of warm brick and stone, has 'Gibbs' windows, and curiously enough the centre is of a slightly later style than the wings. The windows were enriched in the mid-19th century, this being also the period of the *porte cochère* and the towered courtyard face.

The downstairs rooms are mostly panelled, and a modest Vanbrugian fireplace has been moved to the central Drawing Room. The best work is the early Victorian Staircase of carved oak, which evidently fills the former hall. It is 'Elizabethan' in the romantic style of the 1840s, with a strapwork rail

Hanch Hall

and Gothic cornice. Above it is contemporary armorial glass that recorded various families who lived here: 'olim' was for William Orme, a 17th-century Royalist; 'heri' was the Parkhursts; 'hodie', Sir Charles Forster who made the 19th-century improvements. The shield for 'cras' is inscribed *nescio quis*. Mr Haynes bought the house in 1975.

Harewood House, West Yorkshire
(The Earl of Harewood)

Between Leeds and Harrogate (A61)

Of mediaeval Harewood there remain only the isolated church and a ruined castle. Two adjoining estates, Harewood and Gawthorpe, were bought in 1739 by Henry Lascelles. His son Edwin, later created Lord Harewood, decided not only to rebuild Gawthorpe House (which stood to the south, on the opposite hill) but also the village, which had already moved to the main thoroughfare. Either side of the main road are substantial buildings designed by Carr of York; and it was Carr who also designed the house in 1759, with a portico overlooking the valley. At once the ambitious Robert Adam, recently returned from Italy and full of new ideas, suggested improvements, and six years later he was given the whole interior to decorate. All was finished in 1772, when Gawthorpe was demolished and Capability Brown began brilliantly to refashion the park.

Harewood House as recorded in watercolours by Girtin, Turner and John Varley must have been among the great achievements of its day. The house, of local yellow stone, looked down a steep slope to Brown's beautiful lake. Adam's glittering series of rooms, as fine as any he designed, looked superb with Chippendale's furniture and Reynolds's portraits. But it was not enough for the 19th century, and the 3rd Earl of Harewood employed

Harewood House; the entrance front

Charles Barry to build additional floors for bedrooms (which now are redundant). The outside was modified and given a massive Italian balustrade, Carr's portico removed and the slope flattened into a generous parterre with stone fountains and balustrades. Colourful and sociable this may be, but one regrets the loss of a perfectly integrated Arcadian ideal.

The entrance front, massive but low, looks as though sunk into the ground because the drive has been slightly raised. The house appears as a modest seven-bay centre block, flanked by low corridors with narrow end pavilions. This is deceptive and will be forgotten inside. Not only is the house very deep, but Adam's final design filled every square inch, including what appear to be corridors, with fine rooms. Barry made some alterations. He enlarged the Dining Room and turned Adam's Saloon into the Library, filling the apses with curving mahogany bookcases. During the present century the bedroom wing was altered for the Princess Royal, and its original lay-out is no longer apparent. Yet it is Adam's achievement that remains paramount.

He brought in not only light neo-classical plasterwork, but finely matched colouring of walls and ceilings. The Hall shows his mature hand. Doric half-columns round the walls are now painted like red marble, and the ceiling is picked out in terracotta, grey and white. The Saloon or Library that lies on the same axis is in pinks and blues that were matched by the young Turner in two oil paintings that have always hung in the room. On one side is the private wing, with bedrooms and more libraries; on the other are the five State Rooms. Two of them still have carpets designed by Adam, that in the Rose Drawing Room being in a mixture of olive green and dusty rose. The carpet in the Music Room is bolder and brighter, and reflects the ceiling with its roundels painted by Angelica Kauffmann. On the walls are huge decorative classical scenes by Angelica's husband, Zucchi. This room, completed by a Reynolds portrait and furniture by Chippendale, is now rather overpowering because of the Beauvais tapestry chair covers introduced by the 3rd Earl of Harewood.

The climax of the interior is the Gallery, which completely fills one pavilion. It is almost a triple cube, seventy-seven feet long, and in its lofty ceiling are mythological paintings by Rebecca. The walls were designed for pictures, and here will be seen Edwin Lascelles, 1st Lord Harewood, standing in his estate; but more striking is Lady Worsley, an apparition of scarlet and black in her riding habit and feathered hat. Both these are by Reynolds, while others are by Gainsborough, Romney, Hoppner, Lawrence and Winterhalter.

If it were to contain furniture alone, Harewood would still be famous. Here is not only the best of Thomas Chippendale's work but possibly the finest furniture ever to be made in England. It is no longer thought to have been designed by Robert Adam, but to show Chippendale's own mastery of neo-classical style. He seems to have been given a free hand, and made the lofty pelmets in the Gallery, of wood carved and painted to match the curtains. This was practical, for velvet or silk pelmets would not have lasted until our day. The picture frames should not be overlooked. Chippendale's marquetry is of a quality to rival the great French *ébénistes*. The famous Library table has now gone to Temple Newsam, Leeds; but here remain the secrétaire and dressing chest of inlaid satinwood, and magnificent rosewood table-tops on carved gilt frames. The sideboard suite is of rosewood and ormolu. The many sets of chairs are mostly derived from the French *cabriole* chair; they are carved and gilded or painted, but many have been re-covered since the 18th century. The Younger Chippendale also supplied furniture after his father's death in 1779, including the gilded side tables in the Gallery and 'Egyptian' tables.

The Dining Room has no Adam work, except the chimneypiece (designed for the Gallery), because it was enlarged and remodelled by Barry. It is hung with 19th-century portraits, the best being those of Barry's patrons, the 3rd Earl by Grant and his Countess Louisa by Richmond. The Princess Royal, painted by Sir Oswald Birley, is above the fireplace. She was Princess

Harewood House; marquetry and gilt side table made by Chippendale (See also colour plate 9 and illustration on p. 25)

Mary, eldest daughter of King George V, who married the late Lord Harewood and died in 1965. Together they collected the superb Italian paintings that fill two of the main rooms. There are Florentine Renaissance works, but most are Venetian, with madonnas by Bellini and Catena, *St Jerome* by Cima, and portraits by Titian, Veronese and Tintoretto. The full-length of *Procurator Mocenigo* in his crimson robes, by Alessandro Longhi, shows the flamboyant side of 18th-century Venice.

The very fine Stables, built in 1755 by Carr of York, are set out as exhibition rooms showing the history of the house; while close by is the Bird Garden made by the present Earl and Countess of Harewood. Lord Harewood is best known for his interest in music and in particular for the results he has achieved for the English National Opera.

Harrington Hall, Lincolnshire
(Lady Maitland)

Seven miles east of Horncastle (north of A158)

The burst of warmth and colour at Harrington seems natural in this lush, fertile country. The house lies in the south of the wolds. In the 14th century the manor belonged to the Coppeldykes, whose monuments are in the church, and was bought by Vincent Amcott in 1673. After passing by marriage to the Ingilbys of Ripley Castle in 1777 the house was generally let to tenants. It was bought in 1950 by the late Sir John Maitland, M.P.

The long building stands on a mediaeval stone base. The tall projecting

Harrington Hall

porch is an Elizabethan survival, but has somehow acquired two curiously long pilasters above the door. The Amcott rebuilding of the remainder can be dated from the weather vane (1678) and the stone sundial (1681). It was carried out in rose-pink brick under blue-grey Westmorland slates, and has all the charm of its period.

Despite its great length, the house was only one room thick. Panelling in the Drawing Room is late 17th century; but the best of the woodwork is in the Hall, remodelled during the 1720s. The painted wainscot has Doric pilasters supporting a sturdy entablature, and a low brooding arch takes the position of the former screen. The oak staircase, though of the same date, is in a lighter style with slender balusters and brackets carved with hops and wheat-ears.

Tennyson was born nearby at Somersby, and he wrote poems to Rosa Baring of Harrington Hall, with whom he was in love about 1834. By tradition this is the original of Maud's garden; and fifty years later, in his *Roses on the Terrace* he recalled the old terrace which still survives, raised above a wide lawn and borders. The garden is walled, semi-formal still, and wonderfully full of colour.

Hatfield House, Hertfordshire
(The Marquess of Salisbury)

Approach from Hatfield station

Robert Cecil, younger son of Lord Burghley, was five feet three inches in height, with a deformed back and melancholy eyes. Queen Elizabeth called him 'her little elf'. As able and as ruthless as his father, whom he succeeded as Secretary of State, he became Lord Treasurer and Earl of Salisbury; but his greatest monument is this vast house, which was not quite finished on his death in 1612.

When Lord Burghley divided his property between his two sons, Theobalds Park in Hertfordshire, being conveniently close to London, with all its contents and state papers, came to the more talented Robert. However, James I coveted Theobalds, and in 1607 he exchanged it for a property built on a hill overlooking Hatfield town. This, known as The Old Palace, is famous chiefly for having been the enforced residence of two Queens, Mary and Elizabeth, when they were merely unwanted Princesses. It was in fact a 15th-century brick mansion built by Cardinal Morton. When Cecil built his new house he pulled down three sides of the Old Palace for their materials. The remaining wing, largely gutted but still boasting a magnificent timber roof, was used for three centuries as stables. It is now the tea room.

Cecil lost no time in consulting his various friends and starting to build. Like his father at Burghley thirty years before, he seems to have finalised the design himself. The main roof was put on in 1609, but there was great difficulty in keeping up supplies of the eight million bricks that were needed. Financial difficulties ensued, and economies were proposed but not, apparently, adopted. Inigo Jones is known to have visited Hatfield in 1609, and

Hatfield House; the Jacobean forecourt

the very splendid stone colonnade in the south forecourt, with the long gallery above and a magnificent clock tower, could be one of his earliest architectural designs. A carpenter called Robert Liming was also involved with the building, and he showed what he had learnt here shortly afterwards when he built Blickling Hall in Norfolk.

The front door has now been moved to the north side, and the vast structure towers overhead. Its appearance as a grim fortress is really due to later simplifications, because old records show that it was ornamented with turrets and gables, fifty-four heraldic lions on the parapets, and much painting and gilding. The house is in the familiar U-shape with wings broad enough to hold two or three rooms across. An apartment suitable for the King was designed in one wing, an apartment for the Queen in the other. Yet King James I was never to visit Hatfield.

Huge though the Great Hall is, there is yet a floor above it. The oak screen, originally with an open gallery, is heavily but marvellously carved with caryatids, bosses and strapwork, while the second gallery opposite seems to be unique in Jacobethan houses. The Elizabethan relics came from Theobalds. There are two outstanding portraits of the Queen, the 'ermine' portrait by Nicholas Hilliard (the ermine being a chivalric emblem of purity), and the 'rainbow' portrait, perhaps by Zucchero, inscribed *non sine sole iris*. Mary, Queen of Scots, is here, painted just before her execution, and also the two great Cecils. Upstairs will be found Queen Elizabeth's stockings, gloves and straw hat, and a selection from Burghley's papers, including the execution warrant for Mary, Queen of Scots.

The oak staircase is the finest of its date, with posts delicately carved in Renaissance style supporting proud heraldic lions and naked boys playing musical instruments. The carvings were originally gilded. Among the 17th-century portraits is the Duke of Monmouth, Charles II's bastard son, who attempted to gain the throne in 1685; but after his capture and execution, the 4th Lord Salisbury prudently hid the likeness with his own portrait.

Cecil followed the Italian fashion of placing the rooms of state on the upper floor. The Great Chamber leads to the Long Gallery, and thence westwards. Monumental chimneypieces in coloured marbles were supplied by Maximilian Colt. One contains his bronzed stone statue of James I in regal splendour, and another is built around a mosaic portrait of Cecil, made in Venice around 1608. The fine carved and bossed panelling in the Long Gallery, many ceilings, and the Flemish stained glass in the Chapel are also original, but it is not always easy to distinguish them from 19th-century work, particularly as old panelling and chimneypieces – notably that in alabaster in the Dining Room – have been brought from elsewhere. About 1830 the south Colonnade was glazed in and is now the Armoury. Here the original front door will be seen. About 1870 the Chapel was redesigned by Taldini, the Great Hall and other rooms were painted, and the entire ceiling of the Long Gallery was gilded.

The Great Chamber is filled with great portraits. The 1st Marquess of Salisbury, Lord Chamberlain to George III, was painted by Romney, and his Marchioness is by Reynolds. This picture shows something of the character of the spirited woman who was still hunting and gambling at the age of eighty-five, when tragically she died in a fire in the west wing. During the subsequent restorations nearly all the work carried out for her by James Wyatt was removed, but her gilded furniture remains in this room. The 3rd

Hatfield House; the Long Gallery

Marquess of Salisbury, Queen Victoria's Prime Minister, is seen in an interesting portrait by George Richmond; Lord David Cecil, the celebrated man of letters of our own day, was painted by Augustus John (in the Library). Full-length royal portraits, and others of William and Robert Cecil, are in the Dining Room.

Two long and unusually fine refectory tables have always stood in the Hall. A rare Dutch chamber organ, by Hahn, cost no less than £1,084 in 1609; it stood in the Great Chamber, and is now in the Armoury. Late Stuart chairs and cabinets are in the Long Gallery, together with treasures such as mother of pearl furniture and a 16th-century posset set of carved crystal. There are excellent 17th-century Brussels tapestries in the Hall; but the great rarities are the four large Sheldon tapestries of the *Seasons*, woven at that mysterious factory at Barcheston in Warwickshire. Each shows a deity commanding a landscape full of country folk energetically at work and a border of more than forty emblems or 'conceits'. One tapestry is dated 1611. Although precisely of an age with the house, they were not actually made for it but acquired about a hundred years ago.

Haughley Park, Suffolk
(Mr and Mrs A. J. Williams)

Near Wetherden, between Bury St Edmunds and Stowmarket (A45)

Sir John Sulyard was granted the manor in 1527, and his nephew came to the aid of Queen Mary when she fled to Framlington on the proclamation of Lady Jane Grey as Queen in 1553. The family were Catholic. The house was built by another Sir John about 1620, E-shaped, with crow-stepped gables and pinnacles in the traditional and rather old-fashioned East Anglian style,

Haughley Park

while the main windows are surmounted by pediments. The two dormers are modern replacements of the originals, which had disappeared about 1800. At the same time, perhaps, the garden front was rebuilt with bow windows.

Mr Williams bought the house in 1957, but four years later a fire broke out and gutted most of the building. Fortunately the walls survived in good state and the owners decided to rebuild rather than demolish. The architect, Mr Eric Sandon of Ipswich, carried out the task quickly and with distinction, and the reconstructed oak staircase shows that modern craftsmanship can rival that of 350 years ago. Though the house looks large from the outside, it does not seem so within. The width of the centre range is little more than eighteen feet, a convenient span for oak beams.

The excellently maintained garden is often visited for itself alone. The modern buildings adjoining the former kitchen wing are a poultry and egg processing plant, without which the house would not be kept in its present impeccable condition.

Hedingham Castle, Essex
(Miss Musette Majendie, CBE, and Dr Margery Blackie, CVO)

At Castle Hedingham, four miles north of Halstead (B1058)

Standing on a densely wooded hill above an old market town, Hedingham Castle is a landmark for miles around. The Norman Keep dates from about 1130 and was built by Aubrey de Vere, 1st Earl of Oxford, whose father had come to England with William the Conqueror. During the troubled reign of Stephen, de Vere's son followed the rival sovereign, Matilda, but it was here that the wife of Stephen, Matilda of Boulogne, died in 1151. For four

Hedingham Castle; the Norman keep

hundred years the de Veres remained powerful. Their heraldic devices are familiar in churches around Hedingham: the mullet; the badge of a *verres* or blue boar; and the irrefutable motto, *vero nihil verius*.

The square Keep is well preserved, but otherwise the Castle has changed very much. In the Middle Ages, no trees would have obstructed the view of approachers. An 18th-century house (not open) stands in the former outer bailey, where once there were stables, granaries and barracks. The moat and a few foundations of gates remain, but nothing otherwise except for the Keep, which proved to be too strongly built for demolition.

It has about half the dimensions of the White Tower of London. The walls, eleven feet thick, are faced with Barnac stone, a famous hard-wearing material widely used for cathedrals and castles until the quarries were exhausted in the 15th century. The castellations are gone, but two turrets remain. At ground level the windows are mere slits, and they are not much wider on the main floors.

Apart from the undercroft, there are three floors. The Guard Room or Armoury is entered by an outside stair. Here are signs of the 1917 fire which destroyed the timbers and calcined the walls; but the ceiling has been restored, and also the vaulting arch. Rooms and a corridor are built in the thickness of the walls, and the garderobe is in the north-east corner. A wide spiral stair leads to the Hall, where the vaulting arch is original and probably the finest of its kind. The floor, as rebuilt after the fire, is two feet lower than the original. Here is a fine and rare Norman fireplace, with chevron ornament, and corridors and chambers run on two levels. Above this is the dormitory.

Hedingham Castle belonged to the widow of the 18th Earl of Oxford in 1655, and was bought in 1713 by Robert Ashurst, an ancestor of Miss Majendie. With the care that it now receives, it will certainly survive another eight hundred years.

Hellen's, Hereford and Worcester
(Major Malcolm Munthe, M.C.)

At Much Marcle, five miles south-west of Ledbury (B4024)

The name is a corruption of Hellion's Home (or Hellinham Castle), a former monastic house that after 1292 was the property of Hugh Audley, Earl of Gloucester, and his wife Yseult, sister of the infamous Roger Mortimer who caused the death of Edward II. The early history of Hellen's is delightfully told in Major Munthe's book on the house, and fully to appreciate it you should visit the 14th-century monuments in Much Marcle Church. The best is to Lady Blanche Grandison (*née* Mortimer), a sleeping stone figure holding her rosary; but more unusual is the painted oak effigy of John de Helyon in country dress, his legs crossed in token of a pilgrimage to the Holy Land. John's family had been stewards to the Audleys, and by marrying the heiress he became Lord of the Manor. His own daughter Joanna married Thomas Walwyn, who was living here in 1400.

Hellen's; the Tudor wing

It is hard to be precise about the mediaeval house. The low wing with staircase tower is known as the Audley Wing and is said to have been castellated. Its old Hall or Court Room was rebuilt after a fire in the 18th century, the consequence apparently of drinking cider too much laced with brandy. What can be the date of the chimney hood, carved with the Prince of Wales feathers and motto? Tradition says that it was put in by James Audley, the boon companion of the Black Prince, but it looks Tudor. A Gothic altar stone has become a 'refectory table', but during the Second World War it broke in half when German bombs dropped close by. Upstairs, Bloody Mary's Room has a plaster overmantel with her arms and initials. The Walwyns were Catholics and during the Civil War their chaplain was hunted by Roundhead troops and finally seized in this room. There is a hiding hole above the fireplace.

The larger wing is of Tudor brick, but was altogether improved about 1641 when Richard Walwyn, at the age of sixteen, married an heiress, Margaret Pye. Their initials are prominent on the octagonal dovecote outside. The windows of the house were enlarged, rooms plastered and panelled, and a new staircase constructed. The best chimneypiece is upstairs, with oak columns and strapwork, in a room hung with gilt leather. 'Hetty's Room' is named after a Walwyn daughter who had the imprudence to fall in love with a farm labourer and was locked and barred in here. With a diamond ring she wrote a sad couplet on a window pane.

In its greater days Hellen's had been a courtyard house, but by the 17th century was much reduced. The stables with their elegant colonnade are 18th century, but the arms of the Audleys still are to be seen over the arched gate. Ownership was disputed in 1831 and the house became a farm until it was occupied by Lady Helena Gleichen who lived, painted and entertained here up to the Second World War. The house then passed to Hilda Pennington Munthe, wife of the Swedish doctor Axel Munthe (author of *San Michele*), and mother of the present owner.

Hever Castle, Kent
(The Lord Astor of Hever)

Three miles east of Edenbridge

Hever still stands compact within the walls of the mediaeval moated manor whose owner, Sir John de Cobham, received permission to crenellate in 1384. Sir Geoffrey Bullen, newly rich and lately Lord Mayor of London – it sometimes seems as if half the great houses in England were owned or built at one time and another by these ex-Lord Mayors – bought the little castle in 1462. With his ambitious grandson, Sir Thomas, Hever moved briefly and tragically into the mainstream of history. Sir Thomas's elder daughter Mary became Henry VIII's mistress, and it was at Hever that the King later courted her younger sister Anne, destined for three years to be Queen of England and to bring both her brothers and herself to the block. Anne Boleyn – she preferred the more elegant spelling – with her large dark eyes, swarthy complexion, and the 'long neck' that was severed on Tower Green, evidently had immense charm, and Hever calls to memory this girl who, we are told, 'revelled in a joke' and 'enjoyed dice and a glass of wine'.

The unhappy Sir Thomas Bullen died in 1538, two years after his son and daughter, and Henry VIII, with characteristic lack of taste, later granted Hever to Anne of Cleves, his divorced 4th wife. Subsequently new owners came and went. Hever declined in status, and in the second half of the 19th century modest tenant farmers occupied the castle. Ducks and geese swam in the moat; shovels and hoes were stored in the Gate House. Rescue came in the shape of William Waldorf Astor who had been American Minister in Rome before settling in England in 1890, where in due course he acquired British nationality and a peerage. He was a man of taste with exacting standards, and having bought Hever in 1903 he embarked on a vast and calculated programme both of renovation and transformation.

Meticulous restoration characterised his treatment of the outside of the castle. Gabled, with crenellated towers, mullioned windows, and chimneys of diapered brick, and with weathered sandstone walls reflected in a placid moat, the exterior now looks much as it did when the Bullens modernised their fortified manor in early Tudor times. The effect is picturesque in the best sense, and the talkative elevations are rich with architectural incident. None more so than the entrance front, where the machicolated gate house is flanked by little towers with loopholes, and adorned above the entrance arch with quatrefoils and trefoil-headed panels, while windows set with carefree irregularity convey a pleasing sense of the haphazard. The small windows to the right of the entrance are the earliest, in the sense that they are careful restorations of mediaeval work; the bigger square-headed windows with mullions, and probably also the mullioned windows with trefoil heads, date from the Bullen occupation.

Passing under one of the few portcullises in the country which may claim to be original, and crossing a pretty timbered courtyard with bargeboarded gables – all part of the Astor renovations – the visitor enters another world. Few houses present so marked a contrast outside and in. Apart from a 15th-

Hever Castle

century doorway into the screens passage, moulded timbers in Henry VII's Room, and 16th-century panelling in the Long Gallery, few features survive from the old house, for the interior of the castle is a monument to Edwardian craftsmanship and the romantic taste of a wealthy Anglo-American owner. William Waldorf Astor, while exercising the closest supervision, entrusted the transformation of the interior to F. L. Pearson, son of the architect whom he had employed in the 1890s at Cliveden, his house in Buckinghamshire. The intention was to evoke the Age of Anne Boleyn; if the lavish pastiche which resulted hardly does that, it has its own marked character. The craftsmanship is impeccable, and the treatment scholarly. The oak wainscot in the Drawing Room, inlaid with bog-oak and holly, is copied from the famous 16th-century room once at Sizergh Castle and now in the Victoria and Albert Museum; in the Dining Room the elaborate screen and the massive carved chimneypiece of Clipsham stone are in their way highly impressive; so too are Pearson's plaster ceilings and his Library panelled in rare sabicu wood, where the intricate carving was executed by W. S. Frith, a virtuoso who had also worked for the owner at Cliveden. The transformation, effected between 1903 and 1907, is a remarkable expression of craftsmanship in the service of romantic nostalgia.

Reflecting the eclectic taste of a man who was also one of the wealthiest collectors of his day, the contents of Hever strike an exotic note rarely found in English country houses. There are Continental enamels, bronzes, and ivories, and such out of the way furniture as early 'turned' chairs from Scandinavia and 17th-century silver armchairs from Germany, both more curious than beautiful. Perhaps naturally the emphasis is on works of the Tudor period which saw the rise and eclipse of the Bullen family. Thus, among the collection of historical portraits are likenesses of Anne Boleyn and her sister Mary, her husband Henry VIII, her daughter Queen

Hever Castle; the Gallery

Elizabeth, François I and Charles IX of France, and not least a beautiful drawing (attributed to Holbein) of William Warham, the Archbishop of Canterbury who vainly opposed Henry VIII's ecclesiastical reforms. Later paintings include two Guardi's, a luminous Canaletto of Warwick Castle, a Turner, and a portrait by Courbet that comes as a surprise in the context of Hever.

A quantity of sculpture in stone, marble and carved wood, includes numerous French and Flemish pieces of the Tudor period, besides such Italian works as a bust of Christ, attributed to Verrocchio, and an enigmatic portrait head of a woman by Francesco Laurana.

The tapestries and an outstanding collection of armour firmly recall the Bullen period. Two of the Flemish tapestries may have been designed by Dürer, and one of two splendid Burgundian tapestries (late 15th and early 16th centuries) by tradition celebrates the marriage of Henry VIII's sister to Louis XII of France and incorporates the figure of a maid of honour in a red dress, said to represent Anne Boleyn. There are no less than a dozen suits of continental 16th-century armour. One of these, a ceremonial suit of Milanese workmanship was made for Henri II, and there is a gauntlet made at Greenwich armoury for Henry VIII.

Such objects of association, of which there are a great number at Hever, convey an immediate sense of history. Perhaps one might expect to find a headdress worked by Anne Boleyn and her prayer book, or a layette believed to have been embroidered by the Princess Elizabeth for Mary Tudor when the latter imagined she was pregnant. But what of such evocative importations as the enamelled crystal reliquary made for Isabella of Castille, the immense rock crystal casket given by Pope Clement to Marie de' Medici that once contained the swaddling clothes of Louis XIII, a bible signed by no less an owner than Martin Luther, the throne of the 16th-century patriot Doge Pietro Landi, and Cardinal de Richelieu's sedan chair? Yet even such memorials seem commonplace in the context of two extraordinary objects that time and William Waldorf Astor brought to Hever. The first is the silver forearm of the Goddess of Victory presented by the Emperor Varus to the Sixth Legion (stationed in Britain in A.D. 150) and unearthed some 200 years ago. The second is a shapely gilt helmet with enamel inlay that belonged to the unhappy Boabdil, last Caliph of Granada, who fled from his radiant Moorish kingdom in the year that Columbus sailed for America. Such things epitomise the curious and exotic character of the contents of Hever.

The castle is relatively small; in 1903 additional rooms were essential. Nothing is a greater tribute to owner and architect than the distinction and imagination of the 'Tudor village' which they established beyond the moat to house guests and offices. As fanciful as the hamlet which Nash built near Blaize Castle a century earlier, it fulfilled a utilitarian purpose without detracting in any way from the mediaeval exterior of the old house.

Comparable discretion marked the siting of Astor's Italian Garden, which if established closer to the castle would have struck a decidedly alien note. As it is, the fountains and cascades, the loggias and grottoes – providing a setting for perhaps the finest collection of classical marbles (notably sarcophagi) to reach Britain in the last 150 years – are surprisingly at home in a corner of the Kentish landscape.

Hoar Cross Hall, Staffordshire
(Mr and Mrs W. Bickerton-Jones)

Nine miles north of Lichfield (A515)

This vast symbol of optimism, built at the height of Victorian prosperity, quickly turned into a seat of tragedy. It was begun in 1861 by Hugo and Emily Meynell. Meynell is a name associated with foxhunting, and after an accident on the hunting field Hugo died in 1871, the very year in which his house was completed. His widow, living until 1903, built to his memory the adjoining church, a beautiful rose-red temple, high in persuasion and lavish in Gothic; Bodley was its architect. Her family owned the house until 1950, and their visitors' names included Queen Mary, King George VI and Queen Elizabeth when they were Duke and Duchess of York, Lord Curzon and Neville Chamberlain. Then the house remained empty for twenty years until it was bought by the present owners, who have equipped it for hearty mediaeval banquets.

The architect was Henry Clutton, a pupil of William Blore, and this is one of his last country houses. Though architecturally it cannot be called adventurous, it is large and imposing, of a textureless brick with sandstone dressings. The style is Elizabethan, and the long, nearly symmetrical garden

Hoar Cross Hall

front boasts of three large bay windows. The rooms inside are safe and square Elizabethan, expensively panelled, ceiled and floored, and must have made a fine setting for paintings and sculpture.

The Hall has a screen designed by Bodley, and leads to a Long Gallery. The huge Ballroom takes up the centre of the garden front. To the right of this is the former Dining Room, with an 18th-century chimneypiece, and to the left is the Library. The best room, perhaps, is the Chapel, a delightful addition decorated by Bodley with a wealth of oak and gilding. The linenfold panelling and delicate carving are in Henry VII style, and (as Nikolaus Pevsner wrote) all Bodley's typical furnishings and decorations are here. (The chapel is awaiting restoration.)

Hoghton Tower, Lancashire
(Sir Bernard de Hoghton, Bart)

Five miles south-east of Preston (A675)

The Hoghtons came to England at the Conquest and have owned land at Hoghton since the beginning of the 13th century. But the house of somewhat stern aspect dramatically crowning a wooded eminence, on the last spur of the Pendle Hills, was the creation of Thomas Hoghton in 1565. In the 18th century the family moved to their seat at Walton-le-Dale, abandoning Hoghton for over a century. It was largely ruinous when Sir Henry de Hoghton, 9th Baronet, began its restoration in the 1870s under the supervision of Paley and Austin.

In spite of changes and additions, Hoghton conveys much the same impression as it must have done in the second half of the 16th century: a large manor house, with the great hall and living quarters around an upper courtyard, and offices around a lower. The impact of the house derives from

13 Mapledurham

14 Melbourne Hall, from the garden

15 Penshurst Place; the 14th-century Hall

16 Port Lympne; the Moorish Courtyard

its uncompromising air, the dark stone, the heavy stone-flagged roofs, and the small mullioned windows. Thomas Hoghton made no concessions to Renaissance taste and the exterior is notably simple.

The Lower Courtyard is entered through a crenellated gatehouse flanked by square towers. Inside, the range on the left dates from the restorations of the 19th century; that on the right from 1700, though it was put up by the scholar and mathematician Sir Charles Hoghton in the style of Thomas Hoghton's 16th-century work. Steps and fine iron gates, also perhaps of 1700 and curiously situated in the middle of the courtyard, give access beyond two little lawns to the front of the inner courtyard. The gateway here, which carries a swirling achievement of arms, was once surmounted by a high tower from which Hoghton derives its sobriquet.

The upper courtyard dated 1565 is stylistically of a piece and probably all Thomas Hoghton's sober creation. The Great Hall with its larger windows lies on the left and the builder here allowed himself the licence of leaf decoration in the spandrels of the doorway, and above the big bay window that marks the dais end of the hall he gracefully carried the ends of the gable roof on moulded corbels.

Inside the house there are two or three of Thomas Hoghton's original stone fireplaces. One is in the Great Hall where the portrait of the builder hangs and where stands a fine Jacobean table at which King James I is said to have dined when he visited Sir Richard Hoghton, 1st Baronet, in 1617. The hall screen is early 17th century.

Many of the state rooms have attractive fielded panelling, probably dating from about 1700, when (as we have noted) changes were made in the lower courtyard by the 4th Baronet. There is a sturdy staircase with twisted balusters of the same date.

Hoghton Tower; the gatehouse leading to the Lower Courtyard

Holker Hall, Cumbria

(Mr Hugh Cavendish)

Near Cark, fourteen miles south of Windermere (B5278)

The red sandstone house, built following a fire in 1871 by Paley and Austin for the 7th Duke of Devonshire, is an idiosyncratic exercise in Victorian Tudor. Towers, bays, bows, finials, gables, balustrades, octagonal chimneys, and mullioned windows of every size and shape, contribute to its bewildering asymmetry. But for the average visitor it is the interior that matters, for here are rooms that not only in their decoration but in the veriest detail of their furnishing reflect High Victorian taste. Few houses give as good an impression of the surroundings in which many of the grand and the rich lived in the decades before the First World War. Little, one feels, has changed. The eclecticism that recklessly juxtaposed Renaissance bronzes and ladies' beadwork, Louis XV chairs and what-nots, has been carefully preserved, as has the convincing clutter that is so familiar in the faded photographs of the period. The rooms moreover are impeccably shown. The visitor, neither channelled down druggets nor restrained by ropes, wanders at will into a world that fascinates because it is so close to us in time though in all else immeasurably distant.

The Library with chintzes, blue and red Turkey carpet, and oak bookshelves, sets the tone. It is an airy room with large windows: like others at Holker, it dispels the misapprehension that our grandfathers preferred a sombre half-light. The books, three thousand five hundred of them, were brought by the 7th Duke from Chatsworth; they include many of the scientific works owned by Henry Cavendish (1731–1810) who discovered the properties of hydrogen and after whom the Cavendish Laboratory at

Holker Hall

Cambridge is named. The finish both of the linenfold panelling and of the fireplaces in Derbyshire alabaster is notably good, as are the decorative details in other rooms: all no doubt was carried out under the direction of Paley and Austin. Even the electric light switches, installed early in this century, are carefully concealed behind dummy books. Over the Library fireplaces hang two of Richmond's best portraits: they represent the 7th Duke's son, Lord Frederick Cavendish, later Chief Secretary for Ireland, who was assassinated in Dublin in 1882, and his wife. She had a lifelong interest in women's education, and Lucy Cavendish College, the youngest college for women in Cambridge, founded in 1951 is named after her. There is also in the Library a portrait by Riley of James II, and a portrait drawing by Sargent of Lady Moyra Cavendish, grandmother of the present owner.

The Drawing Room, with a vast bay asymmetrically set in one corner, is hung with its original red silk of 1874. Its contents exemplify the hectic mixture of styles and periods which the Victorians found congenial. A naked marble lady surveys with equanimity the juxtaposition of ormolu clocks and ladies' work tables, French 18th-century marquetry and English satinwood, 19th-century chintzes and Gothic Chippendale, Meissen china and engaging family photographs. The exotic blend has not only vitality, but well expresses a certain ducal *insouciance*. Pictures include a Salvator Rosa, a Gaspard Poussin, landscapes by Jacob Ruysdael, cool church interiors attributed to Neefs, and flower pieces in the style of J. B. Monnoyer.

The other rooms on the ground floor speak much the same polyglot language with engaging fluency. They contain some interesting pictures: a seascape by Vernet, four large, French, decorative, 18th-century paintings perhaps by Desportes, an excellent portrait by Jonathan Richardson, an early Reynolds of Sir William Lowther (through whom Holker came into the Cavendish family), and a caricature group by Reynolds.

Most of the bedrooms on the first floor have their Victorian beds and hangings (muslins, dimities, Morris chintzes) and their toilet sets and wash basins of Copeland or Minton. There is a good deal of Gillow furniture, and one of the dressing rooms is decorated with Wedgwood vases and plaques after Thorwaldsen.

Holkham Hall, Norfolk
(The Viscount Coke)

On the north coast, two miles west of Wells (A149)

Holkham is the ultimate achievement of the English Palladian movement. For style, its only rivals are Mereworth Castle and Chiswick House; in size, completeness and furnishing it stands alone. This house is a monument of the Early Georgian period, and of the Whig conviction that the liberties and glories of ancient Rome were revived in England under their rule and influence. While its Augustan dignity represents Whig ideals, the perfection of its classical ornament and proportions shows the mind of a connoisseur.

At the age of ten, Thomas Coke inherited great Norfolk estates. Five

Holkham Hall; Lord Leicester's garden front

years later, in 1712, he started on his Grand Tour and in Italy he collected books, drawings, paintings and sculpture with an extraordinarily mature taste. He consorted with connoisseurs and artists; he studied buildings, concluding that Michelangelo knew nothing about architecture; and he met his countryman, William Kent, who was studying to be a painter. Coke determined to build a house worthy of his works of art. The site chosen was, according to Lord Hervey, 'a most unpleasant place', a windswept heath overlooking the North Sea. Tree planting began in 1720, but the foundations of the house were delayed until 1735 and the interior was still unfinished when, as Earl of Leicester, Coke died in 1759.

The design was due to the famous Palladian triumvirate, Lord Burlington, Lord Leicester and William Kent; but every detail was checked or altered by Leicester himself. The vast centre block was not for everyday use but for 'state and parade'. Its four wings contained, respectively, the kitchen; visitors' rooms; the family apartment, including the Library; and the chapel. Palladio had built many of the Veneto villas of brick, and accordingly, in the absence of stone, brick was baked in the park, of a pale colour that looks from a distance like stone. Thirty different moulds were needed for the rusticated basement storey. Above this are the state rooms on the piano nobile. Plate glass has recently been replaced by barred sashes; the original glazing bars were gilded and burnished. The garden front with its fine portico survives hardly altered, but on the entrance side a Victorian *porte cochère*, a modern convenience, interferes with the original intentions.

The Hall is one of the most striking in any English house. It is based on a cube, and its richness comes from the Derbyshire alabaster, ivory, purple and green, used for the columns and lower walls. Arthur Young said that it all resembled a great bath waiting to be filled. Every detail relies on some classical authority (or that of Inigo Jones); the columns and frieze, for instance, are taken from the Temple of Fortuna Virilis in Rome. At one time a statue of Jupiter was intended to stand at the foot of the stairs that lead to the apse and Saloon.

State Rooms follow in sequence as though pre-ordained by laws of nature. Their proportions, taste and magnificence were highly praised by Sir William Chambers. The Dining Room leads into the Sculpture Gallery, an enlarged version of Lord Burlington's Gallery at Chiswick House, with antique marble statues placed in niches. The Garden front has three main rooms, the coved Saloon at the centre, all hung with crimson Genoese velvet, and with gilded ceilings and doorcases. Numerous gilded chairs and sofas, all covered in velvet, and the side tables were designed by William Kent; the magnificent pier glasses are contemporary, but French and other furniture has been added. Old master paintings include landscapes by Claude and Poussin, and the superb *Holy Family* by Rubens. As for the portraits, two are by Van Dyck, and there are two fine paintings of the young 'Coke of Norfolk' (whom we meet presently), by Batoni and Gainsborough.

The small Landscape Room is entirely hung with Italian landscapes by Claude, Poussin and Gaspard. It was originally part of the Great Apartment which extends all along the north side, consisting of two Bedrooms, two Dressing Rooms, Closet and Ante Room. The great bed is hung with red and olive green velvet and the walls have Brussels tapestries of the *Continents*; the Ante Room has superb Mortlake tapestries of the *Seasons*. In the Apartment there are two portraits of Leicester himself. One, by Richardson, shows him robed as a Knight of the Bath; the other, of a solemnly wigged young man, was painted in Italy by his friend Trevisani. There are plenty more Italian paintings, but the most interesting is a contemporary copy of Michelangelo's *Battle of Anghiari*. Designed in 1504, the work was intended for the Palazzo Vecchio in Florence, but the full-size cartoon is lost and this reduced copy is the best record to survive.

Despite his undoubted taste and scholarship, Lord Leicester had a convivial nature much given to drinking, hunting and cockfighting.

Holkham Hall; left: *the Palladian Hall;* right: *the Sculpture Gallery; (see also p. 15)*

Roubiliac's portrait bust shows the swollen features of his old age. Edward, his son and heir, disappointing and dissolute, predeceased him and in 1759 the property devolved on a nephew. However, Lady Leicester retained a life interest and remained hostile to the next generation. 'Young man,' she said to the young Thomas Coke, 'it is probable that one day you will be master of this house, but understand that I will live as long as I can.' She did so until 1775. Thomas Coke then lived here for sixty-five years. A staunch Whig and reformer, his principal interest was in the estate and the improvement of agriculture. Late in life he too was created Earl of Leicester, but his enduring title is 'Coke of Norfolk'. Fortunately it has always been understood that the Palladian house admitted of little improvement, and so it remains today as close as possible to its original state.

Some of the formal avenues planted in the 1720s are still recognisable, but the park was modified by Capability Brown, and considerably enlarged by Coke of Norfolk. The terrace garden is by Nesfield, and its fountain with *Perseus and Andromeda* is by Charles Smith. The great obelisk visible from here was designed by William Kent and erected in 1729. Corresponding to it on the entrance front, a vast columned monument was raised to Coke of Norfolk in 1845, for which £4,000 was subscribed by his tenants.

Holme Pierrepont Hall, Nottinghamshire
(Mr Robin Brackenbury)

Four miles east of Nottingham (A52)

This ancient property belonged to the Manvers family and came by marriage to Henry de Pierrepont in 1288. Pierrepont tombs in alabaster are a feature of the adjoining church. Today the house consists of the gatehouse range of a late mediaeval building, and its internal courtyard flanked by wings that have been greatly altered at different periods. The main (north) range included the hall: it was enlarged in the 17th century but demolished during the 1730s. The Pierreponts became, for a while, Dukes of Kingston and from the late 17th century they resided at Thoresby, keeping Holme Pierrepont as an alternative house to be used, for instance, by elder sons. When the present Thoresby Hall was being built during the 1860s, the 3rd Earl Manvers lived here, and the formal garden in the courtyard was laid out in 1875.

The house shows work of some three centuries. The front has kept its brickwork of *circa* 1510 (the bricks having come, apparently, from Norfolk) but the crenellated parapet was raised in the early 19th century. Behind it there survives intact a fine 15th-century roof, with trusses and cusped braces (the cusping is said to be unique in the East Midlands). These timbers run the whole length of the front, and were only discovered during recent restorations. The grand Staircase, with elaborately carved floral panels, dates from the time of Charles II and must have come from the demolished hall range. The rooms have Tudor doorways and fireplaces and old oak furniture; some rooms are still in process of restoration.

Holme Pierrepont Hall

After being requisitioned during two wars, the house was left a wreck and dry rot was flourishing. It was rescued by Lady Sibell Argles, a daughter of the 4th Lord Manvers, who lived here until 1968. The wife of the present owner is a descendant of the 3rd Earl Manvers, and thus of the original Pierreponts.

Honington Hall, Warwickshire
(Sir John Wiggin, Bart., M.C.)

A mile north of Shipston on Stour (A34)

To many people Honington will seem to be the 'perfect' English country house: dignified in conception, comfortable in scale, and secluded in a park, with the village church almost at the door and the River Stour flowing just below the garden. The house, built by Sir Henry Parker in the early 1680s, is of warm brick dressed with stone and has all the modest assurance of its period. Probably it once had casement windows, but the niches that hold marble busts of the twelve Caesars seem to be original and are an unexpectedly metropolitan touch. The church was remodelled at about the same time. Like that at Euston, it is a 'Wren' City church in a country setting. A fine monument to Sir Henry and his son stands against the west wall, and it is unfortunate that nothing is known of the architects or craftsmen that he employed.

In 1737 the property was sold to Joseph Townsend who remodelled both the house and its setting. What distinguishes the interior is the marvellous plasterwork. The Hall has an arabesque ceiling with a sunburst and representations of the *Elements*. On the end walls there are two Trojan scenes of Aeneas and four panels of the *Arts*, besides some splendidly rococo brackets. Aurora scatters her morning flowers on the Boudoir ceiling – an odd event in a room that faces south-west. The plasterer may have been Charles Stanley, an Anglo-Danish sculptor who left England in 1747.

Honington Hall; left: *plasterwork in the Saloon, and* right: *plasterwork in the Hall*

Even more exciting is the octagonal Saloon, which was constructed about 1751–2 where previously there had been a staircase. It was designed by John Freeman, an amateur (i.e. gentleman) architect who was rather at logger-heads with the executant architect, William Jones. With its high dome and imposing doorcases, all the basic ideas are Palladian; but Jones would not be restrained from adding the looking glasses and corner 'drops' of wildest rococo that give the room its particular interest. The lower drops have been identified by John Cornforth as representing the Elements and Seasons, but those in the dome remain a mystery. Recently the whole house was found to be active with dry rot and very extensive repairs had to be carried out. At the same time the original colour scheme of the Saloon was renewed, in blues, whites and touches of gilding on the carved window frames.

At one side of the house, under two massive chimneys, a polygonal loggia was added, and on the garden front the Doric temple probably dates from *c.*1760. Against the principal front, the curved arcading (its opposite fellow having been removed long since) conceals the stable court and a very fine 17th-century door hood. The stable block, of limestone and lias, is earlier than the house, and there is an octagonal dovecote close by.

Houghton Hall, Norfolk
(The Marquess of Cholmondley)

Between King's Lynn and Fakenham (A148)

Houghton Hall was built, decorated and furnished between 1722 and 1735 by Robert Walpole, first Prime Minister of England and Earl of Orford. What he created survives, with the exception of his picture collection which was later sold to Catherine the Great of Russia. Walpole's architect was Colen Campbell, with Thomas Ripley as executant, but Gibbs had a hand too and substituted domes at the four corners for pedimented towers à la

Wilton. These enhance the composition by giving it a warmer continental air. In 1727 Walpole turned to William Kent for the interior decoration, including furniture and painted ceilings. The result is the most complete and sumptuous Palladian house in England.

Walpole's grandson, the 3rd Earl of Orford and a near-lunatic, besides selling the pictures allowed the house and grounds to fall into disrepair. When he died in 1791, Horace Walpole inherited but was too old to leave Strawberry Hill. On his death six years later, Houghton passed to his great-nephew, the 1st Marquess of Cholmondley. It now belongs to the 6th Marquess, whose parents restored the house in this century and made good the gaps with paintings, French furniture and Sèvres porcelain from the collection of Sir Philip Sassoon. It scarcely has to be said that everything at Houghton is of the highest quality.

The exterior, faced in Aislaby stone, brought by sea from Whitby, is coolly perfect. Above the central window on the Entrance Front triumphantly recline statues of Neptune and Britannia by Rysbrack. The Garden Front has an attached portico with a richly carved pediment. Flanking pavilions, connected to the main block by Tuscan colonnades, contained the kitchen and picture gallery. The stables form a large detached quadrangle to one side and are faced in brown carstone which forms an effective contrast marking their humbler status. Set in a vast park laid out by Bridgeman, this vice-regal seat is a noble demonstration of Britain's aspirations to Great Power status in the early eighteenth century.

From an unassuming basement the Great Staircase, with a banister of the recently introduced mahogany, mounts to the state apartments on the piano nobile. In the centre of the well, on a tall Tuscan pedestal designed by Kent, is a bronze gladiator by Le Sueur presented to Walpole by the architect Earl of Pembroke. The walls are decorated in grisaille by Kent.

Houghton Hall; left: *the Hall, designed by William Kent, and* right: *the White Drawing Room; (see also colour plate 10)*

Through the Common Parlour, with its family portraits, is the Stone Hall. Few rooms manage such perfect and magnificent elaboration of detail within overall architectural control. It is a cube of forty feet, lined with finest ashlar and adorned with rich carving, particularly Rysbrack's heroic chimneypiece. The full-blooded stucco ceiling by Artari has a frieze of gambolling putti some of whose little legs dangle over the cornice. The contents are no less distinguished. The bronze Laocoon by Girardon was a present from the Pope. A well-known portrait of Sir Robert with his hounds, by Wootton, stands near his bust (by Rysbrack). The chairs, made for the room, retain their original velvet upholstery, as do most others in the house.

The rest of the state rooms sustain this level of magnificence. The Marble Parlour, still used as the dining room, has a further Rysbrack chimneypiece, serving alcoves of white and mauve marble and two full-length portraits of Walpole by Kneller and Van Loo. The Cabinet Room is hung with a ravishing blue-ground Chinese paper while the adjoining bedroom has a magnificent Italian needlework bed in which the future Holy Roman Emperor, Francis I, slept in 1731. The Tapestry Room has a unique set of Mortlake tapestries woven in gold thread with Stuart portraits, while the Green Velvet Bedchamber has a sublime bed designed by Kent with architectural needlework and a large cockleshell on the headboard. The White Drawing Room introduces a Louis XVI note with straw and terracotta Spitalfields silk hangings, pastels by Rosalba Carriera of Horace Walpole and his brothers, and French furniture.

The climax of the house is the Saloon, on axis with the hall. The walls are lined with original crimson Genoa velvet while the deeply coved ceiling has gold mosaic painting by Kent who also designed the gilt sofas, stools, pier tablets and glasses. Over the chimneypiece is a portrait by Roesslin of Catherine the Great, given to the 3rd Earl when he sold her his grandfather's pictures, a loss which has been amply atoned for by the piety of our own century.

Hutton-in-the-Forest, Cumbria
(The Lord Inglewood)

Six miles north-west of Penrith (B5305)

At the end of the drive one is confronted with an L-shaped house of marked character. Though its differing components bridge five centuries, the almost bewildering diversity of taste and style is stimulating. This diversity reflects the contributions of the three families which have been associated with Hutton: the de Hotons who arrived in the late 13th century; the Fletchers, newly-rich men from Cockermouth, to whom the Hotons sold the property in 1606; and the Vanes, forebears of the present owner, to whom it passed by descent in about 1720.

Oddly enough little change was made in the 18th century, and the house is chiefly notable for the highly unusual contributions made in the 17th century and for Salvin's 19th-century additions. The big crenellated sand-

Hutton-in-the-Forest

stone tower that terminates, like an exclamation mark, the main range to the south is Salvin's. Though he did further work at Hutton in the second half of the 19th century, the tower dates from the late 1820s when the architect had just launched on the long career which was to lay so vast a weight of stone on the English countryside. Adjoining Salvin's sandstone tower, rises a contrasting centrepiece of about 1680 in pale limestone. A crowded, rich, indeed almost a swaggering affair, with broken segmental or triangular pediments over the windows, and a coat of arms with swirling draperies set below the cornice, it is by Edward Addison, a little-known Cumbrian architect. Though some of his classical detail may not be text book, he clearly enjoyed his work, as does the visitor today.

This Baroque facade abuts on the oldest part of the castle, a 14th-century Pele tower. As indicated by the proliferation of Pele towers near the Border, Scottish forays were once a constant preoccupation, and such fortified keeps were a necessity in Cumbria until the end of the Middle Ages.

The Hutton Pele, which owes its later battlements, turret and windows, to Salvin, was perhaps never very imposing. Since about 1645 it has also been partly obscured by the attractive and singular wing (forming the upright of the letter L) which buts against it. The wing contains on the upper floor a Long Gallery, an architectural form always uncommon in the North and by the middle of the 17th century somewhat out of date; below stretches an arcaded loggia that was originally unglazed. The front of the wing is broken by a porch-bay on extraordinary pillars composed of clustered shafts. Looking as though they had come straight out of a 13th-century church, they are, for their time, a striking example of mediaevalism.

Entering the house, one finds oneself in a Hall, with a display of arms, whose barrel-vaulted ceiling betrays that it was once the ground floor of the old Pele tower. The Long Gallery was done over in the 19th century when it lost its Jacobean decoration; but high-backed caned chairs, and blue and white china standing on simple oak furniture, give it charm. One of the Fletcher portraits in the Gallery depicts Sir George who was responsible for the Baroque facade in the centre of the house. Behind that facade, there must once have been elaborate Carolean decoration, but its character can now be guessed only from the bold but rustic staircase panels, with well-fleshed amorini clambering among acanthus leaves (the panels are reset in a later 19th-century staircase). On the landing above, similar bold and vaguely lubricious children disport themselves on a Mortlake tapestry of the time, one of the series known as *The Playing Boys*.

In Salvin's big keep-like tower, the Drawing Room retains a nice Victorian flavour: a clutter of furniture, with both good pieces and entertaining trifles like fans improbably mounted with the skins of exotic birds. In the cabinets, the china positively jostles, and there is a collection of Chinese 18th-century armorial porcelain, decorated in black and white in the European taste. The general effect, on a more modest scale, recalls the Victorian rooms at Holker Hall in this same county. The Dining Room is hung with Vane portraits. There is naturally (for the Lancastrian firm makes its contribution to almost every Northern house of note) a Gillow dining table, and also a set of boldly carved mid-18th-century chairs.

The terraces south of the house, where the ground falls away with a generous sweep, were first laid out in the late 17th century and appear on a Kip engraving of 1702.

Ightham Mote, Kent
(Mr C. H. Robinson)

South of Ivy Hatch, five miles east of Sevenoaks

The place derives its name from the old word 'moot', a meeting place where council is held, and not from its protective moat. Yet if any house evokes a 'moated grange', and the romantic associations that the phrase has acquired, it is Ightham. Set in a silent hollow, half encircled by woodland, the manor house seems far removed from this century and its preoccupations, an untroubled survival from the late Middle Ages. Beautiful yet unassuming, Ightham made no mark in history; it knew no great names or great events, and almost no change after the 16th century. A generation ago, when the house seemed gravely at risk, the present owner, a public-spirited Canadian, fell in love with it. One can only hope that its future is now secure.

Both the north and south fronts prettily combine timbered upper storeys that overhang the moat, with ragstone walls below. The only post-Renaissance feature is a single Venetian window. The Entrance Front, with arched or cusped windows of about 1500, is all rough undressed stone. The only exception is the crenellated brick parapet, probably some hundred years later, that crowns the central gatehouse. In the gatehouse wall the squint survives that enabled the porter to scrutinise approaching visitors.

Ightham Mote (also illustrated on p. 29)

Crossing the moat and pushing open the wicket, set in a 16th-century gate of silvery oak with linenfold panelling, one steps into the quiet cobbled courtyard. Opposite lies the earliest part of the house, a stone hall of about 1340 with its original doorway; the big window of five cusped lights was inserted some hundred and fifty years later. Occupying the site of the solar, the adjoining timber-framed building, with oriel window and decoratively carved bargeboards to the gables, is 16th century. So is the timbered north range with a loggia which was unglazed until recent times. To the right of the hall, the windows of the south range introduce a Gothic revival note that is surprisingly acceptable. Even the timbered and gabled kennel intended to house some huge 19th-century mastiff has its appeal.

The Hall is the most important feature of the interior. The arches of the 14th-century roof rest on corbels, rendered as crouching figures, and carved with verve and imagination. There was apparently never a screens passage, but the Gothic doorways to kitchen and buttery survive. When the latter was unblocked the skeleton of a seated female figure was found in the thickness of the wall. The large cusped window was added in about 1500, but the two-light window with a transom is original 14th century and has rebates for fitted shutters. In another early window in the undercroft a shutter can be seen in place. The fireplace is 16th century, but the panelling with a well-carved frieze is by Norman Shaw (1872), and one of the few 19th-century importations at Ightham.

The solar and the old chapel, which has kept its 14th-century doorway, are now reached by a sturdy Jacobean staircase. A squint in the solar enabled the master of the house to attend Mass unseen. The room now has a Tudor roof of unusual construction in that the kingpost rests on two intersecting tie beams. Nearby is a further chapel installed in the early 16th century. Its attraction derives from its wooden barrel roof, with painted decoration incorporating the Tudor rose and the pomegranate of Aragon, and from its woodwork. The linenfold panelling of the sanctuary, the pulpit, the screen, and pews with poppyhead finials, are all of the period.

The last interesting room, the Drawing Room, has an enormous lavishly carved Jacobean fireplace and overmantel, framed by Ionic and Corinthian columns, and a frieze of the same period. The walls are hung with Chinese 18th-century wallpaper. This is the room with the Venetian window, and from it there is a prospect across a wide lawn to vast cedars and the woodland rising beyond.

Ingatestone Hall, Essex
(The Lord Petre)

Between Brentwood and Chelmsford (B1102)

The Benedictine nuns of Barking Abbey had an estate here before the Norman Conquest. In 1539, a month after their suppression, Ingatestone was bought by one of Thomas Cromwell's deputies, William Petre, son of a wealthy tanner from Devon. Petre subsequently was knighted and became Secretary of State under Henry VIII, Edward VI and Queen Mary, thus showing a clever gift for survival. His sympathies finally turned back to Rome, and he went so far as to have his purchase of church property confirmed by Papal Bull in 1555. Sir William and his wife share a fine alabaster tomb in Ingatestone church (attributed to William Cure). The 4th Lord Petre, having already suffered much under the Commonwealth, died in the Tower where he was confined without trial after the Titus Oates Plot. The family has remained Catholic.

The house was built shortly after 1539, when Sir William described the old manorial hall as an 'olde house scant mete for a fermor to dwell upon'. Old plans show the building to have been approached through two courts. The Tudor service dwellings still stand, though refaced in timber, plastered and washed, the Gatehouse supporting an 18th-century clock tower. Of the house itself, only three sides remain because the west range, including the hall, was removed in the 18th century. In 1770 Thorndon Hall, six miles away, became the family's seat until it was destroyed by fire a hundred years later. Meanwhile the remaining three-quarters of Ingatestone Hall was divided as dwellings for Catholic families and their chaplain. After 1918 the 17th Lord Petre returned here, having carefully restored the house to its present homogeneous state. The brickwork, patched but not pickled, has an attractive texture and much old work can be seen in the crow-stepped gables and chimney stacks. Yet the windows seem generally too large and regular, too square and symmetrical to be genuinely Tudor.

The part open to the public is the north wing and Gallery. This is leased to Essex County Council, whose Records Office mount an annual exhibition of documents and photographs. The panelling is Tudor, with some Renaissance carving, but has been cut and patched. The Long Gallery runs above the east range. In 1566 it was described as 'fayr' and 'stately', and it retains some armorial glass, but the timber roof is hidden by a flat ceiling. The furniture includes marquetry commodes and an unusually fine set of Regency tables that came from Thorndon. A long set of family portraits

Ingatestone Hall

runs from Sir William to the 12th Lord Petre. The best are by Romney and Raeburn, while the distinctive family nose persists to the end. Two paintings are specially interesting for their literary associations. Here is Arabella Fermor, with her long hair, and close by is the young and audacious 7th Lord Petre who, in 1712, stole a lock of it. The family feud that resulted was amicably resolved by Pope's mock-heroic poem, *The Rape of the Lock*.

Ixworth Abbey, Suffolk
(Mrs Alan Rowe)

Behind Ixworth church, six miles north-east of Bury St Edmunds (A143)

A Priory was founded here in 1172 by Sir Richard Blount for thirteen Augustine Canons, and held manorial rights over the village. At the Dissolution it was granted to Richard Cuddington, in exchange for Cuddington in Surrey where Henry VIII had decided to build his Nonsuch Palace. The Priory soon became known as 'Abbey'. The principal alterations have been its conversion and use as a dwelling house in the 16th century; additions by the Nortons after 1680; and further additions by the Norton-Cartwrights (a branch of the Aynhoe family) in 1820. Left empty and badly neglected after the Second World War, the house was in piteous condition when saved from demolition by its courageous owner.

Of the Norman church 224 feet in length, only some foundations remain. The cloister too has gone. However, the undercroft of the Dormitory survives complete, beautifully pillared and vaulted with round arches, all of chalk. This was built around 1200, by the same team who worked at Anglesey Abbey near Cambridge. One end was walled off for the Prior's use; the north end leads to the Slype, also vaulted but slightly later in style. The Dormitory above has been remodelled into various rooms, but recently a small window was discovered with an internal shaft for the Dormitory bell-rope at its apex, while the surrounding plaster has false masonry decoration. This window was blocked during the 15th century when a new Prior's

Ixworth Abbey; the monastic Undercroft

lodging was built, a two-storey structure of lofty rooms with closely spaced beams (now in process of restoration). At the other side of the Dormitory building, the Refectory or Frater is divided into North Hall and Drawing Room, and has the 16th-century insertion of a floor. Stone piers that once flanked the reading desk have been found in the thickness of the outside wall.

The old windows have been changed or hidden by subsequent alterations, and panelling and doors are of various dates. The best of the later work is in the Entrance Hall, built about 1690 over the drain of the reredorter. The staircase is a fine and plain construction of oak. Facing it is a large doorway, pedimented, rusticated, and with carved flower panels, in the style of Daniel Marot. The armorial glass of the Norton-Cartwrights was painted by one of the ladies in the family in the last century, and incorrectly pieced together by the local smith.

Kedleston Hall, Derbyshire
(The Viscount Scarsdale)

Four miles north-west of Derby (from A52)

The Curzons have lived at Kedleston for nearly nine hundred years. When Sir Nathaniel Curzon succeeded as 3rd Baronet in 1758 he had already begun to plan the new house, with the intention of creating a setting worthy of his Italian paintings. This involved demolishing the old house, and removing the village a mile or so. His building was well advanced in 1761 when he was ennobled as 1st Baron Scarsdale.

The front of the house should be seen from the lake below. It is vast, yet so quiet and unostentatious that its grandeur needs time to register. No feature is particularly original, yet the whole effect is overpowering. The end pavilions, each large enough in itself to be a Palladian villa, are the earliest part of the design and were begun by Matthew Brettingham who was also working on Lord Leicester's Holkham; 'Sir Nat' appears to have wanted something on a comparable scale. By means of sweeping corridors they are joined to the porticoed central block, which was begun to the design of James Paine in 1760; for, as usual, Brettingham was passed over, and his ideas improved upon by an architect of greater standing. By now Robert Adam had also appeared on the scene, and Paine retired shortly after, saying gracefully that he had too many commitments elsewhere.

Adam set out deliberately to gain clients at no matter what cost to his rivals, and here as at Harewood he was eventually successful. But he gave his patrons no cause for regret, and Kedleston shows all the genius and excitement of his early style. The garden front, entirely Adam's, is monumental and dynamic. The centre has the form of a Roman triumphal arch, while the curving dome and staircase give contrast and 'movement'. Yet sadly his full intention was not realised: the flanking corridors and pavilions were never begun. It seems that Curzon's money had at last run out.

For the inspiration of the Hall we are surely indebted to Brettingham, for its magnificent peristyle of alabaster columns with statues behind was certainly inspired by Holkham. But Curzon found the overhead lighting rather chilling, as indeed it is, and he made repeated attempts to cheer up the room. The columns were fluted (against the advice of Adam), the walls and doors painted with classical scenes, and finally the ceiling worked in pretty stucco (not actually by Adam) and the chimneypieces topped by limp neoclassical virgins. Beyond the Hall is Adam's Saloon, a noble circular Roman temple with a lofty coffered dome and great niches below. It scarcely resembles a room, and was in fact designed to hold sculpture. The green scagliola doorcases are by Bartoli.

Kedleston Hall; left: *the Drawing Room, by Robert Adam and* right: *the Hall; (see also colour plate 11)*

To the left are three great rooms devoted, it has been suggested, to music, painting and literature. Adam had designed these ceilings as early as 1760, and their details are on a larger scale than in his more mature works. A blue-john chimneypiece and the alabaster door and window cases in the Drawing Room show these Derbyshire stones to fine advantage. The coved ceiling was Adam's improvement on Paine's original rectangular design. The paintings remain today as Sir Nathaniel and Adam arranged them; and gorgeous they are, with turbulent works by Carracci and Luca Giordano and others by Cuyp and Mompers (to name but a few). Furniture has become somewhat profuse, and few English works can rival the four gilded sofas, designed and made by John Linnell for the Great Drawing Room. They are carved with merfolk and dolphins, robust, Baroque surely, and oddly Venetian in appearance.

The right-hand side of the house contains the Great Apartment, though it is not so great as that at Holkham. Here are the family portraits which, by comparison with other contents, appear rather homely. The furniture is outstanding, particularly the gilded chairs, and the state bed and pier glasses carved with palm trees and made by James Gravenor. Of all the rooms it is the Dining Room that is most recognisably 'Adam', and Horace Walpole thought it the most tasteful in the house. Its intricate ceiling has lately been redecorated according to the original drawings. Adam designed the sideboards in the apse to show off the silver. On the dining table are blue-john urns, and an ormolu tripod or *athénienne* designed by James Stuart. (We may also note that Stuart had made designs for the interior and sideboard in 1758, which Adam had no difficulty in suppressing.) The chimneypiece, by the Danish sculptor Michael Spang, has figures of Ceres and Bacchus, and many of the fine paintings are somehow concerned with food. In the adjoining corridor there are portraits of Lord Curzon of Kedleston, the supremely dignified Viceroy of India, and of other recent members of the family.

This seat, one of the finest of its century, was built and furnished within seven years by a single country squire, and, moreover, by one who was not outstandingly rich. Horace Walpole remarked that it was 'too expensive for Lord Scarsdale's estate'. Yet the work did not stop with the house. The park was landscaped, for once not by Capability Brown; at the lake Adam built the cascade bridge which might have stepped out of a Piranesi engraving, and the delectable boat house and fishing house. If anything of this Georgian ensemble has to be dispersed it will be to the enduring shame of our age.

Kentwell Hall, Suffolk
(Mr and Mrs J. Patrick Phillips)

Just north of Long Melford (A134)

The two great houses in Long Melford, an unforgettable Suffolk village, are almost twins. Melford Hall, a National Trust property, is slightly the junior and has had more alterations. Kentwell lies further north and, as is recorded in Domesday Book, was once attached to a separate village. The lime avenue, nearly a mile long, is three hundred years old. At the end of it the house bursts into full view: a large open courtyard with walls all of brick, and a roof-line punctuated by dormers, chimneys and paired staircase towers. Water is always an added attraction to an old house, and the wide moat is crossed by an old bridge.

The Clopton family were at Kentwell in 1382. This house was built by Sir Thomas Clopton, whose mother's will of 1563 refers to the 'new mansion house'. Building may have continued over several decades, but the style is mid–Tudor rather than Elizabethan, and the central doorway and window mullions are arched. They are of moulded brick but were faced with stucco to resemble stone. The oriel window to the Great Hall is on the right, and there is another oriel to the left whose original purpose is not clear. Some of the stained glass evidently came from Melford church, but there is armorial glass of different dates from the 15th century onwards. The lead pipes are cast with the arms of Clopton, D'Ewes and D'Arcy, the families to which the house descended. Sir Thomas D'Arcy sold it in 1676, and the avenue was planted two years later. The main staircase, though not in its original position, is as old as the avenue; the Great Hall chimneypiece and some doorcases are early Georgian.

In 1827 a fire gutted the centre block, but the brickwork survived. A new owner, Robert Hart Logan, put the rebuilding in the hands of Thomas Hopper, who, as a versatile romantic, was able to manage any style with ease. His work here is contemporary with the 'Norman' Penrhyn Castle, but at Kentwell he chose to be Elizabethan. The Great Hall has a coved ceiling and a minstrels' gallery. Better still is the Dining Room with its knobbled panelling – actually made of plaster and grained to resemble oak and walnut – a coffered ceiling and a Gothic chimneypiece carved from dove marble. The original decoration of the upper walls, a bronze trellis on crimson,

Kentwell Hall

survives under later paint. These rooms are now (1978) about to be restored. The reception rooms in the west wing are also Hopper's. A plaster cornice contains green men, and the Library is dominated by the smartest of scagliola columns.

When Patrick Phillips bought Kentwell in 1971 it was seriously dilapidated. Taking up an apparently impossible challenge, he and his wife have repaired the roof and brickwork, and, as their long-term work of restoration proceeds, bathrooms are ingeniously fitted in where needed. The moat has been dredged and sifted for relics and broken pottery, the grounds have emerged from jungle conditions and the old walled garden and its surrounding fishponds are clean and replanted. The house itself is certainly a beauty from every angle. At one side stands the 'Moat House', a substantial timber and brick building with garderobe shaft discharging into the moat, clearly several decades earlier than the Hall itself. Nearby is a square dovecote retaining its revolving ladder or potence and 574 nesting boxes.

Knebworth House, Hertfordshire
(The Hon. David Lytton Cobbold)

Between Welwyn and Stevenage (A1)

The Bulwer-Lyttons were talented and versatile. The most famous of them, Edward, Lord Lytton, is remembered chiefly for his numerous (but now seldom read) historical novels. He refashioned this pinnacled palace in 1843, the year he published *The Last of the Barons*, and perhaps symbolically it aped the style of a new era, that of Henry VII. Yet under the elaborate stone and stucco something remains of a genuine Henry VII house.

Old Chenepeworde, 'a village on a hill', has long since been removed to a distance, and the church and manor stand in dignified isolation. Sir Robert Lytton bought the house in 1492 and rebuilt it as a courtyard building. Only his hall range now survives, and on the staircase some exposed brick shows the position of the outside wall. The Lyttons were courtly and urbane. There is a portrait of Sir Robert, able and confident, the friend and Privy Councillor of Henry VII, and another of his grandson Sir Rowland, a young buck grasping his tilting lance. When they died out in 1707 they did so in style, and their three last members are recorded by vast Baroque monuments in the church. Meanwhile the Hall had been modernised. The oak screen is of the style of Inigo Jones, while the pine panelling, with its pedimented arch at the dais end, is late 17th-century.

Knebworth passed to a connection by marriage, William Robinson. Since then, three times it has passed through the female line but the name of Lytton has always been preserved. There is a delightful portrait by Hoogstraeten of Colonel Robinson, who had fought for Charles I, wigged and ribboned in the height of Restoration fashion.

Inheriting a dilapidated house from her improvident father in 1811, Elizabeth Bulwer-Lytton decided to demolish three sides of it. The fourth side she Gothicised and cased in stucco, brick being thought unworthy of

Knebworth House; Lord Lytton's baronial seat

a fine house. Mrs Bulwer was a strong character. She quarrelled with the Rector and held her own services which the village dutifully attended, leaving the church empty. She also quarrelled with her youngest son, Edward, over his marriage and, refusing him all financial assistance, helped to wreck it. Edward determined to live as a man of fashion and turned to writing day and night. Within ten years the separation was final. Yet he treasured his mother's memory and directed that her room and personalia be kept intact. Chinese wallpapers in the adjoining rooms also date from Mrs Bulwer's day.

Edward Bulwer-Lytton had known the old house as a child, and later he said that its memory inspired him to write historical romances. Now he caused the garden front to bristle with towers and pinnacles, traceried friezes, gargoyles and heraldry. John Crace designed the interior. The double Staircase is deceptively Jacobethan; but for the 'State Presence Chamber' (now the State Drawing Room), Crace produced the gayest and brightest of Perpendicular Gothic, the chimneypiece and niched over-mantel being its best feature. Henry VII figures in stained glass, and the ceiling is covered with ancestral coats of arms. Much of the furniture in this room was also designed by Crace.

Maclise's portrait of his friend Bulwer-Lytton shows a forty-six-year-old dandy; while in his large historical canvas, *Caxton's Printing Office*, every character was inspired by *The Last of the Barons*. Dickens was a frequent guest here, and he produced and acted in a play in the Hall. Bulwer-Lytton took to politics, became Colonial Secretary and was subsequently created Baron Lytton. His son, the 1st Earl of Lytton, was a notable poet but is more famous as Viceroy of India. The 2nd Earl was Governor of Bengal and

Acting Viceroy of India, and his portrait in Garter robes was painted by his artist brother, the 3rd Earl. Their sister, Lady Emily, married Edwin Lutyens, the Edwardian architect who redesigned some of the rooms – though we cannot applaud his destruction of Bulwer-Lytton's Library. He also simplified Bulwer-Lytton's garden into the present lawns, beds and shaped hedges.

The Earls of Lytton now live in Somerset, and Knebworth passed to Lady Hermione, who married Lord Cobbold. Since 1972 their son has opened the house and grounds, and adapted the approaches to the needs of a modern public. Symbolically perhaps, one overlooks Stevenage New Town. The prominent restaurant building consists of two 16th-century barns that were recently moved bodily from elsewhere on the estate.

Lamport Hall, Northamptonshire
(Lamport Hall Preservation Trust, Ltd)

Between Northampton and Market Harborough (A508)

This county is famous for great houses and the Ishams may claim to be its oldest landed family. They held the manor of Isham, eight miles east of Lamport, after and probably before the Norman Conquest. From 1310 a younger branch lived at Pytchley Hall. John Isham, again a younger son, was a successful trader in the City of London during the brave days of Sir Thomas Gresham, and with his brother he bought the Manor of Lamport in 1560. Eleven years later he left London to become a country squire and manage the estate.

Of course he rebuilt the house, but on a rather modest scale that proved inadequate after eighty years. A Baronetcy was conferred on the family by Charles I. Their fortunes were not vast, and Sir Justinian contented himself with rebuilding one corner of the court to provide a 'High Roome' fit to receive 'des personnes d'honneur'. In spite of all the difficulties during the Civil War and Commonwealth, he gave the commission to John Webb in 1654, and at one time was actually sending instructions from prison. Webb is an elusive architect. He was son-in-law to Inigo Jones, and this five-bay facade, a miniature *palazzo*, is a rare survival of his work. In the high room, now called the Music Hall, Webb's fine chimneypiece survives, carved by Cibber with the Isham swans. Sir Justinian had asked for something in the Flemish manner, but Webb won the day with his Italian style.

Webb advised his patron about paintings, and accordingly Isham bought Van Dyck's *Christ with St John*, and the copy of the same painter's vast *Charles I on Horseback*. The latter was acquired in 1655, and it was perhaps no coincidence that six weeks later its purchaser was arrested and imprisoned. Van Somer's huge *Anne of Denmark* recalls the Queen's visit to Pytchley in 1605. Sir Thomas succeeded in 1675, only to die from smallpox six years later at the age of twenty-four. Meanwhile he had shown a discriminating taste on his Grand Tour and when in Naples had acquired the two vast cabinets with mythologies painted on glass. There are three

Lamport Hall; the centrepiece is by John Webb

portraits of him, by Maratti, Voet and Lely.

Webb's *palazzo* was enlarged after 1732 by Francis Smith of Warwick (who also built the nearby Rectory and restored the church). This work was begun for the 5th Baronet, Sir Justinian, whose monument in the church by Scheemakers should not be missed. The west (left-hand) wing of the house contains the Library, and a wing the other side completes the symmetry. The resulting facade, long, low and regular, is a well-known landmark from the main road. A new staircase was built, and Webb's severe classicism in the Music Hall was replaced by exuberant plasterwork. In the ceiling, the Isham swan is sporting with nymphs and sea-gods, and on the frieze portrait heads alternate with trophies representing the squire's principal interests: hunting, shooting and agriculture; government, law and music. The ceiling was made by John Woolston in 1740. Hudson's portrait of the squire, Sir Edmund, hangs below.

Early 19th-century alterations included the addition of a pediment above Webb's building, new shelves in the Library, and the removal of the Staircase to a new position. Whatever remained of the Elizabethan house was rebuilt later, the present entrance front of 1861 being the design of the prolific Scottish architect, William Burn. This work was done for Sir Charles, who lived here for over fifty years and was responsible for the edifying but rather depressing texts that are inscribed both outside and in. The garden, though now much simplified, was one of his major interests. He seems to have been the first in the now unglorious fashion of gnomes, and his Alpine rockery near the house was a fairy mine, all alive with goblins at work, play and on strike. The little figures were made in Nuremburg, and one is shown in the Hall.

After its wartime occupations by troops and prisoners, part of the house became, until 1958, the headquarters of the County Records Society. The late Sir Gyles Isham was a distinguished art historian and author of a number of articles on local history. Having coped with extensive dry rot, he rearranged the house as it is now, and in its furnishings and unbroken series of portraits it gives a complete record of four hundred years of Isham ownership.

Langton Hall, Leicestershire
(Mrs Louise D. Cullings)

West Langton, four miles north of Market Harborough (B6047)

From this district, where there are no fewer than five Langtons, came a distinguished family of clerics and scholars, best known among whom is Stephen Langton, Archbishop of Canterbury in the time of King John. The Hall at West Langton appears to be the manor recorded in Domesday Book. Remains of a mediaeval wall and bastion at the right of the drive show it to have been a building of some size. The house was largely rebuilt after 1660, this being the approximate date of the right-hand tower and the staircase. The left tower is refaced in Georgian stone. Early in the 19th century the centre block and Hall within were lightly Gothicised. All this has mellowed and blended into a unity.

The house was bought by its present owner in 1933. It contains two surprises. Two Georgian rooms have been papered with lace; and there is a rare collection of antique Chinese furniture, tables and cupboards of classical grace, made of amber-coloured rosewood, that was bought in the East by Mrs Cullings's grandfather.

Langton Hall

The garden overlooks some of England's finest hunting country. Hugo Meynell lived here during the 18th century, and was Master of the Quorn Hunt for nearly fifty years. Later, the Empress Elizabeth of Austria visited Langton from nearby Althorp, and kept her horses in these stables.

Layer Marney Tower, Essex
(Major and Mrs Gerald Charrington)

Seven miles south-west of Colchester (B1022)

The Marneys, who were ancient but not very grand, are known to have held this manor in the 12th century. Their brief glory came with Henry Marney, who was Privy Councillor to Henry VII at an early age. Henry VIII described him as 'a scant well-borne gentleman of no grete lande', gave him many offices and the Order of the Garter. In 1522 he became Lord Privy Seal, and the next year, only six weeks before his death, he was created 1st Baron Marney. John, his son, died two years later and their line was extinct. They came to an end, wrote Avray Tipping in *Country Life* (February 21, 1914), 'not amid the din of the battlefield or the crowds on Tower Hill, but silently in their beds, at the very moment when they seem to be grasping greatness. But for their "tower", standing like a beacon above the Essex flats, they would be forgotten.'

Their tombs in the church are not only of terracotta but modelled in the French Renaissance style, which shows that the Marneys were following the very latest of court fashions. Terracotta had only recently been introduced to England; it was also used for window mullions on the house, of purest Renaissance design, and no exact parallel is known in England or abroad.

Layer Marney Tower

Though only a fragment of what was intended, the Tower (or, rather, Gatehouse) is one of the most interesting buildings of its date. It was obviously designed to surpass the similar but plainer tower at Oxburgh Hall in Norfolk, to whose owners, the Bedingfields, the Marneys were related by marriage. The entrance was through the present garden, and the court, if built, would have been on the parking area. The bowed turrets that flank the gateway are high achievements of late Gothic brickwork; but this florid Gothic exists side by side with the Renaissance window mullions and the crestings at the top. These crestings are moulded with the initials J and C (for John Marney and his wife Christian) with a true lovers' knot, so they can be dated 1723–5.

Inside the gateway the panelling is modern. On the way up the Tower you will pass through a great number of rooms with bow windows and fine views, but some floors are missing, and the walls are now unplastered. Original building extends either side of the Tower, the far wing having been stables with dormitories above. Very similar was the 'Gallery', a separate building that stands in the garden – the original forecourt. Though its windows are modern, the diapered brickwork is Tudor, and inside there is a splendid timbered roof with curious pincer-shaped posts.

The Marneys departed, their Tower passed to different owners, and by the 19th century it was in sad decay. The long wing became a farmhouse, and the centre part was a barn, its timbers rotten and the windows boarded up. Before 1900 a section to the right was rebuilt in unsympathetic materials. However, the whole building was carefully and sensitively restored after 1904 by Walter de Zoete, who also restored the church. The survival of this unique building stands largely to his credit, but his work is continued by the present owners, who bought the house in 1958.

Leighton Hall, Lancashire
(Mr and Mrs R. J. G. Reynolds)

Two miles north of Carnforth (A6)

From the gates, the park slopes to the house below. Built of pale limestone it shines white in the sun and behind rise the blue curves of the Lakeland mountains. A ravishing setting, and just such as would have appealed to the romantic taste of the early 1800s when Leighton assumed its fanciful Gothic character.

About that time a sober facade of 1763 acquired turrets, finials, and a sense of lively movement. The transformation is attributed to Harrison of Chester, or one of the Gillows. As one comes down through the park the facade seems on the east to terminate in a gabled chapel with a tall church-like window. It is characteristic of the spirit of the building that this should be a light-hearted conceit: the ecclesiastical dress conceals utilitarian stables. A projecting wing to the west, with a high tower, added in 1870, only lends further variety to the composition. It was the work of Paley and Austin, then the most sensitive architects in the north-west, who built

Leighton Hall; the Dining Room; (see also illustration on p. 14)

the new block at Holker Hall some twenty miles away.

In 1822, the house was sold to Richard Gillow, grandson of Robert Gillow of Lancaster, first of the famous furniture makers of that name, from whom Mrs Reynolds, the present owner, is descended. Much of the interest of Leighton derives from the quantity of Gillow furniture it contains. One tends to associate such furniture with later pieces produced after the firm established a London branch in 1770, but the Gillows were in business in Lancaster by about 1730, and at Leighton there are a number of mid-Georgian pieces which Richard Gillow must have inherited and brought with him to the house. The most unusual of these is an altar of about 1750 in a small private chapel. The latter incidentally reflects the Catholic tradition of the county. At Leighton that tradition long antedates the present house; since the Reformation every owner but one has subscribed to the Old Faith.

Leighton inside has that indefinable atmosphere which seems to characterise a well-loved house. Apart from the Gillow furniture there is nothing very unusual, but many things that in combination make a country house attractive. The Hall, with delightful Gothic glazing to its porch, has a screen of clustered columns prefacing an elegant stone staircase, curved and cantilevered. Pictures on the staircase depict both the Georgian mansion of 1763, and the Gothic house before the 1870 wing was built. The Dining Room is nearly all Gillow: dining table, sideboard, wine-cooler, and a set of early Gillow dining chairs. Among the family portraits in the Dining Room is one of the first Richard Gillow, son of the founder of the firm, and the wall panelling is inset with early-18th-century painted landscapes. Gillow furniture of note in the Library and Drawing Room includes an early games table, an architect's desk, and a unique cabinet incorporating religious panels and ivory statuettes from Italy. Almost certainly this was made for Mrs Richard Gillow. There are also pleasant 17th- and 18th-century paintings, among them an evocative seascape by Morland.

Letheringham Water Mill, Suffolk
(Mr and Mrs J. W. Hale)

Two miles north-west of Wickham Market

Not really a country house, but a survival of the typical flour mills that once were plentiful along the rivers of East Anglia. There was a mill here before the Norman Conquest, but the present structure is basically early 18th-century, with walls of brick and weather-boarding. The 14-foot water wheel survives, though shorn of its paddles, and at the various levels inside are the chutes for grain and flour. The Mill-house and garden, with land and water fowl and the adjoining Hall form an interesting and attractive rural group.

Letheringham Water Mill

Levens Hall, Cumbria
(Mr Hal Bagot)

Between Kendal and Carnforth (A6)

When the 18th-century fashion for landscaping swept away formal gardens, those which provide the attractive setting of Levens happily were spared. With yew topiary and great hedges of clipped beech, this rare survival still reflects the formal French layout devised in 1690 by Monsieur Beaumont who was gardener to James II at Hampton Court.

By contrast the front of Levens, grey, gabled and irregular, speaks little of formality but much of the passage of time. Like so many houses in the North, Levens began as a fortified Pele and the solid tower to the right of the entrance marks its site. But the character of the facade is now Elizabethan and dates, as does most of the house, from 1580 when it came into the possession of James Bellingham, later knighted by James I. Little has been altered since, though the south front was added something over a hundred years later, as was the doorway on the entrance front, when a new owner, Colonel James Graham, bought the property.

The outstanding feature of the house is the series of rooms on the ground floor lavishly decorated after 1580 with panelling, richly carved over-mantels, and moulded plaster ceilings. In its elaboration the work is comparable to that carried out a few miles away, and a few years earlier, at Sizergh Castle. The effect of these rooms owes much to the fact that, though Levens has been twice sold since 1580, it passed in each case to a kinsman and the contents were never dispersed. The furnishings are thus an historic accumulation, and not that very different thing, a collection.

The Great Hall, which the visitor first enters, has a deep plaster frieze depicting animals and heraldic shields in panels between fluted pilasters, and incorporating over the fireplace the arms of Queen Elizabeth. On the panelling hang Charles II wall sconces, a Florentine 15th-century Madonna and Child, a Flemish painting of the same subject, and the pistols of Sir James Bellingham who decorated the room (dated 1601 they are among the earliest English-made pistols in existence). There are also many family relics, such as an engraved collar that adorned one of Charles II's dogs, and

Levens Hall from the topiary garden

the gloves removed from Wellington's hands by the ancestress of the present owner of Levens when the Duke entered Paris in triumph after Waterloo. A writing cabinet made for Colonel Graham is by Gerreit Jensen who worked extensively for the Court after 1688. The wide staircase rising from the south-west corner of the Hall is Colonel Graham's addition of the late 17th century.

The decoration of the Drawing Room, dated 1595, is a bewilderingly rich example of late Elizabethan taste: mullioned windows with heraldic glass, geometrical plasterwork ceilings, panelling enclosing diamond lozenges, and exuberantly carved doorcases and overmantel. The last is an astonishing affair, incorporating the three classical orders and deeply-cut heraldic panels. However, much of the furniture must have been acquired by Colonel Graham. Thus (apart from two swirling rococo torchères) it is predominantly 1690–1700 and includes such things as late Stuart mirrors, chairs and tables, and William and Mary chairs in the florid style of Daniel Marot. There are portraits of James Graham and his wife by Lely, of his daughter by Hudson, and not least there is an excellent seascape by Cotman. In the Small Drawing Room that adjoins, the naturalistically carved chimneypiece well expresses the Elizabethan passion for allegory: on either side Samson and Hercules, prototypes of strength, flank panels with figures emblematic of the Senses, the Seasons and the Elements. The whole talkative composition is topped by Bellingham's arms and arabesque strapwork within a broken pediment.

The Dining Room has another of Bellingham's plaster ceilings and a chimneypiece, inlaid with bog oak and holly, dated 1586. The stamped Cordova leather on the walls was introduced by Colonel Graham at the end of the 17th century. The Colonel no doubt also bought the fine late Stuart chairs with scrolled legs and stretchers, and the torchères inlaid with seaweed marquetry.

Littlecote, Wiltshire
(Mr D. S. Wills)

Three miles north-west of Hungerford (A4 and A419)

The house belies its name, the first and enduring impression being of a building of enormous size. Littlecote lies deep in the woods near the edge of the Wiltshire chalk, and the River Kennett flows placidly through the garden. There have not been many alterations to the structure since the Tudor age. The symmetrical brick entrance front of the 1590s is in the familiar Elizabethan shape of E, but pulled out to a great width. The older garden or north side, mostly of flint, is longer still. Less than half of it is taken up by what could easily be a complete Tudor house, and, moreover, one of ample proportions. The whole of the first floor of this section is taken up by the Long Gallery. To the right, among the irregular walls and roofs facing the garden, there remains part of the earlier house of about 1500.

The most famous of the Littlecote legends concerns its haunted rooms.

The estate had passed by marriage to the Darrell family in 1415, and it descended to William, or 'Wild' Darrell. The story tells how in 1575 Mother Barnes, a midwife, was wakened one stormy night, blindfolded and taken many miles to deliver a child, which 'a tall, slender gentleman' immediately flung on the fire. The story became known, the gentleman identified, and 'Wild' Darrell was tried for murder before Sir John Popham. Darrell was convicted but released from his sentence; and, dying without heirs in 1589, he left the entire property to Popham. John Aubrey is one who tells the story, saying that the woman in labour was Darrell's 'Ladie's waiting woman'. She is said to walk still, looking for her child.

Wild Darrell built the Long Gallery, which adjoins the haunted bedrooms. It is 110 feet long, and the plaster frieze has a repeating design made from moulds three feet square. The Darrell crest alternates with trees, birds and animals whose symbolism is not yet understood.

Soon after receiving his inheritance, Popham became Lord Chief Justice and a great person. Aubrey described him, from the portrait here, as 'a huge, heavie, ugly man'. He is said to have revived brick building in London, and the entrance front at Littlecote, all of two-inch brick, has survived in excellent state. Through industry, inheritance, and subsequent marriages the family became enormously rich. There was at least one rowdy member who died with great debts, but otherwise the Puritan persuasion of the family is reflected in the generally solemn character of their house. Colonel Alexander Popham, whose equestrian portrait hangs in the Great Hall, was an active Parliamentarian, and during the Civil War he housed a garrison of soldiers. The quantity of buff coats, arms and armour hung in the Hall was

Littlecote; the Hall; (see also colour plate 12 and illustration on p. 23)

part of their equipment. However, the Colonel later assisted General Monck in restoring Charles II to his throne, and the King was entertained here in 1663.

The Great Hall has no gallery, but its oak panelling and ceiling, though sober, are very fine. Sobriety and a lack of 'enthusiasm' is more obvious in the Brick Hall, panelled in an unusually severe Inigo Jones style, and behind the wainscot there is a recess from which subversive conversations might be overheard. But the Puritan flavour is explicit in the Chapel, the only one of its type to survive intact. A stern authoritative pulpit takes the place of the altar. This, and the pews, screen and gallery, with plain panelling and turned colonnettes seem earlier than the Cromwellian period. This room may have been the ancient Great Hall, but a Gothic piscina shows that at some point it became a Catholic chapel.

The Dutch Parlour is most curious, with painted walls simulating tapestries and closely grouped pictures. The subjects are oddly mixed, with typical Dutch genre scenes, Don Quixote, and nude youths in *louche* dances with nymphs and satyrs. Some of the painting is fine, some crude, and some has been removed for moral reasons. The work seems early 18th century, and is said, improbably, to have been carried out by prisoners of war. The Drawing Room and Library are early 19th century, as is the Conservatory, now a swimming pool, for which part of the 15th-century courtyard was demolished.

The house, with the Popham portraits and much early furniture, was bought in 1922 by Sir Ernest Salter Wills, Bart., whose family now maintain it. Most of the fine oak furniture has always been here, notably the massive thirty-foot table in the Great Hall, which is marked out as a shovel board. Here too is a finger stocks, used by Sir John Popham for keeping prisoners in the dock. The crewel-work hangings in the bedrooms are very fine. In the Long Gallery, royal and family portraits look down on Flemish tortoiseshell cabinets, French commodes, chairs with fine Georgian needlework covers, and much European and Oriental porcelain, the most refined of which are the Ming wares with the Imperial yellow glaze.

A Roman villa, some two hundred yards from the house, was discovered in the 18th century, and this and a Celtic village are now being excavated by the owner.

Little Malvern Court, Hereford and Worcester
(Mr T. P. Berington)

Four miles south of Great Malvern (A4104)

The Priory Church and Court stand together, isolated under the southern Malvern Hills. Founded in the 12th century, Little Malvern Priory was Benedictine and subject to Worcester. The fine church tower and the hall show that it was relatively prosperous, and in 1323 twelve monks are recorded. Shortly after the Dissolution it was granted to John Russell. This younger branch of an ancient knightly family from Strensham remained

17 Raby Castle; the Barons' Hall

18 Rockingham Castle; the Long
Gallery

19 Salisbury Hall, within its mediaeval moat

20 Saltwood Castle; Lord Clark's Library

Little Malvern Court

Catholic, and Russell's descendant owns the house today.

The Refectory or Prior's Hall is wonderfully complete. Raised above a 12th-century undercroft (not open), and retaining a window jamb of the same date, the timber structure dates from the early 14th century. It is of five bays with an open roof and cusped wind braces. The spere truss is a rarity, and has quatrefoil spandrels above the arched posts. The small rooms beyond this were presumably the prior's or guest rooms, and they give a comfortable impression. The original outside door now leads to further rooms in a Tudor addition. Later alterations included the present entrance and the insertion of a floor in the Hall itself, which has now been removed. The present condition is due to the excellent and sensitive restorations recently carried out by the owner.

Long Barn, Kent
(Mr W. S. Martin)

At the west end of Sevenoaks Weald (from A21)

Until this century it was a modest 15th-century house where, by doubtful tradition, William Caxton is said to have been born. The outside is picturesque in its variety of timber and daub, brick nogging and tile. The Hall was modernised in the 16th century by the insertion of a fireplace and a floor to make a room above. A stone fireplace has the initials of Thomas Willoughby, who then owned property in this district.

Long Barn is interesting chiefly as having been the home, between 1915 and 1930, of Sir Harold Nicolson and Victoria Sackville-West. They introduced various exotic but discreet flourishes to the rooms, and, more

Long Barn

important, moved a 15th-century barn from the field below which was converted into a substantial additional wing. Here their many political, literary and artistic friends came to stay, including Virginia Woolf and all the world of Bloomsbury. At the far end was Sir Harold's study where he wrote *Verlaine*, *Tennyson* and *Some People*. Vita's study was at the other end of the house. They lost no time in converting the fields into a garden, with brick terraces and walks, while the Dutch garden with its raised formal beds was designed by Sir Edwin Lutyens in 1925. There is a beautiful and unspoilt view over the Weald.

Longleat, Wiltshire
(The Marquess of Bath)

Four miles west of Warminster (from A362)

The first and finest view comes after Heaven's Gate, when the house appears below in its wooded valley. This was one of Capability Brown's most successful landscapes, and the Long Leat Brook became a series of lakes. Earlier it had fed the fishponds belonging to the modest Augustinian Priory that was bought by Sir John Thynne, the ancestor of the present owner, for £55. Longleat Priory was enlarged twice before being gutted by fire in 1567. At its third rebuilding the house took on its present size and form, and it was far enough advanced for Queen Elizabeth to stay there with her court in 1575.

Sir John Thynne had been at the Court of Henry VIII, and became an officer of the 'Protector' Duke of Somerset. Though he took no great part in politics, the extent to which he enriched himself is evident in this, the first of the Elizabethan prodigy houses. It is remarkable not only in size, but in its advanced (for England) use of classical detail. The work is by Robert Smythson, the most famous of 16th-century country house architects, and a Frenchman, Allen Maynard, but the design was due chiefly to Thynne himself. Some twenty years earlier he had been involved with Somerset House, London, the first serious attempt to bring the Renaissance style to England. Longleat's regularity of detail and its square outline are classical, but the enormous mullioned windows that flood the rooms with light belong essentially to the English Gothic tradition, and are not to be found abroad.

Thynne was rich enough to buy a quarry at Box, and the stone was dragged here across the combes. There have been few alterations to the Elizabethan exterior, except for the Baroque doorway and the statues on the balustrade that were added during the 1690s. The chimneys are classical columns, and the domed turrets were built before 1567 as belvederes; but all this is almost hidden behind the slightly later facade. Inside, the beamed roof of the Great Hall was flattened late in the 17th century when a library was fitted in above it. The mannerist chimneypiece, carved with two-tailed mermaids, was probably the work of Maynard, and the screen is *circa* 1600. On the upper walls there are large horse paintings by John Wootton, about 1740, and in each one appears a stable boy who lost his life when trying to separate two fighting stallions.

For the rest, the interior is 19th century and very spectacular. Most

Longleat; the Hall

rooms were redecorated after 1806 by Wyatville, who built the 'Imperial' Staircase that separates the two internal courtyards. (Note the green men modelled on its corbels.) Some of Wyatville's marble chimneypieces remain, but they look modest among the grandiose transformations of the 1870s, carried out for the 4th Marquess of Bath by the firm of John Crace. Lord Bath had been Ambassador at Lisbon and Vienna and was an avid collector of paintings. In the State Dining Room, a complete set of Venetian mythological canvases of the Titian school were set by Crace into a scrolling gilt ceiling. Most of the ceilings are in Italian style, that in the Drawing Room being copied from St Mark's Library, Venice, while its frieze is composed of an original Venetian painting, attributed to Pietro Liberi. The doorcases inlaid in Renaissance style in the Ante Library are the work of George Fox, who had done similar work at Eastnor Castle. But the finest room is the Saloon, which was the Long Gallery and still looks Elizabethan by reason of its vast windows. The towering chimneypiece supported by figures of Atlas was copied from one in the Doge's Palace. Marvellous tapestries on the walls include a Flemish set of the Life of King Cyrus of Persia. The late Stuart armchairs, covered with red and silver brocade, have always stood in this room, but the gilded Regency chairs and sofas came with Wyatville's improvements and were made for the Red Library below.

The furniture at Longleat is exotic. Many of the continental pieces were collected by the 4th Marquess, whose love of Venice appears again in the scrolled Baroque armchairs, opulently carved side tables, and blackamoors. Two magnificent Louis XIII cabinets of carved ebony are in the State Dining Room. But the Drawing Room is full, indeed overfull, of 18th-century French furniture of the highest quality. The sturdy Louis XVI *bureau plat* once belonged to Talleyrand. In an adjoining gallery are Meissen birds and animals of white porcelain, made by Kändler about 1730 for the Japanese Palace at Dresden.

The great number of paintings is equally impressive. Italian and Netherlands schools will be seen in the Drawing Room, the most notable being Titian's *Rest on the Flight into Egypt*. Turbulent hunting scenes by Snyders hang on the Staircase. The portraits begin with full-length Jacobeans, among them the Earl of Essex, Lady Arabella Stuart and Henry, Prince of Wales. The Duchess of Richmond at the foot of the staircase is by Van Dyck. The 18th century is not too well represented, but the 1st and 2nd Marquesses were painted by Lawrence and Hoppner, and the Breakfast Room has some remarkable portraits by George Richmond, G. F. Watts and Sir William Orpen.

Enormous formal gardens were laid out by George London during the 1690s, with parterres stretching in front of the house, clipped hedges, canals and statues. Though famous in their day, they were much neglected before Capability Brown removed them altogether. A new formal garden has been laid out by the present Marquess of Bath, which, though less extensive, is entirely in keeping with the architectural style of the house. The Orangery was built by Wyatville, and also the Stables which mark the beginning of the 19th-century revival of the Elizabethan style.

Loseley House, Surrey
(Mr James Robert More-Molyneux)

Between Guildford and Godalming (A3100)

Facing almost due north, Loseley looks its best on a summer evening when the cedars cast long shadows on the lawn and the famous Jersey herd idle in the park below. The house is Elizabethan. Its tall white windows and quoins of chalk contrast with the greenish Bargate stone, giving a laced-up appearance, but right-angled gables make it look tubby. The main doorway, of Portland stone, seems to be a Queen Anne addition.

The manor was bought in 1508 by Sir Christopher More, an official of the court of Henry VIII. His equally talented son, Sir William, became a figure of considerable local power, consulted and respected by all the leading statesmen and trusted by Queen Elizabeth. He built the house during the 1560s and the Queen stayed here on three occasions. Similarly, James I was twice a guest of Sir George, to whom he presented his portrait and that of Queen Anne of Denmark that still hang in the Great Hall. About 1600 a large wing was built with additional chambers, a gallery and riding school. This was pulled down in the last century and no trace of it remains.

The Hall is lofty, with a flat beamed ceiling and a fine oriel window with some original heraldic glass. The gallery is made up with various carvings, presumably taken from the demolished wing. The rest of the panelling is said to have come from Henry VIII's Nonsuch Palace and has very interesting Italianate perspectives in low relief. Of some similar Royal origin, too, are the painted panels, one of them bearing the initials of Henry VIII and Katherine Parr. Executed in the full Italian mannerist style, they are attributed to Toto del Nunziata.

Loseley House

The Library has some excellent Elizabethan carving, partly made up into shelves. The Drawing Room chimneypiece is an extraordinary work made of a single piece of chalk. Its urbane caryatids recall the Fontainebleau style, and other classical ornaments are surprisingly advanced for *circa* 1600. Perhaps it was installed for King James's visit, like the plaster ceiling that includes family emblems of a moorhen and cockatrice; while the frieze has a mulberry tree with an appropriate Latin motto.

A quantity of foreign furniture, notably an Augsburg marquetry *Wrangelschrank* and a Flemish wardrobe, were collected abroad by the family's chief traveller, Sir Poynings More (1606–49). The set of late-17th-century walnut chairs, with caned seats and spiral uprights, also appear Flemish. Much interesting English furniture includes a Queen Anne walnut cabinet inlaid with Chinese ladies fishing, and a Vauxhall pier glass in a fine gilt frame.

When the male heirs of the More family failed, the property passed to the descendants of Margaret More who had married Sir Thomas Molyneux in 1684. The heraldic cross molin of this family will be seen on many of the later ceilings. There are many family portraits, the largest of which commands one end of the Hall and shows the family of Sir More Molyneux. It is dated 1739 and said to be by 'Somers'. A notable portrait of Edward VI also hangs in the Hall, and, from a later period, a charming full-length of Felix Ladbrook, a friend of the family, by Beechey. There is an impressive seapiece by Van de Velde in the Drawing Room, and on the Staircase an admonitory 16th-century allegory of the *Judgment of the World*.

Lullingstone Castle, Kent
(Mr Guy Hart Dyke)

Eight miles north of Sevenoaks (from Eynsford, A225)

This sheltered valley of the North Downs has been inhabited for nearly 2,000 years, as the neighbouring British settlement and Roman villa attest. Lullingstone, a manor rather than a castle, is mentioned in Domesday Book, and the Peche family, from whom the owner is descended, were here in 1361. Sir John Peche was a prominent courtier to Henry VII, and as a young man he excelled in jousting contests. His plumed helmet is kept in the house. In 1497, aged twenty-four, he was knighted and probably then he rebuilt the house, making a jousting field beyond the Gatehouse. On his death the property passed to his nephew, Sir Percyval Hart, and later, in 1738, it came by marriage to Sir Thomas Dyke. The adjoining church contains remarkable family monuments and an elaborate early-18th-century ceiling.

The Tudor Gatehouse, one of the earliest survivals of its kind, remains almost entire even to the oak windows and panelled gates. In the Great Hall there is a large oil painting of the house as it was about 1700. There was a second, inner gatehouse and a moat but these were removed about 1760 when the garden was landscaped and the lake shaped to the south. The house is all

Lullingstone Castle; the Drawing Room or Great Chamber

of brick, and the irregular courtyard visible from the staircase is doubtless a mediaeval survival. The fabric is basically early Tudor, but was largely refaced in the time of Queen Anne. The old Great Hall is in the centre, rather dwarfed between two later unsymmetrical wings. On the left or north side there is plenty of Tudor walling, and between two projecting turrets is a splendid Tudor doorcase of oak (better seen from inside).

In a later generation, Percival Hart was a fervent Jacobite and admirer of Queen Anne, who visited the house several times. The remodelling of the interior dates from her time, and the quantity of oak panelling, mostly of bolection type, is fine and impressive work of the highest quality. The Great Hall has a Vanbrugian chimneypiece and a rusticated arch leading to the Staircase with its elegantly turned balusters and, at intervals, the Hart crest of a lion's head. The best room is upstairs. Known today at the State Drawing Room, it was clearly the great chamber but seems more like a gallery. The barrel vault has Elizabethan plasterwork with medallions of Roman heads. There are many interesting family relics here and in other rooms. Queen Anne's portrait hangs on the end wall.

The most interesting picture in the Great Hall is the triple portrait of robust old Sir Percyval aged seventy-nine, and his two sons, each bearing a motto of some appropriately humble sentiment. The painting is dated 1575, and the chased silver knife worn by Sir Percyval appears again in the portrait of his grandson in the Dining Room. The knife itself is also preserved. Two full-length portraits, of Sir Thomas Dyke and his son Sir John Dixon Dyke who remodelled the garden, are unusual 18th-century works by Domenico van Schmissen.

Luton Hoo, Bedfordshire
(The Wernher family)

South of Luton (A6129)

Capability Brown's large and noble park adorned with two lakes strikes the visitor as almost phantasmagoric after the dreary banality of Luton outside the gates. Nowhere else is there so dramatic a visual contrast between late-20th-century urban England and the arcadian ideals of the 18th century. The house is curiously urban, something of a cross between the Ritz, with high mansard roofs, and the British Museum, with a Greek Ionic portico. This is no coincidence, for the Entrance Front was in fact designed by the architect of the British Museum and later altered by that of the Ritz.

Luton Hoo is one of the most modern of great English country houses open to the public. In its present form it is only seventy years old, and the long history of the site is not apparent. The house and collection is the achievement of Sir Julius Wernher, a South African diamond magnate and friend of Cecil Rhodes, who bought the estate in 1903. He completed the remodelling of the house in 1907 as a setting for his discriminating collection of continental works of art. The result is a rarity among English country houses and is closer in spirit to contemporary palaces in the United States such as the Frick house in New York or the Vanderbilt mansion at Hyde Park.

There had been a house at Luton Hoo for seven hundred years before it was acquired by the Wernhers. In 1762 the estate was bought by John, 3rd Earl of Bute, former tutor to King George III and Prime Minister of England. Bute largely rebuilt the existing 17th-century house to the design of Robert Adam, creating a much-admired interior ensemble. None of it survives now. The 2nd Marquess of Bute employed Sir Robert Smirke to remodel the Entrance Front, but in 1843 the house was gutted by fire. It was subsequently sold to a rich Liverpudlian who had made a fortune out of deals in building land. He rebuilt the interior and in the 1870s formed the chapel to the design of one of the best architects of the day, G. E. Street. Unfortunately the chapel was dismantled in this century.

Sir Julius Wernher's alterations involved the total remodelling of the house in the *Beaux Arts* French style by C. F. Mewes, the leading practitioner of that mode in England. Only Smirke's portico and Street's chapel (later dismantled) were retained from the earlier house. The Edwardian work is of the highest order of splendour and has not perhaps received the appreciation it deserves. After the Second World War Sir Julius Wernher's son, the late Sir Harold Wernher, converted half the house into a private residence for the family and the rest into a museum open to the public. The architect for the alterations was Philip Tilden. He closed the central portico and made a small public entrance in a corner of the facade. This unobtrusive approach makes it difficult to appreciate the architecture. The public part of the house is arranged frankly as a museum with the objects displayed in glass cases.

The architectural pleasures of the interior include the main staircase,

Luton Hoo

sweeping up in a circular well round a white marble group of *L'Amore degli Angeli* by F. Borgonzoli, and the Blue Hall in Louis XVI style with a coved ceiling, Ionic columns and charming overdoor paintings of urns and garlands of flowers. The *pièce de résistance*, however, is the Dining Room with rich polychrome marble revetment specially designed to frame superlative Beauvais tapestries of chinoiserie scenes. The opulent gilding of the cornice is complemented by the glitter of a silver-gilt service on the table, made originally for the Duke of Cumberland, King of Hanover.

There are important paintings at Luton Hoo, including works by Titian, Rembrandt, Hals, Memlinc, Rubens, and Filippino Lippi, but the stars of the collection are the St Michael by the rare 15th-century Spanish artist Bartolomé Bermejo and a fine late work by Altdorfer. More important than the paintings, however, are the objects: the ivories, enamels, Renaissance jewels and metal work. Today they are not paralleled in any other English private collection, nor are they rivalled by any provincial English museum.

To the original collection has since been added various purchases of English furniture by the late Sir Harold Wernher, the magnificent 18th-century English porcelain assembled by his mother, Lady Ludlow, and a unique array of imperial Russian objects (including examples of Fabergé's work) inherited by Lady Zia Wernher from her parents, the Grand Duke Michael and the Countess de Torby.

Lympne Castle, Kent
(Mr Harry Margary)

Two miles west of Hythe (B2067)

Perched above Romney Marsh the little castle stands by tradition on the site of a Roman watchtower associated with Lemanis, one of the Kentish ports under the command of the romantically-styled Count of the Saxon Shore. The building is mentioned by Leyland, who in 1536 described it as 'made like a Castelet embatelyd'. So it looks today, though since his time it has passed through many vicissitudes.

Lympne Castle

The village church with its Norman tower lies cheek by jowl with the castle, and the Lympne property for eight hundred years belonged to the archdeaconry of Canterbury. Though the square tower at the east end is of earlier but undetermined date, the castle basically is of the late 14th and 15th centuries: an example of the familiar mediaeval hall-house, with the addition of an unusual stirrup-shaped tower at the west end. The building had come much down in the world before extensive restoration was carried out in 1905 by the imaginative Scottish architect, Sir Robert Lorimer.

As the visitor approaches the house, large mullioned and transomed lights reveal the position of the Great Hall to the right of the entrance porch. The windows, like most of the fenestration, are Lorimer's restoration. The porch once gave access to a screens passage but the screen has disappeared, and one now steps straight into the Hall. As often happened, a floor was inserted (in the 19th century) to give additional rooms at first floor level. This was removed and the roof restored in 1905, when no doubt the wealth of old parchment-fold panelling was introduced. The Gothic doorways – chamfered at the west end, moulded at the east – are original. The fireplace that succeeded the earlier central hearth, whose smoke escaped through a louvre in the roof, is 16th century. East of the Hall, in the old service quarters, there is a good newel staircase, and to the west, where the solar and living accommodation lay, there is a bedroom with a crown-post ceiling and panelling probably of about 1600.

The stirrup-shaped tower at the western extremity of the castle (with another newel staircase) is reminiscent of the gatehouse at Saltwood and perhaps contemporary, that is *c*. 1385. The archdeacon at Lympne may have been inspired by the example of his superior, the archbishop, at Saltwood.

From the summit of the tower there is a memorable view over Romney Marsh. Martello towers on the distant shoreline, and the Royal Military Canal bounding the marsh, recall the Napoleonic wars. Immediately below, at the edge of the plain, are the remains of Roman outbuildings. This cliff-top tower continued its role as a lookout in the Second World War, when a pillbox and support for the telescope were built at the top.

Malmesbury House, Salisbury, Wiltshire
(Mr J. H. Cordle, M.P.)

In The Cathedral Close, north-east of the Cathedral

Situated in the Cathedral Close and thus hardly a 'country' house, Malmesbury has so much the air of one that its inclusion seems justified. The name of the house, to which Handel, Gibbon, Reynolds and Dr Johnson were 18th-century visitors, recalls the Earl of Malmesbury who inherited in 1780.

The squared-limestone facade, almost white in colour, with sober pedimented doorway and strong plain cornice, contrasts with the pinkish brown tiles of the roof. Trim and sedately proportioned, this Queen Anne front gives no hint of the rich mid-18th-century plasterwork inside. The front door opens directly on a hall and ample staircase with twisted balusters; walls and ceiling are decorated with plasterwork, white on a blue ground. In the upper part of the stair-well, niches framed by swags of flowers contain busts of Shakespeare, Milton and Jonson. This bold and masculine treatment contrasts in the ground floor drawing room with a fluent plasterwork ceiling and overmantel in full rococo, though the Kentian chimneypiece

Malmesbury House; the Staircase

recalls an earlier taste. On the first floor one meets with further contrast, a small Gothic library perfect in its sort: white-painted bookcases with ogee-headed canopies, divided by slender pilasters; chimneypiece, overmantel and a little bay that looks on the garden, are treated in the same light-hearted manner. The plasterwork must have been introduced about the middle of the 18th century or soon after. One would suspect the staircase hall to have come first, with the rococo drawing room and library following in sequence over a period of ten to fifteen years.

In the earlier part of the house, at the back, there is a room associated with Handel's visit in the 1720s that has simple Jacobean wainscot, and another room with a 17th-century fireplace and overmantel.

Mapledurham, Oxfordshire
(Mr J. J. Eyston)

Three miles north-west of Reading (A4074, via Caversham)

Only a very few miles beyond the sprawl of Reading, the Mapledurham estate, green and tranquil, miraculously survives. The Elizabethan house, the adjoining church (to which Butterfield made notable contribution), and the hamlet with brick and flint cottages, 17th-century almshouses and a mill standing where a mill has stood since Domesday, resist the encroachments of the 20th century. In the last hundred years no new dwelling house has disturbed the rural harmony. Nearby the Thames moves slowly through the meadows, and Mapledurham is surely the only private house to which thousands of visitors come by water.*

Sir Michael Blount, whose descendants still live at Mapledurham, began his new house in 1588 and faced it firmly eastward as recommended by the Tudor physician Andrew Boorde, who maintained that 'the South wynde doth corrupt and doth make evyl vapours'. Indeed the east front, with its warm diapered brickwork, regular fenestration, and flanking wings, is the only elevation which attempts architectural formality. Though with a convincing 16th-century flavour, it has undergone considerable alteration (like the interior of the house), and much that one sees today – for instance the battlements at roof level, the porch and the flanking bay windows – date from the late 18th and early 19th centuries.

The Entrance Hall, once part of the Elizabethan Great Hall, was re-modelled in 1828, and the panelling and overmantel arrived some forty years later. The peculiar interest here lies in the curious collection of 17th- and 18th-century carved-wood heads of animals that adorn the walls. Naïvely but expressively treated, these bulls, deer, boars, goats and sheep were probably intended to represent virtues and vices.

Off the Entrance Hall lies a chapel, with Gothic plasterwork picked out in white on a pale grey ground. Mapledurham has been a Catholic house for 350 years and the chapel was added at about the time of the Catholic Relief

---

* When the house is open in summer boats ply from Reading at Caversham Bridge.

Mapledurham: left: *the Staircase, and* below: *Martha and Teresa Blount, painted by Jervas; (see also colour plate 13)*

Act of 1791 from which the recusant Blounts were no doubt quick to take advantage.

Among the original features of the interior is a massive oak staircase with continuous-newels rising from floor to floor, and a sensitively moulded plaster ceiling of 1612, with portrait medallions set in strapwork panels. It is one of two or three such ceilings to survive at Mapledurham. The staircase dado, the carved baskets of flowers on the newels, and the pedimented doorway into the Saloon on the first floor, are Carolean additions. The staircase walls are hung with early Blount portraits of the 16th and 17th centuries.

The Saloon has another of the early Jacobean plasterwork ceilings, though the cornice and frieze are some two hundred years later. Here there are lacquer cabinets on stands of about 1690, early Georgian torchères, mid-18th-century rococo console tables, and some plain mahogany chairs of about 1760 upholstered in the early 19th century by the daughters of the house with simple *gros point* needlework. Family portraits continue with the 18th-century Blounts, and include a portrait by Jervas of the sisters Teresa and Martha. Through these ladies Mapledurham entered literary history. Between 1707 and 1715 Alexander Pope was a frequent visitor and both sisters became his close friends. Teresa, the elder, gossipy and feckless, lost his affection (not a difficult thing to do) but the stable Martha, his heir and perhaps his mistress, remained a trusted confidante until his death.

The adjoining Boudoir recalls Martha's long association with the poet. Here hang a version of Kneller's portrait of Pope, and one of Teresa

Plowden as Mary Magdalene. The rococo mirror between the portraits belonged to Pope, as did the classical and Flemish landscapes in elaborate carved frames. Pope left Martha Blount not only furniture, books, and a substantial sum of money, but two urns from his villa at Twickenham. The urns, designed by William Kent, now stand by the steps on the north front of the house.

The Dining Room is a surprise. With its classical frieze and its alcoves for statuary, with sideboards made for the room and late Georgian furniture, it looks impeccably 18th century. It was in fact remodelled in 1828 and is a reversion to a style then going out of fashion. On the walls, balancing a Blount family portrait in the manner of Van Dyck, hangs an early-17th-century full-length portrait of Lady St John of Bletso by William Larkin. This is perhaps one of the earliest English portraits set against a landscape background, but more significant it is a compelling painting, one of the outstanding English portraits of its time.

Markenfield Hall, North Yorkshire
(The Lord Grantley, M.C.)

Three miles south of Ripon (A61)

In 1569 a Yorkshire army gathered in the courts of Markenfield, with the Five Wounds of Christ on their banners. Led by Thomas Markenfield and Richard Norton of nearby Norton Conyers they heard Mass in Ripon Cathedral, joined the Earl of Northumberland's forces, and marched south intending to depose Queen Elizabeth and restore the Faith of Rome. This Rising of the North was quelled in a single skirmish. Eight hundred of the feudal tenantry paid the dire penalty for treason. Markenfield was abandoned; its owner fled abroad.

Two hundred years later the house was bought by Sir Fletcher Norton, 1st Baron Grantley. He was a descendant of the same Richard Norton, and his family have restored and preserved the house. The main restoration was done in the 19th century by J. R. Walbran, and changes between the old and

Markenfield; the courtyard; (also illustrated on p. 34)

new stonework are not easy to detect. The main part is not inhabited now, but the courtyard and outbuildings have been in continuous use as a farmhouse.

It is a beautiful and little known house, isolated among meadows and cornfields and still moated, exactly the romantic idea of a feudal knight's home. The dwelling house is L-shaped. A licence to crenellate was granted in 1310; this is the date of the raised Hall and its traceried windows, but only a scar remains to record its original outside stair. At some point the undercroft was converted into a kitchen; originally it may have been vaulted, like two surviving ground floor rooms in the wing. Also in the wing is the Chapel with its beautiful east window and a later piscina carved with the Markenfields' arms. The other lofty rooms were divided when a floor was inserted in the 16th century. Garderobes discharge into the moat.

The lower ranges in the court, very much in use today, are only mediaeval in fragments. There is a 14th-century doorway, and a row of armorial bearings of the Markenfields, Nortons and other Yorkshire families to whom they were related. The Gatehouse is Tudor and the kitchen once stood next to it. Outside the moat there are stone barns and sheds, late perhaps but solid and very handsome.

Marston Hall, Lincolnshire
(The Rev. Henry Thorold)

Five miles north-west of Grantham (A1)

Opposite the front door stands an ancient wych elm twelve yards in circumference, and not far off there is a laburnum, no less venerable, which experts maintain is the largest in the country. Both trees must have been planted not long after the Thorolds, among the oldest of Lincolnshire families, transformed an earlier building into an Elizabethan house with a central hall set between kitchens and a domestic wing. In the 18th century when the family decided to live at Syston, another property nearby, the house was drastically reduced in size. The domestic wing disappeared and Georgian rooms were fitted into what had once been the dais end of the great hall. The result is an instructive example of the way that halls of the Tudor period were often adapted to later requirements.

The high roof and gable ends of the early hall are clearly identifiable. On the entrance front, the windows have never been sashed and the wooden mullions and transoms reflect the original type of fenestration. The house is still entered through the 16th-century porch and oak door which gave on the screens passage. Though the screens disappeared in the 18th century, the Tudor fireplace and overmantel were preserved and shifted to their present position in about 1720, when the ceiling was put in and the new rooms inserted at the dais end of the hall.

Two internal features of interest, both of them recent introductions, are a rich plaster ceiling dated 1699 which was rescued when about to be destroyed from a Thorold house in Devon, and a marble chimneypiece made

Marston Hall

to a highly unorthodox design by Inigo Jones. Family portraits include an attractive Reynolds of Elizabeth Thorold, daughter of the 8th Baronet, and three Ferneleys of Thorold horses showing this artist at his best. There are also Dutch 17th-century genre and still-life paintings, and two unusual works: *The Geographers* in the manner of Caravaggio, and *St Francis Preaching to the Fishes* by a talented but unidentified 17th-century artist. The furniture includes a number of pieces by Gillow.

Melbourne Hall, Derbyshire
(The Marquess of Lothian)

Seven miles south of Derby (B587)

Long before its name reached Australia, or even the English Peerage, Melbourne was a country town in the centre of England, and to judge from the magnificent Norman church it was prosperous. The parsonage, belonging to the Bishops of Carlisle, was leased to Sir John Coke about 1620. Shortly after, Coke became Secretary of State to Charles I. His portrait by Closterman shows a sharp face, full of humour. Unlike most successful men of his age he liked plain living, and instead of rebuilding what must have been a small and inconvenient old house he merely made some additions. The panelled Dining Room survives from his work. The house, in fact, never was rebuilt and as a result it seems curiously unplanned. It stands close to the town, and is out of alignment with the garden.

The fine portraits of Stuart courtiers show the circles in which this family moved. Thomas Coke inherited as a young man, and later became Vice-Chamberlain to Queen Anne and George I. One of Lely's superb double portraits shows his parents-in-law, Lord and Lady Chesterfield; and Coke himself, in a stylish grey coat, was painted by Dahl. His chief interest was in the garden, and only later did he think of building a new house. In the end he merely remodelled the courtyard (now covered over as a Billiard Room), and built new rooms facing the garden. This garden front must date from about 1720; it is not quite Palladian, and has heavy 'rustic' door and window frames. Inside, the staircase is a fine work of carved joinery, and is hung with paintings of the kind fashionable around 1700, with bird pieces by Hondecoeter and Bogdani, flowers by Baptiste, and a grandly pastoral group of the Coke children by Huysmans. Of special interest are the Jacobean portraits of the Leventhorpes, Coke's maternal family, in a charming primitive style.

Thomas Coke had been greatly impressed by French gardens, and he determined to bring the style of Le Nôtre to his own house. Even before he bought the freehold of the property in 1704, he consulted London and Wise and bought lead statues from Van Nost. The flat parterre just below the house has now been smoothed into a continuous slope and turfed, but its original design is known from an old plan. Below this, the fishponds were shaped into the Great Basin. Coke never realised his idea of a rocky island with Venus and nymphs rising out of the sea, but he ordered the magnificent Arbour of wrought iron, an early work by Robert Bakewell of Derby. Gaily painted in blue, red and gilt, it corresponds to ornaments once in the Versailles gardens, and is popularly and wrongly known as a birdcage. Nost's lead statues set against yew hedges were originally coloured.

Next, Coke formed the Grove out of ten acres of irregular sloping ground to the right of the Great Basin. Though minute in comparison with Ver-

Melbourne Hall; left: *the Arbour, and* right: *the Four Seasons Vase, carved by Nost;* *(see also colour plate 14)*

sailles or Marly, these are known to have been the models that inspired it. The design is intimate and informal. At the lower end of Crow Walk, three basins with small fountains form a vista; at the top, Nost's Four Seasons Vase, presented by Queen Anne, is at the centre of a *patte d'oie*. The character of the grove has subtly changed since Coke's day, but to walk here is still to return to a past age. The famous yew tunnel was one of Coke's earliest garden works.

Formal gardens of this date are very rare in England. The reason for its survival is that its owners were absent for some 150 years. Thomas Coke's daughter and heir married Sir Matthew Lamb, whose grandson was Lord Melbourne, Queen Victoria's Prime Minister. Though their title was chosen from Derbyshire, the family preferred to live at Brockett. Portraits and relics of the family are to be seen: of Lord Melbourne; of his mother, an ambitious and successful woman of the world; and of his undisciplined wife, Lady Caroline Lamb. The house then passed to Melbourne's sister, Emily Lamb, who married another Prime Minister, Lord Palmerston, and descended to the Kerr family by marriage. Admiral Lord Walter Kerr, a veteran of the Crimea and the Indian Mutiny, came to live at Melbourne in 1906 and restored the gardens. He was grandfather to the present, 12th, Marquess of Lothian.

Milton Manor, Oxfordshire
(Surgeon Captain and Mrs E. J. Mockler)

Four miles south of Abingdon (B4016)

The manor, as first seen from the gateway, appears curiously high for its size, and before the short wings were added in the 18th century must have looked as tall and compact as Ashdown Park a few miles away to the south-west. Milton is of two periods. The central block was built, like Ashdown, soon after the Restoration: a square brick house, with the elevations similar on all four sides and a steep hipped roof; the decorative features, such as the giant Ionic pilasters that have odd waist bands with *fleurs de lys* two-thirds of the way up, were executed in plaster. The Calton family built it, who acquired the property in the middle of the 16th century, owned it for over two hundred years, and entertained William of Orange there on his march to Oxford in 1688.

In 1764 it was sold to Bryan Barrett, a wealthy London lace-maker whose descendants still live there. In the following decade he added the wings which are carefully tied to the older building, put in the Georgian front door, and introduced sash windows. His architect was Stephen Wright, who though a Palladian by training was responsible for the Gothic gaiety inside.

The most interesting 17th-century features of the interior are the staircase with solid turned balusters, the overmantel in the hall (not in its original position) which depicts ample ladies nonchalantly supporting a shield and grasping cornucopia, and the plaster ceiling in the Drawing Room with wreaths of oak and laurel set in deep rectangular panels. The rest of the

Milton Manor

Drawing Room – wainscot, chimneypiece and overmantel (the latter inset with an enchanting 17th-century Dutch painting of children with a goat cart, attributed to Thomas de Keyser) – is Georgian and dates, as does the Dining Room with alcoves intended for statuary, from Barrett's changes after 1765. There is also a bedroom done up at the same time with a painted Chinese wallpaper of peonies and birds.

But the delight of the interior is the Gothic library. Bryan Barrett, who is shown here in an overmantel conversation piece by Highmore, was the friend of John Chute of The Vyne who in turn was close to Horace Walpole, and the room was doubtless influenced by Walpole's library at Strawberry Hill. Painted in the original colours, white and mushroom, it is a charming example of Gothic-rococo with clustered columns, a fanciful cornice, and crocketed ogee heads to the bookcases, window frames and chimneypiece. A Pinxton tea set here, depicting the house and doubtless commissioned by Barrett, is a ceramic rarity. The contemporary Catholic chapel, a soberer version of Gothic, is less compelling, but contains Flemish 16th-century glass and some English 14th-century glass from a nearby church.

Moccas Court, Hereford and Worcester
(Mr Richard Chester-Master)

Ten miles west of Hereford (A438)

That Moccas is ancient is clear from the dumpy Norman church that stands, isolated now, a short distance from the house. In the 16th century the manor belonged to the Vaughans, from whom a hundred years later it came by marriage to Edward Cornewall of the distinguished family at Berrington. In 1771 Catherine Cornewall married her cousin, Sir George Amyand, Bart. He took the name of Cornewall and rebuilt the house in its present form.

Moccas Court

A tall crisp villa of brick, it stands on the edge of a plain above the sunken River Wye. This famous picturesque valley was recorded by Thomas Hearne in a series of water-colour views of 1790. The curious thing is that Sir George, having commissioned designs from Robert Adam in 1775, did not use them but went instead to Anthony Keck. Despite his growing practice in the West Midlands, Keck was not as yet well known. The house he built is really an abstraction of Adam's design, its only ornament being the Venetian window under the skeleton of a pediment. The semi-circular porch was a happy addition of 1792. The scarlet brick is cheerful but unexpected, even shocking, in this district of sandstone and timber. The kilns that supplied it were built in the park.

An ingenious double stair leads up to the Hall, and ahead is an elegantly simple cantilevered staircase that floats upward in an oval well. To the left, the Music Room has instruments in the frieze and chimneypiece, while the Library has a chimneypiece of porphyry scagliola.

The climax comes with the round Drawing Room in the centre of the river facade. Drawings by Robert Adam, dated 1781, show that his designs for its doors and plaster ceiling were adopted without much alteration, and also his idea of the walls being painted in 'Pompeian' style. But this colourful decoration was not actually carried out in paint, but in printed papers made by the Paris factory of Reveillon, cut out and arranged *en collage* with some judicious brushwork. No fires were allowed here lest they should smoke the paper, so the room must have been reserved for summer use.

Designs for planting the park were made by Capability Brown, but the former oak clumps have been much thinned out. The view over the river and the red sandstone scar on the opposite bank was greatly improved when Repton cleared ground below the house to form a series of terraces down the hill. Two *cottages ornés* were designed as lodges in 1801 by the younger Repton, who was then working in the office of John Nash.

A chromolithograph from The Royal Horticultural Society's Lindley Library
folio volume, *The Gardens of England,* by E. Adveno Brooke. Published around 1857.
The illustration (15 x 12 ins) shows the garden on the hillside at
Castle Combe, near Chippenham, the seat of G. P. Scrope, Esq., M.P.
The garden is of very early origin and the picture shows all that remains of
an ancient Abbey at the summit of the grass slope.

Unhappily, nearly all the furniture and family portraits were dispersed by a sale in 1946. Sir William Cornewall died in 1962; the present owner, his cousin, has carried out major restoration work and furnished the house anew. The most notable of the contents is the Moccas commode, a splendid mahogany piece probably of the early 1760s. It disappeared after the sale, but recently reappeared at auction in Hertfordshire and has now returned to Moccas.

Mount Edgcumbe, Cornwall
(Cornwall County Council and Plymouth District Council)

West point of Plymouth Sound (B3247 from the west, or by ferry from Admiral's Head, Stonehouse, near Plymouth)

Mount Edgcumbe is a phoenix. Dating from 1547, it was gutted by German incendiary bombs in 1941, and rebuilt in 1958–60 by the determination of Kenelm, 6th Earl of Mount Edgcumbe, to restore and live in the house built by his ancestor, Sir Richard Edgcumbe.

The rectangular outwards-looking house, originally with a round tower at each corner and a substantial central tower over the hall, is quite different from the usual courtyard plan of its day. In 1749 the corner towers were made octagonal. It seems unfortunate that the central tower was not replaced during the recent rebuilding; but the architect, Mr Adrian Gilbert Scott, removed many later additions and the Victorian stucco, revealing once more the simple limestone and granite walls. The windows and front door have Tudor arches; the pedimented door surround is 18th century. Nearly all the contents, with Grand Tour pictures, porcelain and silver, were lost through the bombing, and estate workmen are said to have struggled gallantly to save a grand piano while the flames consumed a series of portraits by Reynolds. Sir Joshua, born at Plympton in 1723, had found his earliest patron in Lord Edgcumbe, and he painted the family from 1740 to 1774. Only one Reynolds remains among the few surviving portraits. The

Mount Edgcumbe

6th Earl's furniture looks well in the restored rooms now occupied by the present Lord and Lady Mount Edgcumbe.

The magnificent park is the real glory of the place. It forms the west side of Plymouth Sound and is steeped in naval history. There are forts and blockhouses, and a spectacular cliff edge walk round Penlee Point to Rame Head on the sea coast. The avenues and groves, the English, Italian and French gardens, their temples and the ruined folly made up one of the most famous of mid-18th-century landscapes: an Arcadia that comes somewhere between the Claudian paradise of Stourhead and the picturesque realisation of Hagley. It was greatly admired by Horace Walpole. This park, forming the backdrop to the westwards view from the Hoe, had long been coveted by the City fathers of Plymouth: but it lay in Cornwall who has always been suspicious of her more commercial neighbours. So an unlikely partnership was formed to buy Mount Edgcumbe House and six hundred acres of the park after the death, in 1965, of the 6th Earl, with the condition that his successor should live in the house.

Visitors should be warned that access is difficult, and the roads from the west are long. The more interesting approach is across the Tamar by ferry from Stonehouse (a western suburb of Plymouth).

Muncaster Castle, Cumbria
(Sir William Pennington-Ramsden, Bart.)

At Ravenglass on the west coast (A595)

With the massif of Scafell for a background and the winding Esk below, the situation of Muncaster is superb. Perhaps the Castle is best seen from Eskdale rising embowered among trees on the high flank of the valley, or when its walls of pinkish granite are glimpsed from the long rhododendron walk to the east of the house. The Penningtons have been at Muncaster since the early 13th century and built, in the fashion of the Border counties, a fortified Pele tower about a hundred years later. However the Castle today is substantially the work of Anthony Salvin, most prolific of architects, who was called in by Gamel Pennington, 4th Lord Muncaster, to remodel the old buildings soon after the middle of the 19th century.

At Muncaster Salvin is in restrained mood, but the Hall, with plain chamfered Gothic doorways, introduces an imaginative mediaevalising feature: the enclosed staircase at the far end is lit with three lancet windows in echelon. This is Salvin at his most original. His octagonal library – its shape survives from an earlier 18th-century room – has a brass-railed gallery above the bookshelves and a ribbed and vaulted ceiling. In the Drawing Room the Salvin plasterwork is believed to have been executed by Italians and there is an imposing late-18th-century marble chimneypiece that came from another family house. In the Bedrooms some elaborate stone chimneypieces of the Tudor period are also apparently late introductions, but one or two cornices, that look about 1700, survived Salvin's extensive alterations.

246

Muncaster Castle; the garden front, remodelled by Salvin

For visitors who are not amateurs of Victorian architecture, the chief interest of Muncaster lies in its contents. These are representative not only of the long family occupation, but of the connoisseurship of Sir John Ramsden, 6th Baronet, who between the two World Wars collected with knowledge and taste. Probably the earliest object in the Castle is the 15th-century 'Luck of Muncaster', an enamelled glass bowl to which a curious story attaches. After his defeat at Hexham Henry VI fled westward, was discovered wandering on the fells near Muncaster by a shepherd, and found asylum with Sir John Pennington. The King, presumably after his restoration in 1470, is said in gratitude to have presented Sir John with the bowl. It is traditionally believed to ensure, so long as it remains intact, the luck of the family and their continued possession of the Castle.

Family history is reflected in a remarkably complete series of portraits, by artists ranging from Lely to Laszlo, that depict the first six Ramsden baronets and their wives. These hang in the Drawing Room with, notably, a Gainsborough, and an enchanting Reynolds of Mrs William Weddell, who was born a Ramsden. Elsewhere among the paintings that call for attention are a very workmanlike Dobson, Ferneleys showing this uneven painter at his best, and a series of interesting 18th-century pastel portraits by H. B. Hamilton.

Early furniture includes a Gothic chest, an Elizabethan refectory table and four-poster bed, but the house is particularly strong in 17th-century pieces. There are many chests of drawers of the type which came into fashion after the Restoration (some markedly architectural in character, others inlaid with bone and ivory), draw- and gate-legged tables, an outstanding set of Charles II walnut chairs and settees, a finely carved armchair of about 1685, greatly elaborated yet confidently elegant, and much other seat furniture of the period.

Probably Sir John Ramsden acquired such collector's pieces as a limewood carving of a Burgundian man at arms, Flemish Renaissance wood carvings of religious subjects, a sensuous alabaster nude by Giovanni Bologna, a large Italian table on lion supports, a bronze attributed to Benvenuto Cellini and others of the School of Giovanni Bologna. Such things, with rare Elizabethan needlework panels, Stuart and early Georgian embroidery, a display of silver by Paul Storr, and fine porcelain, contribute to a rich and varied interior.

Nether Winchendon, Buckinghamshire
(Mrs John Spencer Bernard)

Lower Winchendon village, seven miles west of Aylesbury (A418)

Standing between a retiring old village and the River Thame, this little-known house is an oddity that can deceive experts. The courtyard is seen first through three large and unmistakably Georgian arches. Georgian too are the pointed windows, buttresses and battlements, whose various materials consist of stone, brick, stucco and wood. The effect is overpowering, but regular by comparison with the garden front: a long tapestry of square towers, an off-centre gable, large and small windows of various shapes and a Gothic loggia of cast iron. All this dates from 1798, but above it will be seen some remnants of the old house, namely splendid brick Tudor chimneys and a 17th-century cupola.

Sir Francis Bernard, the 18th-century owner, was Governor of New Jersey and Massachusetts, but lost his American property after the Revolution. Scrope, the youngest son and the brains of the next generation, became Under Secretary of State to Lord Grenville. He was greatly attached to this remote and by then dilapidated house, and bought it against the advice of his eldest brother who said, 'I think you will find you have purchased an encumbrance.' But Sir Scrope, as he later became, was in love with his encumbrance and had the whole exterior remodelled to his own design. Whether it be called naïve or picturesque, its charm is immediate. The various sections make groups with their own symmetry. Those 'mediaeval' towers are really Scrope's recasing of the old structure. At one corner the old timber posts and moulded jetty or overhang can be found inside a false window. The forecourt is marked out by the now isolated Garden Tower. The wide Entrance Hall was completed as late as 1820.

From 1162 to the Dissolution, Nether Winchendon had belonged to nearby Notley Abbey. As Lord of the Manor, the abbot held his Court Leet here, and the Great Hall was probably longer in the 15th century than it is now. The house was let, notably in 1527 to Sir John Daunce, a civil servant at the court of Henry VIII. His chief contribution was the Parlour (and chambers above). The beams and frieze have carving in the sophisticated Renaissance style of about 1530, with scrolls, arabesques, a variety of merfolk and cherubs, green men, and, flanking a portrait head, the initials 'I D'. The frieze has been slightly cut up and added to, and the same is true of the linenfold panelling below it. Two similar friezes are known, both of

Nether Winchendon; the courtyard

them close by. One, formerly at Notley Abbey, is now at Weston Park, and the other is at Thame Park.

The house was sold in 1559 to William Goodwin, from whom it descended to the Tyringhams and Bernards. The long west wing is basically Elizabethan, but little more is known about it. There are many family portraits, though none is of great artistic merit. The Great Hall fireplace has a most curious stone carving with harpies, birds and fruit, and looks like French work of about 1560. It may have come from Eythrope Manor, which was demolished in 1810. Good heraldic glass of various dates in the Parlour includes the muzzled bear of the Bernards and their delightful motto: *Bear and forebear*. The garden is large, and since the war has been carefully planted. The parish church too is worth a visit.

Newburgh Priory, North Yorkshire
(Captain V. M. Wombwell)

Just east of Coxwold, seven miles south-east of Thirsk

The Augustinian priory that settled here in 1145 was a large one. Traces of old buildings, perhaps round the former cloister, may exist in the front court, but over two centuries the house developed into a long low structure, whose shapes and styles are most curiously mixed. Building and rebuilding continued up to the 1770s.

Two Bellasis brothers from Durham, Richard and Anthony, were active in dissolving northern monasteries, greatly enriching themselves in the process. Anthony, a trained lawyer, also did service to Henry VIII by pronouncing his marriage to Anne of Cleves as invalid. The grant of Newburgh Priory to him and his heir was confirmed in 1546, and his descendants still live here. They married into many leading Catholic families of Yorkshire, but each senior male Bellasis seems to have temporised with the established Church as was expedient. Family loyalties to Charles I or to Parliament were similarly divided. Thomas Bellasis, 2nd Viscount Fauconberg, married Mary, the youngest daughter of Oliver Cromwell, and by some means the Protector's body was brought here for burial. As long as his tomb in the attic remains undisturbed this tradition will not be disproved. (Cromwell's head is preserved at Sidney Sussex College, Cambridge.) This Thomas, pardoned by Charles II, was raised to an Earldom in 1689. Long before his death in 1700 he was among the richest landowners in the North Riding.

Apart from the beauty of the setting, with wide lawns and avenues, gates and stables, the fascination of the house lies in its great diversity. Two birds'-eye views, painted before 1700, show the extent then to have been much the same as now. The porch that centres the court is Elizabethan, and another, with tiered columns, is tucked into the garden front. To the right of the court are arched mullioned windows, and more are seen on the end wing, recently gutted by fire but preserved as a shell. Much refacing and rebuilding was done in the 18th century. Part of the court was remodelled about 1720, and the heavy keystones over sash windows suggest the hand of William Wakefield, the Yorkshire amateur architect who worked nearby at Gilling Castle and Duncombe Park. Shortly after this the stables and kitchen wing were rebuilt.

Nothing at the Priory is more notable than the marble overmantel in the Dining Room (the former Great Hall). It was made by Nicholas Stone in 1615, just after he had returned from Amsterdam where he studied under Hendrik de Keyser (whose daughter he married). Altogether in the most advanced Netherlandish style of its day, this suggests that, in spite of the

Newburgh Priory; the entrance front and gutted west wing

*Newburgh Priory; overmantel by
Nicholas Stone, 1615*

building being rather old-fashioned, its furnishings and fabrics were then rich and new. The statues are of Mars and Diana, the putti symbolise spring and autumn, and the central relief shows the court of Venus.

The Black Gallery is so called because it served as a waiting room for the Court Leet, held in the Justice Room next door. Early portraits here include Sir Henry Bellasis, the builder of the house, three nuns of the family, and the young Oliver Cromwell. In the Justice Room there is a charming conversation group of the later Earl Fauconberg with his family, by Andrea Soldi (1755).

The rooms that lie behind twin bow windows on the garden front were rebuilt by Lord Fauconberg after a fire in 1757. They are panelled and columned, and distinguished further by plaster ceilings made by the York craftsman, Giuseppe Cortese. That in the Large Drawing Room is rococo, while the Small Drawing Room, being slightly later, is more classical, with flower branches and musical instruments. In all these rooms, and on the staircase, the numerous family portraits continue. Among them are Mary Cromwell by Huysmans, and again in her court robes as Countess Fauconberg; the later Earl Fauconberg, holding a plan of the Drawing Room (he seems to have designed the improvements himself), by Soldi; two young daughters of the house by Mercier; Lady Anne Wombwell, at full length, by Romney. A set of elegant Georgian chairs have needlework covers that were repaired by the actor, the late Ernest Thesiger.

Since 1802 the house has descended through the female line twice. It came in 1825 to Sir George Orby Wombwell, Bart., who as aide to Lord Cardigan was distinguished for bravery in the Charge at Balaclava. The estate has been divided and reduced, while vicissitudes since 1939 include the lease of the house as a school during the war, serious dry rot, and a fire which gutted the west wing and the long gallery. However, in 1953 Captain and Mrs Wombwell decided to return here, to repair the house and convert the east wing for their residence. Not only is the building completely renewed, but its gardens and courts are immaculately kept, and the spreading lawns extend to a water garden. Captain Wombwell inherited the property in 1913; his grandfather, the previous owner, had done so in 1855. Thus for more than 120 years the house has been occupied by only two generations.

Newby Hall, North Yorkshire
(Mr Robin Compton)

Between Ripon and Boroughbridge (B6265)

Adam's twin lodges indicate that here is the hallowed seat of a classical connoisseur. But Newby was standing long before Robert Adam made his improvements. The house built before the 1690s by Sir Edward Blackett, owner of Northumberland collieries and M.P. for Ripon, survives today, a brick and stone structure very little altered on the outside. On her tour in 1697, Celia Fiennes described it as 'the finest house I saw in Yorkshire'. No longer attributed to Wren, it seems rather a product of the York school – before Vanbrugh brought his more sensational style to the county.

Newby, bought by the Weddell family in 1748, was transformed by William Weddell. As one of the *dilettanti* he delighted in the study of antiquity and the novelty of neo-classicism. On his Italian tour of 1765 he was painted by Batoni, and he returned home loaded with antique sculpture. The portrait bust by Nollekens shows refined and sensitive features, and we may be sure that Weddell was an agreeable patron. Robert Adam's designs for the house appear from 1766. The earlier fabric was hardly altered, so Adam did not make his usual play of covings, domes and apses. But as a true artist he had a proper sense of scale, and in Newby one of his best and most homogeneous interiors survives complete.

Two low wings were added to enclose a new entrance court. In the Hall the walls are solemn, with trophies of Roman arms under a Doric frieze, while the pattern of the ceiling is reflected in the marble floor. The mahogany organ was carved to Adam's design. The former hall became the Drawing Room, with delicate plasterwork on the ceiling, but its chief interest lies in the Gobelins tapestries on the walls. Six sets of such tapestries were ordered and shipped from Paris for English houses, of which

Newby Hall; left: *the Tapestry Room, and* right: *the Sculpture Gallery*

Weddell's was the second. Although their design attempted to be classical, the borders are still of unabashed rococo, as are the abandoned scenes of *les amours des dieux* after Boucher. The flowered chair seats were part of the same order, while the superb gilded chairs themselves were made by Thomas Chippendale. The Library was built as a dining room, with columns screening the apses. The ceiling painting by Zucchi is of Bacchus and Ariadne, and the chimneypiece is also Bacchic.

Two monolith columns of *cipollino* marble facing the staircase were bought in Rome. But the climax of Adam's work is in the Sculpture Gallery, where a new wing was designed to house the marble treasures. It is in three compartments, the centre part domed and, like the Pantheon, carrying an oculus. The stucco work, in Adam's most delicate antique taste, is painted in various salmon pinks, and the rather small scale of the rooms increases the relative importance of the sculpture. This is one of the very few 18th-century collections that survives complete, and it remains today exactly as Weddell arranged it. The best piece is the nude Venus, which was sold by the Princess Barberini ('an expensive woman'), but the lovely body is rather hidden by modern arms. Weddell certainly paid too much for this work, and one hopes he realised how much of it was new. Dealers in antiques were not always honest.

Being without heirs, Weddell left Newby to his cousin, the 3rd Lord Grantham, who appears in an exquisite pencil drawing by Ingres in the Library. Most of the splendid French furniture was collected by him, and he built a new Dining Room, which is hung with Grantham portraits. There is a fine group of children by Mercier, and the portraits by Van Loo of Maria Theresa and her husband, Francis of Lorraine, were given by the Empress herself to the 1st Lord Grantham, Ambassador in Vienna. Subsequently the house passed by descent to Mr Compton through the Vyner family, whose portraits hang in the Elizabethanised Billiard Room upstairs.

A great feature of Newby is its 25-acre garden, mostly created by Major Compton since 1923. The design is centred on the herbaceous border leading down to the river, crossed by the statue walk, and the planting shows the knowledge of an expert. On the park side of the house, the lone equestrian statue has a long history. Originally it represented King John Sobieski of Poland, but in 1672 Sir Robert Vyner had it altered to *Charles II victorious over an Enemy* (undoubtedly Oliver Cromwell), and set it up in the Stocks Market in London. When the Mansion House was built on the site in 1737, the statue was reclaimed by the Vyner family.

Newhouse, Redlynch, Wiltshire
(Mr and Mrs George Jeffreys)

Two miles east of Redlynch, seven miles south-east of Salisbury (B3080)

This curious isolated building was erected by Sir Thomas Gorges, the son and successor of the mysterious Gorges who built Longford Castle. Like Longford it is triangular, and might be thought to represent the Trinity.

Newhouse

This, however, is no clearly defined block round a courtyard, but it points outwards like a figure Y. Started before 1619, it was a hunting lodge on the Longford estate. Its gabled storeys certainly seem big enough, and, placed on top of a hill, it appears larger than it is. The bricks are two inches thick.

In 1633, Newhouse was sold to Giles Eyre, a member of a Wiltshire family, and it has passed by descent ever since. Sir Robert Eyre (1666–1735), a barrister who rose to be Lord Chief Justice of common pleas, will be seen at various ages among the portraits, and also in a fine but anonymous marble bust. Another family link was with Lord Nelson, from whose younger sister, Catherine Matcham, the Matcham-Eyres of Newhouse were descended.

In the 18th century the two front wings were extended and the interior was modernised. The front door leads into an hexagonal Hall with a Georgian staircase. At the end of one wing, the Dining Room has a rococo ceiling; in the other wing a large room was made elaborately Caroline by Maples in 1909. The large and curious 'Hare picture', of Charles I date, shows hares hunting, teasing, executing and feasting upon humans. It is a satire, religious or political or both, condemning the life and habits of the Court party.

Norris Castle, Isle of Wight
(Mrs R. W. B. Lacon)

Between East Cowes and Osborne

When Lord Henry Seymour, the bachelor son of the 1st Marquess of Hertford, bought Norris Farm in 1795, East Cowes hardly existed. James Wyatt built for him this Castle, superbly placed high above the Solent (and incidentally contemporary with Nash's East Cowes Castle, now demolished). It still stands in isolation with its turfed grounds reaching to the sea, like a natural grandstand for the Regatta and the Naval Reviews that take place below.

The whole building is castellated, and the rough stonework ornamented by the traditional galletting of the mortar joints with flints. The main house, not over-large, has round headed windows, is intentionally asymmetrical and is dominated by a noble round tower, inside which is the circular Ballroom commanding splendid views towards the mainland. Wyatt's Library bookshelves are of oak, and Gothic. A lower kitchen and stable wing extends in a long turreted block, while away in the park there are a towered lodge and a substantial farm building, all in a castellated Roman style.

After Lord Henry's death in 1830, Norris Castle was made available to the Duchess of Kent and Princess Victoria, whose bedrooms will be seen inside. The Queen's happy memories led her, in 1845, to buy neighbouring Osborne as her informal family home. She had considered Norris, but the price asked by its new owner was unreasonable. From 1880–1903 the Castle belonged to the Duke of Bedford and functioned as a kind of guest house for Osborne. Kaiser Wilhelm II stayed here often and installed a bath-and-shower of a rather brutal appearance and behaviour. Several changes of ownership and the division of the estate followed, but in 1952 the Castle was saved from demolition by the present owner's mother, Mrs Briscoe-George. The park has been bought back piece by piece, and the house is furnished with a number of curiosities.

Norris Castle, overlooking the Solent

Northborough Manor, Cambridgeshire
(Mr Roy Genders)

Seven miles north of Peterborough (A15)

This rare and exquisite building, visible from all directions across the flat country, is known locally as 'The Castle'. No castle, of course, but a manor house of the 1330s with a noble vaulted gatehouse. It is now established* that it was built by Roger de Norburgh, Bishop of Lichfield from 1322–60. This satisfactorily explains its grace and sophistication, for it was probably erected by the same masons who were then completing the Lady Chapel at Lichfield Cathedral.

The Hall has four large rectangular windows with finely moulded tracery; the ballflower ornament that runs under the eaves is best seen at the back. This too is the best place from which to see the surviving gable, its foliage crockets rising like sea-surf to a lavishly carved chimney. Inside the front door there are three stone arches of an unusual Decorated Gothic pattern. All this was carried out in the shelly Barnac stone that was used for many early castles and cathedrals. It is refined and sturdy: the walls are three feet thick. The Hall roof consists of twenty-six closely spaced courses of timbers.

To the left are the buttery and pantry, with a long Solar above. The porch was an addition of *circa* 1500. Foundations survive for more building on the right, but the Bishop was disgraced in 1340 and his plans seem to have been interrupted. That would account for the subsequent collapse of the end wall and its rebuilding after 1600. Alterations of this later date are obvious on every side of the building, particularly in the mullioned windows and the dormers that have been fitted into the Hall roof. At this time the Hall was

Northborough Manor

* By Mr Andrew Woodger, whose account of Northborough is sold at the house.

21 Sandringham; the Main Drawing Room

22 Sherborne Castle; the 18th-century Library

23 Somerleyton Hall from the garden

24 Squerryes Court

divided by two floors into a number of rooms, the upper tracery of the Gothic windows blocked up, and the Solar was given a long stone fireplace.

These alterations were made about 1618 by the Claypole family, John Claypole having bought the property in 1572. A later John married Elizabeth Cromwell, the daughter of the Lord Protector, and, though far from puritan, the family were staunch Parliamentarians. Several of their members emigrated to America in the 17th century, where they are mentioned in the first tax list of Philadelphia, and the Claypooles were prominent among the fighters for Independence of the Colonies.

To our 'wiser generation' it seems odd that so lovely a building has been neglected for so long. Mr Roy Genders first knew the manor when he was a boy at King's School, Ely, more than fifty years ago, and in 1972–4 he achieved his life's ambition of restoring it. He now lives in the Jacobean range next to the old Gatehouse.

Norton Conyers, North Yorkshire
(Sir Richard Graham, Bart.)

Three miles north of Ripon, one mile south of Wath

Where does one read of a fine old place, a gentleman's manor house rather than a nobleman's seat, with a sunk fence; a square hall all hung with portraits; a spacious, slippery oak staircase with a high latticed window; and – yes – the squire's mad wife confined to a distant attic? There may be other houses that inspired 'Thornfield Hall' in *Jane Eyre*, but Charlotte Brontë is reported to have visited Norton Conyers in 1839, where she heard the legend of its crazed prisoner locked in the top floor.

The Conyers, a great Norman family, were granted extensive lands in Yorkshire after the Conquest, and the Nortons came into the property by marriage about 1370. Richard Norton forfeited his ownership by taking part in the ill-starred Catholic Rebellion of the North in 1569, and it is interesting that his descendants later returned to Markenfield, less than ten miles distant. Meanwhile, Norton Conyers was sold by the Crown, and acquired by Sir Richard Graham, of a Scottish Border clan, in 1624. It passed to his younger son, another Richard, who was created Baronet in 1662, in whose family it has since remained.

The brickwork is concealed by roughcast, but essentially the house is late 15th century, and old chimney stacks are visible. The prominent Dutch gables on the front are 17th-century work, as is the carved doorway. The house overlooks an extensive park, from which it is not so much separated by a sunk fence as raised upon a plateau.

The Hall is doubtless 15th century, but the screens have been removed and a later coved ceiling hides what remain of the roof timbers. The wide oak staircase is Graham work, about 1630, and is lit by Victorian armorial glass. Upstairs is the room where James II, then Duke of York, and his wife Mary of Modena slept while travelling to Scotland in 1679. Since then, however, most of the rooms have been modernised.

Norton Conyers

The most arresting portrait is of Sir Bellingham Graham, the 7th Baronet, painted by Beechey in 1811 as a dashing young officer of the Hussars. Alas, he was wild and extravagant, and on his death in 1866 the house and contents were sold. Twenty years later the family bought it back, but furniture and many paintings were not recovered. Yet portraits still hang like postage stamps in the hall and staircase, many of them 17th century; and there remain three by Romney, a pleasing but anonymous conversation group, and a splendid portrait by Batoni of Sir Humphrey Morice reclining with his hounds in a landscape. There are also Stuart royal portraits, sporting pictures by Sartorius and Emms, and a fine panorama of the Quorn Hunt by John Ferneley.

Nunwell House, Isle of Wight
(Mrs Denys Oglander)

Half a mile from Brading (A3055)

The Oglanders probably arrived with the Conqueror, have been established on their Nunwell property since the 12th century, and at Nunwell House since 1522. The best known member of the family, Sir John, who succeeded in 1609 and married Frances More of Loseley, the poet Donne's sister-in-law, was a member of Parliament and a staunch royalist. Twice imprisoned, he received Charles I at Nunwell after his flight from London in 1647, pressing into the monarch's hand a purse of gold that must have been welcome. A humanist and a gardener, Sir John emerges as a delightful character from his diaries. Not only his political loyalty but his oaken effigy at Brading church indicate that he was also a high romantic. A strangely antiquarian monument for the mid-17th century, it depicts him recumbent in armour with sword and shield, and with his legs crossed in the manner of a Crusader. He has been called 'the greatest man the Isle of Wight . . . ever produced.'

Sir John's Jacobean H-shaped house – 'a fit place' as he said 'for any gentleman' – has grown gracefully over the centuries. His great-grandson, having married an heiress, modernised it in about 1720, adding a well-mannered Georgian front faced with red tiles that have weathered little in two hundred and fifty years. The doorway, based on Vignola's Villa Farnese, is unusual, and the facade retains on the ground floor wooden mullioned and transomed windows.

Overlooking the garden to the east, the main elevation, built in 1765, was conceived on a grander scale. Of three storeys with a bowed central feature, it derives much of its effect from contrasting brickwork: predominantly lilac-grey with pale red dressings for the windows.

The Hall, behind the Queen Anne front, contains panelling and a chimneypiece of the early 18th century, while the Library, situated behind the elevation of 1765, has an Adamesque plaster ceiling, chimneypiece, and mahogany bookcases in the taste of the second half of the century. There is a nice plain staircase contemporary with the Queen Anne front.

The 17th- and 18th-century furniture looks very much at home, as do the family portraits. The best of the portraits are an excellent Lely of a boy (Sir John's grandson), Sir John himself by Cornelius Johnson, and miniatures by Engleheart, Smart, and Ozias Humphries. There is also the most halcyon of seascapes by Dominic Serres, and paintings attributed to Vernet and Gaspard Poussin. In the Hall an oak draw-table with bulbous knees, and a Jacobean chest, must date from Sir John's time, as does a serene likeness of his greatly loved wife. In the Drawing Room and elsewhere there is more good furniture: notably a late-17th-century cabinet in oyster veneer with panels of marquetry flowers, a coromandel cabinet on stand of about the same date, a pair of wide Queen Anne chairs made to take the vast crinolines

Nunwell House; the garden front

of the period, a Kentian giltwood side table, and a set of 'gothic' dining chairs attributed to Ince and Mayhew. The general effect is of a long-lived and long-loved country house.

A more exotic note is struck by a number of Italian objects which came to Nunwell a generation ago. They include two carved wood and gesso bas reliefs of religious subjects in elaborate frames, a number of Florentine 16th-century cupboards, and some naïve but delightful still-life paintings of fruit and flowers.

Oakes Park, South Yorkshire
(Major and Mrs T. Bagshawe)

Four miles south of Sheffield, by Norton church (on A6102)

Relentlessly and inevitably as Sheffield expands, its tentacles have not quite engulfed the pleasant village of Norton. Oakes Park lies, in fact, just over the county border, and faces south over a wide, green, Derbyshire valley. This was not the manor, but a house first recorded in 1468. It was entirely rebuilt in 1668, and twelve years later sold to Henry Gill, whose daughter Elizabeth married Richard Bagshawe, and whose descendants – for the present owners are kin and both Bagshawes – still live here.

Oakes was a 'double-pile' house, nine windows long and with paired doors facing the valley. Its appearance is recorded in drawings made just before subsequent alterations, i.e. before 1811, when the facade was made more regular and the former doors replaced by a central porch. Inside, some very fine joinery seems to be early 18th century. To Richard Bagshawe,

Oakes Park

then, we may credit the oak panelling in the Drawing Room with its finely carved Ionic order, and the staircase with its graceful balusters.

Richard Bagshawe was the younger son of an ancient Peak family, and he became rich through inheriting other estates. In 1801 the male line died out, and Oakes passed to a cousin, Sir William Chambers Darling, M.D., who assumed the name of Bagshawe. It was Sir William who in 1811 made alterations that left the house in its existing form, his architect being apparently Joseph Badger of Sheffield. The East Staircase has a cast-iron rail, similar to one he built at nearby Renishaw. The best of Badger's rooms is the Dining Room with its Adamesque plasterwork. The alcove was intended for a sideboard, but within ten years was filled by the mahogany chamber organ (dated 1792).

Sir William had great talents as a doctor and musician, and besides he was a patron of the youthful Francis Chantrey. This boy, who was to become the most famous English portrait sculptor of the century, was born in the village, and here are some of his early paintings, including a self-portrait made before he lost his hair through an illness. Chantrey became a life-long friend of Sir William's son, and gave him some plaster models which are in the Hall. Another young artist who later became famous was George Frederick Watts; about 1837 he painted two conversation groups of the family. Earlier portraits are hung in the Dining Room where, besides, there is a sumptuous display of Sheffield plate.

On the terrace, the urns are made of composition to Chantrey's design, and from here one looks down on the water or sytch garden, whose lake was dug for Sir William by French prisoners of war. Behind the house, the long office and stable block bears the date 1722. Among the farm buildings will be found a 17th-century Derbyshire dovecote.

Palace House, Beaulieu, Hampshire
(The Lord Montagu of Beaulieu)

Six miles south-east of Lyndhurst (B3056 and B3054)

Cistercian abbeys were vast farms in remote country, and most of them are still in surroundings of great beauty. This is the case with Beaulieu, founded in 1204 by King John in one of his repentant moods and endowed with a great estate next to the King's favourite hunting ground, the New Forest. The river widens here, and the place was called *bellus locus regi* or *beau lieu* – the place of beauty. The church was completed in 1242, and the principal monastic buildings were grouped round a cloister. The refectory is now the village church; the long, lay brothers' wing is used for 'banquets' and a museum. 'Palace House' was the main Abbey gateway. Built about a hundred years after the foundation, it lies a short distance from the Abbey and faces the river and the Abbey's mill and fish ponds.

Within four months of its dissolution this plum was bought by Thomas Wriothesly, later to become Henry VIII's Lord Chancellor and Earl of Southampton. His grandson, the 3rd Earl, is famous chiefly as a candidate

Palace House; the 14th-century monastic gatehouse, greatly enlarged

for the mysterious 'Mr. W.H.' of Shakespeare's sonnets, and his good looks are said to have saved him from execution when he was involved in the Essex plot of 1599. James I visited Beaulieu ten times, and on one occasion watched a game of football. The Southamptons died out, and Beaulieu joined the estates of two illustrious Ducal families: those of Montagu, in 1667, and of Buccleuch, in 1775. The 2nd Duke of Montagu was much at Beaulieu. He developed the shipyard at Buckler's Hard, six miles down the river, intending with a new town and harbour to compete with profit in the sugar trade. For various reasons this project failed, but with an ample timber supply close at hand ship-building continued, and several of Nelson's fleet were launched there.

It was a younger son of the 5th Duke of Buccleuch who made Palace House what it is today. His father gave him Beaulieu as a wedding present in 1866, and he employed Sir Reginald Blomfield to expand the ancient Gatehouse. The alterations were finished before he was created Baron Montagu of Beaulieu in 1885. The Abbey gateway had already been enlarged. The twin gables on the river side are Elizabethan, but of 18th-century additions there remains nothing except two curious little dunce-capped towers, which are said to have been built, with a moat, to repel French invaders.

The most interesting parts of the house are the oldest. The gateway, under a niched statue, led to a wide porch and inner reception hall. These have identical and very lovely rib vaults of the early 14th century. Above there were twin chapels – an odd arrangement, but certain because piscinas survive in both. One is now a Drawing Room, the other the Private Dining Room. Blomfield's additions include stone doorways and windows, baronial chimneypieces and interesting stained glass. The complicated family history can be followed in the portraits in the picture gallery. Specially pleasing are the views of Venice, Naples and Malta by Antonio Joli, a follower of Canaletto. More of these are at the Buccleuch property, Bowhill.

The present owner's father, the 2nd Lord Montagu of Beaulieu, was an early motor car enthusiast, and the National Motor Museum has been made to his memory. This large and fascinating collection, though not within the scope of this book, is housed in a large discreet building that blends well with the surrounding woodlands.

Parham Park, West Sussex
(Mr and Mrs P. A. Tritton)

Four miles south of Pulborough (A283)

As you approach Parham across the park, the smooth shoulders of the South Downs are seen beyond the dense involved foliage of rugged oaks. There could hardly be more satisfying contrast. The grey stone house itself is at home in the landscape where it has stood for just 400 years.

It was once thought propitious for a child to lay a foundation stone: that of Parham was laid in 1577 by the grandson, aged $2\frac{1}{2}$, of Sir Thomas Palmer, the owner. The boy did his work well. Though he went to sea with Drake and sold the property in 1601 to the Bysshopp family, Parham has always been fortunate in its owners. Bysshopp descendants lived in the house for eleven generations, acquiring a baronetcy and (by marriage) the ancient barony of Zouche. When in 1828 a daughter became the Parham heiress, she sensibly married Robert Curzon (1810–73), the distinguished traveller and author of the classic *Visits to Monasteries in the Levant*. Nearly a century later, the 17th Baroness Zouche sold Parham to Clive Pearson, younger son of the 1st Viscount Cowdray. Though many of the contents of the house went with her, fortune remained. Rarely can a great house in our day have fallen into more sensitive hands. Much of the charm and interest of Parham are due to the tact with which it was subsequently restored and the

Parham Park

judgment with which it was furnished. The tradition continues under the present owners – Mrs Tritton is Clive Pearson's daughter – and few houses are presented to the visitor with a better eye for arrangement and detail.

Architecturally among the simplest of Elizabethan houses, Parham turns its shapeliest front to the south and the Downs, revealing the characteristic E plan of the period, with gabled wings at either end and a central porch. The latter, the original entrance, acquired a later doorway surmounted by a swaggering coat of arms, early in the 18th century. To the left of the porch the immensely tall mullioned and transomed windows indicate the position of the Hall. Elsewhere on this front the fenestration is post-Tudor: the other mullioned windows are part of the tactful restoration undertaken a generation ago, and the sashes are Georgian.

The architectural highlights of the interior are the Hall and the Long Gallery. Lit by its towering windows, the double-cube Hall has kept its original stone fireplace (revealed some 30 years ago) and its well-proportioned Renaissance screen that offers a pleasing contrast in its restraint to the over-elaboration of many Flemish-inspired examples. Above the screen, instead of the usual music gallery, two windows give on the hall. They are so contrived that the timber-framing of the wall itself provides the architraves and mullions. Though the paved floor is presumably 18th century, and the ceiling decoration was doubtless due to Robert Curzon in the 19th century, the overall effect is probably much as it was in 1601 when the Bysshopps moved in.

The Long Gallery – so long (158 feet) that the Parham Yeomanry, the local Home Guard of the Napoleonic Wars, is said sometimes to have drilled here – dates from the late 1570s, and is in its own way as fine as the Great Hall. The floor is original, and Ionic pilasters lend a pleasant rhythm to the oak wainscot which has a continuous carved frieze. The ceiling, which recently replaced a Victorian predecessor, is painted with flowing foliage decoration in tempera by Oliver Messel, an effective modern interpretation of an Elizabethan theme. Other contemporary work of good quality characterise the Parlour, and the Solar above it, which regained much of their original character when restored in the 1930s. The new plaster decoration in these rooms, made without moulds, is full of character and recalls the freedom and vivacity of Tudor plasterwork.

The taste of the 18th century has left little mark on Parham, except in a Saloon of 1790. Perhaps because of its low ceiling, the neo-classical decoration here does not make great impact, though the paintings and furniture, more or less contemporary with the room, give it every chance.

When it comes to the contents of Parham, it is impossible to do justice in small compass to the fabrics, furniture, and paintings. Consistent either in high quality or historical importance, they are also displayed with unfailing judgment. Oriental carpets, tapestries, and above all a profusion of rare needlework, lend colour to one room after another. The needlework, which includes pristine wall-hangings in Hungarian stitch and numberless pictorial panels, dates predominantly from Jacobean and Stuart times, but includes a few Elizabethan pieces.

Parham Park; the Hall, with Elizabethan portraits

As suits the character of the house, most of the furniture (except that in the Saloon) is also early. The Great Hall sets the tone with an oak chest and draw-table, both pre-1600, and elsewhere there is a very early example of that useful object, the chest of drawers (*c.* 1600). Jacobean and Carolean furniture are well represented, but the historical sequence virtually ends with early-18th-century walnut, notably a George II mirror with gilt and walnut frame.

However, it is the paintings at Parham, and in particular the series of early historical portraits, most of them collected by Clive Pearson, that are best known. Some two dozen of these portraits were executed before 1600, and half the famous faces of the Elizabethan age look down from the walls of the Great Hall: among them the Queen herself (perhaps by Zucchero), her brother, Edward VI; her successor, James I, and his wife, Anne of Denmark; Lord Burghley, her chancellor; her favourites, Leicester and Essex (the latter by Gheeraerts); and not least Henry Howard, the poet-earl of Surrey, executed by her father, Henry VIII (a splendid melancholy portrait by Stretes).

The paintings in the Parlour evoke Charles I and his family with the same immediacy. There he is, a humourless young man, painted as Prince of Wales by Mytens, and nearby are his sister Elizabeth of Bohemia, 'The Winter Queen', and her husband the Elector Palatine, Anna Maria, the Spanish Princess whom he did not marry, Henrietta Maria whom he did, and his French brother-in-law, Louis XIII. Anne Kirke, his Queen's statuesque attendant, immortalised by Van Dyck, mixes with this royal company.

In the Ante-Room, Charles II, sardonic and confident, presides over a more relaxed gathering, sharing the walls with 'Minette', his favourite sister, with Anne Hyde, his sister-in-law, with his wife Catharine of Braganza, and inevitably with those two alluring ladies, Louise de Querouaille and Barbara Villiers (painted, no less inevitably, by Lely).

Other paintings in the house include two or three of Cornelius Johnson's finest portraits, full-lengths by Reynolds of Sir Joseph Banks and of Omai, the Tahitian boy brought back by Captain Cook (there is another version at Castle Howard), animal subjects by Wootton, Seymour and Stubbs, and a magic view of Venice by Bellotto.

Parnham House, Dorset
(Mr John Makepeace)

A mile south of Beaminster (A3066)

Parnham is a grandiose house, ostensibly Tudor, that lies low in the woods of the Brit valley sheltered by steep, broken hills. It came by descent to the Strodes in the time of Henry VI, and about 1540 Robert Strode, having married advantageously, was able to rebuild it. His work survives in the central Hall and the Solar wing to the left. The right-hand wing, formerly containing the kitchens, was rebuilt by his grandson. The resulting facade is larger and more decorative than most contemporary Dorsetshire manors of this date, and is particularly attractive owing to the use of Ham Hill stone. Though not symmetrical, it is E-shaped with staircase projections, battlements and gables, and a fine oriel window over the front door. Parnham, without alteration, might have suited the 18th-century taste for 'picturesque'. None the less, the improving hand of John Nash came in 1810 to block one side of the Great Hall with a new dining room, redesign the garden fronts and reconstruct the gables with a great display of turrets. The result may offend Tudor purists but is undeniably pleasing.

Parnham House

The house belonged to one family for at least five hundred years, but was eventually sold in 1896, and again in 1910. The interior has been despoiled and refitted. Most of the existing woodwork was bought by Dr Hans Sauer before 1914, and the coat of arms he assumed is over the fireplace in the Great Hall. Above this the roof is still open, and some old heraldic glass remains in the windows. The Gothic beam across the chimney is known to have been originally at Parnham, but was thrown out by Nash and later recovered from another house. In the Oak Room, the linenfold panelling and splendid Renaissance plaster frieze are thought to have come from West Horsley Place, Surrey. The Drawing Room is 17th century; the staircase is a pastiche. Dr Sauer also restored the lawns and terraces, following the lay-out of the Elizabethan garden, and built walls, balustrades and pavilions based on those at Montacute. They make a worthy foreground to the cedars and Turkey oaks.

Since Dr Sauer there have been no less than five successive owners. During the Second World War, Generals Eisenhower and Patton prepared their invasion plans in the Oak Room. Parnham had been empty four years before it was bought in 1976 by John Makepeace and his wife, who transferred their workshops from Banbury, and make furniture in rare and fine woods. The house is now a craft school and every one of its eighty rooms is in use for work, teaching or accommodation. The garden, too, has been revived: the topiary is clipped, water channels run once more, and much planting is being done.

Pattyndenne, Kent
(Mr and Mrs D. C. Spearing)

A mile south of Goudhurst (B2079)

This old house in the heart of the Weald will delight all enthusiasts of the timber-frame. Its Saxon name means 'a forest clearing by a stream'. Built about 1480 as a house suitable for the Manor Court proceedings, it remains today an almost unaltered example of a 'Wealden house'. In this local style the first floor projected in a jetty; but the central part containing the Hall (which was originally open to the roof) has no jetty and appears to be recessed. The jetties at Pattyndenne were on all four sides, and the Hall recessions were on both long faces. The construction rests on four sturdy corner posts, chamfered and moulded, and above them the diagonally placed dragon beams are plainly visible.

The close-studded timbers and moulded fascias have weathered to silver-grey, and the original foundations of Wealden sandstone remain on the north side. The plan was neat and logical. The central Hall was flanked by a parlour at one end and butteries at the other, with chambers above and attics on the second floor. Most of this survives unaltered. Originally the only access from one end to the other was through the open Hall. Under the roof, a massive beam supports a crown post.

In the 16th century the house was sold by the Pattyndenn family to Sir

Pattyndenne

Maurice Berkeley, a younger son of Lord Berkeley, who was Standard Bearer to Henry VIII, Edward VI, Mary and Elizabeth in turn. Four diamond panes of stained glass in the Hall show the rose of Henry VIII and the pomegranate of Katherine of Aragon, who, by tradition, stayed here. Either Sir Maurice or his son modernised the building by inserting the great fireplace in the Hall and additional rooms on two floors above it. The date suggested is 1580, but the deeply moulded beams could be earlier.

The diminutive kitchen wing built about 1600 will have replaced a detached kitchen in the back courtyard. The final alteration came about 1890 in the form of an extension at the back to allow a new staircase. Essential though this is for convenience, it destroyed the original symmetry of the house. The present owners bought Pattyndenne in 1972 and have carried out much restoration. Their early oak furniture looks very well in the house.

Pembridge Castle, Hereford and Worcester
(Mr R. A. Cooke)

Four miles north of Monmouth (between Welsh Newton and Broak Oak)

One of the smaller Border Castles, this rosy-coloured building is isolated among its farmlands, commanding a sweeping view over the valley to the north. The round tower to the left seems to be 12th-century work, the curtain walls slightly later. The fabric, where original, has great beauty and invites a leisurely walk round the moat – which is just wet.

During the Civil War Pembridge was besieged and taken by the Parliamentarians, and stands for their cannon still exist on the higher ground. The result was that the Gatehouse and right-hand wall were 'slighted' or ruined, and remained so until this century. Perhaps the Keep was 'slighted'

268

Pembridge Castle, showing the restored gatehouse

too; the dwelling house is 17th century and was inhabited during the Restoration by George Kemble. His brother John was a Catholic priest who, at the age of eighty, was arrested and executed after the Titus Oates Plot (1679) for having said Mass at the Castle. He is buried at Welsh Newton and was lately canonised.

Drawings of the Castle before it was restored* show that it looked very different from today. In 1912 Dr Hedley Bartlett restored the whole, rebuilding the Gatehouse and curtain wall, fitting pointed windows, and crowning the tower with battlements. The house is a farm and is not open, but visitors may pass through the Court to the Chapel and its simple 13th-century undercroft. The little Chapel itself is late 16th century, but the fittings, the oak screen, carvings and glass, were brought here by Dr Bartlett.

Pencarrow, Cornwall
(Trustees of the Molesworth St Aubyn Settled Estates)

Three miles north-west of Bodmin (B3266)

Like Bodmin Moor, the North and West of Cornwall are bleak and treeless, but four estates near Bodmin – Glynn, Llanhydrock, Boconnoc and Pencarrow – have converted what was open country into a thickly wooded district of great beauty. Pencarrow has an exciting approach. Visitors do not enter the lodges and avenue of monkey puzzle, but join the drive where it becomes typical of Cornish houses, with massed hydrangeas, rhododendrons and azaleas under shaggy trees. Suddenly it swerves round an Iron Age encampment, whose inner ditch is a perfect oval, surrounded by stunted oaks; then comes a glimpse of the house, below and to the right. After all this the building itself may seem conventional and reticent. It is square,

* See *Forgotten Shrines* by Dom Bede Camm, O.S.B. (1910).

Pencarrow; the Palladian front

stuccoed Palladian work of the 1750s, well-proportioned and well-mannered.

The house was begun by Sir John Molesworth, 4th Baronet, but being unfinished at his death in 1766 it was completed by his son. The core of the building is older, perhaps 16th century. The estate was first leased and subsequently bought by John Molesworth, Auditor of the Duchy of Cornwall to Queen Elizabeth, and greatly enriched in 1689 on the death of Sir Hender Molesworth, who left his Jamaican fortune as well as his Baronetcy to his elder brother. From this time the Molesworths were prosperous, and in Pencarrow will be found the contents of several houses which came by marriage: Tetcott and Werrington in West Devon, and Clavance in Cornwall. The present head of the family is Sir John Molesworth-St Aubyn.

In the Music Room, a stucco ceiling of the 1760s depicts the Four Seasons. The maple graining of the walls was commissioned about 1830 by Sir William Molesworth when he extended the room to make a setting for a marble *Venus* brought from Rome. A dramatic effect was achieved by placing it in a triple carved window frame, early Georgian and probably brought from another house. As an advanced radical Sir William was not popular with his neighbours, but he was a determined man and became Colonial Secretary before his death in 1855.

This Music Room is the odd-man-out in a delightful series of mid-Georgian rooms, all with good chimneypieces, excellent furniture and first-rate contents. Besides the family portraits there are subject pictures such as the fine pair by Samuel Scott of *London Bridge* and the *Tower of London*, both dated 1755, and quantities of fine porcelain. Upstairs are two bedrooms, a dressing room and boudoir, and the tour of the house ends *via* the Dining Room in the Ante-Room, with a charming conversation piece by Arthur Devis (showing St Michael's Mount in the background) and other cabinet paintings.

Outside there is much to see. An immense circular lawn on the south front is surrounded by massed woodlands offering long walks and short walks. Many of the trees are rare, and they are listed in the guide book. The visitor should venture at least to the Palm House, standing in a dell shaded by immense trees. Two palms, planted under glass in the 1850s, have long since forced their way through the roof and now stand well above it.

Penhow Castle, Gwent
(Mr Stephen Weeks)

Between Chepstow and Newport (A48)

The Norman castle was one of six outposts that defended Chepstow, the southernmost seat of the Marcher Lords, from Welsh assaults. It can hardly have been convenient for there was no well, and until quite recent times water had to be brought by horse and cart. From the road Penhow appears as a discreet house washed white, almost hidden by trees, and standing high above a quarried rock face. The age of the buildings only becomes apparent from the lane, past the farm. First comes an isolated towered church that was once the castle chapel. The huddle of old buildings beyond this comprise the core of the castle, and their dates span more than five centuries.

Earliest is the rectangular Tower, Norman and 12th century, containing a raised Hall and a Chamber above it. The Hall was entered by an external ladder, while the upper staircases are built in the thickness of its walls. From its earliest time this was the seat of the St Maur family, who came to England in the wake of the Conqueror from their village in the Touraine, France. Their name was corrupted into Seymour, and they are the ancestors of all

Penhow Castle; with the Norman tower on the left

true Seymours. In the 14th century Sir Roger Seymour, a younger son, moved away from Penhow, and from him are descended the Dukes of Somerset and the Marquesses of Hertford. Two generations later, Isabella, the Penhow heiress, married John Bowles, who assumed the Seymour arms.

Meanwhile the Gatehouse had been built and a Hall adjoining it, the latter being divided about 1483 into a Lower Hall for retainers and an upper Great Hall. Timbers of the roof and screen survive. During the more peaceful Tudor age another Hall wing was built opposite, and this was modernised late in the 17th century. Here will be found a most pleasant Dining Room, plastered in the Restoration style, and a sturdy oak staircase leading to the upper floors, while a canopied doorway opens to the narrow and precipitous terrace overlooking the main road.

This proved to be the last of the alterations, because in 1709 Penhow was let as a farmhouse. The Restoration wing was occupied but the remainder, used for stores and animals, became neglected and the tower was gutted. In 1973 Mr Weeks, an independent director-producer of films, bought the property and began the restorations. The tower has been newly floored and roofed, and some kind of reconstruction of the buildings across the court is planned. Meanwhile, excavations in and outside the walls have discovered many old foundations. The two fine manorial gate piers that first greet the visitor have been brought here from the Stroud Valley in Gloucestershire.

Penshurst Place, Kent
(The Viscount De L'Isle, V.C., K.G.)

Four miles north-west of Tunbridge Wells (B2176)

A sense of the epic, of the passage of great men and events, is so strong in certain houses that a description in terms of architecture and works of art fails to convey their distinctive 'personality'. This is particularly true of Penshurst. Few houses have an aura more immediately felt and yet more independent of drawing-boards and the vagaries of artistic taste. The aura derives largely from the associations of Penshurst with the Sidney family. Mrs Montagu, first of the 'blue stockings', wrote after a visit in 1753, 'I know not a family that for arts and arms, greatness of courage, and nobility of mind, have excelled the Sidney race'. She was of course thinking first of Sir Philip Sidney, courtier, ambassador, soldier and poet, the nonpareil of his time; thinking surely also of his brilliant sister Mary, Countess of Pembroke, celebrated by Spenser and Ben Jonson, and nearer her own day of Algernon Sidney, dedicated republican yet resolutely opposed to the trial and execution of the king, who went into exile at the Restoration and, returning after seventeen years, was caught in the political toils of the age, tried by the notorious Jeffreys, and beheaded on Tower Hill. Mrs Montagu, had she lived in our time, would also have had in mind the hinterland of the beaches of Anzio and the Victoria Cross won by William Sidney, Lord De L'Isle, who lives at Penshurst today.

The towers, halls, and galleries of Penshurst, built of warm and now long-

Penshurst Place; the 14th-century Hall and John of Lancaster's Wing; (see also colour plate 15)

weathered sandstone, are supremely romantic, but they have come together in haphazard fashion over the centuries, and their irregular plan makes them difficult to decipher architecturally.* The story begins shortly before 1350 when Sir John de Pulteney, a wealthy financier and lately Lord Mayor of London, built the Great Hall with a block at either end, one to contain the family apartments, the other to contain kitchen and offices.

Some forty years later, when troubled times and the threat of French invasion led to the building of Bodiam Castle twenty miles to the south, a new owner enclosed Pulteney's hall-house with a defensive curtain wall furnished with eight salient towers to provide flanking fire. As the house grew, three of these towers and stretches of curtain were incorporated into later extensions, and one tower stands isolated in the south garden. Otherwise these 14th-century defences have disappeared. The next development came about 1430, when John of Lancaster, brother of Henry V, tacked on the imposing range awkwardly situated at the south-west corner of the solar. The tall mullioned windows, with more than a hint of the French Renaissance, were added by Sir Henry Sidney over a hundred years later.

Penshurst was granted to the Sidneys by Edward VI in 1552, and Sir Henry Sidney (1529–86), father of Sir Philip, made notable changes to the mediaeval house. Having refashioned the solar and state rooms, he linked the Great Hall with a new range and gatehouse to the north, incorporating one of the 14th-century curtain towers. Not least he introduced in his north range an open arcade (now glazed) with Tuscan columns; in 1579 it was a novelty ahead of its time and probably the earliest classical loggia in the country. This is seen from the windows of the State Rooms. The Long

* But see the *Architectural Development of Penshurst Place*, by Marcus Binney and Anthony Emery on sale at the house. An exemplary pamphlet of a sort that many visitors would appreciate at other complex houses.

Gallery was added by Sir Robert Sidney, 1st Earl of Leicester, between 1599 and 1607.

For nearly 250 years Penshurst was then left to mellow; it is thus one of the few great houses which show almost no architectural trace of the later 17th and 18th centuries. Some repairs in a Gothic style were carried out about 1820. Later in the century some of Sir Henry Sidney's state rooms, notably in John of Lancaster's wing, were restored and given their present appearance. But on the whole the 19th century dealt kindly with Penshurst.

The 14th-century Great Hall (the first room seen by visitors) is breathtaking. For its scale, its extraordinary state of preservation, and not least its noble roof, it is unrivalled in any private house. The roof with its massive moulded timbers is of chestnut. The dais, the pinkish tiled floor, and the central hearth may well be original, though the louvre in the roof through which the smoke escaped has gone. The three Gothic archways that led from the screens passage to the kitchen and offices survive intact; the screen itself which bears the Sidney crest, the ragged bear and staff, appears to be 16th century, though the panels which have cast plaster decoration (not carved wood) are perhaps later. Sir Philip Sidney's helm, carried at his funeral on February 16, 1587, is preserved in the hall, and it is curious to reflect that he may have sat at one of the long, elm-topped, trestle tables which had already seen much use in his day.

A wide stone staircase leads up to the state apartments. The first of these, once the 14th-century solar and later the Elizabethan ante-chamber, is now the State Dining Room. Above the 19th-century wainscot hang portraits of 16th- and early-17th-century Sidneys. Among them are a posthumous portrait of Sir Robert attributed to the talented painter William Larkin, and the likenesses of Philip Sidney himself, of his sister Mary with a lute, and of his sister-in-law, Barbara Gamage, with her children (a highly decorative work by Gheeraerts, dated 1596). The crystal and giltwood chandelier carved with cupids and martial busts is probably French and, like the huge silver wine fountain, is late 17th century.

With Queen Elizabeth's Room one is in John of Lancaster's wing (now known as the Buckingham Wing). Transformed in 1575 by Sir Henry Sidney into his Great Chamber, the room was again remodelled in the 19th century when it received its linenfold panelling and traceried window. But the finest things here evoke 1700 or thereabouts. The rare appliqué wall hangings of green and rose damask are of this date; so too the superb daybed with a shell-head and the accompanying chairs, upholstered in the same soft colours as the hangings; also the gesso side table and the torchères which bear one of the Sidney emblems, the pheon (broad arrow). The three rock crystal chandeliers are perhaps a little earlier.

The Tapestry Room, once probably the withdrawing chamber, the apartment that terminated the usual sequence of Elizabethan state rooms, is hung with a pair of handsome 17th-century Brussels tapestries from the set known as *The Elements* and a rare Gothic tapestry of about 1520 perhaps made at Tournai or Arras. A contemporary copy of Van Dyck's equestrian portrait of Charles hangs over the fireplace which is flanked by ebonised

Penshurst Place; Queen Elizabeth's Room with its Baroque furnishings

late Stuart chairs with scrolled stretchers and a settee to match. Other furniture includes an elaborate Kentian giltwood table, and a late-17th-century ebonized cabinet on stand, inset with well executed Flemish paintings.

The Long Gallery, lighted on each side by mullioned windows, made its appearance comparatively late, in 1599–1607. It was elaborately panelled and the array of Sidney portraits looks well against the oak wainscot. There are versions of well-known portraits of Edward VI and Queen Elizabeth, and a mask of the Queen, cast in lead from her monument in Westminster Abbey. Most of the early Sidneys are represented: Sir Philip, his sister Mary, his uncle the Earl of Leicester, and there is a striking portrait of Sir Henry, the builder, perhaps by Hans Eworth, and a decorative likeness of Barbara Gamage, attributed (like that in the Dining Room) to Gheeraerts. Later paintings include a fine Cornelius Johnson, a Lely and a Kneller of more than ordinary quality, and a portrait of Algernon Sidney by Van Egmont, no doubt painted when he was in exile. Blue and white porcelain stands on giltwood side tables, and there is a set of ebonized late-17th-century Indo-Portuguese chairs inlaid with ivory. But the outstanding piece is an octagonal table with a Florentine scagliola top, signed by Lamberto Gori, dated 1753, and portraying the Sidney arms and supporters.

Between walls of Tudor sandstone and yew hedges, the gardens and orchards re-create something of the formal effect seen in Kip's early-18th-century engraving of Penshurst. The layout shown by Kip may well have dated from the 16th century when Sir Henry Sidney was carrying out extensive garden works and was importing fruit trees from Holland. The garden soon became famous for fruit that both Ben Jonson and later John Evelyn praised. Recently an Agricultural Museum has been established in farm buildings to the north, and beyond it a Leisure Park, with rare breeds of domestic animals, has been opened to visitors.

Peover Hall, Cheshire
(Mr Randle Brooks)

Over Peover, four miles south-east of Knutsford (A50)

The Mainwaring family, who lie in their imposing tombs in the adjoining church, owned Peover from the late Middle Ages until 1919. Their red brick Tudor house was built by Sir Ralph Mainwaring whose scrolled coat of arms, dated 1585, appears over the door. The house has undergone many vicissitudes, not least its occupation by the American Third Army when it served as General Patton's Headquarters. On its reversion to use as a private house, extensive renovations were necessary and a large 18th-century wing was demolished.

Late Tudor chimneypieces and wainscot survive in some of the rooms. The 18th-century panelling in the Hall was introduced in this century, as was the virtuoso 17th-century woodwork in the Morning Room. Representing cherubs and pendants of realistically carved fruits and flowers, with twisted Baroque columns framing parcel-gilt Renaissance panels in the overmantel, it must originally have decorated some church. The 16th-century Kitchen has a curious ceiling with cusped braces that play a purely decorative role. Nineteenth-century taste is reflected in the sumptuous Library bookcases and Victorian furniture, which includes pieces such as a great sideboard carved with the meeting of King John and his barons, hardly less elaborate than the famous sideboard at Charlecote Park.

But the notable feature of Peover are the Stables, a long brick range with mullioned windows built in 1654. The interior is a rare survival. Thirteen stalls are set between Tuscan columns, each box spanned by an arch in carved strapwork; above is a strapwork frieze and a plaster ceiling divided

Peover Hall

into large panels with a formal motif in the corners and a central spray of flowers. The Mainwaring horses were nobly housed. So too were their coaches, for the adjoining Coach House, about a century later, is a handsome building. The fine wrought-iron screen and gates near the Stables are mid-18th century.

Port Lympne, Kent
(Mr Michael Aspinall)

Three miles west of Hythe (B2067)

Sir Philip Sassoon's house, built on the cliff overlooking the inhospitable Romney Marsh, was described in 1923 as 'the most remarkable modern house in England'. Its interior is of a style very rarely seen in this country but less unusual in France: expensive, optimistic, colourful and strongly evocative of the society of its day. Sir Philip, who was Private Secretary to Lord Haig and then to Lloyd George, lived among the great figures in politics and art, and his lavish hospitality has become a legend. The list of friends entertained here includes the Prince of Wales and Mrs Simpson, Lloyd George, Lord Curzon, Winston Churchill, Lord Beaverbrook, Charles Chaplin, T. E. Lawrence, and could be extended indefinitely.

The house was designed in the Dutch Colonial style by Sir Herbert Baker just before the First World War. The narrow bricks came from France but the windows are of English oak and the tiles were baked locally. The post-war work is more adventurous. When Baker left England for Delhi, he was succeeded by Philip Tilden, who added the colonnades, extended the garden, and redesigned the interior. To Tilden are due the bronze front

Port Lympne; looking over Romney Marsh; (see also colour plate 16)

door, the black and white marble floor in the hall, and the staircase with its scagliola columns of *lapis* blue below and coral pink above. The luxuriant stair rail in the Wren style, designed by Reynolds Bainbridge, was copied from Caroline Park in Scotland. A door of corded iron leads to Tilden's masterpiece, the Moorish Courtyard inspired by a building at Cordoba. Dozens of marble colonnettes, marble paving with fountains and myrtle borders, pink walls and a green roof make this a place of private and mysterious enchantment.

The rooms on the garden side were badly damaged when the house was requisitioned during the Second World War, and they now form the Wildlife Art Gallery. The Drawing Room had been entirely painted by Michel Sert with elephants and an allegory of *France attacked by Germany*, but this was destroyed by Czech soldiers and survives only in photographs. The Dining Room was decorated before 1923 by Glyn Philpot in a dreamy colour scheme: *lapis* walls, opalescent pink ceiling, and gold chairs with sage green cushions. His Egyptian frieze, in black, white and chocolate, has survived and is to be put up in another room.

Rex Whistler's delightful Tent Room, dated 1931, remains complete and has recently been restored by the Tate Gallery. The shaped ceiling has become a striped awning 'embroidered' with the owner's monogram, and the walls show a lady visiting some ideal Georgian town in her barouche; the townsfolk are idle and innocent. Between the windows is a map of the garden as it then was. The tiny Octagonal Library has also survived with shelves of unstained sycamore glinting like satin. This was completed in 1921, and the Treaty of Paris was signed here by Clemenceau and Briand.

In designing the extensive garden, Sir Philip met the challenge of the cliff face and turned it into a series of terraces with a central swimming pool, walks and enclosed gardens, a vineyard and figyard. This rather flashy lay-out was intended to be 'Roman'; its most impressive feature is certainly the Roman Stair that rises to the top of the hill. Tilden's twin temples have, alas, gone, but the ragstone walls and stone steps are in fine condition. When Mr Aspinall bought the property in 1973 all this had become sadly neglected. The immense work of restoration has been swift but is not yet complete. The surrounding fields are a Wildlife Sanctuary.

Powderham Castle, Devonshire
(The Earl and Countess of Devon)

Between Exeter and Dawlish (A374)

The name of Castle is well suited to Powderham's solid masonry and embattled towers, though originally it was but a defensive manor. In mediaeval times it stood on a dry knoll above the estuary marshes and bogs of the Exe. The ground that stretches towards the estuary, below the garden terrace, was reclaimed as parkland long ago and planted with oak, lime and cedar. On the other side are bracken-clad moors.

The Courtenays, one of the most illustrious old families of Europe, are

Powderham Castle; from the terrace

found in France about the year A.D. 1000, and later their members included three Latin Emperors of Constantinople. The branch that came to England with Eleanor of Aquitaine, wife of Henry II, acquired Powderham by marriage at the end of the 14th century, which is the date of the oldest surviving building. They were ennobled as Earls of Devon, but the title was forfeited by attainder and granted anew to Edward Courtenay in 1553. When he died without direct male heirs it remained dormant until it was successfully claimed in 1831 by William, 3rd Viscount Courtenay, who thus became 9th Earl of Devon.

The 14th-century stronghold consisted of the long centre building and six various towers, of which at least one (to the north) remains intact, while others appear to have been rebuilt. Apart from the Chapel, the only original work to be seen inside consists of occasional arches and uncovered stonework. The Gate and Forecourt are due to rebuilding during the 1840s by Charles Fowler, who is best known as an architect of markets. Since the original Hall had already been divided and transformed, Fowler added a new Banqueting or Dining Hall in an ornate Gothic style. On the chimneypiece, panelling and roof, all the heraldry of the Courtenays' long descent will be found.

The large painting in the Hall, showing the family of the 1st Viscount Courtenay, is by Thomas Hudson, a native of Devonshire who became London's most fashionable portrait painter before Reynolds. Most of his works for Lord Courtenay show the family, as they are here, in Van Dyck dress. Between 1735 and 1765, Lord Courtenay Georgianised many rooms, giving them rococo plasterwork. The finest of all, indeed one of the best interiors of its time, is the Staircase which takes up half of the old Hall. It rises the entire height of the building, and the plasterwork, carried out by

John Jenkins of Exeter, is dated 1755. Profuse drops of flowers and fruit are arranged between panels in a manner that recalls the style of Grinling Gibbons, but their modelling is distinctly rococo. On the upper walls are trophies symbolising the arts of war, peace and love.

Three massive pieces of furniture belong to the same period. The ornate long-case clock has a movement signed by a local maker, but its case must surely have been made in London. A ponderous pair of bookcases, rosewood inlaid with brass, signed by John Channon and dated 1750, show early Georgian furniture at its most ambitious and Germanic. Their columns support wavy pediments, and round the feet are the dolphins of the family crest. They were made for an upstairs library, but the succession of Libraries now occupy ground floor rooms.

The work of another generation will be found in the Music Room, designed by James Wyatt in the 1790s. It is lit by a bow window, has a central dome, scagliola pilasters and musical instruments in the plasterwork. The gilt and white seats, with dolphin arms, are attributed to the firm of Marsh and Tatham, who also supplied furniture for the Prince of Wales at Carlton House. The carved organ is slightly earlier. Within Westmacott's marble chimneypiece is a rare French firebasket of ormolu, signed by Thomire and dated 1788. Above this hangs the portrait of the patron, the 3rd Viscount Courtenay, as a young man, once again in Van Dyck dress. Though he was highly cultivated, his life was overshadowed by having been involved, when a boy, in the notorious scandal with William Beckford. Perhaps this led to his extravagance, and after 1800 he lived in New York and Paris. An only son, he had thirteen sisters, some of whom were also portrayed by Cosway, chastely robed in white and in groups of three.

In 1861 an old granary on the other side of the Castle was consecrated as a Chapel. This is the only mediaeval room to be seen, and it has a good arched and braced timber roof. The old carved bench ends are of particular interest, being in a hybrid Renaissance style and obviously of local craftsmanship.

Purse Caundle Manor, Dorset
(Mr Ralph Egon Winckelmann)

Four miles east of Sherborne (A30)

The grey manor house is at the centre of a shy Dorset village. Stone roofs jut out to the different gable fronts, and a miniature oriel window of great beauty stands above the road, carved with Gothic escutcheons. There were two manors at Purse Caundle in the Middle Ages, both of them ecclesiastical property. This seems to have been the one where a John Alleyn lived in the 13th century with the duty to 'keep and lodge the King's sick or injured hounds at the King's cost'. About 1429 Richard Long bought the house, and a hundred years later it passed to his cousins, the Hanhams. Between them these two families built the house.

The Hall is open to its roof and is 15th century, but five sturdy tie-beams with crown-posts look like an afterthought to strengthen the structure.

Purse Caundle Manor; a 15th-century Hall, with Tudor doorways and tie-beams (See also illustration on p. 30)

They obscure the carved Gothic frieze. Improvements were carried out by William Hanham before 1550, and his initials are carved on a door that formerly led to a newel stair; he also made the dining recess, perhaps out of an earlier porch.

The planning is peculiar because the Great Chamber upstairs lies above the service end of the house. It is a 15th-century room with the oriel window and an unusual and generously arched waggon roof. The big addition at this end of the house came after 1600, namely a long, low, E-shaped wing. This now overlooks the garden, and it comes as a surprise. The ground floor was all taken up with service rooms: buttery, pantry, kitchen and scullery, with lodgings above.

A number of the rooms are panelled, and the oak staircase was built in the 17th century. The Hanhams were Royalists, impoverished by the Civil War, and their occupation came to an end during the Commonwealth. Later owners have included the Huddlestons, also of Sawston Hall, and during this century Lady Victoria Herbert who restored the house to its present excellent condition. In removing Victorian plasterwork she revealed the old doorways in the screens passage. The big Hall window, however, is modern.

Quenby Hall, Leicestershire
(The Squire de Lisle)

Seven miles east of Leicester, *via* Hungarton

This noble house of brick and stone is the best of its period in the county. Its similarity to Doddington Hall in Lincolnshire has often been remarked on, but Quenby was built some twenty years later, about 1615–20. Perhaps it, too, was designed by one of the Smithsons. The exterior is so fine that it seems unchanged since it left the architect's hands. Well, not altogether

Quenby Hall

perhaps. The oaks in the park are too picturesquely grouped for that formal age, and the forecourt is actually an 18th-century enclosure. The central turret has clearly been rebuilt, and some changes have occurred on the opposite front. The elaborate rain-heads are Georgian. Yet all the restoration has been finely done and has caused the minimum of alteration.

The interior is another story. In the 18th century Quenby was bought by Shuckburgh Ashby, a younger son of the Ashby family who had lived here since the 13th century. In restoring a neglected house, Shuckburgh reversed the familiar process. Instead of inserting a floor in the Hall he removed one, together with the screen and panelling. The lofty room that resulted is difficult to visualise, but at the time it was greatly applauded. In 1904 the house was sold to Mrs Greaves, who employed Bodley to put back the floor. Much panelling was recovered from the attics, and a new screen was designed by J. A. Gotch. The Great Chamber above (now the Ballroom) is a brilliant restoration by Bodley, who gave it a plaster ceiling copied from one at Knole. The principal ornament of this splendid room, the magnificent chimneypiece, was recovered from below. It is a monumental piece of carving, with columns flanking the arms of Ashby, mantling in particularly high relief, and interesting filigree detail.

However, the cross wing remains much in its original state. The Brown Parlour has superb carved panelling with four tiers of arches under a rich ceiling. A great oak Staircase central in the wing (in the same position as that at Doddington) has sturdy oak continuous-newels, and leads to two apartments: one bedroom has a plaster frieze of angels, the other has pomegranates very similar to contemporary work at Chastleton House. Old garderobes have been fitted with modern plumbing.

The present owner bought the house from Sir Anthony Nutting in 1972 and has restored the entire house and grounds to their present immaculate condition. The de Lisle family has seats nearby at Garendon and Gracedieu. Garendon House has been demolished, but from it come the pedimented

282

tympanum over the Hall fireplace bearing the March Phillipps de Lisle arms, and a chimneypiece by Pugin in the Library. Family portraits hang in the Ballroom, and more, including fine pastels by Rosalba, are in the Brown Parlour. Many of the works of art have been acquired recently, including Peruvian religious paintings of the 18th century. The William and Mary Room has panelling and furniture of that date, and its great bed, formerly at St Donat's Castle in Wales, has been covered in velvet by Mrs de Lisle.

Quenby is further distinguished in having given Stilton cheese to the world. It was first made here by the housekeeper, and in the 17th century was sold in bulk to the landlord of the Bell Inn at Stilton on the Great North Road, whence it came to London tables.

Raby Castle, Durham
(The Lord Barnard)

Between Barnard Castle and Bishop Auckland (A688)

A great feudal castle set in a beautiful landscaped park is the essence of the picturesque taste. But this is a romantic ideal; in the Middle Ages the appearance was different. This concentration of towers and battlements was set behind a defensive curtain wall thirty feet high, and the untamed parkland looked bleak and brutal.

Raby is first recorded as belonging to Canute. The powerful Nevill family acquired it by marriage after the Norman period, and the castle was certainly fortified before John, Lord Nevill, was granted a licence to crenellate it in 1378. Like the Percys of Alnwick, the Nevills were Wardens of the Scottish Marches. This low-lying position might seem a weakness in defence, but there can be no doubt of the castle's worth as a symbol of power. When James I visited Raby, he was impressed by its enormous size.

The complexity and lack of symmetry that was criticised in the Elizabethan age shows that the castle had grown steadily for generations. The 14th century is the period of much of the visible structure, but the south range is more modern. Raby is worth the time and trouble of picking out its main features. There are nine towers. The gateway is the skeletal remnant of the curtain wall, and leads directly to the massive Clifford's Tower. Left of this is the smaller Kitchen Tower, which is almost unaltered. The vaulted kitchen within is a perfect survival from the 14th century, and its octagonal turret was the louvre to let out smoke. Further left is the curious Chapel Tower, with an 18th-century doorway, and then the projecting Bulmer Tower, which was formerly detached and is thought to have Saxon work at ground level. The long south range over the terrace facing the main road was rebuilt in the 19th century.

The most complete mediaeval survival is on the west side, where some of the walls are twenty feet thick. The very fine Nevill Gateway was the only entrance to the castle's Inner Court, and a gate and drawbridge once crossed the moat. Above the doorway there are three heraldic shields with the Nevill saltire, the cross of St George, and the flowered cross of Lord Nevill's wife,

Raby Castle; the north side, showing the Nevill Gateway (right of centre); (see also colour plate 17 and illustration on p. 17)

all encircled by the Garter which Lord Nevill received in 1369. A tunnel seventy feet long leads directly to the Inner Court, with the old Keep on the right. Ahead, the Hall was originally at ground level; but it was not apparently great enough, for above it Lord Nevill built something finer, lit by tall narrow windows.

In Staindrop church, a mile away, there is a superb alabaster tomb to Ralph Nevill, 1st Earl of Westmorland, who died in 1425. The family remained powerful until the Reformation, when they adhered to the Old Faith. The 6th Earl led the disastrous Rising of the North (1569), intending to place Mary Queen of Scots on the throne; he escaped to a beggarly exile, and Raby was forfeit to the Crown. Sadly neglected, it was acquired in 1626 by Sir Henry Vane, whose descendants own it today. The second Sir Henry believed in freedom and liberty of conscience, and accordingly withdrew his support from Cromwell, only to be executed by Charles II as a man 'too dangerous to let live'. The Vanes became Barons Barnard (1698), Earls of Darlington (1754) and Dukes of Cleveland (1833), but the Dukedom died out and in 1891 Raby was inherited by a cousin who succeeded as 9th Lord Barnard.

Considerable modernisation was carried out about 1783 under Carr of York. His most dramatic alteration was the conversion of the original Hall at ground level, to which he gave a high pointed vault supported by scagliola pillars the colour of ox-blood. The purpose was to allow carriages to enter the Inner Court through a new door under the chapel by way of this room. The court was too small for turning, but from here they could leave by the Nevill Gate. Unfortunately Carr's work involved raising the floor of the Great Hall and Chapel by some ten feet.

Many of Carr's rooms were rebuilt in the 1840s for the 1st Duke by the Scottish 'castle' architect, William Burn. The Dining Room is his, also the octagonal Drawing Room where the doors and ceiling have gilded 'Jacobean' strapwork. Furniture was made by Morant, who hung the walls with yellow silk and supplied the crimson curtains. This lavish interior is reflected to infinity by vast looking-glasses over sculptured fireplaces. Meanwhile the Hall became the 'Barons' Hall', was increased from 80 feet in length to 130 feet, and its original roof beams were replaced. (The floor had already been raised.) At one end are the mutilated remains of Lord Nevill's stone Gallery, while in the Chapel there is a stone arcade through which those in the Hall once assisted at Mass.

The first Lord Barnard was so angered by his son's marriage that in 1714 he sold the entire contents of the Castle, felled the timber and attempted to destroy the building. Consequently all the contents have been acquired since then. Besides superb portraits, the Old Masters include Claude, Ricci and Teniers. The Small Drawing Room is hung with pictures of the Raby hounds and horses by all the best English sporting painters. Victorian taste is evident in the French furniture and porcelain, while among 18th-century furniture in the Barons' Hall will be seen a number of Kändler's porcelain birds made at Meissen (*c.* 1730) for the Japanese Palace of Augustus the Strong. The manacled nude statue of *The Greek Slave* by the American sculptor Hiram Powers is dated 1844. This is the original of a work that caused a sensation at the Great Exhibition of 1851 and became immensely popular on both sides of the Atlantic. An ideal and moral subject was sufficient excuse for an unashamedly erotic work of sculpture.

Ragley Hall, Warwickshire
(The Marquess of Hertford)

A mile south of Alcester (A435)

Once inside the lodge gates, there will be no doubt of the grandeur of this country seat. The park, with raised clumps of trees and a long shapely lake, is Capability Brown's, and after two centuries it is looking its best. At its highest point is the house, with walls of local white lias dominated by a noble portico. The 15th-century castle, long since vanished, was bought in 1591 by Sir John Conway, and descended to Sir Edward Seymour, the ancestor of Lord Hertford. Seymour wrote in 1677, 'here you will find me playing the fool in laying out money upon building, having chiefly undertaken it because my grandfather decided to build here'. His house, the only surviving example by Wren's contemporary, Robert Hooke, was intended to have flanking pavilions. A hundred years later Wyatt added the portico with its paired staircases, and the crowning balustrades. Inside, in spite of the Georgian character of the rooms, the planning is Hooke's. A cross formed by the 'ceremonies' – the Hall, Saloon and two great Staircases – separates each corner into an apartment of four rooms and a back stair. This distinctive arrangement comes from France.

Building proceeded slowly, and the roof was completed only in 1751. Of 17th-century decoration there remains little more than some Gibbons-like carving in the Library (originally intended as a chapel). The rooms were completed by James Gibbs in the 1750s. His Hall, the finest late Baroque

*Ragley Hall; the Hall,
decorated by Gibbs in
the 1750s*

interior in England, shows the last flowering of the style Gibbs had studied in Italy half a century before. Unashamedly rococo plasterwork was certainly executed by Artari, and the seat furniture and its melting strapwork backs would not look out of place in Venice. There are other rooms with excellent rococo plasterwork, most notably the Blue Room, a former dining room, with its vines and Bacchic overmantel.

During the 1780s James Wyatt redesigned a number of the state rooms in anticipation of a visit from George III. Their plasterwork is in the lightest 'Adam' style, elegant and chastely neo-classical. The Main Dining Room was planned for full-length state portraits, to which Queen Victoria was added later. There are three Wyatt rooms on the garden front, ending with the Saloon with its walls hung with crimson silk.

George IV visited Ragley when he was Prince of Wales, and his bed, made with a cresting of feathers, is hung with hand-painted silk. To Lady Hertford, his particular friend (though her influence is said to have depended 'more on intellectual than on corporal qualities'), he gave his portrait bust by Nollekens, now in the Hall. The 4th Marquess, son of the roué immortalised as Lord Steyne in Thackeray's *Vanity Fair*, lived chiefly in Paris, neglected Ragley and spent much of his fortune on French paintings and furniture which, known as the Wallace Collection, has become the property of the nation. None the less, Ragley has its own treasures. There are Louis XV commodes, rococo furniture by Chippendale, Regency chairs, and astonishing late Georgian silver. Among the old master paintings, the landscape by Vernet, the *Raising of Lazarus* by Cornelis van Haarlem, and the *Holy Family* by Cornelis Shut, a follower of Rubens, are outstanding. The long line of portraits of the Conways and Seymours includes canvases by Reynolds of the 1st Marquess of Hertford and his cousin, Horace Walpole, and Richmond's painting of the 5th

Marquess who restored the house after 1870. It was then that the two staircases were rebuilt. One has modern frescoes carried out by Mr Graham Rust. Over the other there is a large painting by the contemporary artist, Ceri Richards, bought by the present Lord Hertford.

Ripley Castle, North Yorkshire
(Sir Thomas Ingilby, Bart.)

Four miles north of Harrogate (A61)

Few country houses have a more perfectly integrated setting than Ripley. The 18th-century model village is a showpiece and its Village Hall, dated 1854, is blatantly French. The cobbled Square narrows towards the battlemented walls of the house and goes down to the Ripley Beck whose valley, beautified by the landscapist's art, is the deer park. The broad shapely lake was dug in 1844.

The Inglebys, a Norman family, have lived here for six hundred years. They assumed the crest of a boar's head in 1355 when Sir Thomas de Ingleby saved King Edward III from a savage boar in Knaresborough Forest. Fifty years later, Sir John was one of the founders of Mount Grace Priory. In the 16th century, Sir William was appointed Treasurer of Berwick. His money chest has been kept, and with sixteen locks it is a fine example of the locksmith's craft.

Like many Yorkshire families this one remained Catholic. During the Civil War they raised troops for the King. After the Royalist defeat at Marston Moor, Cromwell insisted on staying at the castle. In her husband's absence, Lady Ingleby is said to have spent the night with the General on a settle, keeping him at bay with a brace of pistols.

Ripley Castle from the Beck

From its high position, Ripley might seem an ancient stronghold, but there is no record of any actual 'castle' having been here. It was a fortified manor, and the mediaeval Gatehouse survives. Otherwise the oldest part is the Tower, built by the Treasurer Ingleby in 1555. Here are kept all the most interesting of the family's relics. Of the three rooms, the Knight's Room at the top is the best, preserving intact its original beamed ceiling and wainscot, all boarded rather than panelled. During recent repairs a priest's hiding hole was discovered near the window.

The rest of the old house survives only in 18th-century paintings, because it was all rebuilt in 1780 by Sir John Ingilby.* The architect may have been Carr of York. The work is in a semi-Gothic style, with battlements and arches, and the same applies to the buildings round the immense courtyard. The rooms inside are classical, with marbled green columns in the hall and ironwork on the staircase. In the next generation, Sir William Amcotts Ingilby carried out the landscaping of the park and, inspired by his love of travel, added to the village. Although the property has always passed by descent, the title has become extinct three times owing to failure of male heirs, and the present baronetcy is in the fourth creation.

Rockingham Castle, Northamptonshire
(Commander Michael Saunders Watson, R.N.)

Two miles north-west of Corby (A6003)

Not many houses can boast, like Rockingham, of having been a Royal seat for more than four hundred years. The Castle stands high on a hill, a natural defensive post, with views over the Rockingham Forest. A former British and Saxon stronghold, William I made it his own property, a centre for hunting as well as for the administration of his iron-fisted government. Walls, keep, the hall and doubtless a chapel were all built before the Council of Rockingham assembled here in 1095; but of the early Kings, it was John who made most use of the castle. Norman masonry certainly survives, but what mediaeval work is to be seen dates chiefly from the 13th century. Edward I is known to have made many improvements.

By 1530 the castle had become dilapidated, and it was leased to Edward Watson. His grandson bought the freehold from James I, and since then it has always passed by descent, though sometimes to a younger son and sometimes through the female line. In 1646, Sir Lewis Watson was created Lord Rockingham by Charles I, and his grandson was raised to an Earldom. Another Watson was created Lord Sondes in the 18th century. These titles are among the names that are attached to the long succession of family portraits.

The drive leads steeply uphill through a ravine to the old Castle walls. The defensive gate was rebuilt by Edward I with half-round towers. Within the gate, the ancient Outer Bailey will be found much as it was in the 17th

---

* Since 1773 the family have spelt their name Ingilby.

Rockingham Castle; the Outer Bailey showing the 13th-century Hall doorway; (see also colour plate 18)

century: the wide terrace on the open side extends round most of the building. This all lies within the old curtain walls, but the ground was raised and levelled with rubble from demolished buildings. The Norman Keep, described by Leland as 'exceeding fair and strong', was destroyed during the Parliamentarian occupation in the Civil War. Only its mound remains, forming the highest point of the precinct. The whole area has been re-fashioned as the garden, with rose beds and two ancient hedges of yew.

As for the house itself, this was modernised chiefly during the 16th and 17th centuries and it no longer wears the dress of a castle. Additions were made at either end of the 13th-century Hall, which stands behind a Tudor chimneybreast but still has its old doorway. In the left corner, the gabled building is dated 1584. To the right, the long cross wing was begun in 1553, but comprises the work of four centuries, the last consisting of some remodelling in 1850 by Anthony Salvin. Fortunately, as we now think, this shows nothing of the monumental confidence generally associated with his improvements; indeed, the Flag Tower seems a sad apology for the loss of the old Keep.

Visitors enter by a Norman doorway to the service end of the house, passing a delightful cobbled 'street' of brewhouses and laundries to a stairway that Edward I built to Queen Eleanor's apartment. Now comes the Hall. Originally a considerable room of state, this was reduced in size by Edward Watson, who inserted a low beamed ceiling and divided off the far end as a parlour – the present Panel Room, where some 13th-century windows have been revealed. Besides oak furniture, there is an iron-bound chest said to have been left behind by King John, and another with the painted arms of Henry V. The paintings are 16th century, including portraits of François I by Joos van Cleve; of the young Queen Elizabeth; and of Edward Watson kneeling at prayer. He was responsible for the pious text painted on the beams. The Panel Room makes a contrast. The wainscot has 18th-century coats of arms in carved pine, and is hung with post-Impressionist paintings.

After the Hall, the most interesting room is the Long Gallery, begun by Edward Watson but completed in 1631. Two hundred years later, Charles Dickens, a friend and frequent guest of Richard Watson, made Rockingham Castle the model for 'Chesney Wold' in *Bleak House*. He wrote an unforgettable description of this Gallery, its portraits springing to life under the warm rays of the setting sun. Here, to be sure, is a splendid series of canvases, many of them 18th-century portraits of the Sondes branch of the family, including a group by Dahl, two portraits by Reynolds, one by Angelica Kauffmann, and a large hunting scene by Benjamin Marshall. Most attractive of all is Zoffany's group of the children of the 1st Lord Sondes. As a postscript, the Baroque monuments to the Rockinghams in the church below the castle walls should not be missed.

Rousham Park, Oxfordshire
(Mr C. Cottrell-Dormer)

Twelve miles north of Oxford (A423 and B4030)

Lieutenant-General Dormer of the horse-grenadier guards was not only an able soldier and diplomat, but a member of the Kit Cat Club and Pope's friend. He was thus in touch with contemporary architectural taste and on retiring to Rousham he found his Jacobean house unacceptably old-fashioned. Built in about 1635, it was on the conventional H plan with mullioned windows and probably with gables. Three-storey porches rising the full height of the house on the two main fronts, as at Chastleton near by, were the only unusual features.

William Kent in 1738 was invited to transform both house and garden. His treatment of the house was a curious compromise, for while preserving its Jacobean flavour he linked it in Palladian fashion to lateral pavilions. Indeed one of the interesting things about Rousham is that it shows this Burlingtonian architect flirting with romantic revivalism and unashamedly mixing ogee and crenellation with classical motifs. The Entrance Front shows his regard for the outside of the Jacobean house: he merely re-modelled the roof-line, providing a straight battlemented parapet with a cupola behind, at the same time glazing the windows with attractive octagonal panes. Though unhappily most of these were replaced by sashes in the 19th century, this front is otherwise much as he left it. The pavilions, linked to the house by corridors, nonchalantly combine a Palladian plan with mullioned windows and Gothic niches for statuary by Scheemakers and Cheere.

The first thing to note on entering the house are the loops in the original oak door to the Entrance Hall, which Sir Robert Dormer, a staunch Royalist, inserted so that he could train his muskets on approaching Parliamentarians. His portrait and that of his wife by Cornelius Johnson hang

Rousham; the Painted Parlour, designed by William Kent

on either side of the fireplace, and his son and daughter-in-law are also here, painted respectively by Michael Wright and Lely. Kent no doubt put in the simple 18th-century panelling and supplied two fine parcel-gilt pedestals typical of his designs.

On the whole Kent respected the existing plan of the interior with its Jacobean staircases at either end of the Hall, merely dressing the main rooms with Georgian cornices, doorcases and chimneypieces. We must however be grateful that he devised two immensely impressive rooms of his own. The Painted Parlour, purely Palladian, is among the grandest of small apartments. The marble chimneypiece, with a head of Medusa in the frieze and flamboyant overmantel with scrolled pediment, is a splendid thing in itself. Every other architectural feature from skirting to ceiling is similarly enriched with classical motifs, and the doorways, all but one, are dummies, inserted to maintain proportion and balance. Kent supervised every detail. He designed the giltwood side tables, the parcel-gilt chairs, and the carved wall-brackets to display the General's Italian bronzes; he painted the mythological scene, surrounded by 'grotesque' decoration, in the ceiling; he even chose the insipid copies of Italian 16th-century masterpieces set in frames on the walls. One longs to see this ensemble painted as Kent must have intended. The paintwork, now Lenygon and Morant's green and previously grained to simulate oak (probably in Regency times), must surely once have been white and gold.

The Great Parlour, originally a library, is hardly less remarkable, though different in feeling. Here Kent was in his romanticising vein. The extraordinary ribbed and vaulted ceiling has more than a touch of the oriental,

Rousham garden; left: *Praeneste, and* right: *the upper cascade*

and the theme of the Gothic cornice is repeated in a chimneypiece that is otherwise classical. The General's portrait by Van Loo is framed in the overmantel which once was surely not gilded as it is now. A generation after Kent had finished with the room, yet another architectural note was introduced. Books and bookshelves were succeeded in 1764 by the rich rococo frames which now adorn the walls. This virtuoso display, as well as the doors with immensely delicate carving in the friezes, was executed by Thomas Roberts of Oxford. The room lost nothing by the addition.

Kent's most important work at Rousham was the creation of one of the earliest surviving landscape gardens. Drawing inspiration from the Arcadian landscapes of Claude and Poussin he broke with the time-honoured traditions of formal design, parterres, topiaries and constricting regularity. Thus he set the English garden free. He was helped to do so by the fact that Charles Bridgeman had recently introduced the ha-ha, which enabled the 'natural' garden apparently to merge with nature itself. Of course the informality of Kent's design at Rousham is in a sense no more 'natural' than that of older linear gardens. The calculated surprises, the sudden vistas, the romantic references, in Roman temples and ruined Gothic arches, to a classical and mediaeval past are all artificial. They are also charming. Furthermore, as a pioneer conception, they led to the later sweeping informalities and serpentine waters which in the days of Brown and Repton transformed half the parks in the country.

The particular interest of the garden at Rousham is that we see the change from the old to the new in process of evolution. Certain elements, like the Long Walk terminating in a statue of Apollo, and the theatre, were retained from a more conventional layout prepared by Bridgeman some twenty years earlier. The resulting mixture of the formal and the irregular is fascinating. Nowhere more so than when one drops through a wood from the trim bowling lawn north of the house to emerge before the cascades and ponds of Venus Vale, or from some green glade suddenly sees the seven solemn pedimented arches of Praeneste. But if one feature were chosen to epitomise the historic importance of the garden it would have to be the modest channelled rill that twists, somewhat self-consciously, through the Watery Walk. It is apparently the first serpentine motif in garden layout; as such, it has a lot to answer for.

Rydal Mount, Cumbria
(Mary Henderson, née Wordsworth)

Between Ambleside and Grasmere (A591)

Rydal Mount was Wordsworth's home from 1813 until his death in 1850. White-harled and with the tall cylindrical chimneys characteristic of the region (which the poet thought 'the most beautiful shape' for a cottage chimney), it began as a 16th-century yeoman's dwelling; the Dining Room retains the early slate floor and timbers. The building remains, as it was in Wordsworth's day, an unpretentious intimate Lakeland house, and it evokes the long peaceful years which the poet spent there. The gardens covering more than four acres were laid out by himself.

A few years ago Wordsworth's descendant, Mrs Henderson, acquired the house and made it once more the family's home. Unhappily, many of the contents had been dispersed, but the surviving Wordsworth furniture and many objects of association make a visit to Rydal Mount a rewarding pilgrimage. A number of paintings and engravings recall the poet, his family and friends. No less than three oil portraits show Wordsworth in old age. A sensitive likeness, made at the request of his wife Mary in 1844 (the year

Rydal Mount; William Wordsworth, by Inman, and Mary Wordsworth, by Gillies

after he became Poet Laureate), is by H. Inman, an American painter. Another, smaller portrait is by Margaret Gillies, an Edinburgh artist, who painted both Mary and Isabella Fenwick, the latter a friend of Wordsworth's last years, 'the star that came at close of day to shine'. There is also a version of Northcote's early portrait of Coleridge, painted only a few years after the publication of the *Lyrical Ballads.*

The attic Study was Wordsworth's addition to the house, perhaps in 1838, and its ceiling is a copy of one he had admired in Italy. Among the first editions of his works shown here are *The Prelude*, which was published posthumously in 1850, and *Wordsworth's Guide to the Lakes* – the copy which the author gave to his younger son William. The many small objects in the house include the poet's inkstand, the reading glasses he used in his old age, and the squat leather picnic box, with shoulder-strap, that he must have carried on walks across the fells.

In the Library hangs the only known likeness, other than a silhouette, of the poet's sister Dorothy whose diaries reveal such astonishing literary talent. Wearing a shawl and frilly bonnet, she sits in an armchair with a book open on her knees. The eyes are unusually blue and the expression gentle but a little weary. She was sixty-two when S. Crosthwaite, a local artist, painted her. Dora, Wordsworth's much-loved daughter, thought it 'an excellent likeness'. Dora's own portrait in watercolour, done when she was bridesmaid to Sara Coleridge, hangs nearby.

St Mary's, Bramber, West Sussex
(Miss D. H. Ellis)

Seven miles north-east of Worthing (A2037)

Bramber is one of those fascinating old villages in the South Downs that today are thriving and full of activity. In Norman times, and doubtless before, it was a port on the River Adur, and foundations of the old wharf are to be seen in the garden. Posts belonging to the Norman bridge or causeway were recently discovered close to the house, which show that the Adur broadened here into a marsh.

The long, 15th-century structure, with a fine roof of Horsham stone, almost breaks into the road itself, and the closely spaced timbers of the overhang show it to have been an expensive building. St Mary's is still substantial, but what remains is only one side of a courtyard building put up by direction of William of Waynfleet, Bishop of Winchester and founder of Magdalen College, Oxford. Part of an original carved oak gateway is preserved in the house. This was the home of the Wardens of the Bridge, monks from Sele Priory at Beeding; but its plan suggests that it was also an inn for travellers.

After the Reformation it came into private ownership. Rooms were partitioned for dwelling, and additions were made for corridors and a staircase. The Parlour has fine wainscot, Dutch in character, with ebony panels, and a long *intarsia* trophy set in a columned fireplace. Flowered gilt

St Mary's, Bramber

leather, and the curious Painted Room with simulated arcading are 17th century. Later St Mary's became a farmhouse, but was restored and enlarged by the Hon. Algernon Bourke in 1896. Then it was again neglected, and its condition by 1944, after military occupation, can be imagined. A tank had run into the road side. The present owner bought it at auction, outbidding a merchant who wanted only the site and timber, and she has carried out restorations with great determination. The old road has become a freight route, and the vibrations from juggernauts are causing considerable damage. If the traffic problem is not solved, buildings such as St Mary's will not survive many years.

Salisbury Hall, Hertfordshire
(Mr W. J. Goldsmith)

Three miles south of St Albans (off A6)

The moated manor can be seen from the main road, a sheltered oasis among windswept fields. The house is demure, 17th century, and would grace a Dutch painting by De Hooch. Its windows are still of cross-frame type, and the mellowed brick is laid in English bond. Curiously, two-thirds up the bricks change to the narrow 2-inch width. This part was clearly rebuilt, probably about 1670, with materials from a vanished Tudor building, and this fact indicates a complicated history.

The owners of the house, originally Shenley Manor, have been traced

Salisbury Hall; the Hall; (see also colour plate 19)

back to Saxon times. There were two manors of Shenley, and the illustrious name of Salisbury's, or Salisbury Park, was adopted shortly after 1500. It refers to Sir John Montagu, Earl of Salisbury, who married the heiress of Shenley in 1380. He built a fine house here within the neat rectangular moat, and during excavations in the forecourt a panel of 14th-century floor tiles was discovered, decorated with the arms of Montagu. The manor then came by marriage to Richard Nevill, the 'Kingmaker' Earl of Warwick and Salisbury, and his brother John, Marquess of Montagu. In 1471 both were killed at the Battle of Barnet, five miles away, and the house was sacked by the Yorkists.

Salisbury Hall was bought in 1507 by Sir John Cutte, Treasurer to Henry VII. He rebuilt it, but the last surviving Tudor wing was demolished in 1819. The existing building is chiefly due to two later owners: Richard Cole, who bought it in 1619, and Sir Jeremy Snow, a London banker, who came here in 1669. Tradition has it that Snow allowed Charles II and Nell Gwyn the use of his house, and the little building standing over the moat still bears her name.

The interior is generally of 1670–90, but has earlier details of great interest. In the Hall, the Tudor tiled floor has been discovered one foot below the Carolean black and white stones. Oak panelling of Snow's period, though distinguished, is dominated by the earlier carved roundels of Roman Emperors (one being of Cleopatra). They are made of Totternhoe stone (quarried near Dunstable) and are said to have been made for Sopwell Priory, near St Albans. In some way they must be connected with early Renaissance work associated with the Tudor court. Equally surprising are three fireplaces in the Italianate manner of Inigo Jones which must date from about 1640. That in the Drawing Room is of carved, gilded and coloured stone, while those upstairs are of wood. The oak staircase (c. 1670) has carved baskets of flowers on the newel posts. In the main Bedroom there is iron door furniture of about the same date, and the adjoining room, a part of the former Hall Chamber, is wainscoted with Tudor panelling.

During the last war, Salisbury belonged to the de Havilland Aircraft Company, and in the winter of 1940 the first Mosquito was designed and assembled here. This invention, so important in the course of the war, is commemorated by a hangar erected by de Havillands behind the house for the Mosquito Museum. After the war the house was abandoned, and its demolition had actually been ordered when chance brought the present owner here. An artist and restorer of paintings, Mr Goldsmith has interesting pictures and furniture, with excellent English oak and exotic carved and gilded European pieces. In the Hall is a fine Hanseatic chest, inlaid with architectural perspectives. The bizarre Portrait of a Youth in the Study was painted in Italy, about 1650, by Michael Wright.

Saltwood Castle, Kent
(The Hon. Alan Clark, M.P.)

A mile north of Hythe (A20)

Saltwood has always been a strongpoint. One of the towers of the outer bailey incorporates cyclopean blocks that must be re-used Roman masonry, and the place is known to have been fortified in the 5th century, not long after the Romans left. Though in 1026 Canute signed a deed conveying the property to the church, the ecclesiastical tenure seems to have saddled the archbishops of Canterbury with a military garrison whose first loyalty was to the crown. This uneasy dual control became, a century and a half later, one of the prime causes of dispute between Thomas à Becket and Henry II. It was from Saltwood that the four misguided knights set out in 1170 for Canterbury, where after hanging their cloaks on a mulberry tree outside the cathedral they went in and murdered the archbishop. They did not anticipate that this rash action would firmly establish the church at Saltwood for nearly four hundred years, until Cranmer, foreseeing another clash with the crown, ceded the castle to Henry VIII in 1540. Queen Elizabeth stopped off at Saltwood a generation later with Sir Walter Raleigh (whose horse was reshod at a cost of ten pence). In 1580 the castle was so badly damaged by earthquake – a rare fate in England – that it lost much of its importance and gradually became ruinous. Major restoration took place in the years preceding the Second World War.

The oldest part of the castle is the Inner Bailey, dating largely from the 12th century, and probably built on the line of earlier earthworks. It was a naïve fortification, with little provision for flanking fire from towers along the curtain wall, and no true keep (no trace exists either of an earlier earthen motte). There was, however, a substantial gatehouse which is now concealed

*Saltwood Castle;
Archbishop
Courtenay's
Gatehouse, built
circa 1380
(See also
colour plate 20)*

in the massive structure, with tall, twin towers flanking a machicolated entrance, put up about 1380 by Archbishop Courtenay. This building, highly sophisticated by contrast with the 12th-century work, is really a substitute for a keep, one of those elaborate strongpoints that were then in fashion. It was placed, rightly and in contradistinction to early keeps, where the terrain offered least natural defence. The building is attributed to Henry Yevele, the celebrated mediaeval mason who was employed by the Crown at Westminster. (The windows date from the 20th-century restoration by the architect Philip Tilden.) To secure the approach to his strongwork, Archbishop Courtenay at the same time constructed the Outer Bailey to the north and east. Now largely ruinous, it was furnished with bastions of liberal projection to give flanking fire.

The Inner Bailey contains, most unusually, two Great Halls: one perhaps episcopal, and the other for the use of the garrison. The latter is in ruins, but seven beautiful windows survive with intersecting tracery of the late 13th century. Below the windows runs a curious stringcourse with the roll and fillet moulding often associated with Jacobean work. The Episcopal Hall, with a splendid stone floor above a 13th-century undercroft, was re-roofed and restored by Philip Tilden. Now hung with Renaissance tapestries, perhaps from Tournai, it contains the library of Lord Clark, the renowned art critic, author of television's *Civilisation* series, and father of the present owner.

But it is beside the point to talk of Saltwood only in architectural terms. The Inner Bailey is a garden and one looks outward from the *chemin de ronde* into the tops of oaks and tulip trees. What one most recalls is the felicitous

298

marriage of stone and vegetation: figs basking against sundrenched masonry, a gigantic white buddleia pushing thirty feet to the battlements, and trailing plants gracefully crowning them. Though the marriage would give the inspectors of the Ancient Monuments Department a fit, it is enchanting. Even the house-martin approves it, making 'his pendant bed, and procreant cradle' in the shelter of this most verdant castle.

(N.B. The private rooms, with interesting furnishings, in the 14th-century gatehouse are not regularly shown but are open from time to time.)

Sandringham, Norfolk
(Her Majesty, Queen Elizabeth II)

Between King's Lynn and Hunstanton (B1140)

When the future King Edward VII came of age in 1861, his parents decided that he should have a house of his own. The attraction of Sandringham for the Prince may partly have been its privacy and remoteness; but in addition, the estate offered great possibilities for shooting and he developed it into the best game reserve in the county. The clocks were kept half an hour fast so that guests should be early at the coverts. The house was, externally, no beauty, and after his marriage to Princess Alexandra it was quite inadequate. By 1870 it had been replaced by the present structure built to the designs of A. J. Humbert who, among other works, had recently built Prince Albert's Mausoleum at Windsor.

Sandringham is the private and personal home of the Royal family. Here ceremony was laid aside and King Edward became the local Squire. George V wrote that his 'dear old Sandringham' was the place he loved best in the world, and the affection in which it is held today by Her Majesty is well known. It was by her particular wish that the grounds and part of the house have been opened to the public.

The house is solidly Jacobean, of scarlet brick generously relieved with stone dressings. The long low wing on the garden side contained a bowling alley (now the library) that stretched from the billiard room – the conservatory of the earlier house. This wing, by contrast, is built of local carstone, a glowing brown sandstone that recalls the sandy soil from which the place takes its name.

The front door leads to the Saloon which has the form of a Jacobean Hall; the carved balustrade of the gallery resembles that on the staircase at Crewe Hall. The Main Drawing Room has richly carved panelling and plaster reminiscent of the Grand Trianon, the informal retreat of Louis XIV. Coloured white with a painted ceiling, it was said in 1902 to be all 'sweetness and light'. On comparing the rooms with eighty-year-old photographs one can see how little has changed since King Edward VII came to the throne. Though some woodwork has been lightened, palm trees and hundreds of knick-knacks have been cleared away and chintzy sofas are replaced by painted furniture, the atmosphere remains late 19th century. This is specially true of the Royal portraits. In the Saloon there are pictures of the

Sandringham; view from the upper lake; (see also colour plate 21)

Prince of Wales and his family (by H. von Angeli, 1876) and earlier portraits by Winterhalter of Queen Victoria (1845) and Prince Albert (1850). A delightful full-length of Queen Alexandra as Princess of Wales dominates the Drawing Room; it was painted by Edward Hughes in 1896. The Small Drawing Room has portraits of her parents, the King and Queen of Denmark.

The tapestries in the Dining Room, two of which are woven after cartoons by Goya, were a present from the King of Spain in 1876 and when new were thought to be rather crude in their colouring. There are collections of carved semi-precious stones and other treasures, some fine Worcester porcelain, and pleasing marble statues. Many of the sporting pictures in the Lobby and Ballroom Passage feature King Edward VII, and they hang above an interesting collection of bronzes, several of which are by Count Gleichen (King Edward's cousin). The bronze inkwell in the form of a harpy is a self-portrait of the actress Sarah Bernhardt.

The Victorian gardens are now much simplified, and the lake is bordered by carstone rocks and flowering shrubs. The walks are specially memorable for daffodils and massed camellias in the spring, azaleas, rhododendrons and primulas in summer. On the main road the massive wrought-iron gates were made by Thomas Jeckyll for the Great Exhibition of 1862 and subsequently given to the Prince of Wales by the County of Norfolk. Everything at Sandringham has its own particular association. North of the house, the great gilded Kuvera – a Buddhist divinity – was given by Admiral Sir Henry Keppel in 1869. The formal North Garden was laid out by King George VI, and the 18th-century statue of *Time* close by was bought by Queen Mary in 1950. The church is full of memorials and gifts (the silver altar was presented in 1911 by Mr Rodman Wanamaker) and should not be missed.

Seaton Delaval, Northumberland
(The Lord Hastings)

Between Tynemouth and Blyth (A190)

Sir John Vanbrugh liked his houses to stand high and to face north. That is how he built Seaton, in defiance of its inhospitable windswept site scarcely a mile from the North Sea. The view stretches bleakly towards the coast and industrial Blyth, and the house has little protection save that given by its own long drooping wings. It looks like a sorcerer's castle, a stage set for tragic opera. Did Vanbrugh foresee it as a dark, sightless ruin?

Everything about Seaton Delaval supports the legends of brilliance, dissipation, violence and death. The 'gay Delavals' were famous in the 18th century. Lavish entertainments given by Sir Francis transformed Seaton into 'an Italian palace, and the grounds were a perfect fairyland of light, beauty and music'. Yet the family had their serious side. Reynolds's portrait of Sir Francis (at Doddington, Lincs) shows him as a dashing young volunteer ready to invade France; and his brothers, John, Lord Delaval, and Thomas developed Seaton Sluice and established many local industries. It was predicted that no male of the family should die in his bed until a certain restitution of property had been made. This proved correct, but after the curse was lifted Seaton's destiny was sealed by a fire which destroyed the interior in 1822. For nearly 150 years the house was gutted and the windows boarded. Lord Hastings recently undertook the partial restoration. Once more the house is glazed, damaged stonework has been replaced, the courts

Seaton Delaval; Vanbrugh's main block

are tended and a new garden laid out. On a grey day Seaton Delaval is grim and forbidding; but as the evening sun reaches its face, the house by some enchantment springs back to life.

The de la Vals recorded at Seaton in the 12th century were probably descended from Hamo, who took part in the Norman Conquest. The estate has passed by descent to this day; the name Delaval survived until 1814. After the Reformation they became Protestant zealots and Parliamentarians. Industrious Sir Ralph in the 17th century built Seaton Sluice which, by sending salt and coals to London, became a port of some consequence. Owing to peculiar terms in his will his direct descendant could not afford to inherit, and Seaton was bought in 1717 by a distant cousin, Admiral George Delaval. Though he was nearing sixty he persuaded Vanbrugh to design the new house for 'the entertainment of our old age'. Neither he nor Vanbrugh was to see it completed. The Admiral died after a fall from his horse in 1723, and an obelisk was erected on the spot where this occurred.

Vanbrugh was never dull, but he packed more shocks into Seaton than into any other building. Except for the four corner turrets and a symmetry around the central axis, every surface was given a different treatment. There is enough variety in the centre block alone for three or four houses. The restless facade is crowned by a top floor 'like a Greek temple sailing above the clutter of an acropolis'. Either side of the door there are three massive Doric columns, as decorative and useless as a guard of honour; the frieze is carved with nautical symbols. As in all of Vanbrugh's houses, the stonework and carving is very fine. He liked to introduce archaic features such as the corner turrets, and the taller towers at the side which contain staircases. Something similar may have existed on the previous house (as it does at Chastleton). The south front is only a degree more cheerful. Its principal feature is the deep portico, whose fluted columns are of the genial Ionic order.

The Hall, now open as far as the roof, is in monumental style. In the upper niches, plaster statues of the Arts survived the fire, though some were undressed by it. The chimneypiece remains almost intact, but the iron gallery has lately been restored. The whole south front was taken up by a saloon, formerly divided by columns into three sections. Stone corridors lead to the vaulted basement; while at the top, the staircases become belvederes, brilliantly lit by Venetian windows. Some mahogany-panelled rooms survive in a corner. Here are shown portraits of the Delavals, views of the house, plans and documents. It will be seen that a wing was added to the garden front by 1811; this has quite gone, but the scar is visible on the east staircase tower.

The long arcaded wings were not burnt. The Stable is even grander inside than out, and its cathedral-like arches, apse and stalls are very impressive. The vaulted Kitchen opposite is on the same scale. Since 1822 the Kitchen Wing has been the family's residence. In a long corridor upstairs there are portraits of Lord and Lady Delaval and their five children by the Newcastle artist John Bell. Lord Hastings is the descendant of Rhoda

Hussey-Delaval who in 1751 married Sir Edward Astley. Two pastel portraits of the Astleys of Melton Constable, Norfolk, are by Francis Cotes. A long set of needlework chair covers were worked by the Astley ladies, and the matching settees show two combats of Sir John de Astley, at Paris and Smithfield, in 1438 and 1441. An oil painting of these is at Arbury Hall.

Sheffield Park, East Sussex
(Mr and Mrs P. J. Radford)

Between Haywards Heath and Uckfield (A275)

The manor of Sifelle, whence Sheffield Park derives its name, appears in Domesday and was in the ownership of three kings: William I, Henry III and Henry VI. But the history of the existing house begins with John Baker Holroyd, later 1st Earl of Sheffield, and the close friend of Edward Gibbon who is said to have written some of the *Decline and Fall of the Roman Empire* in the Library. Holroyd bought the property in 1769 and a few years later employed James Wyatt, who was later to be recognised as the most imaginative Gothicist of his day, to transform the existing house, and Lancelot Brown to lay out the grounds which form the enchanting prospect from the south front. In the 19th century, the 3rd Lord Sheffield, a dedicated cricketer who initiated the Australian Test Matches (and ensured that his

Sheffield Park; the Gothic Staircase, designed by James Wyatt

property had the finest cricket ground in the country), made Sheffield Park famous for other reasons. A. G. Soames, a distinguished gardener, bought the property in 1909, making a notable contribution to the gardens (owned by the National Trust since 1954) but alterations to the house that are best forgotten. It was rescued in 1972, when its future seemed to hang in the balance, by the present owners.

Tasteless changes, introduced mainly in the first decades of this century, make it easy to underestimate Wyatt's building. On the present entrance front one must overlook the heavy porch and bays to appreciate his composition. The centre with regular fenestration is basically Georgian, except for battlements and hood-moulds to the windows. It is flanked, however, at either end by blind Gothic arches, a storey higher and surmounted by stepped gables and pinnacles, which provide a marked vertical contrast. Round the corner on the east front, a boldly asymmetrical composition, this vertical emphasis finds an echo in a vast 'ecclesiastical window', similarly stepped and pinnacled. On the garden front Wyatt's design, which incorporates a tall, turreted, tower-like gatehouse, suffered by the addition of a service wing, and a later sun-parlour (c. 1912).

Wyatt's happiest contribution to the interior is the Staircase. Light and restrained, rising to a glazed dome, it is, in Wyatt fashion, simultaneously classical in conception and Gothic in detail. In the Drawing Room, sphinxes and lions confront each other, no doubt in some surprise, on an imaginative Wyatt frieze. Here the ceiling is also attributed to Wyatt, but looks like a later pastiche of Jacobean work. The State Bedroom, white picked out in gold, has a delicious painted ceiling in the classical manner. The work of Charles Catton, R.A., it dates from Wyatt's transformations, 1775–8. The cove is decorated with garlanded lions, tigers and leopards, while cupids sport among festoons on the ceiling above.

Sheldon Manor, Wiltshire
(Major Martin Gibbs)

Two miles west of Chippenham (A4 and A420)

The manors of Sheldon and Chippenham were among the estates that came by marriage to Sir Geoffrey Gascelyn in 1256. His family held them for some 200 years, and his coat of arms is still used by the town of Chippenham. A village that once stood behind the Manor seems to have dwindled and departed before the end of the Middle Ages, leaving the stone house in isolation.

The Hungerfords bought Sheldon in 1424. Since they rebuilt the right-hand wing and added the Chapel they may have intended to live here, but in fact the house was leased almost continuously to tenants. The Hungerfords were ambitious and powerful, and owned great estates in Wiltshire. As late as 1625 John Aubrey noticed 'in the windows in the Hall were severall of the escutcheons' – that is, armorial glass – but by the end of the Civil War the house was in such poor condition that the tenants themselves rebuilt the entire left-hand side. The Hungerfords, impoverished, sold the property in 1684, and its architectural history really ends here. However, an 18th-century owner built the two long barns, dated 1723, and, probably, the forecourt and back of the house.

Rather hidden behind two ancient yew trees stands a buttressed 13th-century porch, the finest of its date in the country. It is vaulted, and the lofty 'Priest's Room' above has a waggon roof with closely spaced beams. Inside the porch is the original water cistern, made of stone and fed by pipes from the roof. In the Hungerfords' wing (15th century), the Dining Room has fine beams, and the Library upstairs was presumably the Solar. As for the left side of the Manor, rebuilt about 1660, it is of fair size, with a low Hall. The oak staircase looks rather earlier.

Sheldon Manor

The Manor became a farm, and little improvement was done until 1911 when a new owner made alterations to fireplaces and put in the linenfold panelling. The Gibbs family bought Sheldon in 1917, and have made it their home since 1952. Their furniture was mostly collected by Major Gibbs's grandfather. Among much early oak are a 15th-century buffet, a Cromwellian settle-table, Lancashire chairs, and a country-made cupboard with its original painting. Spanish vargueños, some excellent seaweed marquetry, two 17th-century Dutch ebony cabinets with painted interiors, and a large cabinet of brilliant red tortoiseshell all show the taste of a cultivated romantic.

Sherborne Castle, Dorset
(Mr Simon Wingfield Digby)

Just east of Sherborne

Two castles, divided by a lake, stand on opposing hills. The Norman fortress, 'slighted' and ruined after two sieges in the Civil War, was originally owned by the Bishops of Salisbury. Sir Walter Raleigh coveted its grandeur and position, and Queen Elizabeth, taking it from the Bishop in 1592, conferred it on her favourite. When Raleigh was disgraced and banished from court on account of his secret marriage, he built the new 'castle' where before there had been a smaller, alternative house or lodge. Until 1800 this was still known as Sherborne Lodge, but 'Castle' describes better the address of its towers and heraldic pinnacles. This extraordinary building, an example of Elizabethan romanticism, is as exotic as Sir Walter himself. He made it rectangular and high, with a picturesque skyline. Towers, however, seem to have existed in some form in the earlier lodge, and a Tudor window will be found in the cellar.

On Raleigh's attainder the property was seized by James I, and for a short time it belonged to Henry, Prince of Wales. In 1617 it was granted to Sir John Digby, later Earl of Bristol. Though this title became extinct before the end of the century, the property has continued in his family down to the present owner. In 1625 Lord Bristol retired to Sherborne, disgraced owing to his failure to negotiate the Spanish marriage of Charles I, and extended the building by four long wings, all terminating with towers. The resulting letter 'H' is thought to be a tribute to Prince Henry. The walls were of rubble and probably were always rendered. The gateway to the forecourt is of an interesting Jacobean design, and the pedimented windows that survive

Sherborne Castle (see also colour plate 22)

on the right flank are also 17th century, but whether early or late is hard to say.

The planning of the rooms is not easy to follow. In one of the wings, the Oak Room has an internal porch. Some of the plasterwork seems to be Raleigh's, as his coat of arms is on a plaster ceiling in the Green Drawing Room; but the great chimneypiece has the Digby arms, with their *fleur de lys*, and the ostrich crest. The interior was restored in the 19th century in Jacobean style, and the lavish alabaster fireplace in the Dining Room (the former Solarium) is of 1860.

These restorations destroyed most of the Georgian work, but happily the Library remains complete and altogether delightful in chastely white Strawberry Hill Gothic. There is much excellent Georgian furniture, with grandly gilt pier glasses set above tables carved with ostriches, marquetry commodes in the style of Langlois, and sumptuous Japanese lacquer cabinets; also quantities of porcelain, with Meissen services, Chelsea and Sèvres, Kakiemon vases and Chinese blue and white wares. The numerous family portraits run continuously from the 17th century, when the Digbys employed Cornelius Johnson, Van Dyck and Lely, through Reynolds and Gainsborough, Batoni and Angelica Kauffmann, down to Landseer and Sir Francis Grant. Raleigh himself is recalled by the famous *Procession of Queen Elizabeth*, the Queen being shown in a litter, surrounded by her court. The actual occasion for this picture is still unknown.

When Alexander Pope frequented the Castle, the gardens were still laid out in hanging terraces, groves and topiary. Capability Brown redesigned the slopes to look natural, widened the lake and built a cascade. The view from the Castle, away from the sprawling town, remains essentially as he left it. The Orangery seems to be by Adam, and a Gothic dairy stands close by. Under the old Castle, the Lake Walk passes by Raleigh's Seat, where, according to legend, Sir Walter was smoking when a servant, supposing him to be on fire, extinguished him with a bucket of water.

Shipton Hall, Shropshire
(Mr C. R. N. Bishop)

Between Ludlow and Much Wenlock (B4378)

Raised on a hill behind its garden forecourt, from the valley road the house appears larger than in fact it is. Flanked by the church and a circular dovecote on the higher ground the ensemble is perfect, and the dusky warmth of the walls blends perfectly with the Corve Valley. The date given for the house is 1587.

Shipton belonged to Wenlock Priory in the Middle Ages. In the time of Elizabeth the owner was John Lutwyche, whose son Robert replaced a timber-frame house by the present one of stone after a fire. In 1759, the Lutwyche heiress married Thomas Mytton, and Shipton descended in this family until 1894 when it was bought by Charles Bishop. The house was modernised during the 18th century, but the Elizabethan facade remained

Shipton Hall

intact and some of the windows still retain their original leaded diamond panes. The oddity of the house is the porch with its side tower and door, which looks like an addition. Otherwise the building is a regular H-shape, with right-angled gables and wide bay windows.

The 18th-century additions consist of rooms at the back: two staircase projections are separated by a large polygonal bow. The year 1769 is recorded on a rain-head. The architect was Thomas Pritchard of Shrewsbury, who is most famous for his later Iron Bridge in Coalbrookdale. The Georgianised Hall has pedimented doors, a fine plaster ceiling, and the carved fireplace is of stone.

The cast-iron stove was made at Abraham Darby's Coalbrookdale works. In the Staircase the plasterwork is altogether more intricate, the mixture of Gothic and rococo being reminiscent of Croft Castle in Herefordshire where Pritchard was also employed. The Library upstairs is Pritchard's and has a delicately carved overmantel and another Coalbrookdale grate with an interesting iron hearth designed to retain heat.

Elizabethan oak panelling survives in several of the rooms, but in some cases it is painted. That in the Yellow Room, for instance, is blue. In the principal bedroom or Hall Chamber, the panelling has a carved frieze. About 1900, part of the old kitchen wing became the Dining Room and was fitted with panelling brought from another house. This is 'Elizabethan' in style and belongs to the romantic taste of the 1840s.

Sledmere House, Humberside
(Sir Tatton Sykes, Bart.)

Between Malton and Great Driffield (B1251 and 1253)

This estate on the Yorkshire Wolds is signalled by thick belts of beech, and the village, excessively neat with its stables and paddocks, is peppered with curious monuments. Great trees hide the house and its park that was laid out in a semi-formal design by Capability Brown. The village formerly lay near the bottom of the valley, but was removed to a dry position out of sight of the house. The whole ensemble has in fact been created by the Sykes family since they inherited the property in 1748, and shows the result of careful estate management over two centuries.

The core of the house, roughly square, was built by Richard Sykes, elder brother of the first Baronet. In the next generation Sir Christopher added two cross-wings, resulting in the form of an H. Romney's portrait of Sir Christopher Sykes and his Lady (1786) is contemporary with his additions, and shows the scholar-squire to have had a dignified presence, a long nose and determined chin. By 1823 the estate passed to his second son, Sir Tatton, who was interested chiefly in racing, hunting and breeding horses.

In 1911 a fire gutted the entire building. Heroic teams from the village rescued not only all the furniture and sculpture but many fittings, doors, and also the original designs for the house. The moulds for the plasterwork were still in existence, and the architect, Mr W. H. Brierly, restored the house so brilliantly that it looks like the original work. Recently, the whole interior has been very well decorated.

Sir Christopher seems to have been largely his own architect. The outside, austere and very impressive, is advanced in style for the 1780s, and the recessed triple-windows anticipate the later work of the Wyatts. The proportions of the park front have the optical effect of reducing its apparent length: it is in fact no less than 120 feet. The interior is less austere. A mid-Georgian ceiling survives in the Dining Room, but otherwise the plaster-work has all the elegance and delicacy of the style Robert Adam had introduced to England twenty-five years earlier. Joseph Rose, the plasterer, had previously worked for Adam at Kedleston, Harewood and Syon. The Music Room is judiciously simple, but the Drawing Room has a more elaborate ceiling and an ormolu-clad chimneypiece. The Staircase Hall now runs the length of the house. But the climax comes with the Library above, which takes up the whole of the park front. With a semi-circular vault based on the Baths of ancient Rome, it is divided into three compartments. During

Sledmere

bad weather Sir Tatton would take his exercise here, covering miles by walking up and down. His energy was undiminished at the age of eighty when he was painted by Sir Francis Grant. Unfortunately he was no scholar, and he sold his father's valuable book collection.

The contents are of high quality, even for a house of this period. There are Elizabethan portraits and large 17th-century Italian works, but the majority are 18th and 19th century, those by Pine, Maron, Romney, Lawrence and Grant being specially notable. In the Dining Room, the large *Countryman reciting Gray's Elegy* is by Benjamin West. There are two sets of 'Chinese Chippendale' chairs, a set of Louis XVI seat furniture (from the Orleans collection), another in Gallic style made by John Robbins (1792), and fine French marquetry. The greatest rarity is an early-18th-century tea table of Canton enamel. The cast-iron stoves upstairs are identical to those at Kedleston and were made at the Carron Iron Works, of which Adam was a Director.

As for 20th-century work, the Turkish Room dates from after the fire and its tiles were obtained in Damascus by the Armenian designer, David Ohanessian. Outside, an enormous post-fire service wing has recently been demolished and replaced by an Italian garden. The 18th-century stables were the nucleus of the famous Sledmere Stud.

Somerleyton Hall, Suffolk
(The Lord Somerleyton)

Between Lowestoft and Great Yarmouth, four miles inland (B1074)

After a long drive across the pastoral uniformities of East Anglia, Somerleyton will come as a shock. As early Victorian houses go it is not vast, but belongs to a time when designs and materials were valued more highly if they were exotic and novel.

Sir Morton Peto was able and enterprising. He served his apprenticeship as a bricklayer, inherited a small building firm and took full advantage of the steam boom by constructing railways in Europe and as far afield as Canada, the Argentine, Australia and Russia. In 1844, aged thirty-three, he bought Somerleyton and proceeded at once to bring it up to date. The 17th-century house, a brick and stone affair with scrolling 'Dutch' gables, was the basis of the new one. In 1848 it was reported that 'very extensive repairs now in active progress promise to preserve the ancient character of the place', and all was complete by 1852. The architect, John Thomas, was really a sculptor and had done ornamental work on the Houses of Parliament, but occasionally he designed commercial buildings. Between them, Peto and Thomas produced the Victorian ideal of a new, expensive and cheerful house, yet one whose every detail was borrowed from some older building.

The architecture was described as 'Elizabethan transformed into a rich and noble Italian'. There is also a strong French flavour, not least from the copious use of Caen stone, whose pale texture resembles fudge. Unfortunately it weathers badly, and much of it has recently been renewed. The

Somerleyton Hall; showing the site of the former Winter Garden; (see also colour plate 23)

towering south porch is all of this stone, and has collared pilasters, a Tudor bow window and Baroque pinnacles. The dormer windows are Henry IV, and the walls are of vivid scarlet brick. The Italianate tower on the right not only breaks up the symmetry, but was useful as a water tower. The pepperpot tower was designed for Vulliamy's clock, this being a model intended for the new Houses of Parliament but rejected on account of its expense.

By contrast with the brightness of the exterior, the rooms are muted by oak panelling. In the Oak Parlour the 17th-century wainscot survives with luxuriant doorcases and a fruity overmantel. Beyond this, the present Library was once a two-storeyed Banqueting Hall. The oak shelves, moved in from next door, were carved with a lively fret pattern by Willcox of Warwick, whose work can also be seen at Charlecote and Warwick Castle. In the Dining Room (the former Library), there are two magnificent war paintings by Clarkson Stanfield. One shows *H.M.S. Victory towed into Gibraltar after Trafalgar*; the other, perhaps the finer, is *The Siege of San Sebastian*, an episode in the Peninsular War. They were ordered by Sir Morton Peto about 1850.

The Staircase Hall has some excellent panelling, but the Vestibule has more exciting woodwork of dark oak relieved by panels of marble, Minton floor tiles, and a stained glass dome painted with game birds. This sophisticated essay in the Loire style is further enlivened by stuffed polar bears and sculpture. Finally, the Drawing Room, in red, white and gold, with sculptured chimneypieces, rococo window pelmets and huge plate looking-glasses, is strongly evocative of crinolines and the domestic pleasures resulting from hard-won affluence.

The Drawing Room windows look out over the vanished Winter Garden. This was a literal and huge pleasure dome of glass 'evoked by a magician's wand', but unfortunately it had to be removed in 1914. The sunken lily pond that now occupies the site is bordered by an ornate conservatory and loggia with flower maidens smiling down from the arches. In front of the house, the open terraces, lawns and rose beds are such as any Victorian would have been proud of. Twelve acres of undulating lawn and meandering paths, spot-planted with conifers, shrubberies and oddly-shaped borders must have delighted many a house party. The enormous yew maze was designed by William Nesfield in 1848.

It is sad to learn that Sir Morton's business failed, and that in 1863 he was forced to sell his house. The new owner was Sir Francis Crossley, Bart., the carpet manufacturer from Halifax, whose son was created 1st Baron Somerleyton in 1916. Their family portraits hang in the Staircase Hall, while a marble statue of the 1st Lord Somerleyton as a child, made by Thomas Durham, stands in the Vestibule.

Squerryes Court, Kent
(Mr J. St A. Warde)

Just west of Westerham (A2)

Looking confidently across a lake and landscaped foreground, the red brick house, built in the last years of Charles II, is an exercise in symmetry. Regular fenestration, matching pediments, balanced chimney stacks, the whole tied neatly together by a white wooden modillioned cornice: a well-mannered building if a little lacking in personality.

The interior by contrast clearly reflects the personality of the squires who have lived at Squerryes for nearly two and a half centuries. The Wardes arrived in 1731, when John Warde, son of a Lord Mayor of London, acquired the house; its atmosphere derives largely from the accumulated family contents. John Warde II, who succeeded in 1746, bought pictures with discrimination and through his younger brother George Warde, the boyhood friend of James Wolfe, many Wolfe relics entered the house. There is striking 18th-century furniture, much of it made for the Lord Mayor shortly before the family came to Squerryes. The Lord Mayor must also have ordered from Canton the great armorial service of about 1720, one of the finest in the country.

The convincing flavour of the house comes out well in the Dining Room, which is hung with Dutch cabinet paintings, mainly acquired by John Warde II: Hondecoeter, Steenwyck, Jacob Ruysdael, Van Goyen, a contemporary version of a well-known Cuyp, and a splendid burgher family group by Van der Helst. Giltwood mirrors, surmounted by the Warde crest, and a set of upholstered chairs with seaweed marquetry, are early 18th century, and both are out of the common run.

No less unusual are the tapestries and furniture in the Tapestry Room, which has kept its corner fireplace and panelled Carolean dado. The highly decorative arabesque tapestries, depicting large vases of flowers on marble tables, and bearing the Warde arms, were woven by Joshua Morris at Soho and must have been ordered about 1720. Of about that date is a set of unconventional settees and stools, ebonized, parcel-gilt, and upholstered in contemporary needlework.

Mention has been made of the Dutch cabinet pictures, but among other paintings of note are two vast Luca Giordanos, a Guido Reni, a Rubens, a *Martydom of St Sebastian* by Van Dyck, and a small classical landscape attributed to Nicolas Poussin. Family portraits include paintings by Wootton, Dandridge, Romney, Opie, and a likeness painted in 1829 of a John Warde, who was a famous master of the Pytchley and known as 'The Father of Fox Hunting'. He is shown on his horse Blue Rubin, so named because it was bought from a gin merchant at Newbury.

Squerryes Court; the Dining Room; (see also colour plate 24)

A room is devoted to the memory of General Wolfe. His family moved to Westerham not long before the Wardes came to Squerryes, and he formed a close boyhood friendship with his contemporary George Warde. To judge by Opie's portrait, the latter, who was also to become a general, was the most open-countenanced and reliable of men. He eventually became Mrs Wolfe's executor and she left him many of the Wolfiana now at Squerryes. These include a sensitive portrait of James Wolfe at the age of thirteen (the only portrait known to have been taken from the life), his first commission, the short sword he wore during the Quebec campaign, and the letter of condolence written by the Elder Pitt to Mrs Wolfe on her son's death.

Squerryes is also the home of the Kent and County of London Yeomanry Museum, which contains a display of military uniforms, banners, and regimental relics.

Stanford Hall, Leicestershire
(The Lord Braye)

Five miles north-east of Rugby (east of M1)

The Cave family owned land at Stanford by 1430, and in 1540 Sir Thomas became Lord of the Manor by purchasing property surrendered by Selby Abbey. In the church he has a superb Renaissance monument of alabaster. Some hundred and fifty years later Sir Roger Cave decided to rebuild the house, which then stood close to the church, and moved to higher ground across the River Avon (incidentally transferring from Northampton to Leicester). The family, careful over extravagance, built their house slowly: so slowly, in fact, that it occupied four successive owners over fifty years.

Sir Thomas succeeded Sir Roger in 1703, and married Margaret Verney, the descendant of the Lord Brayes who had been statesmen during the 16th century. This Barony lay dormant for nearly three hundred years before it was revived in favour of the heiress of Stanford, Sarah Otway-Cave, who thus became 3rd Baroness Braye in 1839. A tireless traveller, she brought to the house many treasures from Italy.

Isolated and dignified, the house stands in an open park overlooking the river. It was begun by the brothers William and Francis Smith of Warwick in 1697, and documents show that the actual fabric was estimated at precisely £2,138 10s. 3d. The mixture of details is curious. Originally the side elevations had cross-windows rather than sash, and ashlar was used only on the front. This facade, of a tranquil dove-grey sandstone, is a textbook example of the William III style. It has tall sash windows that still retain their old frames, and a hipped roof. Whereas the centre windows have Italian mouldings and are placed above balustrades, on the

Stanford Hall; and stables

projecting wings the mouldings, and panels below, are of the Dutch type.

William Smith died in 1724, and Francis, who was by now a prominent Midlands architect, continued in rather a different style. The idea of stable blocks flanking the forecourt was abandoned, and the present stables, of brick and ironstone, were built in 1737. The same date is suggested for the east front, overlooking the river, with its Gibbs-style basement. The monumental double-stair, remodelled in 1880, leads to the side entrance door.

The panelled Grey Drawing Room and the East Staircase are of the first period. The work after 1730 became more spectacular. Francis Smith designed the Grand Staircase with slender carved balusters that repeat continuously three different forms. The Hall was remodelled by his son William in the 1740s. It rises through the first floor, its ceiling 'sunk by a cove'. The plasterwork is by John Wright of Worcester. Agreeable hunting scenes were painted by a Frenchman, M. Joubert, in the 1880s, and the room is now known as the Ballroom.

Family portraits are very numerous in the staircases, passages and rooms, and the painters include Cornelius Johnson, Kneller and Hudson. There is a bust of Thomas Otway-Cave by Chantrey, and a full-length statue of his sister, Lady Beauchamp, made in Rome by Gibson. Particularly interesting are the paintings and objects that their mother, Lady Braye, bought in Rome about 1842, including a collection that had belonged to Henry, Cardinal of York (known to Jacobites as King Henry IX). In the Ballroom is the Duke of Buckingham (favourite of James I), James III and his Queen, and a fine Charles III, painted in Rome in 1770 by Laurent. There are also two portraits of the Cardinal himself.

The ample furnishings include fine 17th-century Flemish tapestries and Dutch marquetry in the bedrooms, and an unusual rococo-Gothic table in the Library. Two sculptured Italian *cassoni* are 16th century, perhaps Venetian. The greatest rarity is the mediaeval refectory table that must have come from the old house.

The Aviation Museum in the stables is dedicated to the memory of Lt Percy Pilcher, R.N., a close friend of the 6th Lord Braye and the first man to fly in this country. A replica of his machine, 'The Hawk', is shown. Pilcher was killed in 1899 while gliding in the park, and on the spot where he crashed, beyond the river, a monument was erected by the Royal Aeronautical Society.

Stapleford Park, Leicestershire
(The Lord Gretton, O.B.E.)

Four miles east of Melton Mowbray (B676)

The Sherard family, who acquired Stapleford by marriage in 1402, held the property for nearly five hundred years. In 1894 it was bought by John Gretton, grandfather of the present owner. The house, built at three distinct periods, is chiefly renowned for the curious salient wing on the north front that has no parallel in this country. Dating from 1500, it was extensively

Stapleford Park; the early Tudor wing, altered in 1633

altered in 1633 by Lady Abigail Sherard who added the fantastic pedimented Flemish gables with inverted scrolls and much of the applied sculpture from which its unusual character derives. Twelve sculptured figures under Gothic canopies adorn the front. Six are early Tudor (three of these represent Knights of the Round Table); the other six, which include William the Conqueror, portray Lady Abigail's putative ancestors. We also owe to her a number of religious reliefs presumably from a church; their introduction at this date represents an eccentric and early example of mediaevalism.

The main house, in finely dressed stone with regular fenestration and hipped roof, followed in about 1680 and has the assurance of its period. The original entrance front on the south with projecting wings must once have looked somewhat like the front at Belton. One would wish to have seen it before the late 19th century when, in the third and last phase of building, the space between the projecting wings was filled and the house received a south facade of Jacobean character with a prominent central bay and, behind the big mullioned and transomed windows of the upper floor, a Long Gallery.

The house today is entered on the restrained east front of the Stuart building, not the original approach. Inside there are two remarkable rooms with late Stuart decoration. The Dining Room, not in its original position but faithfully transferred from the first floor, has an 18th-century fireplace but a plasterwork ceiling of the 1680s and wainscot enriched with 'prodigious' carvings – the adjective is Pevsner's – in the manner of Gibbons on the mantel, overdoors, and elsewhere. Two of the Lelys here are particularly good and in their original frames. The Ante-Room, with realistic carving to doorcases and overmantel, is in the same taste but even richer, though the fireplace again is 18th century. The room has French 18th-century furniture, an inlaid Italian cabinet made in 1643, and a Reynolds portrait in a fine rococo frame. The vaulted Old Kitchen, also probably of the 1680s, contains two decorative full-lengths by Marc Gheeraerts of Lady Abigail, who embellished the north wing, and her husband William, 1st Lord Sherard.

The 18th century left its mark on the Entrance Hall which has a chimneypiece and delicate plaster ceiling of the 1770s. The ceiling might well be by James Wyatt, who in 1776 was working fifteen miles away at Belton. There are also hall chairs of the same date. The walls are hung with sporting pictures by Sartorius and Ferneley.

In the late-19th-century addition, the Drawing Room with an Aubusson carpet made for the Duc d'Aumale, son of Louis Philippe, contains more French 18th-century furniture, and a number of interesting paintings: Venetian views by Guardi, a Bellotto, and works attributed to Van Goyen and Jacob Ruysdael. The Library owes its character to a quantity of ormolu-mounted Empire furniture: wall lights, firescreen, desk, commodes, and chairs. Other objects of note in the Victorian rooms include a huge 17th-century Mortlake tapestry of two rearing horses, representative surprisingly enough of the Destruction of Niobe and her children, and a rare dessert service enamelled in yellow or deep pink with floral panels. It was made thirty miles away at Church Gresley in Staffordshire, where a shortlived factory was established in 1794.

No visitor to Stapleford should miss the adjoining late-18th-century church of St Mary Magdalene which has its original reredos, pews and furnishings; also marble Sherard monuments, among them one of about 1640 depicting Lady Abigail and her husband, and another, a stupendous affair, by Rysbrack, some hundred years later.

Stoke Park Pavilions, Northamptonshire
(Mr R. D. Chancellor)

By Stoke Bruerne, three miles east of Towcester (A508)

A pair of wings to a vanished house stand in a garden overlooking unspoilt farming country. They may be dated almost precisely. Sir Francis Crane, a man of obscure origins, became Secretary to Charles I when Prince of Wales, and in 1619 was appointed Director of the new Mortlake tapestry factory. So fine and costly were the tapestries that Charles quickly fell into his debt, which was discharged by grants of lands and manors in this county. Crane acquired the manor of Stoke in 1629, and died in 1636. The house may have been already standing, but since it was destroyed by fire in 1886 it can no longer speak for itself. As for the wings, it was said that Crane 'brought the design out of Italy'; but no architect in England would have been capable of executing such learned and urbane Palladianism except Inigo Jones. To Jones, therefore, they are attributed.

The curved colonnades survive, though incomplete, and their low columns form loggias in the much taller portals of the pavilions. One pavilion was a library, the other a chapel. This was the first appearance of the Palladian format of colonnaded wings in an English house; yet the classical details derive not actually from Palladio but from his pupil, Vincenzo Scamozzi, whom Inigo Jones had known in Italy. The former complex roof lines were simplified in the 18th century but the grandeur of the buildings is unimpaired. The walls are of the local limestone that is used in the village, but columns and details are picked out in tawny ironstone of which neighbouring Towcester is built. The contrast adds distinction without being in the least overpowering.

Stoke Park Pavilions

Stoke Park passed by marriage to a branch of the Vernon family, whose arms remain in a cartouche on the west pavilion. After the fire of 1886 they brought the balustrades, pool and fountain from Harefield Hall, Middlesex. Less judicious was their rebuilding of the house in red brick, attached to and uglifying the east pavilion. Neglected almost to complete ruin, the property was bought by the present owner in 1953. He removed the upstart house, restored the stonework and planted the garden anew. The pavilions are not open; but a visit to this enchanted garden on a summer evening will not quickly be forgotten.

Stokesay Castle, Shropshire
(Sir Philip and Lady Magnus-Allcroft)

At Craven Arms, six miles north-west of Ludlow (A49)

No true castle, this, but a fine and unique fortified manor. Lying low, and built of the local Silurian limestone, it is not only picturesque and evocative but altogether genuine. Stoke means dairy farm, and Say was the family who owned it from 1115. Of their house only the moat remains and the lower part of the North Tower. By 1281 the house had been bought by Lawrence of Ludlow, the greatest wool merchant of his day, to whom we owe the building in its present form. He built the Hall and Solar, and in 1291 obtained a licence to fortify the manor, the result of this being the embattled South Tower.

In 1620 the house was sold to Dame Elizabeth Craven whose son, the romantic Lord Craven, was an ardent Royalist and the devoted follower of Queen Elizabeth of Bohemia. Stokesay, indefensible against cannon, quickly surrendered to Roundhead troops in 1645, and whatever remained of the curtain wall and ancient gatehouse were removed. From 1648 the house was leased to the Baldwin family and, later, to farmers. The Hall became a cooper's workshop, the Solar a granary, and the South Tower was damaged by a fire in the basement where there was a blacksmith's shop. Mr J. D. Allcroft bought Stokesay from Lord Craven in 1869. Though no longer inhabited, the structure has been carefully and expensively restored.

The cheerful timber Gatehouse, black and yellow, is likely to have been built by the Baldwins after the Civil War. The brackets are carved with

Stokesay Castle; from the north showing the 17th-century gatehouse; (see also colour plate 25)

dragons, devils, Adam and Eve. The house itself, except for 19th-century buttresses remains much as it was first built, though the surrounding wall and all subsidiary buildings, including the kitchen, have disappeared.

In the Great Hall the central hearth is still to be seen. The roof is formed of oak crucks, but their lower ends have decayed and been replaced by stone brackets. Originally they were 34 feet long, and the fact that so many curved beams could be cut and matched gives an idea of the great forests that once covered England. As for the windows, Lawrence could afford glass in their upper tracery, while the lower lights were shuttered. The original oak stair leads to an upper room with a 14th-century fireplace. The attractive overhang visible from outside still has most of its original timbers.

The Solar at the south end is approached by a separate stair. It has fine oak panelling and an overmantel brought here when the room was the Baldwins' dining room. But the climax comes with the Tower. This is a separate building and once it had a drawbridge. An irregular polygon, it has two projecting bays placed where the narrow lancets would catch the most sun. Both of its main rooms have fireplaces, and the staircase is in the thickness of the wall. Garderobes discharge into the moat. From the roof you will see three chimneys, rare survivals from the 13th century.

Stonor Park, Oxfordshire
(The Lord Camoys)

Four miles north of Henley-on-Thames (B480)

This famous house, 'climbing on a hill' in an isolated Chiltern combe, is of very ancient origin. So is the Stonor family. Possibly they are descended from the Herveys, of British descent, who lived here before the Conquest. A Robert de Stanora ('stony hill') is recorded in the 12th century; and a Norman arcade that survives in a corner of the house cannot be much later. Once it supported the roof of a two-aisled hall, and the curious way it runs into the hill suggests it may have developed from an earlier room hollowed out of the chalk.

Since the Reformation the Stonors have been distinguished by their loyalty to the Old Faith. During penal times they gave shelter to many priests, including St Edmund Campion whose *Decem Rationes* was secretly printed here in 1581, the year of his arrest and execution. The Stonor estates had been considerable, but Recusancy fines and confiscations up to the 18th century reduced the properties. This history emphasises the importance of the Chapel. Built of flint, it is 13th century (or earlier) with a 15th-century brick tower, but the interior was Gothicised by 1760. It contains mahogany 'Gothic' furniture, stained glass by Eginton, and a fine collection of sacred vessels and embroidered vestments.

An impressive display of heraldry recently set up in the Hall shows the Stonor marriages with numerous Catholic families, including the Blounts of neighbouring Mapledurham, the Pastons, Towneleys and Blundells. The Barony of Camoys was a mediaeval honour that fell into abeyance in 1426.

25 Stokesay Castle; a 13th-century house

26 Sutton Park

27 Thoresby Hall, by Anthony Salvin

28 Wilton House

Stonor Park, looking towards the Chapel

Over four hundred years later it was determined in favour of Thomas Stonor by inheritance through the female line. Thus it was not associated with this ancient house until comparatively recently.

About 1540, Leland wrote that the house was built round two courts, 'of tymbar, brike and flynte'. Some sixty years later the accumulation of four centuries' building was concealed behind a regular gabled front and the forecourt was enclosed by a wall and gatehouse. By 1760 this Elizabethan facade had given way to the long open courtyard of warm brick and sash windows that remains today. Only one gable was retained, that over the front door. The cornice is of wood.

Alexander Pope likened the interior to a rabbit warren. In spite of many puzzling alterations, the various components of the Tudor house remain: screens, hall, great chamber (now the Library) and long gallery. The Hall, like the Chapel, was heavily Gothicised in 1754–60; but only a ghostly fragment remains, because in 1834 Thomas Stonor, already Member of Parliament for Oxford and soon to be elevated to the House of Lords, turned the front part into a Drawing Room. What survives of the Hall retains its Gothic chimneypiece and some good Flemish Renaissance glass. The Library upstairs is a noble room with a long barrel ceiling. The Gallery has Georgian panelling and opens directly on to the garden.

There were unfortunate sales of furniture in 1938 and 1975, but a great deal is still to be seen. The family portraits date from the mid-16th century, and most of the Recusant library has been kept. Some excellent mahogany furniture is an early production of the Catholic firm of Gillow of Lancaster. Older furniture and tapestries have been lent by Mrs Eyre Huddleston, a cousin of the family, and among her paintings is a portrait of the youthful

Queen Mary by William Scrots. A more colourful note is provided by the exotic collection of the late Francis Stonor: painted wood sculpture of North Italian or Germanic Baroque; a pair of immense bronze andirons after Algardi; and a rare pair of sculptured globes taken from Coronelli's *Atlas* of 1699. The huge bed in the form of a shell is perhaps Italian, *circa* 1820. One room is hung with French wallpaper of *Les Monuments de Paris*, printed by Dufour in 1815.

Stratfield Saye, Hampshire
(Trustees of the Duke of Wellington)

Between Reading and Basingstoke (A33)

If the glittering apartments and noble works of art at Apsley House recall the international figure, the Grandee of Spain and Prince of Waterloo, whose strength of character and military genius made him for over a generation the best-known man in Europe, Stratfield Saye by contrast movingly evokes the great soldier at home. Objects of association create an atmosphere independent of architecture and works of art. Here are rooms furnished for his pleasure, here is the reflection of his life and tastes as he grew older (for he was most often at Stratfield Saye after his wife's death in 1832). Here one sees him, as Thorburn painted him, with his grandchildren, and here, stepping as it were into the wings of history, one is confronted by his hairbrushes, his cupping bowl, and the hearing aids of a man deafened by the cannonades of twenty years' campaigning. Here even hangs the funerary armour that accompanied his bier through silent crowds to St Paul's. He bestrides the house like an aging colossus.

It was not a house that his contemporaries, with the exception of sensible William Cobbett, thought much of. When a grateful nation after Waterloo offered him £600,000 for a country mansion and estate, he considered many (rejecting Uppark with characteristic practicality because the steep approach would have unduly taxed his carriage horses). Having in 1817 chosen Stratfield Saye, perhaps partly on account of the setting and the river, he declined, no doubt in some measure on financial grounds but with his unfailing good sense, to demolish it and build the vast neo-classical palace that was expected of him. Thus nothing came of the colonnaded grandeurs for which Benjamin Wyatt, Cockerell and others, submitted plans. As usual the Duke knew his own mind.

Stratfield Saye was, in fact, a house of unusual interest. Built in about 1630 by Sir William Pitt, at one time Comptroller to the Household of James I, it relates architecturally to a small group of houses with pedimented gables expressing strong Dutch influence, such as Swakeley's, Raynham, and West Horsley. The visitor approaching the entrance may with a little imagination still envisage how the confidently proportioned front looked in the 17th century. The two outer gabled wings are later additions, but the central block and the first gabled projections preserve the rhythms and character of the Jacobean house. In Georgian times the brickwork was

Stratfield Saye; the entrance front

stuccoed, mullions gave way to sash windows, and at roof-level the white wooden cornice probably replaced a stone cornice such as survives on the gable ends. Finally the porch was added for the Duke by Benjamin Wyatt in 1838, an unfortunate but highly convenient addition.

Inside little now recalls the 17th-century house, except the staircase with elaborate Jacobean balusters, for the main rooms were altered in about 1745 and again towards the end of the century. These alterations are at once apparent on entering the Hall with fireplaces of bold early Georgian character, and a screen of marbled Ionic columns which may be a little later (and from which hang Napoleon's tricolours, beautifully worked in silver thread). The Hall also introduces the visitor to the furniture and works of art which Wellington bought in 1816 when the collection of Cardinal Fesch, Napoleon's uncle, was dispersed in Paris. They include here antique busts flanking the fireplace, and two Empire side tables in the style of Jacob, on which stand Houdon's splendid head of Napoleon when First Consul and Pistrucci's head of Wellington. The Duke also ordered from C. D. Rauch (1777–1857) the marble busts of Blücher, Frederick of Prussia, and the Czar Alexander (who gave him the great malachite tazza in the Hall). Let into the Georgian slats and limestone floor are mosaic pavements from the Roman villa at Silchester nearby.

The Duke had been a reader of history from his early days in India, and the Library (many of the leather-bound volumes once belonged to Napoleon) was his favourite room. It has changed little since his day. The parcel-gilt doorcases, entablature and ceiling, are mid-18th century, but most of the furniture is Regency. The adjoining Music Room, entered through a pillared archway inserted somewhere about 1800, is dedicated to the memory of Copenhagen. Paintings and bronzes portray the bay charger of fifteen hands which carried the Duke through the long day at Waterloo.

Stratfield Saye; left: *the Duke of Wellington's Library, and* right: *the Gallery*

Copenhagen, descended from the Derby winner Eclipse, spent his last years at Stratfield Saye and is buried in the grounds.

The Gallery is a room that evokes superlatives. Its disparate elements create a sumptuous glow and glitter, achieving simultaneously profusion and balance. The architectural elements – screen of Ionic columns at either end, cornice, doorcases, grey marble chimneypieces – are mid-18th century. The prints, edged with gilt beading, that decorate the walls were introduced some fifty years later, and the master stroke came at the end of the 19th century when burnished gold-leaf was applied to the wall surfaces that remained exposed. This is the glowing background for bronze busts (some of them 17th century and most of them parcel-gilt) which stand on Boulle pedestals and cabinets. The Boulle marquetry is by Etienne Levasseur (1721–98). Both the bronzes and Boulle furniture were bought in Paris by the Duke. A recent and wholly appropriate addition to this gallery was the Savonnerie-type carpet woven in 1951 by the Spanish Royal Carpet Factory in Madrid for the 7th Duke, an architect and connoisseur whose taste and knowledge did much to conserve and embellish Stratfield Saye.

Other rooms combine an 18th-century structure with decorations of the Duke's choosing. The Drawing has a rococo ceiling (resembling Vassalli's work at Petworth) and rococo chimneypiece and looking-glasses set against a delightful French wallpaper put up in 1838. There is plenty more French furniture here, collected by the Duke. The Dining Room, an addition of about 1775, has a Palmyra 'sunburst' ceiling, and its furniture makes an interesting mixture: it is mostly Regency, but four splendid gilt torchères by James Moore (*circa* 1710) stand next to Empire console tables.

The Drawing Room paintings, mainly Dutch and Flemish, have a romantic history. Like much of the collection at Apsley House, they were part of the spoil captured with Joseph Bonaparte's baggage-train after his flight from the field at Vitoria in 1813. When it later appeared that many of the pictures had been filched from the Spanish Royal Collection, the Duke courteously proposed their return to King Ferdinand. The King reacted no less courteously, replying: 'His Majesty, touched by your delicacy, does not wish to deprive you of that which has come into your possession by means as just as they are honourable.' Elsewhere in the house may be seen part of the vast Sèvres dinner service, decorated with views of Egypt after drawings by Vivant Denon, that Napoleon offered to Joséphine and that Louis XVIII later presented to the 1st Duke.

Sudeley Castle, Gloucestershire
(Mrs Dent-Brocklehurst)

Just south-east of Winchcombe (A46)

Sudeley commands the lofty hill overlooking Winchcombe, a prosperous trade centre that became capital of Mercia in the 8th century. It was royal property in Saxon days, but this castle was built in 1442 by Ralph Botelar. Rendered almost uninhabitable after the Civil War, it was occupied by farmers until 1837 when it was bought and restored by the brothers John and Edward Dent, merchants from Worcester.

The history of the castle was published by Emma Dent (*née* Brocklehurst) in her work of 1877. Botelar's wealth came from the spoils of the French wars of Henry V and VI, and the Portmare Tower near the Gatehouse was so called after a French admiral, one of many prisoners held to ransom here. Botelar's castle had the same extent as the present building. To the left was the Outer Court; to the right, the Inner Court with the Keep or Dungeon Tower at one corner. Kitchens were on the entrance side, and apparently the courts were divided by a Great Hall. In 1469 Botelar, a Lancastrian, was forced to sell the property to the Yorkist King. Improvements made by

Sudeley Castle; the entrance front, showing the Portmare Tower

Richard III in 1484 included a new and magnificent Hall raised above an undercroft, which, despite its ruined state, is still the chief ornament of the castle.

St Mary's Chapel, detached to the east, is a survival from Botelar's work. Highly decorated with pinnacles and gargoyles, it looks like a garden folly. The outside has been authentically restored, but within all is polished Victorian.

For nearly eighty years Sudeley remained Royal, and about 1540 John Leland wrote that 'it goeth to ruine, more pitye'. In 1547 it was granted to Sir Thomas Seymour, created Lord Sudeley, the brother of Jane Seymour and uncle of Edward VI. He married the Queen Dowager, Katherine Parr, but she died here the next year after giving birth to a daughter, and by her own wish was buried in the chapel. Seymour's lofty ambitions soon led him to the scaffold. Queen Mary granted Sudeley to Thomas Brydges, 1st Lord Chandos, whose family owned the property until 1812. Much rebuilding was done about 1572 and Queen Elizabeth was entertained here three times. The 5th Lord Chandos was known from his lavish hospitality as 'King of the Cotswolds'; his son, the handsome 6th Lord Chandos, was Royalist and for a time Sudeley was the headquarters of Charles I. The eventual defection of Chandos to the Parliamentarians did not prevent their order to 'slight' the Castle and make it indefensible. It was then that part of the inner courtyard was removed.

The rebuilding was carried out partly by Sir George Gilbert Scott for the Dent brothers in the mid-19th century. It was done with a care unusual at that date, and the restorations are not easy to distinguish from the original fabric. But inside, the rooms are altogether of 19th-century character, though 'Katherine Parr's Room' still has its 15th-century window, and a delicately carved Renaissance chimneypiece survives bearing the Chandos motto.

The Dents bought a remarkable number of paintings and treasures associated with the history of their castle. Some, like the painting by Hans

Sudeley Castle; the Sheldon tapestry cover

Eworth of *The Tudor Succession*, had belonged to Horace Walpole and came from the sale of his house, Strawberry Hill, in 1842. Many early portraits and relics have been arranged as a special exhibition in the Dungeon Tower. Even so, the rooms are crowded with interest. Special mention should be given to a large and rare Sheldon tapestry cover, woven with biblical scenes and a hunting border. Of a different age is the flowered bed-hanging of Aubusson tapestry, worthy of the taste of Marie-Antoinette who is said to have owned it. The paintings include really fine works by Rubens, Van Dyck, Poussin, Claude, Ruysdael and Greuze, two of Turner's subject pictures of the Thames and *A Boat Passing a Lock* (1824) by Constable.

Extensive gardens were laid out in the 19th century. They are mainly on the site of the ancient 'pleasaunce', and the formal Queen's Garden can be seen from 'Katherine Parr's Room'. The ruined Inner Court has also become a garden, part of the moat is transformed into an ornamental pond, and from the terraces there are marvellous views over Cotswold country.

Sutton Park, North Yorkshire
(Mrs Sheffield)

At Sutton-on-the-Forest, eight miles north of York (B1363)

Sutton, one of the tidiest villages in the Vale of York, once lay on the edge of a royal forest. Though dignified and Augustan, the early Georgian house is an essential part of the village, and, like the cottages, it is built of the local rosy-coloured brick. The architect was perhaps Thomas Atkinson of York, the patron John Harland, the date about 1760. The main part of the house is narrow, of five unornamented bays, but rises high and with impeccable proportions. With its flanking pavilions connected by curving passages, it is the embodiment of the true Palladian spirit. Inside, plaster ceilings were fashioned in the lightest rococo style by Giuseppe Cortese, an Italian who worked at many Yorkshire houses. Some of the chimneypieces are also rococo, making a play of white and coloured marbles, and the Chinese wallpaper, painted with birds and flowering trees on a pale green background, is kept in pristine condition. One room has original marbled wainscot; but in the Morning Room, the carved pine panelling was brought from Potternewton Hall, demolished in 1930, and is said to have been designed by the joiner-architect, Henry Flitcroft.

Sutton Park was bought by the late Major Sheffield and Mrs Sheffield in 1963. He was descended from that Duke of Buckingham whose London House, dating from 1705, has grown into Buckingham Palace. The Sheffields once owned estates in Yorkshire, but for four hundred years their country seat was Normanby Park in Lincolnshire. This will explain why the contents at Sutton are of so fine a quality. The furniture which has been kept for this house is mostly English mahogany of the middle and late 18th century, but there are also Dutch pieces which came from Major Sheffield's mother, and French furniture bought by his father, Sir Berkeley Sheffield, while in the diplomatic service in Paris. Chimneypieces in the Adam style and bookshelves designed by Smirke have been moved from Normanby Park. In the hall one is greeted by a large early drawing of Buckingham House, and elsewhere there are 18th-century views of London. The Sheffield family portraits will be of interest to historians as well as art lovers. Some, by Hayman and Highmore, show the gentle English rococo style at its best. There is a little known self-portrait of the American artist, Benjamin West.

Visitors should allow ample time to enjoy the garden, and may be surprised that anything so complete could have been created since 1963. Three long terraces with broad flowering borders descend to a half-moon of still water, with views over the 18th-century park. A garden such as this should be visited every month of the year.

(See colour plate 26)

Syon House, Middlesex
(The Duke of Northumberland, K.G.)

West of London, between Brentford and Twickenham (A315)

In the 18th century Syon was one of the many riverside houses and villas that bordered on the Thames in a continuous line as far up as Hampton. The road approach was along Brentford High Street with all the traffic to Hounslow, Reading and Bath. On this narrow and untidy thoroughfare, Adam built an exquisite gateway, surmounted by the proud lion of the Percys. Though oddly out of place here, battered, and now out of use, its delicacy gives an idea of what will be found in the house.

The Syon we know was largely the creation of the 1st Duke of Northumberland, Robert Adam and Capability Brown. Its earlier history had not always been happy. The Brigittine Abbey had been founded by Henry V in expiation of his father's part in the murder of Richard II, and it came to the Crown after the Suppression. Katherine Howard was confined here before her execution, and Henry VIII's coffin, resting at Syon on its way to Windsor, burst during the night, the contents being dishonoured by dogs. Later occupants included the Protector Somerset, who rebuilt the house, and John Dudley, father-in-law to Lady Jane Grey, both of whom were executed. James I gave Syon to Henry Percy, 9th Earl of Northumberland, but on being unjustly accused of complicity in the Gunpowder Plot he was sent to the Tower for fifteen years. His son, the Parliamentarian 10th Earl, had the children of Charles I under his charge, and they lived here during the London plague. Princess Anne stayed here for a time when she quarrelled with her sister Queen Mary II.

The history of Syon should be read with that of the other Percy properties, Alnwick and Petworth. All the Percy estates passed to the 'proud' 6th Duke of Somerset, but were divided in 1750 when Syon, Alnwick, and Northumberland House in London came to Lady Elizabeth Seymour. Her husband, Sir Hugh Smithson, assumed the name of Percy and became 1st Duke of Northumberland. He employed Robert Adam to modernise all

Syon; left: *The Hall, and* right: *the Long Gallery, both remodelled by Robert Adam*

three houses, of which Syon came first. Improvements started in 1762 and continued for ten years, resulting in a remarkable series of state rooms formed out of the 16th-century house. The embattled exterior was not altered, and, though refaced with Bath stone about 1825, it still looks much as it did when painted by Canaletto.

Adam published an account of his intentions and ideas for Syon. His Hall is the coolest of rooms, furnished with statues like a Roman *atrium*, but was intended to be enlivened by footmen in blue and gold livery. This had been the old Great Hall, and its floor was low. Adam's steps in a columned recess gave 'an additional picturesque'. By contrast, the dazzling Ante Room was designed 'for the attendance of servants out of livery'. The patterned floor is of scagliola, and lavish greens, mahogany and gold suggest both Imperial Rome and Napoleonic France. The twelve monolith columns of *verde antico* marble are said to have been dug out of the Tiber, and are arranged to make the room look square.

The Great Apartment continues with the Dining Room, fitted with elegance and splendour because, as Adam said, the English habit was to spend much time here. Marble copies of antique statues were ordered from Italy. The Drawing Room, principally for the ladies, has a high coved ceiling with tiny Pompeian figures painted by Cipriani, walls hung with plum-coloured silk from Spitalfields, and a filigree chimneypiece mounted with ormolu. The Gallery had to be designed within the old Long Gallery, a room 136 feet long but of a width and height of only 14 feet. Adam's intricate stucco-work was 'to afford great variety and amusement', and the Gallery was intended for the ladies' retirement after dinner so that the noise of the men in the Dining Room would not reach them.

All the rooms have that meticulous decoration for which Adam is celebrated, combining spatial ingenuity with light stucco-work and carefully chosen colouring. Much of the furniture was designed by the architect, and there are original sets of chairs, side tables and gilded looking-glasses. More Adam furniture came from Northumberland House when that great house was demolished in 1878. The carpet in the Drawing Room, one of the finest of its kind, was also designed by Adam, is signed by Thomas Moore of Moorfields and dated 1769. The walls here are hung with portraits of the Stuart monarchy.

The remaining side of the courtyard, intended as the private apartment, was not finished to Adam's design and dates from the 19th century. In the Print Room and Oak Gallery there are portraits of those who made the history of the house, among them the Lord Protector Somerset and Lady Jane Grey. Gainsborough's fine portrait of the builder Duke of Northumberland contrasts with the excellent but matter-of-fact picture of his military son and successor by the American painter Gilbert Stuart. Here are also two marquetry cabinets and a bureau that belonged to the 'proud' Duke of Somerset. In the staircase there stands a vast and highly decorated Sèvres vase, ordered by Charles X of France in 1825 for the 3rd Duke.

Rare and exotic trees were planted in Capability Brown's park by the 3rd Duke of Northumberland, who also built the Great Conservatory, designed by Charles Fowler, about 1830. His botanical gardens were famous and open to the public. In 1965 the present Duke formed the Gardening Centre Limited, a national horticultural exhibition occupying fifty-five acres of parkland around the lake. The sales department is the delight of many a London gardener.

Tanyard, West Sussex
(Mr M. R. Lewinsohn)

Between Sharpthorne and Horsted Keynes, five miles south of East Grinstead

A picturesque house probably of late mediaeval origin, with timbered additions of the 16th and 17th centuries, now much restored. Its primary interest derives from the fact that it was an ancient tannery. Outside, the long rectangular pits for washing hides survive, and the tanning process was carried out close by in the old stone wing of the house.

Thoresby Hall, Nottinghamshire
(The Countess Manvers)

Three miles north of Ollerton (A614)

The vast and well timbered park is part of Sherwood Forest, celebrated today chiefly for the romantic legends of Robin Hood. His effigy stands in the forecourt, but it is unlikely that he would approve of this solid pile erected in the heyday of a great aristocratic family. Highest of high Victorian, it is a late work by Anthony Salvin and seems just the right setting for a Trollope novel. Thoresby was built in 1865–71 for the 3rd Earl

Thoresby Hall; the Drawing Room (See colour plate 27)

Manvers, the heir to the Dukes of Kingston and the Norman family of Pierrepont. There were two earlier houses here. The first was by William Talman, the architect of Chatsworth. A painting by Tillemans of 1725 shows the first Duke of Kingston wearing his Garter star, shooting in the park. The house burnt down in 1745, but something of its great Baroque pleasure grounds survives in distant lakes and avenues. It was replaced by a neat classical house designed by Carr of York, but after a century this was found inadequate.

Salvin's Jacobethan house stands solidly among open terraced gardens. Though not exactly picturesque, every front has been made carefully asymmetrical, and its jagged bow windows, dormers and chimneys seem to be based on Burghley. A spiky gabled tower marks the position of the grand staircase, and over the front door is a clock tower and lantern. Inside, the entrance stair is lined with weapons and arms, and round the corner it bursts open to the Great Hall, a lofty mixture of Romanesque and Renaissance under a hammerbeam roof. The Hall looks best from the galleries. Conscientious and scholarly though he was over details, there is said to be a coldness about Salvin's later houses. Even in that age of gas the house was lit by oil. An indoor staff of nearly fifty was necessary to maintain it.

Spacious reception rooms occupy the whole of the south front overlooking the terraces. The ceilings are more or less Elizabethan, and the joinery, in light and dark oak and fine walnut, is of superb quality. The Blue Drawing Room, hung with damask silk, looks Second Empire chiefly because of its rococo chimney glass, sumptuous Boulle cabinets and Louis XVI needlework chairs. A huge *boutonné* pouf gives a promise of pneumatic bliss. Here are portraits of the builder of the house, Lord Manvers, and of his French wife Georgine, daughter of the Duc de Coigny, who brought French furniture and sculpture to Thoresby; and a charming picture of their friends, Napoleon III and Eugénie in the *salon* at the Tuileries. In the Dining Room there are not only full-length portraits of the Emperor and Empress riding (by Boutibonne, 1857), but another of their son, the Prince Imperial, painted by Llusse in 1870.

The Victorian furniture in all the rooms is fine, from ebony and fruitwood dining chairs to the exotic mixture in the Great Hall. Most of the Pierrepont treasures are said to have been burnt with the first house in 1745, but a considerable number of excellent portraits remain. The young Charles II and his brother the Duke of Gloucester were painted in exile by Nason, and in the Dining Room a triple portrait by Dahl shows the Duke of Kingston, Lord Burlington and Lord Berkeley drinking at table, young but solemn in their copious periwigs.

Thurnham Hall, Lancashire
(Mr and Mrs S. A. Crabtree)

Five miles south of Lancaster (A588)

North Lancashire with its flat coast, pastoral hills and wild moors was, until the 19th century, as remote as it still is picturesque. In this rugged locality, far from the metropolis yet easily furnished by sea with priests from the Continent, Catholic recusancy flourished as nowhere else in England. Venerable dark stone houses with secret chapels and priest holes served as Mass centres for wide areas. Thurnham is one of those houses.

Its antiquity is not now immediately apparent because a symmetrical gritstone facade in an elegant Gothic style was added in 1823. Twin octagonal turrets, sash windows, castellated parapet and projecting porch indicate the hand of the same architect as nearby Leighton Hall, possibly

Thurnham Hall

one of the Gillows. But this is merely a stone skin varying in thickness from four to eighteen inches and attached to an irregular mid-16th-century house behind – which in turn occupies the site of a 13th-century Pele tower.

In early times Thurnham belonged to various families including the Flemings and the Grays, but in 1566 it was bought by Robert Dalton and remained in the Dalton family until 1973 when it was sold to the present owner. Badly damaged by fire in 1959 and in near-ruinous condition five years ago, it is now undergoing a radical restoration. Much of the earlier fabric is being revealed, and timber-studded partitions, old stonework and blocked archways show the palimpsest nature of the house.

Thurnham's recusant past is attested by two priest holes. A Catholic chapel added by Miss Elizabeth Dalton in 1854, perhaps to the design of Charles Hansom, is in the Decorated Gothic style with characteristic Victorian stained glass and pitch pine woodwork. Of the other interiors, the best is the Hall with a 16th-century ribbed plaster ceiling, a moulded frieze with vines and grotesque heads, and panelling from Park Hall, Charnock Richard, recently brought in. Stained-glass roundels in the windows show the arms of the Daltons and their kinsman Sir Thomas More. Some Dalton portraits still hang in the rooms as an accompaniment to old oak furniture.

Tiverton Castle, Devonshire
(Mr and Mrs Ivar Campbell)

By St Peter's Church, Tiverton

The castle dominates the crossing of the River Exe, its natural defence to the west, and stands on a steep bank near the fine parish church. The face of the Gatehouse is late 14th century, but behind this is an earlier Gatehouse of *circa* 1300; beneath the two a dark vaulted tunnel leads into the courtyard, now laid out as a garden. The walls enclose about an acre of ground. A round corner tower survives, but the old principal range is in ruins. Nothing remains of its former hall, but traceried windows and hooded fireplaces indicate vanished splendours of the solar and chapel. All this is in the local dusky red sandstone.

Tiverton Castle was begun in 1106 by Richard de Redvers, created Earl of Devon by Henry I. It passed with the title to their kinsmen, the powerful Courtenays (later of Powderham). Sir William Courtenay married the daughter of Edward IV, Katherine Plantagenet, who could describe herself as 'the aunt, sister and daughter of Kings'. They lived here in great state and the splendour of her funeral in 1527 is still remembered in the town; but her son, created Marquess of Exeter, stood too near the throne and was executed by Henry VIII. The castle was given to the Duke of Somerset and later bought by Roger Giffard, who in 1588 rebuilt a substantial part. The great destruction during the Civil War was ordered by Fairfax after capturing the castle from its Royalist defenders.

A late-17th-century wing was built with the old stone by Peter West, a rich wool merchant of the town. This part is occupied by the present owners

Tiverton Castle; the gatehouse and corner tower from the courtyard

who came here in 1960. They have excellently restored the older buildings in which several rooms, though shorn of most original features, are shown to visitors. There are Persian rugs, oak chests and Continental furniture, and on the walls are copies of scenes from the Bayeux tapestry. Most interesting is the upper floor of the Gatehouse, now called the Joan of Arc Gallery. It is arranged to illustrate the theory that the Maid of Orleans was no peasant but the illegitimate daughter of Queen Isabeau of France and, far from having been burnt at the stake, she died peacefully in her bed in 1449. This is supported by copies of portraits of the period – an odd collection to find in a market town in Devonshire.

In the circular south-east Tower one can peer down a cavernous garderobe surrounded by the *Collecteana Campbelli Curiosa*, a multitude of timepieces that tick the hours together in a bizarre clock symphony.

Trewithen, Cornwall
(Mr Michael Galsworthy)

Between St Austell and Truro (A390)

Most Cornish houses lie within deep woods with the romantic approach of a long drive. Trewithen on the contrary is urbane. Spruce white palings either side of the gate lead into a small park planted early in the 19th century with big clumps of ilex. Plain but finely proportioned, the house appears at the top of a slope with a pond below making a neat, relaxed setting. Stable blocks frame the forecourt, each with a cupola, one of which has a turret clock dated 1769.

Philip Hawkins, having bought the estate about 1715, 'new built' the house. It was continued after his death by his nephew Thomas Hawkins, and decorated and furnished by another Thomas who succeeded in 1766. In

334

size the building seems modest, nine bays wide, but this is deceptive as it is six bays deep. Little has been altered since the time of George III; it descended, twice through the female line, from Hawkins to Johnstone and now to Mr Galsworthy, grandson of the late Mr George Johnstone.

The ground floor rooms are filled with an excellent miscellany of family possessions, well arranged by the late Mrs Johnstone. Everything in the house has quality, is related to its history and is in keeping with its background; Trewithen is very much the better for being emphatically not a 'collector's house'. The panelling in every room is set off by many paintings. Reynolds's *Market Girl* in the Dining Room has particular charm, and there are paintings by Reynolds and Northcote in the Oak Room and Dining Room. The latter, filling five bays on the south side, is the *chef d'oeuvre* of the house. Its great length is relieved by arcades at either end forming vaulted alcoves, and the walls are graced by light-hearted rococo plaster-work. This was installed by the first Thomas Hawkins before 1766. At the far end are portraits by Reynolds of Dr Zacchariah Mudge and his wife, friends of Samuel Johnson. Mrs Mudge counted sixteen cups of tea drunk by the Doctor, too many altogether for her patience. The teapot, the centre of the trouble, is preserved in the house.

The Dining Room windows look down on the long lawn which is the glory of Trewithen: it was here that Mr G. H. Johnstone, V. M. H., created his beautiful and world-famous garden. The broad grassy ride leading into the wood was here in the 18th century, but Mr Johnstone extended it to two hundred yards wide at the house and tapering gradually along its length. The shrubs at the edge merge into extensive woodland gardens behind. Many of them were raised at Trewithen as their names show: *Camellia reticulata* Trewithen Pink, *Rhododendron Johnstoneanum*, *Rhododendron* Alison Johnstone, and *Ceanothus* Trewithen Blue. The sensitive touch apparent in the house is equalled in the garden. Trewithen, in short, is a masterly ensemble, discreet, quiet, a place of distinction.

Trewithen

Upper Slaughter Manor, Gloucestershire
(Mr Eric Turrell)

Three miles south-west of Stow-on-the-Wold (A436)

The honey-coloured village, lying in a meandering valley off the Gloucestershire highways, is altogether typical of the renowned beauty of the
Cotswolds. The Manor stands high where the ground falls away sharply
to the south east, and distant views over the wolds give a feeling of isolation. 'Slaughter' is a corruption of the Saxon *Sclostre*, meaning 'muddy
place'; the Slaughter family were Lords of the Manor, until they migrated to
America in 1738. The Manor became a farmhouse, and was restored
during the present century.

The entrance and garden fronts of the Slaughters' house are typical
Cotswold Elizabethan, with three gables apiece, all sporting finials. A two-
storeyed porch was added early in the 17th century, with classical columns
in two orders, a fan pediment and the family's arms over the doorway. In
1913 the house was extended on the left by another gable. The change in
ground level is so abrupt that the back door is a full storey lower. From here
the house is seen to be L-shaped, the towering structure showing the
patchwork of centuries. The various openings, overhangs, mouldings and
chimneys defy any precise dating.

Inside, the single-storey hall and drawing room have stone fireplaces with
simple Renaissance mouldings and columns; panelling and the oak stairs,
rather restored, are a little later. The rooms on the lower level are older, and
in one there survives a ribbed vault of stone that is certainly 15th, and
perhaps 14th, century.

Upper Slaughter Manor

Upton Cressett Hall, Shropshire
(Mr William Cash)

Four miles west of Bridgnorth (from A458)

The Saxon village, high in the Shropshire hills, was appropriately named Upton. Now there remain only the manor house, once moated, and the diminutive church with its fine Norman chancel arch. John de Upton was the Norman Lord of the Manor, and in the 14th century his descendant married a Cressett. Hugh Cressett in the 15th century was Constable of Mortimer Castle, and High Sheriff and Member of Parliament for Shropshire. His son Robert, a Yorkist by allegiance, is said to have lodged the boy King Edward V here on his last journey from Ludlow to London. The oldest parts of the house may be dated about 1380 and 1480.

The Cressetts remained Catholic and Royalist; Francis Cressett was one of those who tried to rescue Charles I from Carisbroke Castle in 1648, and was his Treasurer in that last fateful year. Yet eventually they changed their loyalties, and James was Envoy to Hanover during the negotiations for the Hanoverian succession. The family lived at Upton until 1701, but then they built a new house, Cound Hall, in this county. Upton was let, became a farmhouse, and was finally sold in 1919. By 1970 it was derelict: crumbling and overgrown, it might have been thought beyond repair. Yet in very few years, the new owners have restored the house to fine condition.

Remote from public highways, the house first appears on the skyline as a solid mass, with two prominent chimney stacks. Adjoining it is the Gatehouse, a substantial late Elizabethan building of diapered brick with polygonal turrets. The newel stair leads to good rooms, obviously built as

Upton Cressett Hall; from the gatehouse

additional lodgings, with plaster ceilings. The narrow gateway is aligned with the original main door of the house.

Doubtless the Manor once enclosed a courtyard, but half of it was demolished by the early 18th century and whatever remained of the old timber building has been cased in red brick. The Dining Room is the lower part of the original Great Hall, and once was longer than it is now. Two oak piers that rise from the floor suggest that this is a rare survival of an aisled hall, while in the bedroom above the roof survives in fine condition. The date for this may be 1380, when the families of Upton and Cressett were united by marriage.

The long cross-wing, at least half of which is 15th century, undoubtedly replaced an earlier structure. Two fireplaces, one of them serving the kitchen, three brick chimneys and some windows look early Tudor. But substantial remodelling was carried out in 1580, and the panelling in the Drawing Room and the bedroom above it is dated 1600. At some point the oak staircase was moved from the cross-wing to its present position. So many alterations and dates add to the fascination of this house, and it deserves a detailed and expert study.

Weston Park, Staffordshire
(The Earl of Bradford)

Nine miles north-west of Wolverhampton (A5)

More a village than a house, the tightly-packed complex of rose brick and grey stone is the capital of a large domain. Today the 14,000-acre estate is among the most efficiently managed in the country, famous for experiments in organic farming and pioneering forestry.

Like most great houses Weston occupies a mediaeval site; as the proximity of the parish church bears witness. Though it has always passed by inheritance, it has seen more changes of family than most owing to successive failures of male heirs. From the de Westons it passed to the Myttons, the last of whom – Elizabeth – married Sir Thomas Wilbraham in the mid-17th century. They had no son and so Weston passed, again by marriage, to the Newports, Earls of Bradford of the 1st creation, and after one generation to the Bridgemans of Castle Bromwich, who were descended from Charles II's Keeper of the Privy Seal. The present owner is the 6th Earl in the Bridgeman line, this title having been created in 1815.

Weston Park is a very early example of the classical style. It was designed in 1671 by Lady Wilbraham herself. Her annotated copy of Palladio is in the library, but the house owes as much to French example as Italian, particularly in the two semi-circular pediments on the Park front. Despite its size it has a cosy domestic feeling. The warm brick was stuccoed in the 19th century and only revealed again in the 1930s. Lady Wilbraham also designed the stables and parish church. The latter contains a typical series of family monuments, the finest of which is that by Peter Hollins to the 1st Countess of Bradford (1842), a masterpiece of neo-classical sculpture.

Weston Park; the facade, designed by Lady Wilbraham in 1671

Inside the house nothing survives from the 17th century, the light cheerful rooms which the visitor traverses being the result of three later remodellings. The mid-18th century brought columns to the Library and Drawing Room and splendid marble chimneypieces. From the 1860s to the 1890s the house was re-orientated and the large Dining Room and marble staircase installed. Lastly, in the 1960s the Victorian rooms were remodelled and several others redecorated with flair and sensitivity by the present Countess.

One is glad, however, that two rooms are unaltered and still have that elusive mellow quality of a true country house. The Library with its grained woodwork has great charm. The Tapestry Room is hung with one of the six sets of Boucher-Neilson tapestries woven at the Gobelins factory in the late 18th century for English clients.

The palatial Dining Room is the most dramatic of the recently redecorated rooms, with its lofty ceiling embellished with new stucco by Jacksons and rose-coloured wallpaper specially made in Italy. It was finished in time for the coming of age of Viscount Newport in 1968. The former Billiard Room and Smoking Room in the centre of the house, rearranged as picture galleries, are redolent of English 18th-century and early-19th-century taste with Dutch cabinet pictures and landscapes by Vernet and Salvator Rosa.

One of the purposes of the rearrangement of Weston has been to display the pictures to the best advantage. The most interesting smaller portraits, including Holbein's Sir George Carew, are now hung in the Breakfast Room, while the Dining Room is ablaze with newly cleaned Van Dycks of the highest quality. Perhaps the most important picture at Weston is Jacopo

Bassano's *Way to Golgotha*, a gift to Charles II from the people of Holland in 1660. (It is not clear how it left the royal collection!) Curiosities which might attract the visitor are 1,100 letters from Disraeli to Selina, wife of the 3rd Earl of Bradford, and a stuffed (male) yellow parrot which laid twenty-three eggs on twenty-three consecutive days in 1903 and then died.

The park was landscaped by Capability Brown. It contains subsidiary buildings designed in the 1760s for Sir Henry Bridgeman, one of the great 'improvers' of his generation. The Home Farm is 'one of the noblest architectural products of the agricultural revolution'. There are two lakes, a Roman bridge, Swiss Cottage, an obelisk, a Grecian mausoleum, a Gothic tower, boat houses, seats and well-sited urns. Architecturally, the finest building is the Temple of Diana, by James Paine, which contains in a small compass an orangery, tea room, music room, and china room. It commands arcadian vistas, including a glimpse of the house framed by cedars.

The White House, Aston Munslow, Shropshire
(Miss Constance Purser)

Eight miles north of Ludlow (B4368)

The ruined dovecote in the garden tells us that this house was probably the mediaeval manor. It is first recorded as 'The White House' in 1694 when occupied by Thomas Stedman, whose family had already lived in it for many generations. His descendants remained the owners until 1946, after which it was bought by Walter Purser.

The White House

The long low wing, though now entirely cased in stone, is in fact a cruck-framed Hall of, at latest, the 14th century. The crucks have been cut at their bases and are best seen in the roof where is also the spere truss – an early form of screen. The massive chimney stack, serving six hearths, was a 17th-century insertion, as was the floor that provides chambers overhead. The kitchen fireplace has bake and cream ovens. This long Hall had been built against an earlier solar wing, of which there remains a cellar of two rooms hewn out of solid rock. The solar was rebuilt in the 16th century as a timber-frame construction, and this was enlarged after a fire some two centuries later.

The house and old farm buildings are now a Museum of Country Life. Among many exhibits are a Montgomery hay wain of 1891, a complete cider house, and threshing and winnowing machines which, though used within living memory, already call for some explanation.

Wilton House, Wiltshire
(The Earl of Pembroke)

Three miles west of Salisbury (A30)

Few great houses so immediately evoke a talented family as does Wilton, where the Herberts have lived for over 400 years and where successive generations have made a contribution. William, who established the Herbert fortunes, charmed François I, had the good luck to marry Anne Parr (later Henry VIII's sister-in-law), and achieved the unusual feat of enjoying favour and office under four Tudor sovereigns. In 1542 Henry VIII gave him the abbey and lands of Wilton, Edward VI made him Earl of Pembroke, and he was still in high regard at the Elizabethan court on his death in 1570. By all accounts a fortunate and remarkable man.

In his son's day, Mary, sister of Sir Philip Sidney and 'the immortal subject of all verse', was mistress at Wilton. 'The greatest patronesse of wit and learning of any lady of her time', she made of Wilton, as Aubrey says, 'an academie as well as a palace'. Spenser celebrated her virtues, Sidney wrote his *Arcadia* at her suggestion, and *As You Like It* may well have received its first performance under her roof. The 3rd and 4th Earls, 'the incomparable pair of brethren' to whom Shakespeare dedicated the First Folio of his plays, continued the tradition. Even if the 3rd Earl's mistress, Mary Fitton, was not the 'Dark Lady' of the Sonnets, or the Earl himself the 'Mr W. H.' to whom the Sonnets were addressed, Shakespeare held him in regard, Ben Jonson was his friend, and Pembroke College, Oxford is named after him.

The 8th and 9th Earls were hardly less distinguished. The former, founder of the Wilton carpet factory, was a notable collector and President of the Royal Society. His son and successor was 'the architect earl': captious, eccentric, but a man of outstanding probity, he played an important role in the Palladian movement.

Though the visitor enters the precincts of Wilton through William

Wilton House; the Palladian Bridge; (see also colour plate 28)

Chambers's triumphal archway (*c.* 1755) surmounted by an equestrian bronze of Marcus Aurelius, the landscape setting which so becomes the house is only revealed after passing from the forecourt to the western lawns. The water meadows, the huge dark cedars (is there another such group in the country?), the pellucid stream, and the Palladian bridge, are the 9th Earl's memorial. In the first decades of the 18th century, he swept away the earlier parterres, planted the first cedars, and designed the incomparable bridge. Though acknowledging a debt to Palladio, this entrancing structure is highly original, and was so regarded by the Earl's contemporaries who proceeded to copy it at Stowe, Prior Park, Hagley, and even in Russia.

From the Palladian Bridge, the gentle Chilmark stone of the house is seen across suave and cedar-shadowed lawns. Little is seen of the Tudor mansion built by the 1st Earl other than its plan, and the tall frontispiece on the east elevation, but a richly ornamented porch (its design perhaps rightly associated with Holbein) now serves as a garden temple. It is the South Front that focuses attention. Designed about 1636, probably by Isaac de Caux but certainly with the advice of the great Inigo Jones, this is one of the most famous elevations in England, and architecturally one of the most influential. It is a simple and effective composition, and for all its Italian inspiration has a distinctly English character. The central feature is a Venetian window surmounted by reclining classical figures. The gabled corner pavilions were in some sense dictated to the architect by the surviving towers of the Tudor house. All this was to be much copied in the 18th century.

When the interior was gutted by fire in 1647–8, it was rebuilt by John Webb but again with the help of Inigo Jones, now aged seventy-six. Whether the south front was altered at this time is doubtful, and some rooms at the south east seem to have survived from the earlier phase. But the finest room of the Great Apartment, indeed the most famous 17th-century interior in Britain, emerged from the ashes and was designed by Jones and Webb: the Double Cube room, decorated in white and gold (measuring 60 × 30 × 30 feet). The immense Corinthian doorcase, carved swags of fruit, the haughty marble fireplace flanked by gilt statues, and not least the rich unifying entablature, all these emphasise a strictly architectural intention to which even the painted *trompe l'oeil* ceiling and the series of glittering Van Dyck portraits are subordinate. The very floorboards, of wide oak so different from the restless narrow floorboards of our day, are perfectly in scale, as are William Kent's heavy gilt settees and side tables though made nearly a century later. The imposing Single Cube (30 × 30 × 30), carved, painted and gilded has a coved ceiling of arabesques. Besides these noble rooms there is the former great apartment; and in spite of later alterations and delightful ceilings painted by Clermont during the 1730s, these interiors give an idea of how Whitehall Palace might have looked if Charles I and Inigo Jones had ever succeeded in building it.

Wilton offers a further architectural pleasure, though of very different character: the early-19th-century cloister with which James Wyatt surrounded the interior courtyard of the house. Airy, spacious, picturesque as Wyatt understood the term, the cloister, one of his last works (1814), shows the same talent for imaginative Gothic that he expressed at Fonthill and Ashridge.

The architecture and the setting might seem enough, yet much of the attraction of Wilton lies in the paintings (one of the great collections in private hands) and the objects of association acquired over the centuries. Edward VI, Elizabeth, James I and Charles I, all knew the Tudor house, and lesser visitors have been admitted to wonder at the riches of Wilton for over two hundred years. Apart from the famous Van Dycks, there are a series of Reynolds portraits, Lelys, Richardsons, and a sequence of views of Wilton that show Richard Wilson at his topographical best. The old masters

Wilton House; left: *the Double Cube Room, and* right: *the Single Cube Room*

of Italy and the Netherlands are magnificently represented by really fine works of Andrea del Sarto, Lotto, Lucas van Leyden, Van der Goes, Mabuse, Rembrandt, Rubens, and many others. The collection should be studied at leisure, and with the help of a catalogue written by the late Lord Pembroke. There is a magical little landscape by Claude; and in the Large Smoking Room hang an unusual set of mid-18th-century gouaches depicting *haute école* as elaborated by the Spanish Riding School in Vienna.

The Cloister contains the residue of the classical and 17th-century marbles collected by the 8th Earl, and elsewhere the work of Roubiliac is well represented, notably by his busts of Sir Andrew Fountaine, an antiquarian, and Martin Folkes, P.R.S., as well as of the 9th Earl and his Countess. The furniture includes an unusual number of Kent's solemn pieces and many examples of Chippendale's craftsmanship. Among the objects of association are Henry VIII's grant of the abbey lands of Wilton, a lock of Queen Elizabeth's hair, a manuscript poem by Sidney, Napoleon's dispatch box, and Fred Astaire's twinkling shoes. The impression is one of accumulated history.

Woburn Abbey, Bedfordshire
(Trustees of the Bedford Estates)

Six miles north of Leighton Buzzard (A418)

Woburn opened its gates to the public in 1955. Before that, the eleven-mile wall round the park had done an efficient job in keeping people out. The three late Dukes of Bedford were not sociable, and their Abbey had become as aloof and mysterious as a forbidden city. Its seclusion ended dramatically and Woburn has become a household word, largely owing to the successful public approach of the present, 13th Duke. The house itself, seat of the liberal and far-sighted Russells, has seen depredations in recent years, but still it is one of the most majestic and best filled treasure houses in the country.

The suppressed Cistercian Abbey was granted in 1547 to John, Lord Russell, who soon after became 1st Earl of Bedford. The family had settled at Chenies, and Queen Elizabeth's decision to stay at Woburn on her Progress of 1572 was disrupting as the house was scantily furnished and in poor repair. The Russells made Woburn their principal seat only after they happened to take refuge there to escape a London plague in 1625. Some rebuilding was put in hand almost at once. The north wing became the private apartments, and its Grotto or fountain room still remains, a remarkable work of shells and stucco quite in the Italian mannerist tradition and probably designed by Inigo Jones's assistant, Isaac de Caux. Next to this is a room retaining its ceiling and chimneypiece; but more work of the period survives than is apparent, because under their 18th-century dress the State Rooms still preserve their Carolean shape and order of progression.

The 4th Earl, the builder of Covent Garden, was a close friend of Charles I; but his son the 'Puritan Earl' became an active Parliamentarian, served

Woburn Abbey; the Palladian west front

under Cromwell, and at the age of eighty was created a Duke by William III. The honour was probably granted as atonement for the execution of his eldest son at the time of the Rye House Plot (1683). The Bedfords became front-line Whigs and the 4th Duke, who remodelled the house, was one of the party's most active and influential members in the mid-18th century. Of greater and more lasting benefit than their politics has been their agricultural work. Already in the 1630s they had begun draining the fens, a project that nearly resulted in bankruptcy (relieved, however, by the inheritance of the Bloomsbury estates of the Earl of Southampton), and their pioneer work throughout the 18th and 19th centuries contributed towards England's supremacy in farming.

Until 1950 the house kept the form of an enclosed quadrangle – the legacy of the Cistercian cloister – but then, owing to dry rot, the eastern half was demolished. So numerous are the objects at the house that this wing might well have been kept for their overflow. However, the late Sir Albert Richardson healed the scars and designed the steps that now lead up the hill towards twin Stable Blocks, bold and accomplished 18th-century work by Henry Flitcroft. It was Flitcroft too who gave the Abbey a Palladian park front during the 1750s, its very correct Ionic centrepiece linked to the wings by two lower ranges, and who designed the State Rooms within. They start on the first floor in the old private wing with the Chinese Room, with superb wallpaper bought in 1753. Six yellow and blue rooms lead without a break through the State Apartment, the State Bedroom on the corner being always reserved for Royal visits. Charles I stayed here three times, and Queen Victoria and Prince Albert came in 1841. The Bedroom has a Palmyra sunflower ceiling, while the other ceilings are either rococo or regular Palladian.

The central Saloon has recently been painted by Roland Pym with murals showing various achievements of the Russells and their historic properties. Beyond it lie the State Dining Room (hung with Van Dyck and 17th-

Woburn Abbey; left: *the State Bedroom, and* right: *the Grotto*

century portraits) and the Breakfast Room containing superb portraits by Reynolds. Behind these rooms, the Long Gallery overlooking the Quadrangle is Flitcroft's remodelling of the Carolean gallery. Here are Royal and other Tudor portraits, the most famous being the Armada Portrait of Queen Elizabeth. The Jacobean Earls of Bedford are seen on the Staircase, as well as Velasquez's painting of *Admiral Pareja*. The Blue Drawing Room has a Claude and two Poussins, the State Dressing Room has Netherlandish masters (including Cuyp, Steen and Teniers). In the Bedroom is Bonnington's *Normandy Coast Scene*, and in Prince Albert's Dressing Room 19th-century portraits have recently given way to horse pictures. These examples give only an idea of what will be found in the State Rooms. And there is yet the furniture: magnificent gilded pier glasses, chairs and the state bed all made by Samuel Norman; sumptuous marquetry commodes by Pierre Langlois; Palladian mahogany, 'Chinese Chippendale', French marquetry and Boulle.

A new era began in 1787 when the young 5th Duke commissioned the 'Whig' architect, Henry Holland, to rebuild the south wing (which has now become the private wing). The Library (not always open) is referred to as the architect's finest interior. The corner room has twenty-two Canaletto paintings of Venice, each one a masterpiece, that were brought here in 1800 when Bedford House in London was demolished. Outside, Holland's pretty Chinese Dairy is still to be seen, but the vast Tennis Court and Riding School he built beyond the Stables was demolished, as well as his east wing, in 1950. Against the South Stables, Holland designed a huge Conservatory that shortly after was converted by the 6th Duke into a Sculpture Gallery. This superb room, adorned with eight ancient columns of marble, is now used for catering and the sculpture, which includes Whig portrait busts by Nollekens, is put around the house. But at one end of the Gallery, Canova's *Three Graces* remains in the circular Temple that Wyatville designed for it in 1816.

There seem to have been exotic birds and animals here since the 18th century, but from 1893 the 11th Duke and the 'Flying Duchess' enormously increased their number by collecting from all over the world. There are now nine varieties of deer, including the Père David from China which the Duke saved from extinction. These and numerous mammals make up the Wild Animal Kingdom.

The remarkable Duchess was a person of compulsive enthusiasms, and having made several record-breaking air flights she disappeared when flying alone, aged seventy-two, in 1937. The present, 13th Duke inherited the estate in 1953 and had to find staggering death duties, partly as a result of which he quickly became the leading figure in the stately homes business – indeed he virtually invented it. Before his retirement to France, rooms were arranged in the Crypt for yet more family treasures: marvellous porcelain, including a Sèvres dinner service presented to the Duchess of Bedford by Louis XV; silver and gilt plate, snuff boxes and miniatures. Woburn Abbey is now shown and the estate managed by his heir, the Marquess of Tavistock.

Wolfeton House, Dorset
(Captain N. T. L. Thimbleby)

A mile north of Dorchester (A37 and A352)

This curiously shaped grey Manor was the seat of the Trenchards, a family of Wessex landowners whose wealth came from extensive sheep farming. Between 1495 and 1630 (if we except the years 1550–7) there were only two owners: Sir Thomas Trenchard, and his great-grandson Sir George. Between them they built the house, whose architecture therefore can satisfactorily be dated to their respective reigns. But around 1800 the building was brutally dismembered, and what remains is little more than the Gatehouse and one side of the courtyard. Even the Hall was removed. But enough survives to show originality and even eccentricity.

Wolfeton's *grand siècle* began in January 1506, when the future Sir Thomas Trenchard entertained the Archduke Philip and his wife, Joanna of Castile. The royal couple had been on their way to claim the throne of Castile, but were forced by storms to land at Weymouth. After some days at Wolfeton the illustrious guests proceeded to Windsor. The house was presumably large enough and warm, but nothing of it is known except possibly the two surviving circular towers that flank the Gatehouse. They are unequal in size, and their upper storeys were formerly pigeon houses. Built of silver-grey stone, the centre of the Gatehouse is dated 1534. What remains of Sir Thomas's courtyard house must be seen from the garden, namely a stair tower and a garderobe projection, with windows between. In spite of later alterations, the fine quality of the original carving remains. The jambs have stepped plinths, and luxuriant vines trail under the hood mouldings.

The rest of the garden front is Elizabethan and was built by Sir George.

Wolfeton House

The centre windows once protruded as a bay. Inside there is an extraordinary mixture of decoration, but, owing to later demolition, the plan is hard to make out. There are overmantels which, being similar to work at Montacute, may be dated around 1600. A vast oak doorcase and chimneypiece are overpowering and self-indulgent. More interesting are the vaulted corridor, stone staircase and doorway above, an ensemble carved with great refinement in the Renaissance style. Dr Girouard has suggested they were carved by Allen Maynard, a Frenchman who was working from 1563 at Longleat. The upper floor is mostly taken up by a Gallery or Great Chamber that formerly had a curved plaster vault.

The last Trenchard of Wolfeton removed the splendid armorial glass that was once seen in nearly every room, and clearly he took away other spoils besides. The manor descended to the level of a farmhouse, was sold and partly demolished. Restorations were attempted after 1862, when chimney-pieces were moved around and old woodwork rearranged. The Great Chamber was divided up, and since the last war the Manor has been let as three separate residences. The present owner has removed many intrusions, and much reinstatement is still to be done. From a fireplace he has recovered late Gothic panels carved with the *Occupations of the Months*, which will now be seen in a Gatehouse room that has been furnished as a Chapel.

Wotton House, Buckinghamshire
(Mrs David Gladstone)

At Wotton Underwood, between Aylesbury and Bicester (south of A41)

Grenvilles were certainly at Wotton by the 11th century. Richard Grenville, the builder of this Queen Anne house, married Hester Temple, eventual heiress of the renowned Stowe estate that lies fourteen miles away. When she succeeded as Countess Temple in her own right in 1749, Wotton was united with Stowe and used as an alternative residence by the family who

348

became Marquesses and Dukes of Buckingham and Chandos. It was, for instance, the country place of George Grenville, First Lord of the Treasury, whose brother-in-law William Pitt, Earl of Chatham, had a great affection for its fine and luxuriant gardens.

The forecourt is flanked by delightful twin pavilions, each topped by a lantern. In style they are not so advanced as the house, which bears the enigmatic Latin inscription 'conceived in 1704' on its garden door. Even though it has lost the former attic storey, the building still gives an impression of considerable height, its outline defined by Corinthian pilasters. Oddly enough the garden front has two bays fewer than the entrance. The relationship – for this cannot be doubted – between Wotton and the original Buckingham House (now Buckingham Palace) begun in 1705 has not been discovered, and the architect of Wotton is unknown. Thornhill painted the stairs and saloon, but these were destroyed in the fire of 1820.

The fire can have done little damage to the outside walls, but the 2nd Marquess of Buckingham commissioned Sir John Soane to redesign the whole interior. This was one of Soane's last country house commissions and it survives almost complete. This architect had no love for tall buildings. He removed the attic storey, and by reducing the height of the first floor rooms was able cleverly to conceal a new attic behind the frieze and cornice. Inside, the Entrance Hall was, unfortunately, remodelled in 1929 by A. S. G. Butler, but Soane's arches remain, opening to his narrow oval staircase with its high coffered vault. Tijou's original wrought-iron balustrade dating from the Queen Anne building was re-used. Hanging arches and opposing curves

Wotton House from the forecourt

give elusive effects of perspective and shadow, both here and in the corridors.

Three fine rooms occupy the garden front, while upstairs were the apartments of Lord and Lady Temple. The immediate impression is one of dazzling light. Soane's details are not demonstrative: delicate beaded cornices with rounded corners, shallow reeded mouldings and arched doorcases make for an illusion of fragility. All this shows the unmistakable hand of John Soane, who distilled his vast architectural knowledge into these simple and primitive forms.

The pleasure grounds so much admired by the elder Pitt were originally laid out by Queen Anne's gardener, George London, to whom were due five avenues that radiated from the house (recent victims of elm disease). Capability Brown in 1757–60 expanded the lakes and may have built the bridge. The large number of trees recently planted will help to restore the park. When the late Patrick and Mrs Brunner discovered Wotton the house was within two weeks of demolition. Not without great difficulty they effected its last-minute rescue, bought four hundred acres of parkland from five different owners, and worked on the restoration of this unique house.

SCOTLAND

29 Abbotsford; Sir Walter Scott's study   30 Glamis Castle; the Drawing Room

31 Inverary Castle; the Drawing Room

32 Kellie Castle, Arbroath

33 Manderston

Castles and Mansions of Scotland

by Colin McWilliam

Mountains and valleys, lochs and islands; these, with their impassive, eternal challenge to human endeavour, make up the vision of Scotland in the mind of the traveller. Nearly every scene is linked with the name of a famous Scots family, and that name with a famous event in history.

As to what it was like to be a lord, a farmer or a merchant in the days when that history was being made, the best answer is provided by the houses in which they lived. And the reason why so many of these have survived is that they are built of stone, the one resource in which no part of Scotland is lacking. Only a man of some means was ever able to build with stone, let alone quarry and work it, so most of the humbler houses have gone, leaving only archaeological evidence behind. Even the grander ones are built mainly of stones picked up in the open, their rubble walls being weatherproofed where necessary with a blanket of harling (rough rendering) which has a sculptural beauty of its own. A fully dressed stone house was a sign of uncommon wealth, and remained so right up to the late 18th century, by which time the story told by Scotland's buildings has changed, from rivalry and conflict to development and improvement.

Buildings survive in a variety of ways and roles. Many now exist with the main purpose of being visited. Ancient Monuments, for example, are in direct government care, usually preserved as ruins and in no case inhabited. A number of complete houses and castles, notably in the north-east, belong to the National Trust for Scotland who set a high standard in their care and interpretation. Many houses can be visited as hotels. But by far the most, despite the difficulties of keeping them up, are still lived in by their owners. An opportunity to see some of the finest, just when their gardens are at their best, is given by Scotland's Gardens Scheme. But the Scottish part of this volume is devoted to those houses still in private hands where visitors are welcomed under more formal and regular arrangements.

The first thing you notice is that most of the houses are in fact castles – each one the focus of territorial responsibilities or ambitions. On the rugged coastline of the west, and the islands of the west and north, castles lie in wait for seaborne attack. Of the Vikings, who were only slowly dislodged from these regions, the main evidence today is in the physical appearance and the traditions of many of the islanders, and in the great Romanesque Cathedral of St Magnus at Kirkwall on the island of Orkney. The castles came later, not principally for the defence of the realm but for the territorial security of the chiefs and their loyal clansmen. Later still came the tragic drama of the Jacobite risings in the first half of the 18th century; and out of this, in time, a revival of family and national pride, splendidly expressed in Highland dress and 19th-century baronial architecture. Two castles sum up this story. First is Dunvegan, seat of the MacLeods on the island of Skye, whose grand feudal austerity can be admired today as Doctor Johnson admired it two centuries ago. Second Eilean Donan, wonderfully resurrected after an extraordinary and violent history so that with its modern turrets, standing guard at the entry to Loch Duich, it forms the ideal picture of Scotland's romantic past.

But for the first generation of stone-built castles we must look towards the Lowlands, Dirleton Castle, an Ancient Monument, was first built in the early 12th century by the family of Vaux, one of those to whom baronial powers had been awarded by the monarch of a broadly united Scotland. It had, and still has, a perimeter curtain wall punctuated by big drum towers. Later castles were on a smaller scale. Still adjoined by a walled courtyard, they concentrated their accommodation in a single tower such as can be seen most clearly at Lennoxlove,* but still lies at the heart of many castles, as at Dunrobin where it is obscured by subsequent work. Cawdor, perhaps, is the most perfect of these compound Scots houses.

Most of these massive towers date from before the battle of Flodden (1513). Even afterwards, however, when the main need was for defence against marauding neighbours rather than full-scale military attack, the tower remained the most important type for every scale of domestic building. Shortage of timber for roofing had much to do with it, and when wood was used for ceilings (generally imported from the Baltic), it was often gaily decorated in tempera; the house of Northfield* at Prestonpans has some of the best preserved of these paintings. The leaping hound with trails of foliage that appears on a timber partition is strikingly similar to one that forms part of a hunting scene in a much earlier example (on a plastered masonry wall) at Traquair.

In plan, the tower-house of the 16th and 17th century often forms a capital L shape; a substantial staircase turret, round or polygonal, was set in the internal angle, with a yett or iron gate at the bottom. Glamis Castle is the most magnificent specimen of this basically simple type and shows its final development, with the old roof-top capehouse now burgeoning into candle-snuffered bartizans and Renaissance gables; it was finished during the reign of Charles II. Muchalls and Kellie are less formidable, but still on the defensive, while some, like Traquair, break away from the 'angular' tradition altogether so that the successive building stages form a single range. Indeed, Traquair, with its late-17th-century forecourt, must be one of the loveliest of old Scots houses – perhaps because it is the simplest.

All these buildings have hints of the Renaissance, especially in their internal details. The new style, which had suddenly dawned in the 16th-century palaces of Falkland and Stirling, originally came from France. Italy and the Low Countries, as well as England, were the source of further ideas,

* Houses marked with an asterisk are open by special request, which should be made well in advance.

Left: *Dunrobin Castle; the ancient tower in the centre of the building*
Below: *Glamis Castle; the staircase and yett*

but these continued to enter Scotland chiefly through the court. Winton,* in the 1620s, was the first house to aspire to the full classical treatment with pedimented windows and moulded string-courses, and its builder was William Wallace, the King's master mason. Significantly, it still uses the old-style L-plan, and its elaborately ribbed plaster ceilings are the grandest examples of a type which is basically English but is found in the houses of many Scots loyalists of the early 17th century, such as Glamis and Muchalls. But of all Scots Renaissance houses the most spectacular is Drumlanrig; a century later than Wollaton in England, it presents an even more daring mixture of old and new ideas.

A real understanding of classical architecture comes with dramatic suddenness in the last years of the 17th century, making a complete break with tradition. Kinross House,* built for himself by the courtier-architect Sir William Bruce, is followed by the ducal palace of Dalkeith (its noble forecourt visible from the road through the park), whose architect was James Smith. Both buildings owe much to Holland. Then at the turn of the century Bruce designs the highly original house of Hopetoun; the exterior Palladian with a French accent, the interior comfortably panelled in the old style, with a wonderful top-lit stair in the centre. But this soon proved insufficiently grand, and the whole of the entrance front is transformed into the semblance of a colossal Baroque palace by William Adam senior, with magnificent rococo interiors (after his death) by his distinguished sons. Thus Hopetoun is a sort of cross-roads in Scottish classicism, though its excellence is by no means alone; the lovely interiors at Blair, which are known to be the work of Thomas Clayton, are of equal quality.

The Act of Union was passed in 1707, and there will always be more than one opinion about the rights of it. On the one hand, many Jacobite sympathisers were to forfeit their estates. On the other, there were plenty of landowners who wanted to make the Union work; prosperous partnership between Scotland and England was a declared aim of many lowland improvers as they planned their parks and mansions, their farms and their new towns or villages. Their foremost designer was William Adam senior, who has a splendidly diverse series of houses to his credit. Floors was an austere, symmetrical castle, subsequently romanticised by Playfair. Elsewhere his work was grandly Palladian-Baroque, and at Hopetoun and Arniston* he redesigned not only the house but the park as well. Money for all these 18th-century improvements generally came from local development. For example the Penecuik* estate, where Sir John Clerk himself laid out the park, was supported by farms and coal-mines. But later in the century a second type of landlord comes to the fore; the Scot who has made his fortune abroad and returns to buy and improve an estate in his homeland, like the remarkable Dr James Mounsey of Rammerscales.

Parks were generally laid out before the new houses were built, and their impressive size is indicated by far-flung lodges or, as at Floors, by mile upon mile of boundary wall, always of stone. As for the gardens, they are almost always sited at some distance from the house. Stone walled and often brick-lined, they continue to be planned in the 17th-century manner, divided into four parts by two intersecting paths.

The practice of architecture in Scotland tends to run in families, of which Mylne, Adam and Playfair are the best known. On William Adam's death in 1748, his sons were already established as architects in their own right. Robert Adam's achievement in England is well known, but his contribution (and that of his brothers) to the Scottish house is only now being fully appreciated. It is seen most distinctively in the design of castles, of which the best known is Culzean (National Trust for Scotland) on its cliff above the Firth of Clyde. Mellerstain, which has more the look of a toy fort, is earlier; it contains perhaps the most beautiful series of Adam interiors in Scotland. Why build a castle when there is no need to defend yourself? Scottish tradition has much to do with it, but the reason Adam most often gave to his patrons was the suitability of his great round-towered, castellated houses to grand natural landscapes. Inverary, designed by Morris, though significantly William Adam was put in charge of the work, was in many ways the prototype. Rossdhu, very much in the Adam manner, is a rare example of a large, late classical house in a majestic natural setting.

Scottish painters were active and well patronised by their countrymen. George Jamesone died in 1644 and belongs to the late Renaissance period. Of later generations, Sir John Medina, a Spaniard who settled in Edinburgh, has left portraits at Glamis, Blair and Inverary; his pupil William Aikman settled in London; David Allan, best known for his conversation groups, worked for some years in Rome. Who can forget the noble sweetness of a portrait by Allan Ramsay, or the authority of one of those speaking likenesses by Raeburn? Clayton was the best of Scottish plasterers, Trotter

356

Left: *Allan Ramsay: the 18th Countess of Sutherland (Dunrobin Castle)*. Right:
Sir Henry Raeburn: Sir Walter Scott (Bowhill)

of Edinburgh (in the Regency manner) the outstanding cabinet maker. But
the strength of the Union with England is clear also in many portraits by
Reynolds and Gainsborough, and in the London-made furniture at Hopetoun, Blair and Inverary. No less than their English counterparts, the great
Scottish houses formed collections of old master paintings, while French
furniture in all its magnificence can be seen at Scone, Bowhill and Floors.

Sir Walter Scott is rightly credited with the romantic revival of interest
in Scottish history and architecture. But Abbotsford, surprisingly, is more
like an English manor than a Scottish laird's house, despite the wealth of
Scottish allusions (and a number of fragments of actual Scottish buildings)
within its walls. The genuine baronial revival, for which Scott had created
the climate and encouraged the architectural research, was further stimu-
lated by the visit of George IV in 1822, and the return of Highland dress. In
building it was initiated by the great William Burn[1] at Tyninghame (1829)
whose park is open. Burn lived and practised in the first half of Victoria's
reign, and all over Scotland the lead was followed by his former pupil David
Bryce, who added to old castles like Blair or built new ones. Now, as much as
in England, the need was for huge houses of a functional complexity never
imagined by Georgian designers, for the entertainment of guests (accompanied by their servants) in the grand manner. Burn and Bryce performed
the considerable feat of developing an old and very different tradition to
these modern needs, and their houses are now admired (where they have
survived) for their own qualities, their boldly picturesque composition,
their fine interior sequences and their consummate craftsmanship. The
royal Castle of Balmoral, popularly but erroneously thought to be the father

[1] Camperdown* by Dundee (1822) is his neo-classical masterpiece.

The Armoury Hall at Inverary; weapons of the Clan Campbell; (see also illustration on p. 358)

of the baronial revival, is not in fact particularly Scottish. But Queen Victoria's enthusiasm for the Highlands undoubtedly set the royal seal of approval on a style uniquely suitable to the Scottish scene.

The supreme country house of Edwardian Scotland is Manderston; the rooms a sophisticated adaptation of the Adam style, the dairy Gothic, the boathouse a Swiss chalet, all by John Kinross, in the setting of an earlier park. But the real story of the Scottish house, and particularly the castle, was brought into the 20th century by Sir Robert Lorimer. His was a gentler sort of restoration than Bryce's though he could still be grand, as in the interiors he supplied at Lennoxlove, Rossdhu and Dunrobin. But he was not the last architect in the Scots tradition; Sir Basil Spence's Broughton Palace near Peebles, built in the 1930s and at present partly open as an art gallery, is a direct and eloquent tribute to it. Quite recently Maxwelton House, the birthplace of Annie Laurie, has been ingeniously restored to make the most of its older features. Even the massive-walled tower-house has now come back into its own, and fine examples, roofless for a hundred years or more, are taking their place with surprising ease in modern life.

Houses in Scotland

Abbotsford, Borders
(Mrs Maxwell-Scott, O.B.E.)

Between Melrose and Galashiels

Walter Scott had always been in love with the Border country and thanks to the success of his poems (even by 1800 *The Lay of the Last Minstrel* had sold 40,000 copies) he was able in 1811 to satisfy an innocent longing to become a laird on Tweedside. For £4,000 he bought a stead with a farm of some 110 acres (which later grew to 1,400), and he romantically christened it Abbotsford, since the property had once belonged to the Abbey of Melrose and monks had used the nearby ford. In the modest farm house, to which he moved with his family in the following year, the Waverley novels were written, bringing him a vast reputation, temporary wealth, and a baronetcy from George IV. A wing was added in 1818, and by 1822 he was in a position to pull down the old farm and build his new Abbotsford. This, apart from a small west wing added twenty years after his death, is the Abbotsford we see today. William Atkinson was the architect, but 'authentic' details were contributed by Edward Blore, whom Scott had discovered as an illustrator of books on Gothic.

Of vaguely Tudor appearance, with battlemented tower, crow-stepped gables, conical turrets, and strips of machicolation, all prefaced by castellated gateway and portcullis, the house was among the precursors of early Victorian Baronial. It was not a distinguished building, not even a predominantly Scottish one, but Scott loved it. Ruskin might condemn it and Queen Victoria, years later, pronounce it 'rather gloomy', but the public (to whom it was first opened in 1833, the year after Scott's death) took it to their hearts. Meanwhile, partly owing to his encouragement of research, the more distinctive baronial style spread its roots over the length and breadth of Scotland.

Baronial revival is but one aspect of the wide influence exerted by the novelist's romantic passion for an idealised Scottish past. Two decades of Waverley novels healed the wounds of Culloden, gave the country a new self-confidence, and launched the cult for Scotland and all things Scottish which has obsessed the English ever since. It was an extraordinary achievement, and the mediaevalistic gallimaufry of Abbotsford is fascinating as a reflection of the brave and lovable man who brought off, perhaps to his surprise, this political and cultural conjuring trick.

With moulded ceilings, dark polished panelling, fires roaring in the pseudo-mediaeval grates, and Brussels or thick Turkish carpets on the floors, the interior of Abbotsford must once have had much the same warmth as Scott's own personality. Even today, though the floors are alas carpetless and the temperature has dropped in a century and a half, that

Abbotsford (see also colour plate 29)

same personality dominates the house. Everything reflects the life of the man and the writer, his enthusiasms and his friendships. Raeburn's portrait (of which the first version is at Bowhill nearby) hangs on the wall, and in Chantrey's marble bust he stares firm-mouthed down the length of the Library where some of the books that most influenced him – Percy's *Reliques of Ancient Poetry*, an early-18th-century *Life of Rob Roy* – lie open in the showcases. In the Study is the desk at which he wrote, and at which, when financial disaster struck soon after Abbotsford was finished, he toiled unremittingly.

Presents from the great and the humble are witness to the esteem and affection Walter Scott inspired: Goethe's medallion portrait was handed to Carlyle by the great German to pass on to Scott, and in the Drawing Room, which is hung with Chinese 18th-century painted paper, an ebony desk and chairs were presented by George IV, and a silver urn by Byron. But the rooms derive their predominant and characteristic flavour from the objects of romantic and antiquarian interest that Walter Scott himself collected. Among them are an engraved tumbler that belonged to Robert Burns, a lock of Prince Charles Edward's hair and his quaich, Rob Roy's portrait, sporran, dirk and broadsword, Bonnie Dundee's pistol, and Montrose's cabinet taken with his baggage after the defeat at Philiphaugh. Scott also amassed a quantity of armour, some of it highly interesting. There are 15th-century maces, German 16th-century suits of field and tilt armour, a German wheel-lock gun of the same period, and notably a superb set of French Louis XIV *coûteaux de chasse* mounted in silver gilt that once belonged to Prince Charles Edward.

The last clothes Scott wore are preserved at Abbotsford – a grey beaver hat, a black cut-away coat, and plaid trousers – but they do not seem a *memento mori*, for though he died here in 1832 his living presence still fills the house.

Blair Castle, Tayside
(Duke of Atholl)

Eight miles north-west of Pitlochry (A9)

Blair was fortified before the end of the 13th century, and a military strategist would recognise that its situation at the entrance to the inhospitable reaches of Glen Garry, one of the few feasible routes into the Highlands, called for a castle. Yet to the layman it comes as a surprise to find so large and ancient a mansion, with the setting a great house deserves – trees like sailing-ships on seas of sward, an avenue of shady limes, assured terraces – three miles above the Pass of Killiekrankie and in a mountain setting where winter roads must have been impassable for weeks before the advent of snow-ploughs.

The character of the castle offers further surprise. The massive white-harled house, though pleasant enough, seems at first sight but another Scottish mansion with pronounced baronial flavour, strong on clan history and legend, but hardly the polite home of the 18th-century arts. Appearances are deceptive. Blair's baronial facades conceal a Georgian interior of unusual distinction.

The architectural history is curious and illustrates the compulsive force of the tides of taste. The early castle, where Edward III had stayed in the 14th century, was conferred in 1457 on Sir James Stewart, ancestor of the present owner, the 10th Duke of Atholl. In 1530 a new Great Hall was built, but Blair retained its mediaeval character for another two hundred years. Then

Blair Castle

the 2nd Duke, seduced by the growing vogue for Georgian architecture, sliced off turrets and gables, and between 1747–58 conjured up a more regular mansion within sight of the Grampians. Rather over a century later, when romantic taste had set in a different direction, the 7th Duke called in David Bryce, a competent exponent of Scots baronial, to undo, as far as the exterior of the castle went, the work of his predecessors. After 1869 castellations, crow-stepped gables, and bartizans reappeared. But happily the 18th-century interior was spared.

The outside offers little hint of what is in store. Even the Entrance Hall is Bryce's work, though commanding enough it looks with its gleaming trophies of arms. The unexpected series of 18th-century rooms is to follow. The architect responsible was James Winter and the interior decoration was apparently supervised by Abraham Swain. Little seems to be known of these men, but Thomas Clayton, who had worked for William Adam at Holyroodhouse Palace, executed the stucco, and Thomas Carter of Piccadilly, the sculptor and stonemason who left his mark on so many English houses and years later was employed by the Prince Regent at Carlton House, was responsible for the marble fireplaces. (Perhaps he was a Jacobite, for he christened his daughters 'Sobieska' and 'Clementine'.)

The decoration of the mid-18th-century rooms is a telling tribute to the confident taste of the time. The Picture Staircase, though the plaster and woodwork were grained (and well grained) in the 19th century, epitomises the robust character of the Georgian work, as does the green and white Dining Room. In the latter Clayton's assured plasterwork is seen at its most exuberant: luxuriant swags of fruit over broken door-pediments, a baroque overmantel, and a ceiling that combines both Baroque and rococo elements. Hardly less imposing are the Drawing Room, hung in crimson damask, with a noble ceiling, coved and richly plastered, and the Tapestry Room (so called for its Brussels tapestries that were made for Charles I), with a tall

Blair Castle; left: *the Picture Staircase, and* right: *the Dining Room*

damask-hung William and Mary bed that flaunts tufts of ostrich feathers and still wears its period fringes, as do the mid-Georgian chairs in the room.

Thirty-two rooms ending with the immense 1877 Ballroom are shown to visitors, and no attempt can be made here to describe them all. Their contents are remarkable, and Blair has been called with pardonable exaggeration a 'Highland Victoria and Albert'. As was usual at the time, most of the best Georgian furniture (but not all: notably two mid-18th-century pieces by Sanderman of Perth) is English-made. Much of it is documented oak hall-chairs by Cobb, mahogany seat furniture with attractive fish-scale decoration by Gordon, side tables by Hodson, a rococo bed and chairs by William Masters, mirrors with rococo giltwood frames by Cole (all these more or less contemporary with the 2nd Duke's Georgian interior), Neo-classical chairs and settees of c. 1780 by Chipchase, and Regency cabinets by Bullock. The formidable list could be extended.

Paintings, if less outstanding, include competent portraits by Lely, Ramsay, Raeburn (a talented likeness of Neill Gow, fiddler and musician to three Atholl Dukes in the 18th century), Lawrence, and not least two enchanting conversation pieces of the 3rd and 4th Dukes by Zoffany and David Allan. The bravura full-length of the 1st Marquess of Atholl by Jacob de Witt (on the Picture Staircase) looks like one of Louis XIV's marshals. Built into the Dining Room walls are large romantic paintings of views on the estate by the little-known Charles Steuart, one of the earliest of Scottish landscape painters, who was a native of Atholl and spoke Gaelic. He was patronised by the 3rd Duke, as was his architect brother George who is best known for having designed Attingham Park.

Pre-Georgian Blair – the visit of Mary Queen of Scots, the occupation of the castle for eight years by Cromwellian forces, Prince Charles Edward's stay – is evoked by Stuart miniatures and portraits, and such moving relics as the helmet and breastplate worn by Bonnie Dundee when he fell mortally wounded at Killiekrankie. In the Stewart Room there is early oak furniture, most of it pre-1650.

Bowhill, Borders
(The Duke of Buccleuch and Queensberry)

Three miles west of Selkirk (A708)

Unlike Boughton and Drumlanrig, two other great Buccleuch houses, Bowhill offers little to the architectural purist. The large rambling house, which entombs an earlier 18th-century mansion, took somewhat haphazard shape in the 19th century: first at the hands of William Atkinson who began to transform it in 1812 (and who was later to work for Walter Scott at Abbotsford nearby), and secondly after 1831 at the hands of William Burn. None the less, set above the gracious Vale of Ettrick, associated with the poet James Hogg known as the Ettrick Shepherd, one can see why Scott called the place 'Sweet Bowhill'. It has an easy-going air and for all its size is very much a family home.

Bowhill; Mortlake tapestries in the Gallery Hall

Today Bowhill largely reflects the interests and personalities of two agreeable men, the 4th and 5th Dukes of Buccleuch. The 4th Duke was the close friend of Walter Scott, a relationship that is commemorated in the Study, where hangs the earliest of Raeburn's portraits of the poet, and the manuscript of *The Lay of the Last Minstrel* and other Scott relics are preserved. The 5th Duke, a notable agriculturalist and among the most enlightened of Victorian landowners, succeeded in 1819. He was master of Bowhill for sixty-five years, and much of the friendly aura of the house must be due to him and his competent Duchess.

For the average visitor atmosphere and some remarkable contents will be the attractions of Bowhill. When Montagu House in Whitehall, the family's London seat, was closed in this century, many of the furnishings were brought north, and works of art from yet another family house, Dalkeith Palace, have also enriched the collection.

On entering the Gallery Hall, the visitor receives a first impression of the high quality of much that awaits him. Three superb Mortlake tapestries above the gallery were woven after Mantegna's cartoons at Hampton Court that depict *The Triumph of Julius Caesar*. Below hang works by Lely and several imposing full-length portraits that in many houses would be confidently given to Van Dyck. It is somehow characteristic of Bowhill that they are modestly attributed to his School. The Gallery Hall also provides an introduction to the French furniture which is one of the specialities of the house. There are signed Louis XV chairs with Aubusson upholstery, a signed *bureau plat* of the same period, a Boulle bracket clock of about 1710, Louis XVI candelabra, pale blue Sèvres bowls mounted in ormolu, and not least a Louis XIV mirror of ebony, tortoiseshell and ormolu, given by Charles II to the Duke of Monmouth.

The Duke, the natural son of Charles II and Lucy Walters, married

Bowhill; the Drawing Room; (see also illustration on p. 357)

Anne, heiress to the Scotts of Buccleuch, and the Monmouth Room is dedicated to his memory. A full-length portrait of the Duke in his Garter robes by Lely faces the door, and an unusually attractive Kneller portrays his Duchess with their two boys. Relics of Monmouth and his unhappy rising include the Duke's cradle, his seal, his sword, his sumptuous saddle worked in gold thread, and the white linen shirt in which he was executed.

In the Monmouth Room there are also a series of topographical views by the 18th-century landscapist, George Barrett, which recall his large murals in Surrey. With their romantic overtones, they provide an interesting contrast to another collection of topographical paintings by Francesco Guardi and Antonio Joli, which hang, with works by Marieschi and Pannini, in the Italian Room nearby. But the finest topographical work at Bowhill is in the Dining Room – a wonderfully luminous view of Whitehall by Canaletto. It hangs, comfortably enough, with a dazzling series of family portraits. They include three vintage Gainsboroughs and half a dozen works by Reynolds, among them *The Pink Boy* (the sitter was to become the 4th Duke of Buccleuch), and his sister Caroline Scott enchantingly portrayed as *Winter*. Other notable objects in the Dining Room are a pair of gilt mirrors of about 1720 and a vast silver wine-cooler of 1711. Boulle pedestals support *bleu du roi* Sèvres.

In the Drawing Room, still retaining its faded silk brocade and curtains of about 1840, there is another notable Reynolds, a full-length of the 3rd Duchess, the Montagu heiress who brought in Boughton and united the two noble families of Montagu and Scott. It hangs here with an early Kneller of the Duke of Monmouth, Dutch 17th-century paintings, a landscape and seascape by Vernet, and two early Claude Lorraines. As remarkable as the pictures in this room is the wealth of French furniture by famous designers. There are signed mid-18th-century chairs and settees, covered in Aubusson tapestry, from sets made by three of the foremost craftsmen of the time, a games table of about the same date, a signed parquetry Régence commode, and a number of Boulle pieces. To such furniture 18th-century Meissen, Sèvres, and oriental porcelain mounted in ormolu, make a perfect complement.

In spite of the Duchess of Monmouth's imposing marble fireplace and overmantel (brought from Dalkeith Palace), the Library with its chintzes and old green brocade, with half-length family portraits (four by Beechey show this artist at his best) hung above simple white bookcases, strikes a more informal note and provides an introduction to the rooms of predominantly Victorian character which follow. First of these is the Boudoir, associated with the wife of the 5th Duke, which despite an 18th-century Chinese painted wallpaper has a rich mid-19th-century flavour. It is a flavour that comes out as strongly in the recently restored Bedroom and Sitting Room. In the adjoining Corridor there are drawings of the family by George Richmond. Executed between 1851 and 1876, they show how good this prolific artist could be. Beside them hangs a striking sketch of the Duke of Wellington by Lawrence.

Braemar Castle, Grampians
(Captain A. A. Farquharson of Invercauld)

Forty-two miles north of Perth (A93)

The point where the pass from the south that now crosses the skiing terrain above Glen Shee descends to the upper waters of the Dee has always been strategically sensitive. It was here, near the village of Braemar, that John Erskine, Earl of Mar, High Treasurer of Scotland and once guardian of the young King James VI (later to become James I of England) built his castle in about 1628. The neighbouring Farquharson clan were traditionally at loggerheads with the Erskines. Some sixty years later Grahame of Claverhouse, 'Bonnie Dundee', raised the Stuart standard, and the Earl of Mar made no move to join him. John Farquharson, a romantic Jacobite known as 'The Black Colonel', took the opportunity to burn Braemar Castle, thus denying it to the government forces. It remained a ruin for more than half a century.

Following the rising of 1715 another Earl of Mar, who on this occasion had espoused the Stuart cause, forfeited his Deeside estates, and in 1732 the ruined castle was sold to John Farquharson of Invercauld. The burnt-out shell was of no use to him, and the Laird sixteen years later leased it for £14 a year to the Hanoverian government who, immediately after the '45, were establishing strongpoints to control the Highlands. The castle was duly restored and garrisoned. But quieter times came when garrisons were no longer necessary, and in 1807 the Farquharsons of Invercauld regained possession. Later, in the high tide of the Victorian era, they welcomed the Queen there when she attended the Braemar games.

Rising from a little knoll, the castle confidently overlooks the valley of the

Dee. Architecturally it is of great interest, for the building of 1628 represents one of the later and most convenient developments of the defensive tower houses of the north. It is built on the characteristic L plan, with a substantial newel staircase in the angle (giving easy access to the rooms on either side). Isolation, great height, and the corbelled bartizans on the outer angles give a curious and top-heavy appearance that Gustave Doré captured in his romantic and melancholy painting; yet there is nothing here that is not essentially part of the traditional Scottish way of building.

Braemar Castle

When the Hanoverians leased and restored the castle in 1748, the architect responsible for the work was John Adam, son of William and elder brother of Robert, who at that date was Master Mason to the Board of Ordnance in Scotland. He heightened the staircase tower and the bartizans, replacing their conical tiled roofs with flat battlemented tops that were better adapted to the needs of a garrison post. He also threw round the castle the curtain wall, with six sharp-angled salients whose gun-slits were designed to cover the approaches. This no doubt replaced some earlier form of protective enclosure. Within this courtyard, five storeys of harled granite tower overhead. Inside, the best feature is the granite staircase that rises the full height of the building. Otherwise the scale is intimate and the rooms are pleasantly furnished: a miniature castle in which it would be agreeable to live. When not looking across the meadows to the Dee, one would have the solemn pleasure of contemplating the world's largest cairngorm, weighing no less than fifty-two pounds.

Cameron House, Strathclyde
(Mr Patrick Telfer Smollett, M.C.)

On Loch Lomond, three miles north of Alexandria (A82)

Tobias Smollett's description of Loch Lomond was 'romantic beyond belief', and the Empress Eugénie, when visiting Cameron in 1860, said that the views surpassed those of the Italian Lakes. Cameron House stands near the less dramatic southern end, looking towards the islands and mountainous banks. Its name comes not from any Cameron clan but from the small piece of land that juts into the Loch and is shaped like a crooked nose – in Gaelic *cam sron*.

The Smolletts, originally from Dumbarton, were among the earliest of the Clydeside shipbuilders. Sir James bought the Palace of Bonhill near Alexandria in 1684, and another James bought the Cameron estate in 1763. Twelve years later it came to his daughter Jane, who married Alexander Telfer. Better, indeed universally known is her brother, the wit and satirist Tobias Smollett. Educated at Dumbarton Grammar School and Glasgow University, he studied medicine before staking his career on writing in 1739. Later generations of the family have been distinguished in the armed forces. Alexander Smollett, after whom nearby Alexandria is named, commanded the Coldstream Guards at the Battle of Alkmar (1799); Admiral Rouet Smollett served under Nelson and died in 1842. General A. P. D. Telfer Smollett was Commander-in-Chief of the International Garrison in Shanghai in 1937, and his son is the present Laird.

Cameron House

Of the old tower only foundations remain, for in the 18th century Cameron was rebuilt low and square, and the house was greatly altered in 1806. Substantial additions made after a fire in 1865 resulted in the building at the back of the house that reaches, by stages, a baronial tower with its castellated turret and bartizans.

A great number of rooms are open, some of them laid out with family collections of an endearing and personal kind. The front rooms have good discreet plaster ceilings dating from 1806. The many portraits begin with the 17th century. Jane Smollett appears as a lady of mid-Georgian charm and elegance, and the Admiral was painted by Raeburn. In the Dining Room will be found a portrait of the Abbé Grant, a well-known Scotsman resident in Rome during the 18th century, where he acted as cicerone and guide – but only to the grandest of Grand Tourists. In the Library, a fine canvas by Francis Wheatley (1779) shows Ferdinand and Miranda from Shakespeare's *Tempest*; it is typical of the interest in literature that produced Boydell's Shakespeare Gallery in Pall Mall.

The several portraits of Tobias Smollett, made at different times of his life, are of very particular interest. Two are by Verelst. The Smollett Museum, upstairs, has his waistcoats and many personal belongings, and a unique collection of editions of his literary works formed by the late Professor Lewis Knapp of Colorado University.

The garden was laid out by Mr Lanning Roper, one of the best landscapists of our time, and is planted with a fine variety of shrubs. The walled garden is now a Zoo Garden, and the parkland is largely given up to the Cameron Loch Lomond Wildlife Reserves, the woods being stocked with bison, yaks and various deer, while on the banks of the Loch there are sanctuaries for beavers, otters, seals and waterfowl.

Cawdor Castle, Highlands
(The Earl of Cawdor)

Five miles south-west of Nairn (B9090)

Thane of Cawdor. The phrase carries the deep resonances of *Macbeth*.

> '. . . nothing in his life
> Became him, like the leaving it; he died
> As one that had been studied in his death,
> To throw away the dearest thing he ow'd,
> As 'twere a careless trifle.'

But Shakespeare cared little for the niceties of time. Macbeth died in 1052, and the Cawdors, or Calders as they were then called, enter history over two hundred years later. Yet, overhanging dark Cawdor burn, their castle, now the home of the 25th Thane, carries without embarrassment the mediaeval overtones with which Shakespeare's tragedy invests it. But while evoking the troubled distance of clan strife, of feud and raid, of Cawdor Thanes murdered or killed in battle, the once-forbidding fortress has moved with

Cawdor Castle

the centuries. Fine gardens and urbane parkland surround it; a castle has become an informal house and home. Such transitions are familiar, but distant past and present rarely seem to meet with so little loss.

The 1st Thane arrived at Cawdor towards the end of the 13th century. In 1498 the 8th Thane died leaving only a posthumous daughter who was promptly abducted by the Campbells of Argyll, and in due course married to a young John Campbell. From this union, surprisingly enough a happy one, the Campbells of Cawdor are descended. Though making no undue stir in the world they have produced their fair share of talent: members of parliament, a Lord of the Admiralty, a poet. 'Good plain cooking with an occasional pinch of red pepper,' as the present Lord Cawdor puts it. Yet there is more to the story than this. The Campbells of Cawdor have enjoyed the enviable gift of courage, and the bold ventures of early Thanes have found a notable echo in our own times. In the last hundred years, members of the family have won, not counting lesser military honours, 3 Croix de Guerre, 15 DSOs, and no less than 3 VCs.

As one approaches the castle across the lawn from the east, the assured grey stone buildings might be of any age. In fact the tower-house – the central keep-like structure with later pepper-pot towers – was probably begun about 1370 by the 3rd Thane, though the royal permission to crenellate was not given until nearly a century later. As often happened, the early entrance to the tower-house was situated, for security, at first floor level and the entrance arch is still clearly visible in the masonry on the east front. The tower-house would have been initially surrounded by a curtain wall within which the clansmen could take refuge. It has long since disappeared and the buildings with crow-stepped gables about the little courtyards to the east and north date substantially from the 17th century when the castle assumed a more domestic character. Further alterations in the 19th century were tactful and the pedimented dormers carrying the Cawdor arms on the east front, dated 1855, are attractively in keeping.

In the centre of the ground-floor chamber of the tower-house there rises, surprisingly, from floor to vaulted ceiling the trunk of a famed and venerable hawthorn. Legend states that the 3rd Thane 'having decided to build a new castle, had a dream instructing him to let a donkey, laden with gold, wander about the chosen area; wherever the donkey lay down to rest in the evening, there he should build his house.' No doubt to the Thane's annoyance, the animal lay down beneath this very hawthorn. The fascinating part of the story is that modern techniques date the wood to about 1370, the decade in which the building of the castle most probably began. Adjoining the Thorn Tree Room is a doorway that must have served as entrance to the castle from the date that the first-floor access was blocked until the mid-17th century. Like a number of Scottish doorways of the period, it is protected by a massive iron yett or grille, but it is appropriate to the stormy mediaeval past of Cawdor that this example should have been carried away by the 6th Thane from the Moray stronghold of Lochinborb when he demolished it in 1456. Another unusual feature of the castle is the well which is sensibly, but exceptionally, situated in the floor of the Old Kitchen itself.

Today the main entrance to the castle, approached through the little north courtyard which displays the arms of Sir Hugh Campbell, 15th Thane, leads into the 1663–76 additions which he built. The Drawing Room (the old Hall) contains family portraits, notably two sparkling oil sketches by Lawrence of the 1st Earl Cawdor and his wife, and a full-length of the 1st Baron Cawdor by Reynolds. The Baron is associated with the last invasion of Britain, for he accepted the surrender of Napoleon's ill-conceived expeditionary force at Fishguard in 1797 (some of the French arms he captured are displayed in the Thorn Tree Room). In the Tapestry Bedroom are a four-poster, with an Italian Baroque bedhead, retaining its original velvet hangings, and a series of late-17th-century Arras tapestries depicting the Story of Noah. Six tapestries of similar date, but of Brussels manufacture, hang in the Tower Room. A further, and highly unusual, set of tapestries (c. 1700), illustrating the Adventures of Don Quixote, hang in the Dining Room. Bearing no resemblance to the familiar Mortlake set of the same subject, their provenance is uncertain but their style recalls the 'grotesques' associated with the Soho factory. The singular fireplace in this room is c. 1670, but with its relatively primitive stone carvings might well be taken for Jacobean work of fifty years earlier.

Druminnor Castle, Grampians
(Mr Andrew Forbes)

South-east of Rhynie, twenty-four miles north-west of Aberdeen (A97)

From the 13th century the Druminnor property was the seat of the Forbes family and passed in direct male descent until its sale in 1770. Nearly two hundred years later, in 1954, the castle was bought and devotedly restored by a descendant in the fifteenth generation of the 1st Lord Forbes, who had built it about 1450. A satisfying story.

Perched on a steep slope above a stream, the harled and pink-washed castle with crow-stepped gables consists now of a single block with a staircase tower at one end. It was not always so. The castle when first built was L-shaped, with a massive keep-block projecting at the end of the existing front. This block, probably ruinous by the early 17th century, was replaced about 1815 by a Gothic villa. It must have married strangely with the old wing and was swept away in 1960 when the castle restorations began.

Today the vaulted basement and ground floor, and probably the lower part of the staircase tower, are much as they were when built *c.* 1450. The upper floors suffered drastic alteration. In the mid-17th century the Hall on the first floor was subdivided, and the capehouse was corbelled out over the circular staircase. Further changes, primarily on the second floor and at roof level, occurred in the 19th century.

The ground-floor rooms retain 15th-century fireplaces, decorative ceiling bosses for lighting, garderobe, and so on. The Hall, now restored to its original dimensions, has a fireplace dating from the mid-17th century. Probably the most impressive thing is the generous newel-staircase. The

Druminnor Castle

moulded doorway to the tower is set, unusually, in the face of the tower rather than in the angle between the tower and the main building. Though one of three handsome coats of arms above the doorway is dated 1577, there is little reason to think that the lower stages of the tower are not 15th-century work. The angle of the gun-loop at door level indicates that it was intended to cover the entrance to the vanished keep-block.

Drumlanrig Castle, Dumfries and Galloway
(The Duke of Buccleuch and Queensberry)

Three miles north of Thornhill (A76)

Once seen, Drumlanrig haunts the memory, for it combines the evocative quality of a castle in a Claude landscape with the drama that Vanbrugh achieved at Seaton Delaval. The park-like slopes of green Nithsdale, the carefully planted woods, and the perfectly devised approach, no doubt have something to do with its impact. Oddly enough, the plan of the house, deriving from the castles of the later Middle Ages, is very simple. A rectangle, with a muscular tower at each corner, encloses an open courtyard. In keeping with this simplicity three of the elevations are so plain as to be severe, but the entrance front – here comes the surprise – rises clothed in the rich and formal splendour of Carolean Baroque: curving perron, arcaded loggia, giant pilasters, ranks of pedimented windows, balustrades, and a lavishly decorated porch with trophies and swirling coats of arms. This burst of exuberance is echoed by the forest of turrets breaking the skyline over the four corner towers. The improbability is breathtaking.

The Douglases had already been at Drumlanrig over three centuries when, between 1679 and 1691 William Douglas, Earl of Queensberry, built the present castle of rose-red sandstone. He also laid out vast formal gardens, which have now completely disappeared. The cost nearly ruined him, but with poetic justice he was advanced to a dukedom while the work was in progress. The architect was probably James Smith, or his father-in-law Robert Mylne; but whoever was responsible had recourse to drawings made over fifty years earlier, which might account for a certain archaism and the resemblance, often remarked, to Heriot's Hospital in Edinburgh begun in the 1620s. Moreover, to some extent the plan was governed by the existing castle. The central courtyard has a newel staircase in each of the slender turrets in its four corners. The entry to the house must originally have been even more dramatic than it is today: having swept up the perron and through the Carolean frontispiece, one found oneself in an open loggia whence, traversing the courtyard, one finally gained admission to the Hall. The loggia was glazed early in the 19th century when it became the entrance lobby, and the original hall was converted into a dining room. Other changes included the insertion of plaster ceilings and some panelling; but the staircase and the fine overmantels and overdoors carved in the style of Grinling Gibbons are original to the building.

The visitor will do well to observe one small detail: a winged heart

Drumlanrig Castle

surmounted by a crown that recurs on the stonework. With the motto 'Forward', it forms the Douglas crest. It was assumed for the following reason: when Robert Bruce died in 1329 without achieving his wish to crusade in the Holy Land, his heart was entrusted to Sir James, 'The Black Douglas', that he might take it on crusade against the Muslims in Spain; when the Douglas fell mortally wounded, he hurled the heart in its silver casket towards the infidel ranks, with the cry 'Forward, brave heart'. It is appropriate to the boldness and grandeur of Drumlanrig that this dying gesture should so often be recalled on its walls.

Drumlanrig passed for thirteen Douglas generations in the direct male line, until in 1788 it went, with the dukedom, to a cousin, the notorious rake 'Old Q'. When he died without an heir, Henry Scott, 3rd Duke of Buccleuch, succeeded to the property and dukedom through his Douglas grandmother. This accounts for the fact that the furnishings of the castle reflect both the Queensberry and the Buccleuch inheritance. The Buccleuch descent from the Duke of Monmouth brought in such things as two astonishing Louis XIV cabinets given to the Duke by his father Charles II, a great ebony cabinet with gilt metal mounts that the Duke probably acquired in Flanders, Daniel Marot chairs with needlework reputedly worked by his wife, and two of her settees upholstered in crimson velvet.

The collection of French furniture is particularly rich. Tables, chairs, commodes, encoignures, and smaller *pièces ambulantes*, include signed pieces by such notable cabinet makers as Charles Cressent, J. C. Saunier, and Pierre Roussel. The English furnishings are hardly less exceptional: Charles II stools that were once in Whitehall Palace, Queen Anne day-bed and chairs with their original cut velvet, early Georgian chairs and settees by Giles Grendey with original needlework, a vast silver chandelier of the time of Charles II, William and Mary silver wall sconces, giltwood wall sconces in Chippendale's 'Director' style, and carved giltwood mirrors attributed to Matthias Locke. The list of fine things could be extended indefinitely: clocks by the best makers (Knibb in London, Leroy in Paris), late-17th-century *verre eglomisé* mirrors, 18th-century wine cisterns and Monteith bowls, ormolu-mounted Sèvres, Chelsea 'red anchor', and, in the room in which Prince Charles Edward slept on his retreat from Derby, a superbly embroidered Carolean bedcover.

For the masterpiece one would choose Rembrandt's moving portrait, *An Old Woman Reading*, painted in 1655. Family portraits inevitably include the Duke of Monmouth, but perhaps the most attractive is a lovely early Reynolds of Lady Elizabeth Montagu. The Dining Room hung with representative paintings by Richardson, Kneller, Hudson, and a likeness of 'Old Q' by Ramsay, sets the standard. Historical portraits elsewhere include Francis I by Clouet, Holbein's staring evocation of Sir Nicholas Carew, and James I and his Queen attributed to George Jamesone, the earliest Scottish painter of distinction. The Boudoir contains Dutch cabinet paintings by Cuyp, Ostade, Teniers, van der Neer, and Jacob Ruysdael, while in the Servery hangs an unusual series of portraits of the Buccleuch chef and household servants in about 1817. Though far more competent, they recall the portraits of former servants preserved at Erddig in Denbighshire.

Drumlanrig Castle; right: *the Staircase, and* below: *Louis XIV cabinet given by Charles II to the Duke of Monmouth*

Dunrobin Castle, Highlands
(The Countess of Sutherland)

North of Dornoch Firth, between Golspie and Brora (A9)

The fairy-tale palace is perched on the edge of a cliff whose seaward face has been tamed into terraces and gardens. The green luxuriance of these reclaimed coastal plains contrasts oddly with the vast barren moors further inland. Remoteness and the timeless mystery of the Highlands add to the fascination of Dunrobin. Its origins are very ancient. The Scottish kings who regained Sutherland from the Norsemen in the 12th century conferred it on Hugh de Moravia, whose son William was created Earl of Sutherland about 1235. Dunrobin is mentioned as the family's stronghold in 1401, but the tower that survives in the heart of the building may be older than that.

The Earldom is the oldest in Scotland and in default of male heirs it may pass through the female line. When this happened in the 16th century it caused a bloody dispute. The second occasion, in 1766, was more peaceful but the law-case was long and costly. Judgment was eventually given by the House of Lords in favour of Elizabeth, whose father, the 18th Earl, had died when she was just one year old. As 19th Countess she married an Englishman, George Leveson-Gower, who shortly after succeeded as Marquess of Stafford and, just before his death, was created Duke of Sutherland. This famous alliance gave rise to one of the richest and most brilliant of 19th-century families. Elizabeth, known as the Countess-Duchess, lent her clothes to Marie-Antoinette for the ill-fated flight to Varennes in 1791, her husband being then ambassador to France; before she died in 1838 she had travelled to Sutherland by steamship. The 1st Duke inherited the Duke of Bridgewater's fortune in addition to his own and was described as a 'Leviathan of Wealth'. He was an active Whig reformer and patron of the arts, and his enormous statue by Chantrey stands on a mountainside near Golspie. But in Sutherland he is remembered, and not kindly, for his Highland Clearances by which the time-honoured crofters had to leave the moors and settle in more prosperous coastal districts. It is fair to say that the suffering this caused was due to the harshness and greed of the local factors and ministers. The 3rd Duke, with his estate of 1,300,000 acres, was the greatest landowner in western Europe, but much of his property was moorland. When the 5th Duke died without heirs in 1963 the English dukedom passed to a cousin, the Earl of Ellesmere; while the ancient Scottish earldom and estates came to his niece who is the present and 24th Countess.

What is seen of the Castle, outside at least, was largely built by the 2nd Duke. Succeeding in 1833, he commissioned Sir Charles Barry to design additions to the 18th-century harled house (which still stands forming the west wing). The style chosen was French Renaissance, complete with dormers and steep conical roofs, and the yellow sandstone has a curious resemblance to that used on the châteaux of the Loire. The building was executed, and slightly modified, by W. Leslie of Aberdeen. When Barry visited Dunrobin in 1848 he designed the imposing entrance tower and the gardens.

Dunrobin Castle (see also illustrations on pp. 355 and 357)

Caen stone, too soft for outside use, was imported for the staircase. Architecturally, this is the best part of the interior because most of the castle was gutted by fire in 1915 when in use as an Auxiliary Naval Hospital. After the war the rooms were redesigned by Sir Robert Lorimer, who also recapped Barry's entrance tower.

In Lorimer's panelled Dining Room there are five large portrait canvases, the earliest of which is Ramsay's 18th Earl of Sutherland wearing his tartan kilt. This was painted shortly before his death in 1766; his Countess, in a very delicate work by Ramsay, will be seen in the Breakfast Room as well as their daughter, the Countess-Duchess, painted by Lawrence. As for the Leveson-Gowers, the father of the 1st Duke stands in his Garter robes, painted by Romney. The Dining Room is dominated by Lawrence's picture of the 2nd Duchess with her child, while in a later portrait by Winterhalter she is seen standing in the vast staircase of her London home, Stafford (now Lancaster) House. This Duchess was Harriet, daughter of the Earl of Carlisle, Mistress of the Robes and a great friend of Queen Victoria who stayed at Dunrobin several times.

The long Drawing Room was created by Lorimer out of two previous rooms. Two really magnificent Canaletto views of Ambassadors' Receptions at the Doge's Palace hang between three Mortlake *Diogenes* tapestries, woven after the engravings of Salvator Rosa. The furniture is mainly French, and good. The Library is again Lorimer's, fitted up in natural sycamore wood, and over the fireplace hangs a commanding portrait by de Laszlo of Eileen, 5th Duchess, who was Mistress of the Robes to Queen Mary and died in 1943. The upstairs rooms were decorated to her taste. From the vaulted corridor, which contains an interesting portrait by Michael Wright of an Irish Chieftain, the ancient tower and courtyard can be seen.

In the garden below the terraces stands the Museum. A former banqueting house, during the 19th century it filled up with a magpie collection of curiosities. There are heads from four hundred species of game, an iguana, a horned frog, weapons, coins, hundreds of historic seals, a tawse, Lord Raglan's cap, Garibaldi's slippers, Queen Victoria's handkerchief (1874), skulls of the sons of King Lochlin of Denmark, and plenty more. This remarkable exhibition may well shock the principles of modern museum officials. Let us hope it will not be dispersed.

Dunvegan Castle, Highlands
(John MacLeod of MacLeod)

On the north-west coast of the Isle of Skye (A850)

For over seven centuries the MacLeods have been established on this rock, where the high tides of Loch Dunvegan lap the curtain wall, where seal-heads bob on the waters of the bay, and eider and merganser cruise almost within gunshot. Few inhabited castles have a longer history or are more romantically set. The rock on which Dunvegan stands was fortified probably about 1270 (shortly after the Scots regained the Western Isles from Norway) by Leod, 1st of the MacLeod Chiefs, the reputed son of Olav the Black, King of the Isle of Man. The seaward curtain at its base is Leod's work, and here is the sea-gate which, defended by two massive doors and a portcullis, was until 1748 the sole entrance to the castle. Harling has latterly obscured the rugged character of the old stonework; yet under the baronial additions of the 1840s is the clear outline of a 14th-century keep, its walls nine feet thick in places.

The east, the present entrance front, was defensively the weak point; and

Dunvegan Castle from Loch Dunvegan

Dunvegan Castle; left: *Norman, 22nd Chief of McLeod, by Allan Ramsay, and* right: *the Dunvegan Cup*

until the mid-18th century there was no gate here. Old prints show this front severe and imposing, with scarcely any windows. To the left is the Fairy Tower with its crow-stepped gables, built about 1500 and hardly altered. It is now connected to the Keep by a Victorian high range. Lower down is a roof walk with a stretch of 17th-century Baroque balustrading – a surprise on Skye – and the new entrance of *circa* 1810, flanked by low turrets.

Most of the furniture that Doctor Johnson must have found when he came to Dunvegan with Boswell in 1773 has disappeared. Fortunately some distinguished MacLeod portraits survive: the 22nd Chief and his wife by Allan Ramsay, unusual full-lengths by Zoffany (notably that of General MacLeod, 23rd Chief) painted in India, and General MacLeod and his wife by Raeburn.

But Dunvegan, as the shrine of the Clan MacLeod, offers something other than architecture and works of art. The family have faithfully preserved certain sacred objects which epitomise the legend and history of this Hebridean stronghold. Most remarkable is the so-called Fairy Flag, the talisman of the Clan. It is believed that when waved it brings victory to the MacLeod arms – as it did twice in the 15th and 16th centuries – but that it cannot be waved thrice without losing its potency. It is of eastern origin, and scientific tests have revealed that the tattered silk dates from the 7th century. There is a theory that the Fairy Flag is the same as the 'Land Ravager', the banner that Harald Hardrada brought to Yorkshire in 1066, but the argument is a tricky one.

Hardly less curious is an ancient wooden mazer or drinking cup, seemingly given to Rory Mor, 16th Chief, by the O'Neills of Ulster in gratitude for the contingent of five hundred MacLeods who crossed in 1595 to support a rising against Queen Elizabeth. The elaborate silver filigree mounting bears an Irish inscription and the date 1493, and once was studded with precious stones; the simple wooden utensil itself may be much older, and tradition (perhaps handed down by the bards) connects it with Niall of the Black Knees, a 10th-century King of Ulster. With Rory Mor is also associated an ox-horn banded with silver. It holds $2\frac{1}{4}$ pints, and each Chief is expected to drain it of claret at a single draught. The feat was last performed in 1956 by John MacLeod, the present and 29th Chief. Of honourable antiquity is the claymore or two-handled sword of the 7th Chief, William Longsword, who died in battle in the late 15th century. No less evocative are the celebrated pipes that belonged to Iain Dubh MacCrimmon, and the pipe mouthpiece of a MacCrimmon who fell at Culloden. This family were for thirteen generations hereditary pipers to the MacLeods of MacLeod.

Though a MacLeod force followed Charles II to Worcester and died almost to a man, the 22nd Chief, seeing no prospect of success, did not bring the Clan out in the '45. Yet memorials of Prince Charles Edward reached Dunvegan through Flora MacDonald's daughter who married the illegitimate son of the 22nd Chief. The courageous Flora's stays indicate a shapely waist. There is also a rare Jacobite glass, dated 1747 and inscribed to 'The Faithful Palinurus'. This was one Donald MacLeod who, like Aeneas's helmsman, faithfully piloted his royal master through stormy waters. Finally, woven over a thousand years after the Fairy Flag, there hang in the Castle the colours of the Loyal MacLeod Fencibles raised by the family in 1799 to meet the threat of Napoleonic invasion. It is such relics of the past and the castle's long occupation by a single family that distinguish Dunvegan.

Eilean Donan Castle, Highlands
(Mr J. D. H. MacRae)

At Dornie (A87)

On a black rocky islet, Eilean Donan stands guard where Loch Alsh divides round the mainland. Approached by land over a narrow bridge, it looks the perfection of an ancient Scottish castle, and the wild uninhabited hills, yellow gorse and purple heather all make up the romantic picture that has become world-famous. But the building dates, in fact, almost entirely from the 20th century. It was reconstructed from complete ruin after the First World War by Colonel MacRae, a direct descendant of the last Constable of the Castle. It is said that the evidence for the reconstruction came to him in a dream, but the result looks authentic enough and it certainly makes a fine view. The interior, with bare stone walls, tartans, antlers, clan and Jacobite relics, conforms as closely to the popular image of Scotland as does the exterior and its evocative setting.

The original castle was built about 1220 by Alexander II as one of a chain of coastal fortresses to protect Scotland from the Norseman, who were still occupying Skye and the Islands. For centuries it was held by the Macken-

Eilean Donan Castle

zies, Earls of Seaforth, and met its unlikely doom as a result of naval warfare in 1719, when the garrison of Spanish Jacobites was bombarded from the Loch by an English man-of-war. The castle was reduced to rubble, and so it remained for two centuries until its recent and unexpected resurrection.

Floors Castle, Borders
(The Duke of Roxburghe)

North-west of Kelso (A6089)

The Kers had been settled north of the border for some four hundred years when Robert Ker acquired property at Floors, thus establishing the family fortunes. Ancestor of the present owner of Floors, he was created Earl of Roxburghe in 1616. Something over a hundred years later the vast castle was put up by John Ker, 5th Earl, who was described by a contemporary memorialist as 'a man of good sense, improved by so much reading and learning that he was perhaps the best accomplished young man in Europe'. As Secretary of State for Scotland, he vigorously promoted the Act of Union of 1707 and in the same year was rewarded with a dukedom. His cultural interests were inherited by his grandson, the 3rd Duke. This eminent bibliophile, who gave his name to the Roxburghe Club, built up the famous library at Floors which, with its unrivalled collection of Caxtons, was unfortunately dispersed after his death.

John Ker certainly had an eye for a ducal setting. Situated on the brow of suave green slopes, the castle surveys an idyllic pastoral landscape, a stretch of shining Tweed, and the distant spire of Kelso church. The Duke's building, flanked by lower pavilions enclosing a forecourt, and built between 1721 and 1726, was essentially a massive four-storey block with square towers at the corners. There has been much debate as to the architect and

Floors Castle; the entrance front

Vanbrugh's name is often mentioned. But the Duke had no need to look across the border for such a design when there was Heriot's Hospital in Edinburgh, and Drumlanrig to the west. The architect is now thought with reasonable probability to have been William Adam, father of the more famous son.

In the last century the appearance of the 1st Duke's house greatly changed, for extensive alterations were carried out by William Playfair after 1838. Playfair, whose neo-classical buildings make a notable contribution to Edinburgh, worked at Floors in a different and romantic vein. Though he linked the main block to the flanking pavilions, added the large carriage porch on the entrance front, and a ballroom to the east, his most striking contributions are seen at roof level. Here, with his proliferation of corbelled pepper-pots and castellated parapets, with simulated gun-barrels projecting from the frieze, purists may think that he took leave of his senses. Others will be attracted by his very extravagance and a skyline almost as exotic as that of Chambord.

Half the charm of the interior of Floors is that the main rooms are ranged along the south front. From every window one looks over the landscape to the Tweed. Though Playfair's vast and florid Jacobethan Dining Room is unaltered, much else was remodelled early in this century by Mary, Duchess of Roxburghe, grandmother of the present Duke. An American heiress with a life-long interest in the arts, she not only inherited or bought the superlative collection of tapestries, French furniture and oriental porcelain now at Floors, but substituted decoration in the manner of the early 18th century for much of Playfair's Victorian work.

In the Hall, with a Playfair ceiling but doorcases and dado panelling of the 20th century, the walls are hung with paintings of the School of Canaletto, and topographical views by English artists. With the Ante Room one reaches the south front. The ceiling is again by Playfair but the cornice, like that in the Drawing Room, may be of about 1725. A rare Gothic tapestry, woven with wool and gold thread in Brussels in the late 15th century and representing *The Pentecost*, hangs over the fireplace. A later 16th-century tapestry, *The Court of Love*, hangs in the adjoining Pine Room. The *Madonna and Child* by N. B. Landi is an Italian work of the second half of the 15th century; and the painting of Floors by William Wilson shows the Castle as it was in 1808 before Playfair's embellishments.

In the next rooms the furniture is predominantly French: sets of gilded chairs with tapestry covers, writing tables richly embellished with ormolu, kingwood and marquetry commodes. A commode in the Drawing Room was made by Joubert in 1773 and the stamp and number of the royal inventory show that once it belonged to the Comtesse d'Artois. In the Ballroom (an addition by Playfair) there are besides some very fine English pieces, notably a set of six James II armchairs, carved and gilded and upholstered in old crimson velvet. The cream japanned cabinet on a lavish gilt stand may be Dutch.

The walls of the Ballroom were repanelled in this century to take two immense Gobelins yellow-ground tapestries. Woven after designs by Claude Audran le jeune in 1699, and forming part of a famous series known as *Les Portières des Dieux*, they depict various gods framed by arabesques. The five early-18th-century Brussels tapestries in the Drawing Room show the Triumphs of the Gods in a more pictorial way.

Among the portraits in the Ballroom, two stand out: Sir John Thorold by Reynolds, and Captain Cook in naval uniform by Gainsborough. The picture most strongly evocative of the 18th century is Thomas Patch's delightful caricature of the 3rd Duke of Roxburghe and his friends at Florence. Among the company the artist has included himself on the extreme right.

Glamis Castle, Tayside
(The Earl of Strathmore and Kinghorne)

Ten miles north of Dundee (A928)

'Very singular and striking in appearance, like nothing I ever saw,' wrote the poet Thomas Gray when he stayed at Glamis in 1765. From the first sight of the castle, framed at the end of a long and wide avenue of oaks, it is the oddity that strikes one most: massive and very high, with a busy skyline of clustered and pointed turrets. This Scottish verticality must have been even more pronounced before the wings that flank the soaring central block lost their gabled roofs. A castle of great antiquity, Glamis commends itself also to our affections, for it was the childhood home of the youngest daughter of the 14th Earl of Strathmore, later to become Queen of England and Scotland and now Her Majesty Queen Elizabeth the Queen Mother.

A royal hunting lodge from the 11th to the 14th centuries, Glamis is where King Malcolm is thought to have died in 1034. It passed in 1372 to Sir John Lyon, known for his fair complexion as the 'White Lyon'. On his marriage to the daughter of King Robert II, his grandson became the 1st Lord Glamis. In the 16th century the Castle was seized by James V, who not only stripped it of its contents but ensured that the widowed Lady Glamis, for whose family – she was born a Douglas – he nursed an implacable hatred, was burnt as a witch, without shred of evidence, on Castle Hill in Edinburgh in 1540. It is one of the most unsavoury episodes of that unhappy century in Scotland. Her young son was able to re-establish himself in the castle of his family, but it sheds strange light on the sensibilities of the times that Mary Queen of Scots, James V's daughter, stayed at Glamis some twenty years after the immolation and seemed, in the words of the English Ambassador, 'never merrier, never dismayed'.

In the 17th century the Lords of Glamis acquired successively the Earldoms of Kinghorne and Strathmore. The 5th Earl was the close friend and follower of Montrose. Stuart sympathies lingered on; indeed, the Chevalier de St George, James VIII (known pejoratively across the Border as The Old Pretender), was entertained in the castle. His sword and watch, and his coat and breeches, in Royal Scottish tartan, are preserved at Glamis. In 1767 a fortune came to the Strathmores when the 9th Earl married Mary Bowes, the heiress from Co. Durham. From that date the family name has been Bowes Lyon.

The core of the castle dates from the 15th century, when it was surrounded by a defensive curtain wall. By the early 17th century the castle was largely remodelled and its splendid internal plasterwork introduced. After the Restoration, Patrick, the 3rd Earl of Strathmore and Kinghorne, added the west wing (thus modifying the typically Scottish L-shape of the tower) and heightened the central block, leaving it with its very distinctive roof-line. He placed the stone armorials on the face of the staircase tower, where his own portrait bust also appears. This and the sundial in the garden are thought to be the work of a Dutch sculptor, Santwoort, while the lead statues of James VI and Charles I either side of the avenue are by Arnold Quellin. There was little further alteration until about 1800 when two wings exchanged their old gables for a crenellated roof-line.

The Dining Room, which the visitor first enters, though uncharacteristic

Glamis Castle (see also colour plate 30 and illustration on p. 355)

of Glamis has great interest as a little-touched example of 19th-century decoration. Ceiling, chimneypiece and dado, armorial glass, furniture and even the fire-dogs make up the ensemble, all in Elizabethan style. There is a sharp contrast between this and the simplicity of the tunnel-vaulted crypt that lies beyond, its unplastered walls set with armour and hunting trophies. This was a dining hall, and steps lead down to the circular staircase tower and entrance where a massive yett still guards the doorway into the castle.

Above the crypt is the Jacobean Great Hall, now known as the Drawing Room, the finest of the 17th-century apartments. Its splendid plasterwork is dated 1621, and doubtless the huge stone overmantel is of the same date. The walls are mainly hung with family portraits, many in sumptuous 17th-century frames. The 1st and 2nd Earls of Kinghorne survey the room they jointly created, and the large family group of Patrick, the 3rd Earl, was painted by Medina. There is a sensitive French 16th-century portrait of the 9th Lord Glamis, whose mother died so tragically on Castle Hill, with (on the reverse) a likeness of his tutor. Grahame of Claverhouse, 'Bonnie Dundee', is also here in a portrait attributed to Kneller.

More plaster decoration occurs on the ceiling and overmantel of King Malcolm's Room, with motifs that were repeated shortly afterwards, and doubtless by the same craftsmen, at Muchalls Castle. The Chapel, consecrated in 1688 (and thus part of the later Stuart work done for Earl Patrick) has ceiling and walls lined with panels painted by a Dutch artist, Jan de Wet, showing the Life of Christ and the Twelve Apostles. Though not of great artistic value, perhaps, the complete survival of a Laudian decorative scheme is unusual, and particularly so in Scotland. The suite of Royal Apartments was arranged by the 14th Countess of Strathmore for her youngest daughter when Duchess of York, and is still used by Her Majesty the Queen Mother when she visits her early home.

The 17th century has left its mark in a quantity of good furniture, notably pre-Restoration chairs and fine Netherlandish cupboards, a four-poster bed with carved giltwood and painted decoration, and a number of late Stuart ebonised or lacquer chests on elaborate gilt stands. From the same century are the Mortlake tapestries depicting the Story of Nebuchadnezzar. But perhaps the strangest object at Glamis dates from early in the next century: the Strathmores were the last family in Scotland to maintain a jester, and his silken suit of motley has been preserved.

Hopetoun House, Borders
(Hopetoun Preservation Trust)

On the Firth of Forth, three miles west of Queensferry

The great stone dramas of Hopetoun will be appreciated best if you can manage to find its main gates, just west of Queensferry. A long drive runs within view of the two Forth Bridges, and finally sweeps into a wide forecourt and the welcoming arms of Scotland's largest and most sensational country house.

The Hopes of Hopetoun were descended from John de Hope, who is said to have come to Scotland in the train of Madeline de Valois, the first wife of James V. They became prosperous Edinburgh merchants, acquired estates in West Lothian, and in 1678 they bought the land on which this house is built. The young Charles Hope in 1699 married the sister of the cultivated and eccentric Marquess of Annandale, and four years later, aged twenty-one, was created Earl of Hopetoun. His descendant, the 7th Earl, was Governor-General of Australia and created Marquess of Linlithgow; the 2nd Marquess was Viceroy of India from 1936–43, and his son, the 3rd Marquess, now lives here.

The original house was designed and built in 1699–1703 by Sir William Bruce, an architect who broke completely with the Scottish tradition of defensive tower-houses. His urbane Palladianism, tempered with French influences, will be found on the garden side which has been little altered. Bruce's house had a grand entrance forecourt, but it was hardly twenty years old when Lord Hopetoun, encouraged by Annandale, started to transform it into something greater. One wing was extended by William Adam in 1721; the curved colonnades were begun in 1725; and two years later a contract was signed for a completely new facade. The stonework was completed in 1748.

William Adam was on his way to becoming the most prolific and out-standing of Scottish country house architects. His style, bizarre, vigorous, and never dull, shows the influence of Vanbrugh and Gibbs. This is the greatest of his houses, and its super-human scale is emphasised by the fluted giant pilasters. The original design had proposed a central portico and a curved double stairway; these were omitted, possibly for economy, but the broad stone steps that were actually built are all the more noble for being

Hopetoun House; the central block, by William Adam

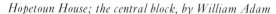

Hopetoun House; left: *the Staircase, and* right: *the Red Drawing Room*

simple. The house was completed by Adam's sons, John and Robert. The courtyard pavilions and their remarkable towers are among Robert Adam's earliest independent works.

The Entrance Hall is cool Palladian. On the walls there are full-length portraits of the 1st and 2nd Marquesses, both robed as Knights of the Thistle, and paintings by John Wootton of George II at Dettingen and the Duke of Cumberland at Culloden. From here one proceeds to the earlier part of the house, built by Bruce. The secondary staircase has a fine and typically Scottish scrolled iron balustrade; the main staircase is central and lit from above, octagonal in shape with panelling and rich carving by Alexander Eizat, who had worked at Holyrood Palace. Mural paintings by W. McLaren have been added as a memorial to the late Lady Linlithgow. The apartments upstairs are panelled and fitted with Brussels tapestries. A large number of allegorical paintings over doors and fireplaces were commissioned from Philip Tideman, of Amsterdam, and there is superb Dutch Baroque furniture, painted and gilded. The panelled central room downstairs and the Libraries are also part of Bruce's house.

The work of the Adam brothers comes in the state apartment of three large rooms. These were built as the Dining Room,[1] Drawing Room and Bedroom, but the last was altered early in the 19th century when it became the Dining Room. The first two retain generous coved ceilings that show Robert Adam in an unexpected role as exponent of rococo. He had learnt this style during a visit to England in 1749, and the plasterwork, probably carried out by Thomas Clayton of Edinburgh, has great vitality. Lord Hopetoun was without doubt pleased with Robert's work, and suggested in

[1] Now the Yellow Drawing Room.

1754 that he should accompany his brother, Charles Hope, on an Italian tour and share expenses. By the time they reached Rome Robert was complaining that he had to bear most of the expense while Hope took all the credit. None the less this famous visit was to prove crucial to the course of English architecture. A design was sent from Rome for the huge marble chimneypiece in the Red Drawing Room, which was carved by Rysbrack.

The rococo console tables in the same room were also designed by Robert Adam. Most of the mid-Georgian furniture was supplied by James Cullen of London: massive mahogany seat furniture for the Drawing Room as well as its crimson silk wall hangings; carved and gilded pier glasses; and two monumental bombé commodes, beautifully inlaid. The last have no cupboards in front, and seem of little practical use. They were intended for the State Bedroom, and there are delicate night tables to match. The gilded State Bed itself, now moved to another room, was designed and probably made by Matthew Lock, the earliest of the rococo furniture designers in London, and was sent by Cullen in 1768.

The large Baroque portrait of Lord Annandale is by Andrea Procaccini, the pupil of Maratti. Near it hangs a less flamboyant portrait of the builder, the 1st Earl of Hopetoun, by David Allan, with the house in the background. The 2nd Earl is by Ramsay; his sons, Lord Hope and the 3rd Earl were painted in Rome by Nathaniel Dance. The Annandale collection of old master paintings was mostly sold in the 19th century and replaced, on the advice of Andrew Wilson, by those that are now to be seen. There are fine Venetian portraits, a delightful group of four Musician Brothers of the Manaldini Family by Passerotti, an Italian painting showing Emperor Charles V out hunting, and distinguished Flemish and Dutch pictures.

The view from the roof is magnificent, with the Forth estuary on one side and the gardens and farmlands on the other. The layout of Adam's garden remains, with its radiating avenues; the central parterre was removed long ago, but the pattern of its box hedges shows up in the grass during a hot summer.

Inverary Castle, Strathclyde
(The Duke of Argyll)

On Loch Fyne, 60 miles north-west of Glasgow (A83 and A819)

Like some realisation of Utopia, Inverary makes up its own self-contained microcosmic world. The wild mountainous background contrasts with the long still waters of the loch; and in between, on a strip of reclaimed and cultivated land, stand the lochside harbour and town in dignified grey and white, and, a discreet distance away, the presiding castle, trim, towered and turreted.

The Campbells, Headsmen of a great Clan, have been Earls of Argyll since 1457. The 10th Earl, a vigorous anti-Jacobite and the champion of William of Orange, was raised to the Dukedom in 1701. Their ancient stronghold was Innischonnel Castle, now a ruin, on Loch Awe. The 3rd

Inverary Castle; (see also colour plate 31 and illustration on p. 358)

Duke, Archibald, inherited the title and estates in 1743 at the age of sixty, and began at once to plan a new seat at Inverary. The walls and roof were up within ten years; by the time of Doctor Johnson's visit with Boswell in 1773 the rooms were fully occupied. The Doctor's host was the 5th Duke, who, during the next decade, transformed the interior as we see it now. Meanwhile the decaying 15th-century tower was demolished and the old Royal Burgh of Inverary, which lay across the present garden, was rebuilt further away.

The castle's architect was Roger Morris. A Londoner best known for his Palladian works, he seems an odd choice for the 'castle style'; yet Morris had already built Clearwell Castle in Gloucestershire, and both buildings are among the earliest of the Gothic revival. Gothic for Duke Archibald did not imply defensive towers with their panoply of enclosures, bartizans and gables. His castle was to be low, urbane and convenient, and the result is not at all Scottish. Morris seldom visited the site, and supervision was given to William Adam and his sons John and Robert. The fabric is built of a singular slate-like stone from Creggans on the opposite bank of the Loch. Kitchens and offices lie in the basement, so the isolated building is complete without flanking wings or courts. Doctor Johnson felt the Castle would look better if raised by an additional storey. Something of the kind happened after the upper floors were gutted by fire in 1877, when the battlements were removed and dormer windows superimposed. This was done by Anthony Salvin, the Victorian castle expert, who also built conical roofs on the corner towers. Fortunately his improvements went no further than this, but already they detract from the importance of Morris's central tower.

Gothic outside, but classical within. The rooms were originally Palladian, but during the 1780s many were brilliantly re-cast to the designs of Robert Mylne for John, 5th Duke of Argyll. First the windows were lengthened to reach floor level; next, the main entrance was changed from the south to the north side, where a former gallery was divided up into an Entrance Hall

Inverary Castle; the Dining Room

(with a Gothic ceiling) and rooms either side. Duke John and the Duchess were often in Paris, and a light French touch gives glitter to these rooms. The Dining Room is perhaps the finest painted room in Britain. Its delicate arabesques and figures would not look out of place at Bagatelle or Fontainebleau, and it is no surprise to learn that they were in fact carried out by French painters. In the Drawing Room the coloured and gilded ceiling has more English character, but the walls carry seven Beauvais tapestries (as well as overdoors) from the *Pastorales* set, woven after designs by Huet. Over the chimneypiece is Hoppner's portrait of Lady Charlotte Campbell as *Aurora*. Among the gilded chairs is a set made by John Linnell of Berkeley Square; but in the Castle there are no less than ten different sets of gilded chairs, some of them French. All are covered with French tapestry.

The Saloon on the opposite side of the house was originally the entrance hall. The four dado-to-cornice girandoles were made about 1790, and the damasked walls are hung with portraits. The 1st Duke was painted by Medina, the 2nd and 3rd by Ramsay. The full-length portrait by Gainsborough is of Henry Seymour-Conway, brother-in-law to the 5th Duke, while the children of the 5th Duke are seen in four delightful portraits by John Opie. His Duchess, the Georgian beauty Elizabeth Gunning, had previously been married to the Duke of Hamilton, and was thus wife to two Dukes and mother of four more. Her second son, the 8th Duke of Hamilton, was painted in Rome by Batoni.

The central tower is seventy feet high and is flanked, Vanbrugh-wise, by twin staircases. The state rooms escaped the fire of 1877, but the tower was gutted and redesigned by Salvin. It is known as the Armoury Hall, and the arms, magnificently piled in wheels and fans, include 'Brown Bess' muskets that were used in the '45, Lochabar axes and Highland broadswords. More portraits hang on the stairs, and above, the Victorian Room has relics of Queen Victoria and her fourth daughter, Princess Louise, who married the 9th Duke of Argyll in 1871. On this occasion the entrance bridge was covered by glass and iron to a design by Matthew Digby Wyatt, who had already done this kind of work on a mammoth scale at Paddington Station.

In November 1975 the Castle was again gutted by fire, but prompt action saved the state rooms and most of the contents. The damage has been made good with astonishing speed by the present, 12th Duke, but the expense was enormous and has mostly fallen on the estate. Besides restoration of the building, the painted rooms have been restored and tapestries are repaired and cleaned, so the Castle now appears in finer condition than it has done within living memory.

The Castle is only the nucleus of a landscape that has been considerably improved since the time of Duke Archibald. The new town was laid out by Morris, Adam and Mylne, the latter being also responsible for its bridge. Further north, the double-arched bridge over the Aray is again by Mylne (Adam's turreted bridge having collapsed during a storm in 1772), while the Garron Bridge at the head of the Loch is by Morris. Farmlands extending up the Garron valley were reclaimed from heath and marsh. The legacy of so much improvement and of two Castle fires is a grave financial problem.

Kellie Castle, Tayside
(Mr Angus Kerr Boyle)

At Arbirlot, two miles west of Arbroath (B9127 and A92)

Kellie Castle – not to be confused with another of the same name in Fife – stands within sight of the sea, where the narrow coastal plain starts rising to the Sidlaw Hills. The ancient history is obscure, but it seems that early in the 12th century the Norman Philip de Moubray built his tower here, on the banks of the Eliot Water. The barony of Kellie was granted to Robert Stewart in 1309 but by 1402 the Ochterlony family were described as 'of Kely'. Traces of a 15th-century building have been detected in the cellar.

What can be seen outside dates from the 17th century when Kellie belonged to Sir Alexander Irvine and his family. It was sold with all his Angus estates to the Earl of Panmure in 1679. The next Earl, famous for his Stuart loyalty during the '15, was wounded and taken prisoner at Sheriffmuir but was heroically rescued by his gallant brother, Harry Maule. The Earl refused to take the Oath of Allegiance and died in exile. Harry, however, capitulated and he and the Countess reoccupied their houses at Panmure and Brechin. Kellie, abandoned and roofless, is said to have been used by smugglers. It was restored in 1864 by Fox Maule, 11th Earl of Dalhousie, with whose family it remained up to the present century, passing in 1924 to the late Captain Archibald Maule Ramsay. Mr Kerr Boyle acquired the Castle in 1973.

A strategic outpost, then, rather than a principal seat, Kellie may seem modest by comparison with more lordly castles but it remains remarkably complete. The first sight is the best, with the tower of red and grey sandstone and its bartizans rising sheer above a courtyard. The building seems principally 17th century, the tower earlier than the wings, and some window pediments are of Renaissance character. The main door leads into a small stone Hall with a fireplace, a boldly moulded doorway and an oval newel stair which is unusual in that it rises in a right-handed spiral. The old Kitchen, though for long out of use, survives in the cellar.

The character of the dwelling rooms is Victorian. In the beamed Dining Room there are portraits of Harry Maule, the 10th Earl of Dalhousie, and various Ramsays. Above this, the Drawing Room has the initials of past Barons of Kellie in its frieze and on the ceiling are recorded the principal building dates: 1442, 1613, 1697 and, finally, 1864. Higher up is a guest suite incorporating a watch-tower chamber. In the courtyard wing, the Victorian Library has been converted into a Gallery for contemporary paintings and crafts.

(See colour plate 32.)

Manderston, Borders
(Mr Adrian Palmer)

Two miles east of Duns (A6105)

Country life reached a twin peak of comfort and opulence in the Edwardian period. Rarely could this have been more evident than at Manderston, now a unique survivor from that lavish epoch and still lived in by a descendant of Sir James Miller who largely rebuilt it after 1900. A commission of heady extravagance, the ensemble remains in our day complete; and happily so, for its architect, John Kinross, was one of the most sensitive of his generation. At a time when craftsmanship was unusually high, he demanded work of the finest possible calibre. This will be appreciated in every detail, from the razor-sharp edges of the masonry, down to the joining of the oak panelling in the boat house and its fixing with wooden nails.

Sir James Miller's father was a Baltic merchant and made a fortune of millions out of hemp and herrings. Part of this his son devoted to racing, and his horse, Rocksand, won the Triple Crown in 1902. Sir James married at the age of twenty-nine, and decided to build on the property his father had bought in 1864. Before everything came the stables (dated 1895), which are among the most memorable of his buildings. The grooms' room is panelled in mahogany, the horses' stalls are in teak surmounted by brass-framed marble plaques bearing each occupant's name. Every one is headed by 'M' – for Miller and Manderston.

The house was completely remodelled in the first five years of this century. Lady Miller was a daughter of Lord Scarsdale, and either from affection or one-upmanship the house took its inspiration from Kedleston, her family home. This accounts for the use of the Adam style. The earlier

Manderston; the Ante Room to the Dining Room (See also colour plate 33)

house dating from the 1780s survives on the garden front; a wing was added, a substantial new entrance front and a service court. The severe classical style was continued but enriched with carved medallions. Inside, the new work is complete 'Adam', with domes, covings, apses and columns. The Hall in the centre of the house has a dome with elaborate arabesques, and a chimneypiece that exactly reproduces that at Kedleston. On it stand candlesticks and urns, part of the house collection of blue-john; the organ case too is of an Adam design.

The string of reception rooms was intended to impress visitors and attract house parties: among them are the Billiard Room, Ballroom (whose ceiling copies that in the Dining Room at Kedleston), Drawing Room and Morning Room, the last retaining its Georgian ceiling. The plasterwork in the Dining Room is the most elaborate; but the set-piece is the Drawing Room opening into the Ball Room, whose walls are hung with coloured velvet embossed with silk and curtains of gold and silver thread. The furniture everywhere is reproduction Louis XVI and sumptuously upholstered by any standards. Meanwhile great importance was attached to having efficiently arranged servant's quarters. The basement runs the length of the house, and besides the usual offices and a huge kitchen there are five marble-clad larders.

Before starting work on the house Sir James had already built the home farm and the village of Buxley close by. Farm buildings, accommodation for gardeners and farm hands, and an electric generating station are all in the baronial style. The Dairy has a Gothic vault and walls hung with coloured marbles from seven different countries, while in the Tea Room above, the oak panelling and carving is joined without the use of a single nail. At the house, the terraced garden lies within view of the distant Cheviot Hills. An extensive woodland garden has been planted since the Second World War with a specialist collection of rhododendrons.

Maxwelton House, Dumfries and Galloway
(The Maxwelton House Trust)

Thirteen miles north-west of Dumfries (A702 and B729)

This attractive old house, which has a complex architectural history, was rescued, shorn of its Victorian accretions, and extensively restored a few years ago by its occupant, Mrs Stenhouse. Set round three sides of a courtyard, the walls harled, with sandstone dressings, crow-stepped gables and external turret staircase, the outside now conveys the impression of a post-Renaissance Laird's dwelling. The rooms inside have also been carefully restored. An early vaulted undercroft survives, a tower room with robust quadripartite vault, a huge open kitchen fireplace with sandstone lintel, and 17th-century chimneypieces.

Maxwelton House

Stephen Laurie, a Dumfries merchant, acquired the property in 1611 and it descended in his family until 1848. Robert Laurie, notable for his support of the Stuart cause, was made a Baronet in 1685. Three years earlier his daughter Annie Laurie, immortalised in one of the best known Scottish love songs, was born at Maxwelton. She was said to be the beauty of Dumfriesshire and her portrait, which will be seen in the house, reveals a girl with a charming oval face and regular features.

Mellerstain, Borders
(The Lord Binning)

Between Kelso and Gordon (A6089)

Robert Adam must have been delighted when George Baillie, ancestor of the present owner, invited him in 1770 to build a house at Mellerstain. In spite of a soaring reputation, and the mark he had already left on many great Whig interiors, he had found little opportunity, except at Mersham-le-Hatch, to build *de novo*. It was also his first important commission in his native Scotland.

Adam at Mellerstain was confronted by a curious situation. In 1725 his father, William Adam, had put up two low, robust, early Georgian wings, but the mansion to which they were to be the adjunct was never built. For nearly half a century the wings (one of them a stable block) had remained isolated. Adam now linked them.

For all its castellated roof-line, simulated machicolation, and hood-moulds over the windows, his house, seventeen bays wide, was Georgian in character. Without the easy sense of movement that was to distinguish Culzean a few years later, it was, in spite of its honey-coloured stone, somewhat forbidding and rigid. But the interior decoration, always Adam's strongest point, is among the architectural delights of Scotland. If the staircase is perhaps uneasy, the state rooms with classical motifs interpreted in his own fashion – lightly, delicately, and gaily – have the assurance and vitality of 18th-century music. In two hundred years little has been altered; the rooms are complete with the ceilings, friezes, and fireplaces that Adam designed.

Mellerstain; the entrance front

The Library, with fireplace in green and white marble, mahogany doors (beautifully finished like all those at Mellerstain), and mellow leather-bound books on the shelves of the white carved-wood bookcases, is particularly cool and assured. Above the bookcases, the walls carry panels with classical figures and niches with portrait busts of earlier date than the house. Two of these, of Lady Grisell Baillie and her daughter Lady Murray, are remarkable works by Roubiliac. The white plaster relief of the ceiling stands out against pale green and pink, with medallions of slate grey.

The adjoining Music Room takes the place of honour, central on the garden front, and strikes the same lucid note. Beyond it is the Drawing Room, followed by the former bedroom with two dressing rooms. When ground-floor bedrooms went out of fashion the two last were opened up into a single room, but their ceilings remain. One cannot avoid mentioning more of Robert Adam's remarkable work: the apsed Entrance Hall, in a low-key Doric; the corridors and Sitting Room (the former dining room) in the lightest of Gothic; and, oddly placed at the top of the house, the Great Gallery whose curved ceiling, alas, never received the plasterwork that the architect had designed for it.

In speaking of such perfectly composed rooms, it seems almost superfluous to mention furniture and pictures. Yet the setting gains from English 18th-century pieces such as one would expect in a great house, though (with the exception of some looking-glasses and side tables) Adam did not at Mellerstain, as he sometimes did elsewhere, design much of the furniture. The paintings include a darkly mysterious Van Dyck portrait, a girl by Nicholas Maes, an early Gainsborough and half a dozen Ramsays, among them a delightful conversation piece. Berchem, Jacob Ruysdael, Van Goyen, and Constable (some small studies), contribute landscape or genre; there are religious subjects attributed to Lorenzo Costa, Previtali, and Bassano.

Bold garden terraces were laid out in 1909 by Blomfield, one of the best practitioners of his time. They preface a splendid sweep of lawn that slopes to a distant lake in the form of a Dutch canal. The view reaches to the Cheviot Hills.

Muchalls Castle, Grampians
(Mr Maurice Simpson)

Between Stonehaven and Aberdeen (A92)

The castle, not far inland, stands neighbour to an old rookery. One looks out to the grey waters of the North Sea; there is the agitation and cawing of rooks in great trees. The north range, incorporating an earlier building, was transformed in 1619 by Alexander Burnett, the owner of Crathes, the famous house twelve miles away (National Trust for Scotland). The family once controlled vast estates hereabouts. The south range was added before 1627 by his son, Sir Thomas, who thus transformed Muchalls into a characteristic L-shaped Scottish house of the period. Though the original fenestration has disappeared, little else has happened architecturally since

Muchalls Castle

then. None the less, the first impression of the harled house, in spite of weathered coats of arms, corbelled turrets, and stepped gables, is vaguely disappointing. One must be patient.

From the entrance in the south wing a broad stone staircase spirals to Sir Thomas's hall. This is the first of three rooms with Jacobean plasterwork ceilings of exceptional interest, dated 1624. They are worth going far to see. The craftsmen responsible were probably active a year or two earlier at Glamis Castle where identical motifs occur, but there is no reason to suppose, as has been maintained, that they were Italian.

The Hall ceiling is the most elaborate. Animals of weird aspect peer from long, scrolled, pendant bosses; medallions depicting heroes and biblical figures, and the armorials of Sir Thomas and his friends, punctuate flat broad strapwork with floral decoration; there is a delicate frieze of flowers and fruit. The shields of arms are coloured, and the painting has been exceptionally well done. Over the simple stone chimneypiece, pairs of terms – a bearded gentleman and a lady with linked arms, and naked to the waist – flank the royal coat of arms. In this room is preserved the factor's rent-table from Ballochmile House on which Robert Burns may be supposed to have paid his rent, if he ever did such a thing, for he was at one time a tenant on the estate.

The Withdrawing Room and Solar are more simply but no less delightfully treated. In both rooms the Burnett arms appear over the chimneypieces, and there are classical and biblical figures taken from the same moulds as those in the Hall. The Solar, with wainscot in elm and oak, has panels divided by strapwork, while those in the Withdrawing Room, enclosing heart-shaped floral designs, are divided by thin moulded ribs.

Rammerscales, Dumfries and Galloway
(Mr A. M. Bell Macdonald of Rammerscales)

Between Lockerbie and Dumfries (B7020)

Born on a modest farm not far away, James Mounsey, the builder of Rammerscales, was, like Charles Cameron, one of many Scotsmen to make a name and fortune in Russia in the 18th century, where his outstanding medical ability commended him to the Imperial Court. After rising to the rank of Lieutenant-General as an army doctor, he was in 1761 appointed head of the Medical Chancery by the Empress Elizabeth, a post which entailed control of medical administration throughout the Russian Empire. Following the murder of the Czar Peter, who had confirmed his appointment, his position became politically difficult and possibly dangerous. He retired to Scotland in 1762, bringing with him the first rhubarb to be propagated in Britain. The precious seed had reached Russia from China whence it had been smuggled by the Imperial Medical Service.

Dr Mounsey had bought Rammerscales two years before his return and began building at once. Perhaps it was as a contrast to the rich splendours of the Russian Court that he chose a sober symmetrical Georgian. The three-storey house is a little tall for its width, but the stone is a finely jointed ashlar, the uncompromising elevations are relieved by a cornice and balustrade, and on the entrance front by a recessed loggia with a screen of Tuscan columns. The inclusion on the second floor of a Long Gallery (now the Library), with bowed ends, is an unusual feature for the second half of the 18th century. The builder is unknown but the curiously wide spacing of the modillions on the external cornice suggests that he was not a metropolitan architect.

Rammerscales

The doctor died in 1773 but how much he or his heirs lived at Rammerscales is a puzzling question. It appears that the Library had no floor until 1801, and most of the fireplaces, cornices and joinery, are early 19th century. Even the doctor's elegant spiral staircase cannot have received its rail and balusters until after 1800.

The most interesting contents are the books, associated with William Bell Macdonald, who inherited in 1837. He was an outstanding linguist in his day, and the specialised library of several thousand volumes is representative not only of the Classics but of his studies in Coptic, Hebrew, Samaritan and other minority tongues of the Eastern Mediterranean. There is also a collection of modern works of art which in a fairly remote country house in Scotland must be something of a rarity. It includes sculptures by Rodin and Barbara Hepworth, a Lurçat tapestry, and paintings and drawings by such artists as Forain, Despiau, Segonzac (a ravishing nude), Wyndham Lewis, and Lowry.

Rossdhu, Strathclyde
(Sir Ivar Colquhoun of Luss, Bart.)

On the west bank of Loch Lomond, south of Luss (A82)

Nowhere in Scotland is the contrast between mediaeval rivalries and the Enlightenment of the 18th century so well illustrated as at Rossdhu where, in one of the most beautiful of settings, the ruins of the 15th-century castle stand close to its demure Georgian successor. Rossdhu is Gaelic for Black Headland, and the house stands on a low peninsula jutting into Loch Lomond against a sublime backdrop of island-dotted waters, mountains and hills. The views are framed by the park landscaped in 1797 by Thomas White, an English gardener and pupil of Capability Brown. In this arcady, the ruined castle stimulates hair-raising memories of blood feuds, murder, treachery and witchcraft.

Very different are the associations of the house built in 1772 by John Baxter to the designs of Sir James Clerk of Penecuik for Sir James Colquhoun, 25th of Luss, and embellished by his successor, another Sir James, friend and correspondent of Horace Walpole. His son, also James, married a daughter of Sir John Sinclair, the prophet of agricultural improvement in Scotland, and added the wings and Tuscan portico as well as building the triumphal arch at the south entrance to the park. Thus the ensemble is the creation of three eminently civilised men. It is interesting to see that, as in the buildings of Glasgow, the stone was once 'blacked' – surely a depressing cosmetic for a country house.

The interior of Rossdhu shows charming variations in style. The Entrance Hall, remodelled by Lorimer in this century, is painted a striking green. The Large Drawing Room, remodelled after a fire, has a 20th-century barrelled ceiling and limed oak panelling, against which the family portraits include works by Reynolds, Raeburn and Allan Ramsay. In an adjoining room is an interesting collection of stuffed birds and animals

Rossdhu

gathered together in the mid-19th century by John Colquhoun, author of the classic *The Moor and the Loch*. The Library has its original ceiling and a magnificent pair of pedimented mahogany bookcases obviously made for the room, as well as a set of chairs with needlework seats worked by Lady Colquhoun and a *Last Supper*, dated 1528, attributed to Bernard van Orley. In the early-19th-century wing, the Dining Room is more monumental, with a Doric frieze, attached marble columns at one end, and stout mahogany furniture contemporary with the architecture.

The contents of the house were resolutely sold by the widow of the 5th Baronet in 1907, but fortunately many were bought back and it has subsequently been possible to trace and acquire a few more; thus a gilded enrichment bearing the family's crest has recently been found, which matches two looking-glasses in the Chinese Room. Some rooms are currently being re-arranged and re-decorated.

Scone Palace, Tayside
(The Earl of Mansfield)

Two miles north of Perth (A93)

Scone is not only a great mansion but a national shrine. A hundred yards north of the house rises the Moot-Hill that in a sense is the heart of the Scottish kingdom: here the Pictish kings held council in the first centuries of our era, here early in the 8th century King Nectan embraced the Christian faith, here successive kings were enthroned, and here on New Year's Day in 1651 Charles II was crowned before his fatal march to Worcester.

With the Moot-Hill was associated the famous Stone of Scone, until Edward I carried it away to Westminster where it forms part of the chair on which the kings of the joint kingdom have been crowned since the time of James VI. When Scottish nationalists in 1951 daringly spirited the stone from the Abbey on Christmas Eve, it was at Scone that they naturally planned to lodge it after an absence of six and a half centuries.

A religious foundation existed at Scone from the 6th century, and after 1580 the powerful Ruthven family, Earls of Gowrie, built themselves a house on the ruins of the monastic buildings. (Intoxicated by the pulpit oratory of John Knox, a Dundee rabble had sacked the place a generation earlier.) Following the enigmatic Gowrie conspiracy (1600), James VI conferred the property in gratitude on Sir David Murray who may have been instrumental in saving the king's life. Thus began the association of Scone with the Murray chieftans which has lasted nearly four centuries. Sir David, created Viscount Stormont in 1621, was buried in the early-17th-century church on the hill and his alabaster memorial is one of the finest things of its kind in Scotland.

In the '15 and the '45, Jacobite Murrays, the 5th and 6th Viscounts, successively entertained Prince James and Prince Charles Edward at Scone. But it was in London, in the generation after the '45, that the most distinguished of the Murrays achieved fame. The outstanding jurist of his day, William Murray was twice Lord Chief Justice and Chancellor of the Exchequer. Such was his eloquence that Lord Chesterfield said of him, 'One might have heard a pin fall when he was speaking' in the House of Commons. By a judgment in favour of a runaway negro slave in 1771, he played a decisive role in the beginnings of the Anti-Slavery movement. He became Earl of Mansfield in 1776.

Scone Palace

Replacing an earlier gabled house, Scone today is the creation of the jurist's great-nephew, 3rd Earl of Mansfield, for whom it was designed in 1802 by William Atkinson (d. 1839), the talented pupil of James Wyatt. Built of the same red sandstone from which the Stone of Scone had been quarried, Atkinson's castellated building is very much in the Georgian Gothic style of his master: square, sober and reasonable, it has little to do with his later Abbotsford and the romantic baronial style. The rooms are ample and well-lit, with Gothic details down to the pelmets and chandeliers. The halls and Gallery are vaulted or beamed. The building was complete in 1813, and its consistency speaks for the architect's controlling hand.

By contrast the furniture and works of art at Scone surprise by their variety. Among the early objects are embroidered velvet bed hangings associated with Mary, Queen of Scots and said to have been worked by the queen and her ladies. The 17th century contributes exotic cabinets and tables from Germany and Italy; inlay of marquetry, of ebony and scarlet tortoiseshell, of agate and lapis lazuli. Among the English pieces there are side tables attributed to William Gates, Lord Mansfield's brass-mounted library table, and half a dozen superb lacquered pieces in the taste associated with the Brighton Pavilion.

Much of the important French furniture was presumably bought by the 7th Viscount Stormont (later 2nd Earl of Mansfield), ambassador in Paris from 1772–8. The Boulle includes 18th-century pedestals, commodes, tables, clocks, and a pair of wildly extravagant marriage caskets. Among the best inlaid pieces is a small marquetry writing table made by the incomparable Riesener for Marie-Antoinette. This, with a set of Louis XV armchairs covered in highly unusual needlework, is in the Drawing Room which retains its classical green wall-silk of 1841 and an English carpet.

The Gothic shelves in the Library are now filled with porcelain: two

Scone Palace; the Drawing Room

Meissen tea and coffee services of *c.* 1740, a large Ludwigsburg dinner service, early Sèvres of the 1750s, a Paris service decorated with birds, and Chelsea 'red anchor' botanical plates. More unusual, though uneven in quality, is the large collection of continental ivories in the Dining Room, which includes a few good 17th-century pieces, among them some exuberant examples of Augsburg Baroque. A collection of *vernis Martin* vases and *objets d'art* – over seventy of them, mounted in silver-gilt or ormolu – merit, for once, the adjective 'unique'. The technique of painting on *papier mâché* under a lacquer varnish, developed by the Martin brothers of Paris, died with them, and the Scone collection has no parallel. It is displayed in the Gallery where the 16th-century parquetry floor, inlaid with bog-oak, was rightly spared by Atkinson when he incorporated the room into his new building.

Good sculptures include a bust of Newton by Guelfi; another of the Earl of Mansfield who built the house, by Nollekens; and one of the jurist, by Rysbrack. Reynolds's seated portrait shows the great jurist looking wise and benign; and Zoffany's portrait of the ambassador's daughter, Lady Elizabeth Murray with her maid is a painting that sums up the grace of English portraiture.

Traquair House, Borders
(Peter Maxwell Stuart of Traquair)

South of Innerleithen, six miles south-east of Peebles (A72)

Coming over the pass down to the young Tweed one reaches a point where for the first time the encompassing Peebles hills allow a reasonable width of tilth and pasture. A place where in early days a house would have been situated – and suddenly, glimpsed through trees, there it is, Traquair, tall and silent. Not to be assessed but felt, it is one of those rare houses with a luminous quality that seem to stand under the protection of a tutelary spirit.

A place of such atmosphere is difficult to describe in conventional terms. Once it was a hunting lodge of Scottish kings, and the first recorded royal visit was in 1107. Later in the century William the Lion signed at Traquair the charter authorising the establishment of 'Bishop's Burgh' on the banks of the Molendinar – now the City of Glasgow. Traquair is said to be the oldest continually inhabited house in Scotland; proof is impossible and it hardly seems to matter. The main front, solid, non-committal yet curiously friendly, lifts its harled storeys to an attic of pedimented dormers and a vast roof of steep pitch. The oldest part of the house, to the left, has the remains of a Pele tower with narrow newel staircase, probably of the 14th century. The house was greatly extended in the late 16th century, and before the middle of the 17th it had acquired its dormers and roof, and the block which protrudes slightly on the entrance front and contains a more spacious newel staircase. At the end of the 17th century the name of an architect, James Smith of Edinburgh, is recorded. Probably owing to lack of money his plans to give the house a much more formal appearance were never carried out;

Traquair House

but he added the iron gates and screen that complete the forecourt, and on the east front he built the terrace and two little pavilions with ogee roofs. Excepting a 19th-century entrance porch, there has been little change outside since then.

Traquair came to the Stuarts in 1491, and James Stuart, the first Laird of Traquair, fell at Flodden in 1513. (His descendant, the 20th Laird, owns the house today.) Half a century later Mary Queen of Scots and Darnley were entertained here, and among the many Jacobite relics are her rosary and crucifix, and a silk bed-cover believed to have been worked by the Queen and her ladies. The 7th Laird, whose portrait hangs in the Dining Room, enjoyed the unstable confidence of Charles I, was advanced to an Earldom and became High Treasurer of Scotland, only to end in disgrace and penury. Perhaps he was not robust enough for the troubled temper of the times, and is now unhappily remembered as the Laird who closed his door to Montrose when the latter sought a night's shelter after his defeat at Philiphaugh. His son, born in 1622, reverted to the Old Faith, and Traquair has been a Catholic house ever since. In 1664 it was sacked by a Presbyterian rabble, which seems the only disaster recorded in its long history.

The 4th Earl was involved with the Jacobite rising of 1715 and imprisoned in Edinburgh Castle; his son the 5th Earl was confined for two years in the Tower after the '45, where he was joined by his devoted wife. A story relates that one day in the late autumn of 1745 Prince Charles Edward, the Earl's guest, rode out through the Bear Gates – 'the Steekit Yetts' – that stand at the end of the main avenue. As the gates closed, the Earl promised that they would not be reopened until the Stuarts were restored to the throne. It is not only the gates that have made no concession to later times. Stuart loyalties, recusancy, and the resulting fines withdrew Traquair from the mainstream of Scottish history and left little means for renovation. In a sense they preserved this rare house.

The brass knocker on the door bears the initials of the 4th Earl and his wife, with the date 1705. His son remodelled the Drawing Room, and introduced the delightful *trompe l'œil* overdoors and overmantel. Part of an earlier ceiling has been revealed: painted with strapwork, grotesques and floral motifs, it gives an idea of how the room must have looked in the 17th century. There is a harpsichord made by Andreas Ruckers in 1651 and a Flemish ebony cabinet of about 1700, the interior painted with biblical scenes. Among the portraits in this room is one of the poet, John Dryden, by John Riley. The most important family portraits hang in the Dining Room. They include a fine Flemish 16th-century work on panel, and canvases of five of the first six Earls of Traquair.

The Library, created in the first half of the 18th century, has a cove painted in grisaille with the heads of philosophers. The collection of books is almost intact, and its treasures include an illuminated psalter of the 14th century and a copy of the *Nuremburg Chronicle* printed in 1493. In the Museum Room a section of the original mural decoration of *circa* 1530 survives, showing a hound, dromedary, and other animals against a con-ventionalised background of vines and grapes. Of roughly the same date are a series of Flemish carved wood panels in the Chapel, depicting scenes from the Life of Christ. Once belonging to Mary of Guise, they were later acquired by the 5th Earl.

Special mention must be made of the Royal Stuart relics at Traquair, which include collections of miniatures, Jacobite glass and King James VI's cradle. There is early Jacobean needlework in pristine condition, and two rare examples (*c.* 1700) of silk embroidery on paper. Visitors should not miss the Brew House where a potent Traquair Ale is brewed by the traditional process in old vats.

Traquair; left: *16th-century painting on the Drawing Room ceiling;* right: *the Library*

Glossary

artisan baroque   Provincial architecture from *circa* 1660, in which classical details are pleasingly if ignorantly arranged to give a decorative pattern.

bailey   An enclosure or court of a castle. The inner bailey contained the keep or principal dwellings. Also known as a ward.

banqueting house   A garden house, often quite small, for informal entertaining.

barge-boards   The fascia boards of gables, which might be elaborately carved.

baronial   The romantic revival in the 19th century of Scottish pre-classical architecture. The result was highly picturesque, particularly at roof level.

Baroque   The highly-charged artistic style of the 17th and early 18th centuries, the hallmark of the Papacy, the royal courts and nobility. Classical forms become massive or ornate, and the intention is to impress or overwhelm the spectator.

bartizan   (Scotland) A turret, usually round, supported on stone brackets (i.e. corbelled out) at the top angle of a building. A corbelled turret.

belvedere   (Italian) An elevated building or room giving a fine view.

blue-john   A decorative fluorspar, marked with blue, purple and brown, mined in Derbyshire. Used extensively after 1743 for fine ornaments.

Bomarzo   The garden of the Villa Orsini at Bomarzo, near Viterbo, created after 1561, famous for its temples and fantastic carved monsters.

Boulle furniture   Furniture veneered with marquetry of brass and tortoiseshell, and sometimes other materials. Associated first with the Parisian *ébéniste* André Charles Boulle (1642–1732) and Louis XIV, it was imitated outside France and revived in the 19th century.

braces or wind braces   Subsidiary beams, set diagonally, which strengthen a timber roof.

brickwork   In **English bond**, a row of stretchers (bricks laid lengthways) alternates with a row of headers (laid head-on). In **Flemish bond**, which had become general in England by about 1700, each row contains alternate stretchers and headers. **Diapered** brickwork, associated with the Tudor period, has a lozenge or other pattern picked out in bricks of contrasting colour, usually grey. **Moulded** bricks are baked in particular shapes, for, e.g. a door surround. **Rubbed** bricks are cut into shapes, often *in situ*.

capehouse or cap-house   (Scotland) A gabled chamber on top of a tower, within the parapet wall.

cartouche   A tablet, often shield-shaped and elaborately bordered, to contain an inscription, coat of arms or painting.

caryatid   A sculptured human figure, generally female, when used like a column to bear a structure overhead.

chinoiserie   Imitation of Chinese arts, which began in the 17th century. In the 18th century it became distinctly rococo.

cipollino   Marble, of strongly veined sea-greens, quarried by the Romans on the Island of Euboea (and since 1888). Used as monolith columns and wall linings.

classical   In architecture or decoration: based on the forms developed in ancient Rome or Greece.

clearstory or clerestory The row of windows in the upper walls of a church or hall, which provide the main light.

collar-beam A tie-beam set higher up in the pitch of a roof.

commode (French) A chest of drawers. In English furniture, any sufficiently ornamental chest of drawers or low cupboard.

console A bracket attached to the wall; a side table in the form of a large bracket.

corbel A bracket built into the wall, supporting a beam, vault or other structure.

cottage orné A picturesque cottage built of various rustic materials but architect-designed (late 18th – early 19th centuries).

crewel work A bold style of needlework in coloured wools on pale-coloured linen. Most familiar in 17th-century bed-hangings.

crown-post Similar to a king-post (q.v.) but, rather than the roof ridge, it supports a collar-beam or braces (q.v.).

crow steps Gables which rise in steps; a Netherlandish and German form, found also in Scotland and East Anglia.

cruck Simple but massive form of timber-framing. Two crucks, matched and slightly curved, form an inverted V and support both walls and roof.

cupola A dome, large or small. Sometimes used incorrectly for a lantern or small bell-tower.

curtain wall A wall that supports no structure; the outer wall encircling a castle, punctuated by bastions.

Decorated The middle phase of Gothic architecture in England, *circa* 1290–1370, characterised by ogee arches, abundant naturalistic carving, and interesting spatial effects.

Domesday Book The census of England made by order of King William I and completed in 1086.

ébéniste A cabinet-maker in France.

entablature The structure supported by the column of classical architecture. It consists of an architrave, frieze (which may be carved), and cornice.

escutcheon A shield such as carries a coat of arms.

feudal system The system of land tenure in the early Middle Ages, depending on the relation of lord and vassal.

French Hepplewhite An established misnomer for English furniture, *circa* 1770–90, and especially chairs, of serpentine or bombé forms derived from the Louis XV style.

galilee A vestibule, sometimes large, placed usually at the west end of a mediaeval cathedral or church.

garderobe A wardrobe; but also the privy of a mediaeval house.

Garter The Most Noble Order of the Garter is the highest order of Knighthood in England. It was instituted by King Edward III about 1348, and the number of Knights-Companions is limited to twenty-five.

gatehouse The main entrance to the courtyard of a house. When it leads to the inner courtyard, it will be towered and contain fine rooms.

gesso A white composition of chalk and glue. In the early 18th century it was applied to furniture, then carved in low relief, and gilded or silvered.

giallo antico (Italian) One of the fine marbles removed from the ruins of ancient Rome. It is cloudy yellow with purple veins, and was quarried in Algeria.

giant columns or pilasters These rise through two storeys.

'Gibbs' opening The accepted term for a particular form of door or window opening with rusticated jambs and pronounced keystones.

Gothic architecture The structure and character depend chiefly on the use of the pointed arch. Mainly 13th to 16th centuries, but it survived regionally through the 17th. It features stone vaults and huge traceried windows.

Gothic revival The revival of Gothic architecture and decoration is associated with the circle of Horace Walpole, from 1749, but it had been attempted earlier. From about 1795 the style became by degrees less naïvely decorative, more structural, and, largely owing to Pugin, it finally took on a moral character.

Great Hall The central room of a mediaeval house where, in early times at least, the entire household would assemble for meals, was called the 'hall' or, later, 'great hall'.

green man A fertility symbol of ancient but uncertain origin. In decoration he appears as a face with leaves sprouting from the mouth.

grisaille Monochrome painting in tones of grey.

grotesque A stylised form of decoration with human figures or heads and animals among flowers and architectural fancies, based on the Roman wall paintings found in buried buildings or 'grottoes'. Not to be confused with grotesque = exaggerated, bizarre.

guilloche A running pattern of two or more interlaced bands which form ovals or a plait. A classical feature.

ha-ha A sunken ditch, intended to be invisible from the house, to keep the park animals away from the lawn; said to have been invented by Charles Bridgeman, early 18th century. 'Ha-ha!' expressed the surprise on its discovery.

hammerbeam Short beams projecting from the wall at the foot of the roof. Supported from below by braces, hammerbeams support further braces or an arch.

herm A head, bust or half-figure whose base develops into a plinth.

Imperial staircase An imposing form with a single lower flight that divides into two upper flights.

Jacobethan This useful word avoids the tedium of 'Elizabethan and/or Jacobean'; often particularly suitable for the Victorian revival of those styles.

jetty On a timber-frame house, the floor joists which project beyond the lower wall and carry an overhanging upper storey.

keep The centre and most strongly built part of a castle, where the lord would have his lodgings. The last defence against invaders, it took the form of a tower.

king-post A vertical post which supports the roof ridge, and normally stands on a collar- or tie-beam (q.v.).

leet The jurisdiction of a mediaeval court of law.

Leviathan A mighty monster, described in the Book of Job (chapters 40–41).

louvre An opening with slanted boards, to release air or smoke; a louvre of lantern form was placed in the roof of a mediaeval kitchen or hall.

machicolation The projecting parapet of a castle wall, with holes through which to drop missiles or boiling lead on assaulters.

mannerism The tormented artistic style of the 16th century, which followed in the wake of Michelangelo. In English architecture it is used for the deliberate misuse of classical motifs, as found e.g. in the Elizabethan style.

Manor The unit of territorial organisation in feudal times. More often used as an abbreviation of 'Manor House', the home of the Lord of the Manor.

marquetry A decorative veneer of contrasting or stained woods, sometimes with other materials (e.g. ivory, mother of pearl, brass, pewter) making a floral or figurative pattern. When set in a formal mosaic pattern it is called **parquetry**.

mathematical tiles Tiles made to look deceptively like brickwork. The key behind is only visible, if exposed, at the corners. Commonly used in south-east England after the brick tax (1784).

motte A steep mound on which an early castle keep was built.

mullions Uprights, of stone or wood, that divide a window.

muntin *See* panelling.

Nash, Joseph (1808–78) A water-colour painter, best known for his lithographs, *Mansions of England in the Olden Time* (1840s), which epitomise the romantic nostalgia for the Gothic, Tudor and Stuart periods.

neo-classicism Of all the various revivals of classical style that have occurred since the days of Charlemagne, this word refers to that of the mid-18th century, which included a Greek revival about 1800, and continued into the 19th.

ogee A form of Gothic arch whose head is formed of serpentine curves meeting in a point.

orders of classical architecture The 'order' is the entire column, complete with plinth and entablature (q.v.). Order also refers to the type, of which there are five, ranging from the sturdy to the elegant and ornate: **Tuscan**, simple; **Doric**, whose frieze is punctuated by triglyphs (q.v.); **Ionic** with a scrolled (voluted) capital; **Corinthian** with a capital of acanthus leaves; and **Composite**, with both leaves and scrolls.

Palladian The classical style of architecture adopted by the Whig establishment, *circa* 1714–60. Intending to combine nobility with simplicity, they imitated the villas and street buildings of Andrea Palladio (1508–80) and Roman temples.

panelling Plank and muntin is a primitive or country form, often used as a dividing wall: muntins are the weight-bearing uprights, planks form the panels. **Linenfold** is late Gothic: the panels are finely carved in relief with a design said to resemble folded linen. Purists may prefer to call it **parchmentfold**. In late-17th-century work the panels are large, often raised, and bordered by **bolection** mouldings (broad serpentine curves). **Fielded** panels have their edges stepped and chamfered.

parcel-gilt Partly gilt.

peristyle A row of columns that forms a walk around a building or courtyard.

Perpendicular Late phase of English Gothic architecture (late 14th to 16th centuries) in which vertical and horizontal lines are greatly emphasised.

picturesque 'What would look good in a picture'. The cult of The Picturesque was at its height in the 1790s and caused intense debate. A 'picturesque' view should look natural but have a balanced composition and afford variety and contrast. Romantic architecture is called picturesque when judiciously varied and ornamented.

pier A sturdy, square column or short stretch of load-bearing wall.

pier glass A looking-glass made to hang on a pier between windows.

pietre dure (Italian) Semi-precious stones (agate, jasper, carnelian, lapis, amethyst, etc.), as fashioned by the Grand Ducal Workshops of Florence. Table tops and cabinets of *pietre dure* were bought by Englishmen on the Grand Tour.

porphyry A hard volcanic rock quarried by the Romans in Egypt. Of purple flecked with white, it suggests opulence and was always associated with the Roman Emperors. Porphyry of a duller colour was quarried in Sweden from the late 18th century. There are also green and black porphyries.

porte cochère A porch large enough for wheeled carriages to pass through.

pulvinated frieze A convex frieze.

putto (Italian) A plump, naked infant used decoratively in Baroque ornament. Cherubs and Cupids, though similar, are winged.

quit-rent A small charge put upon an estate in lieu of other services.

quoins Dressed stones that run up the corners of a building, generally projecting and rusticated.

Renaissance The revival of classicism which began in Italy, particularly Florence, in the early 15th century. It reached France about 1480, and England a few decades later.

rocaille (French) Literally 'rocky'. Known in England as shell-work or rock-work, rocaille is one of the main decorative motifs of the rococo style.

rococo The light-hearted sequel to Baroque, intended not to impress but to give pleasure. Formulated in France, it reached England after 1730 and remained for thirty years. The decoration is characterised by rocaille, C-scrolls, and flowers and animals of peculiar vitality.

romanticism By its nature, the romantic impulse cannot easily be defined, but it covers a multitude of sins. Though launched in the 18th century, the movement was strongest in the 19th, and produced revivals of every known style of architecture. For country houses, Elizabethan and mediaeval were among the most popular.

rosso antico (Italian) A decorative red marble quarried by the Ancient Romans in southern Greece.

rustication The deep channels on a wall which look like joints between massive blocks of stone. Most commonly seen on the basement storey or quoins (q.v.) of a classical building.

scagliola A composition using powdered selenite, coloured and polished. Used particularly for table tops in 18th-century Florence, and for columns simulating marble during the neo-classical period.

screen or screens stood at the kitchen end of a mediaeval hall, in line with the main doors, where they helped to keep away the draught, thus forming a screens passage. Above the passage was a gallery – the 'minstrels' gallery'.

seaweed marquetry A style of marquetry (q.v.) fashionable in Holland and England from the 1690s. It is of an intricate and even design of trailing fronds.

'slighting'   In the Civil War (1642–8), the action of the Parliamentary forces after capturing a Royalist castle or fortification. The defensive walls, keep and perhaps more would be partially or wholly demolished to make them indefensible.

solar   From *solarium*, literally a room designed to catch the sun. Used for an upper living room in a mediaeval house, but not, apparently, before the 19th century.

spere truss   An early form of screen in a mediaeval hall: a wooden arch with stout piers, the latter attached with trusses to the wall.

strapwork   takes various forms. It is a decoration of interlaced, scrolling or curling bands, derived from leather or iron straps, and belongs to the Tudor and Jacobean periods.

Strawberry Hill Gothic   18th-century Gothic revival in its most decorative form, so called from Horace Walpole's house, Strawberry Hill, which he re-modelled, room by room, from 1749. It was pretty and colourful, but the true structural principles of the Gothic were not understood before the 1790s.

tempietto   (Italian) Bramante's Tempietto, built in Rome in 1502, is a circular temple, domed and surrounded by columns, and has always been acclaimed a classical masterpiece.

tie-beam   An internal beam across the base of a roof, to counteract the outwards thrust.

transoms   The horizontal bars that may divide a window.

triglyph   In classical architecture belongs to the Doric order (q.v.). It is a channelled block that is placed at regular short intervals along the frieze.

undercroft   A low vaulted room at ground or cellar level of a mediaeval building. The main room above it is thus free from rising damp.

Utopia   An ideal commonwealth, described by Sir Thomas More (1516), whose citizens live and work peacefully under prescribed conditions.

vault   An arched roof. **Barrel** or **tunnel** vault: an arched roof of continuous semi-circular section.

Venetian window   A triple window whose central section is heightened and arched. Not much used in Venice, but developed by the English Palladians.

vernacular   Native or domestic. It describes regional styles which show no pretensions in aping cosmopolitan fashions.

Versailles parquet   A floor of oak or walnut parquet laid in a particular squared pattern. French in origin, and copied in England after the 1680s.

waggon roof   An arched timber roof with closely spaced rafters and braces; it may also be panelled or plastered.

yett   (Scotland) A massive iron gate placed for protection at the main door of a house, or at the foot of the main stair.

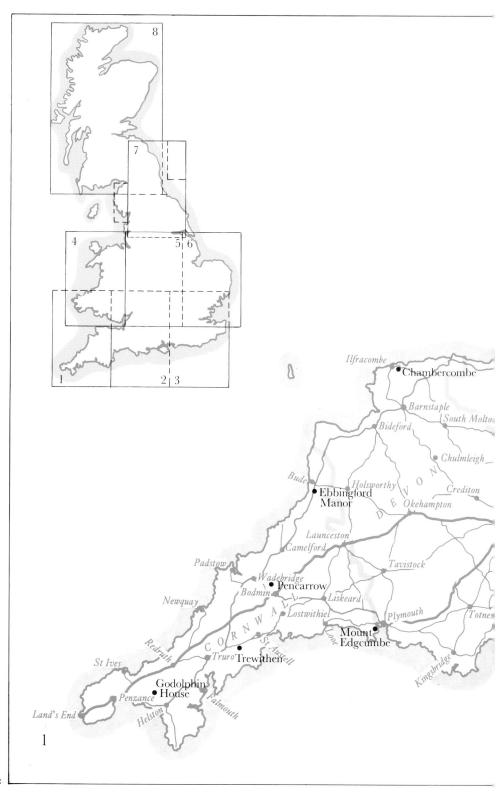

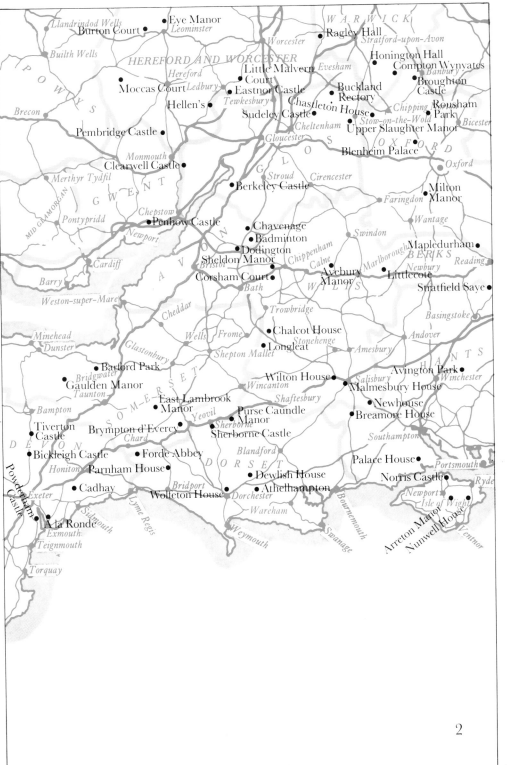

Llandrindod Wells
Burton Court
Eye Manor
Leominster
WARWICK
Ragley Hall
Stratford-upon-Avon
Builth Wells
HEREFORD AND WORCESTER
Worcester
Honington Hall
Compton Wynyates
POWYS
Little Malvern Evesham
Court
Banbury
Broughton
Castle
Hereford
Moccas Court Ledbury
Eastnor Castle
Buckland
Rectory
Brecon
Hellen's Tewkesbury
Chastleton House
Rousham
Park
Chipping
Sudeley Castle
Stow-on-the-Wold
Bicester
Pembridge Castle
Cheltenham
Upper Slaughter Manor
OXFORD
Gloucester
GLOS
Blenheim Palace
Monmouth
Oxford
Clearwell Castle
Merthyr Tydfil
Stroud
Cirencester
GWENT
Milton
Manor
Berkeley Castle
Faringdon
Pontypridd
Chepstow
Wantage
MID GLAMORGAN
Penhow Castle
Newport
Chavenage
Swindon
Mapledurham
BERKS
Cardiff
AVON
Badminton
Dodington
Chippenham
Calne
Marlborough
Newbury
Reading
Sheldon Manor
Barry
Corsham Court
Bristol
Avebury
Manor
WILTS
Littlecote
Stratfield Saye
Weston-super-Mare
Bath
Basingstoke
Cheddar
Trowbridge
Minehead
Wells Frome
Chalcot House
Stonehenge
Andover
Dunster
Glastonbury
Shepton Mallet
Longleat
Amesbury
HANTS
Barford Park
SOMERSET
Avington Park
Bridgwater
Wilton House
Salisbury
Winchester
Gaulden Manor
Taunton
Wincanton
Malmesbury House
Bampton
East Lambrook
Manor
Shaftesbury
Newhouse
Tiverton
Castle
Brympton d'Evercy
Chard
Yeovil
Sherborne
Purse Caundle
Manor
Breamore House
DEVON
Sherborne Castle
Southampton
Bickleigh Castle
Forde Abbey
Blandford
Palace House
Honiton
Parnham House
DORSET
Norris Castle
Portsmouth
Powderham
Castle
Cadhay
Bridport
Dewlish House
Athelhampton
Newport
Ryde
Exeter
Wolleton House Dorchester
Isle of Wight
A la Ronde
Lyme Regis
Wareham
Arreton Manor
Ventnor
Exmouth
Weymouth
Swanage
Nunwell House
Teignmouth
Bournemouth
Torquay

2

413

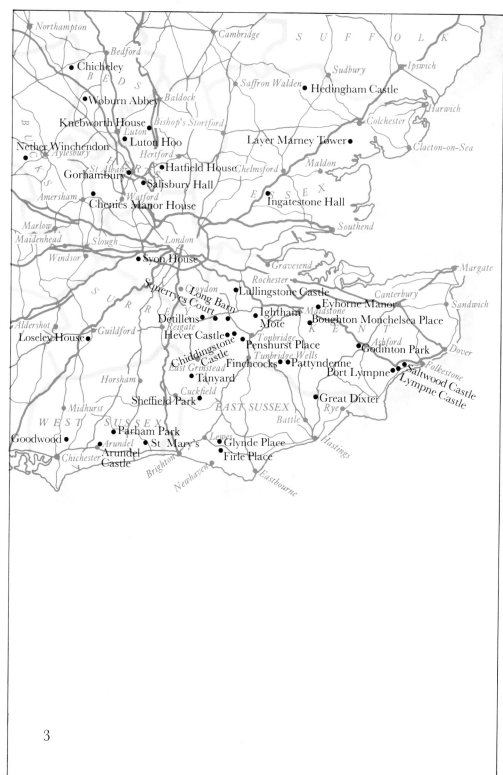

3

Holyhead

Llandudno

Rhyl

Conwy

● Bodrhyddan Hall

Bryn Bras Castle ●

Bangor

Denbigh

● Gwydir Castle

Caernarvon

Llanrwst

C L W Y D

Betws-y-Coed

G W Y N E D D

Portmadoc

● Ffestiniog

Llangollen

Pwllheli

Bala

Oswestry

Harlech

Barmouth

● Dolgellau

Welshpool

Machynlleth

Montgomery

Aberystwyth

Clun

P O W Y S

New Quay

Llandrindod Wells

Builth Wells

Lampeter

Cardigan

Llandovery

Brecon

Fishguard

Carmarthen

Llandeilo

Milford Haven

Merthyr Tydfil

GWENT

Tenby

Llanelli WEST GLAM

M I D

Pontypool

Pembroke

Swansea

Neath

GLAM

Port Talbot

4

Cardiff

SOUTH GLAM

Barry

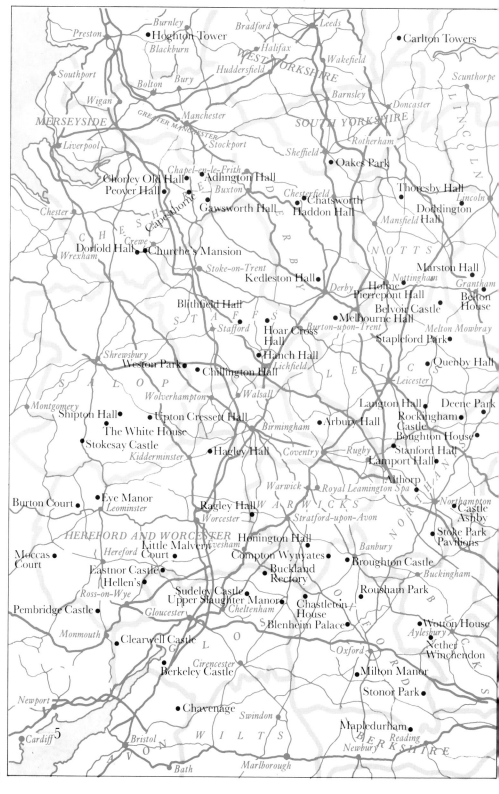

Preston
Burnley
Bradford
Leeds
Carlton Towers
Hoghton Tower
Blackburn
Halifax
WEST YORKSHIRE
Wakefield
Southport
Huddersfield
Scunthorpe
Bolton
Bury
Barnsley
Wigan
Manchester
Doncaster
MERSEYSIDE
GREATER MANCHESTER
SOUTH YORKSHIRE
LINCOLN
Liverpool
Stockport
Rotherham
Sheffield
Lincoln
Chester
Oakes Park
Chapel-en-le-Frith
Thoresby Hall
Chorley Old Hall
Adlington Hall
Chesterfield
Peover Hall
Buxton
Chatsworth
Doddington
Gawsworth Hall
Haddon Hall
Hall
Capesthorne
Mansfield
Crewe
DERBY
Dorfold Hall
Churche's Mansion
NOTTS
Wrexham
Marston Hall
Stoke-on-Trent
Kedleston Hall
Nottingham
Grantham
Derby
Holme
Belton
Blithfield Hall
Pierrepont Hall
House
STAFFS
Belvoir Castle
Melbourne Hall
Stafford
Burton-upon-Trent
Melton Mowbray
Hoar Cross
Stapleford Park
Hall
Shrewsbury
Hanch Hall
LEICS
Weston Park
Lichfield
Quenby Hall
Chillington Hall
Leicester
SALOP
Wolverhampton
Walsall
Langton Hall
Deene Park
Montgomery
Shipton Hall
Upton Cresset Hall
Rockingham
The White House
Birmingham
Arbury Hall
Castle
Boughton House
Stokesay Castle
Hagley Hall
Coventry
Rugby
Stanford Hall
Kidderminster
Lamport Hall
Warwick
Althorp
Eye Manor
Royal Leamington Spa
Northampton
Burton Court
Leominster
Castle
WARWICKS
Ashby
Ragley Hall
Stratford-upon-Avon
Stoke Park
Worcester
Pavilions
HEREFORD AND WORCESTER
Honington Hall
Banbury
Moccas
Little Malvern
Evesham
Compton Wynyates
Broughton Castle
Court
Hereford
Court
Buckingham
Eastnor Castle
Buckland
Hellen's
Rectory
Rousham Park
Ross-on-Wye
Sudeley Castle
Upper Slaughter Manor
Chastleton
Pembridge Castle
Gloucester
Cheltenham
House
Wotton House
Monmouth
Blenheim Palace
Aylesbury
Clearwell Castle
Oxford
Nether
GLOS
Winchendon
Newport
Cirencester
Milton Manor
Berkeley Castle
Stonor Park
Cardiff
Chavenage
Swindon
WILTS
Mapledurham
BERKSHIRE
Bristol
Newbury
Reading
AVON
Bath
Marlborough

416

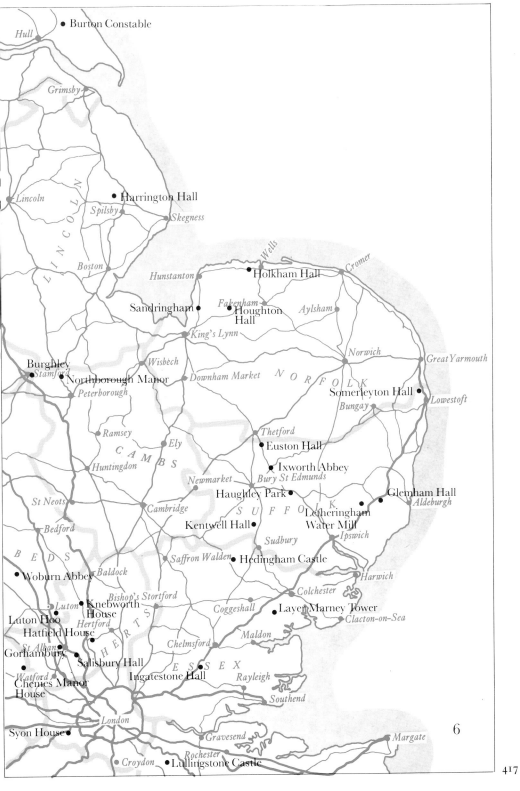

Hull
● Burton Constable

Grimsby

Lincoln
Spilsby
● Harrington Hall
Skegness

Wells
Cromer
Hunstanton
● Holkham Hall

Boston

Fakenham
Aylsham
Sandringham ● ● Houghton
Hall

King's Lynn

Norwich
Wisbech
Great Yarmouth
Burghley
Stamford
● Northborough Manor
Downham Market
N O R F O L K
Somerleyton Hall ●
Peterborough
Lowestoft
Bungay

Ramsey
Thetford
● Euston Hall
Ely
● Ixworth Abbey
Huntingdon
Newmarket
Bury St Edmunds
Glemham Hall
St Neots
Haughley Park ●
Aldeburgh
S U F F O L K
Bedford
Cambridge
Letheringham
Water Mill
Kentwell Hall ●
Ipswich
Sudbury
B E D S
Saffron Walden
● Hedingham Castle
Harwich
● Woburn Abbey Baldock
Colchester
Bishop's Stortford
Luton ● Knebworth
Coggeshall
● Layer Marney Tower
Luton Hoo House
Clacton-on-Sea
Hatfield House Hertford
Maldon
St Alban's
H E R T S
Chelmsford
Gorhambury
Watford Salisbury Hall
E S S E X
Chenies Manor ● Ingatestone Hall
Rayleigh
House

Southend
London

Syon House ●
6
Gravesend
Margate
Croydon ● Lullingstone Castle
Rochester

417

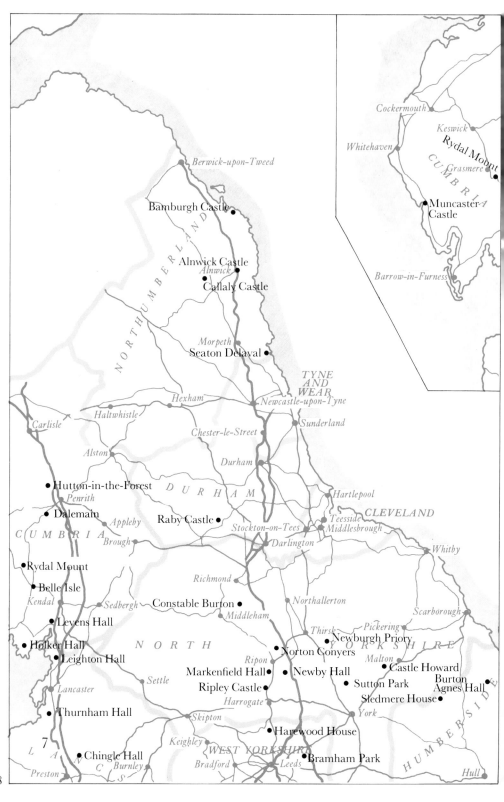

Cockermouth
Keswick
Whitehaven
Rydal Mount
CUMBRIA
Grasmere
Muncaster
Castle
Barrow-in-Furness

Berwick-upon-Tweed

Bamburgh Castle

NORTHUMBERLAND

Alnwick Castle
Alnwick
Callaly Castle

Morpeth
Seaton Delaval

TYNE
AND
WEAR

Hexham
Haltwhistle
Newcastle-upon-Tyne
Carlisle
Chester-le-Street
Sunderland
Alston
Durham

Hutton-in-the-Forest
DURHAM
Penrith
Dalemain
Appleby
Raby Castle
Hartlepool
Teesside
CLEVELAND
CUMBRIA
Brough
Stockton-on-Tees
Middlesbrough
Darlington
Whitby

Rydal Mount
Richmond
Belle Isle
Kendal
Sedbergh
Constable Burton
Northallerton
Scarborough
Middleham
Levens Hall
Thirsk
Pickering
Holker Hall
NORTH
Newburgh Priory
Leighton Hall
Norton Conyers
YORKSHIRE
Ripon
Malton
Markenfield Hall
Newby Hall
Castle Howard
Settle
Burton
Lancaster
Ripley Castle
Sutton Park
Agnes Hall
Harrogate
Sledmere House
Thurnham Hall
Skipton
York
7
Harewood House
L
A
Keighley
WEST YORKSHIRE
N
Chingle Hall
Bradford
Leeds
Bramham Park
C
Burnley
HUMBERSIDE
S
Preston
Hull

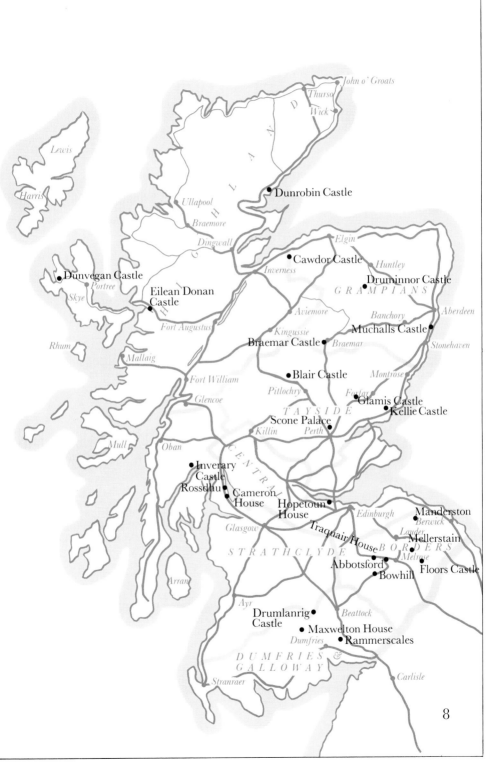

Lewis

Harris

Ullapool

Braemore

Dingwall

HIGHLAND

Thurso

Wick

John o' Groats

• Dunrobin Castle

Elgin

Cawdor Castle

Inverness

Huntley

Druminnor Castle

GRAMPIANS

• Dunvegan Castle

Portree

Skye

Eilean Donan
Castle

Fort Augustus

Aviemore

Banchory

Aberdeen

Rhum

Mallaig

Kingussie

Muchalls Castle

Braemar Castle • Braemar

Stonehaven

Fort William

Glencoe

• Blair Castle

Montrose

Pitlochry

Forfar

Glamis Castle

Mull

Killin

Scone Palace

TAYSIDE

Kellie Castle

Oban

Perth

CENTRAL

• Inverary
Castle
Rossdhu •
Cameron
House

Hopetoun
House

Edinburgh

Manderston

Berwick

House

Lauder

Mellerstain

Glasgow

Traquair House

BORDERS

STRATHCLYDE

Abbotsford

Melrose

Floors Castle

Arran

Bowhill

Ayr

Drumlanrig •
Castle

Beattock

• Maxwelton House
• Rammerscales

Dumfries

DUMFRIES &
GALLOWAY

Stranraer

Carlisle

8

Acknowledgments

The authors and publishers are most grateful to all those house owners who have allowed photographs of their property to be published, to those who have kindly supplied photographs, and to the following who have allowed the use of their copyright: Her Majesty the Queen, for colour plate 21; James Austin, MA., F.I.I.P., p.32; Baron Publishing Company, Woodbridge, pp. 184, 208; Birmingham Museum and Art Gallery, pp. 36, 37; British Tourist Authority, pp. 12, 182, 194, 355, 381; *Country Life*, pp. 14 left, 14 right, 15 left, 16 right, 17 left, 23, 24, 28, 30, 40 left, 40 right, 55, 56, 58, 59, 61, 62, 64, 65 left, 65 right, 67, 71, 73 left, 74, 76, 79, 81, 83, 86 left, 86 right, 92 right, 95, 97 left, 97 right, 101, 102, 104, 105, 108, 109, 114, 116 left, 116 right, 130, 132, 133, 135, 142, 145, 147, 152, 154, 155, 161, 163, 164, 166, 172, 173, 175 right, 180, 197 left, 197 right, 200 left, 200 right, 203, 215, 217, 219, 223, 229, 231, 241 left, 243, 245, 249, 250, 251, 259, 263, 265, 270, 273, 275, 279, 281, 287, 292 left, 292 right, 296, 298, 309, 314, 321, 326, 335, 339, 343 left, 343 right, 348, 349, 361, 362 left, 362 right, 364, 365, 374, 375 left, 375 right, 386, 393, 397; Courtauld Institute of Art, p. 15 right; *Coventry Evening Telegraph*, p. 316; *Dorset County Magazine*, photo by Colin Graham, p. 306; *East Anglian Daily Times*, p. 211; English Life Publications Ltd, Derby, pp. 17 right, 33, 43, 209 right, 227, 284, 289, 313, 319, 331, 358, the jacket photo, and colour plates nos 1, 8, 10, 14, 17, 18, 20, 24, 25, and 27; the *Field*, p. 143; Howletts and Port Lympne Estates, p. 277 and colour plate 16; Jarrold Colour Publications, p. 404 left, colour plates nos 6 and 23; A. F. Kersting, pp. 209 left, 329 left, 387 right, colour plates nos 9 and 11; Michael Laird and Partners, photo by Henry Snoek, p. 394; Antony Miles, A.I.I.P., Salisbury, colour plates nos 4 and 28; National Monuments Record, pp. 92 left, 125, 129, 193, 201 left, 201 right, 221, 233, 235, 240, 324 left, 324 right; National Motor Museum, Beaulieu, p. 262; Photo Precision, St Ives, Huntingdon, pp. 183, 237 left, 237 right, colour plates nos 5, 12, and 26; Picturepoint – London, colour plate 3; Pilgrim Press, pp. 355 left, 357 left, 357 right, 390, colour plates nos 30 and 31; Royal Commission on Ancient Monuments, Scotland (Crown Copyright) p. 405 right; Helen Sandon, p. 311; Tom Scott, Edinburgh, pp. 367, 384, 387; Scottish Tourist Board, pp. 370, 402, 404; Geoffrey Shakerley for Patrick Lichfield Studio, p. 303; The Marquess of Tavistock and the Trustees of the Bedford Estates, pp. 345, 346 left, 346 right; Trustees of the Goodwood Collection, p. 16 left; Bertram Unné, p. 252 left, 252 right; Jeremy Whitaker, pp. 47 left, 47 right, 53, 85, 158, 175 left, 196, 244, 247, 323, 329 right; Woodmansterne Ltd, colour plates nos 2 and 22 photos by Clive Friend, F.I.I.P., colour plate 29 photo by Nicholas Servian, F.I.I.P.

Photographs on pp. 360, 372, 382, 398 were taken by Robbin Fedden, and on pp. 29, 34, 41, 73 right, 78, 90, 98, 110, 113, 118, 119, 122, 123, 128, 137, 140, 157, 159, 167, 170, 177, 185, 187, 192, 205, 225, 226, 238, 241 right, 254, 255, 256, 258, 266, 268, 269, 271, 282, 300, 305, 308, 325, 336, 337, 342, 368, 377, 389, 395 by John Kenworthy-Browne. The authors would like to acknowledge also the following photographers: John Almond, p. 151, colour plate 7; Keith A. Bowden, p. 99; Ian Graham, p. 318; Beric Tempest, colour plate 13; and Jean White, p. 111.

Illustrations on pages 184, 208, and 311 were first published in *Suffolk Houses – A Study of Domestic Architecture*, by Eric Sandon, FRIBA (Baron Publishing, Woodbridge, 1977). Particular thanks for their help are due to Baron Publishing, *Country Life*, *English Life*, Messrs Jarrold, A. F. Kersting, Photo Precision Ltd, Tom Scott, and Jeremy Whitaker.

Index

Bold numbers indicate the main entry for a house; names in italics indicate house owners or life tenants.